Eva Perón

Eva Perón

✦

ALICIA DUJOVNE ORTIZ

Translated by
Shawn Fields

WARNER BOOKS

A *Warner* Book

First published in Great Britain in 1997
by Little, Brown and Company
Reprinted 1997

Copyright © 1995 by Editions Grasset & Fasquelle
Translation copyright © 1996 by Shawn Fields

The moral right of the author has been asserted.

A CIP catalogue record for this book
is available from the British Library.

ISBN: 0 7515 1945 6

Typeset in Berkeley Book by
Palimpsest Book Production Limited,
Polmont, Stirlingshire
Printed and bound in Great Britain by
Clays Ltd, St Ives plc.

Warner Books
A Division of
Little, Brown and Company (UK)
Brettenham House
Lancaster Place
London WC2E 7EN

Acknowledgments

❖

First of all, I would like to thank Alicia Dujovne Ortiz for writing a biography as fascinating as its subject. I would also like to thank Matt Bostock for his endless support and enthusiasm. And above all, I dedicate my translation to Laura Dail, my agent, adviser, *hermana*, who, like Evita, is a unique woman whom I will always admire.

Contents

Eva Perón

Part One

Chapter 1

✤

ILLEGITIMATE

The espadrilles were black and the pinafore white, but the children's uniform would turn completely grey in one week's time. By Friday, the stark contrast between black and white would be erased by the dust from the road. President Domingo Faustino Sarmiento, the nineteenth-century idealist who had made the white pinafore mandatory for public school students, had not foreseen its impracticality. He believed that the uniform, which he described as 'the colour of a dove,' would abolish all differences among rich and poor students. It would be as if pure snow – the great equaliser, very European but rarely seen in Argentina – had fallen over them like a miracle. A noted author, President Sarmiento had published a book called *Facundo, Civilization, and Barbarity*, which had placed an indelible idea in the national consciousness: Europe was civilised; Argentina barbaric. This accepted truth was to be embodied in the image of the young schoolchildren rendered free, equal, and fraternal by their 'civilised' pinafores. But the worn-out espadrilles of the poorer children could never deny the reality of their barbarity. For in his lyrical flight of fancy, Sarmiento had forgotten that rich children wear leather shoes while poor children wear espadrilles.

Eva Duarte belonged to the latter group, although not all the time. In the fragile life of little Evita, seemingly anything could happen. Sometimes, she would gaze at her reflection in the patent leather shoes handed down from her sisters. Other times, she would make circles in the mud on the road to school with the roped soles of her espadrilles. Only her cleanliness never changed. Doña Juana, her mother, a fleshy but beautiful woman who smelled of soap, washed, starched, and ironed her daughters' pinafores twice a week. On Thursdays, Eva and her older sister, Erminda, went to school dressed as immaculately as they did on Mondays. It was a rare luxury, for even the schoolchildren who wore leather sandals were ink-stained by Thursday. However, it was also a suspicious luxury and many who knew Doña Juana wondered what mistakes this very clean woman was trying to wash away.

✣

'You are not a Duarte, you are an Ibarguren.' When Erminda walked into her classroom, she found these words scrawled on the blackboard and she started to cry. The other girls either sympathised or laughed, depending on the quality of their hearts. Now, sitting on the rock in the village square, Erminda confided in her little sister. As she shamefully explained, Evita was silent.

Los Toldos square, much like the squares of all Argentinean villages, was framed by the school, the church, the town hall, the bank, and the general store. Right in the middle of the square rose a statue of General José de San Martín: the soldier who crossed the Andes in 1817 to liberate Argentina and Chile from Spanish rule, the man who had founded the Argentinean tradition of exile. San Martín had retired to Boulogne-sur-Mer, where he died, leaving behind both admiration, born of his prowess, and a troubling question: what did his 'voluntary ostracism' mean? Many generations of Argentinean children asked themselves if civilisation meant Europe. And had San Martín, the *Libertador*, gone there to cut himself off and die? It all seemed very strange, but in these villages of the pampas that stretch out like a long yawn, most people are not very curious. The hero must have had a good reason for being here, in the centre of the square, with his sword and his horse. Nor were Evita and Erminda worried about the Legend of San Martín as they sat on their rock, confused and wondering why in the world people said that their name was not Duarte.

San Martín was not the only hero to have a statue erected in his honour in the town square. There were other, less imposing ones, as well as two emblems: one from Argentina of a Phrygian cap and a laurel wreath, and one from the small town of General Viamonte, named for another nineteenth-century military hero, Juan José Viamonte. The latter's crest contained a cow, an ear of corn, an Indian spear, and a white hand shaking a copper hand that was now tarnished and green. The town's entire history was reflected in that crest. The town of Los Toldos was named after the Indians of yesteryear who lived in tents (*tolderías*), Indians who were now symbolised by that green hand. Los Toldos was a little village in the province of Buenos Aires, founded on the dreary but fertile land that is called the 'wet pampas.' Evita no longer lived at *La Unión*, the ranch just outside Los Toldos that belonged to her father, Don Juan Duarte. But during the happy times when she still visited there, she would ride into Los Toldos with Juan Duarte. He would hoist her onto the light and graceful carriage, and she would sit by his side. Shaken by the trotting that her father controlled by quickly pulling on the reins, the little girl would crouch down to look at the Indians. The Indians lived somewhere on the plains, halfway between her father's *estancia* and the village. They were called the Coliqueos and worked for Juan Duarte as porters transporting wheat to the train station.

The Coliqueos' presence in the middle of the province of Buenos Aires was unusual. In 1879, Julio Argentino Roca had 'cleansed' the pampas of the last few Indians. Furthermore, the Coliqueos were *mapuches*, of Chilean origin, so the fact that they were there in the first place was indeed strange. They had settled in the region in 1862, with their leader, Ignacio Coliqueo, who served in the ranks of General Urquiza, governor of the Entre Ríos province and victor over Rosas, the tyrant. After having helped to overthrow Rosas, the Coliqueos founded a village in the exact spot where Los Toldos now stood. Their village was twice destroyed by other tribes, partisans of Rosas.

Crouched in the bottom of the carriage, Evita could not know any of this. She had not learned it in school. Textbooks, quick to dismiss the Indians in two sentences, described nothing more than their traditional pottery. She had not learned it in the village, either, for who in Los Toldos could remember it all? Argentina cultivates forgetting. But Evita knew that she had a debt to pay to the Indians. Her mother had told her that the midwife who had come on May 7, 1919 – that rainy dawn when Eva was born – was a Coliqueo. (Just like her mother, the midwife's name was Juana, Juana Guaquil. She could not have gone by any other name. Throughout Evita's life, everyone who meant something to her had the same name. Her father, her brother, and her husband were all named Juan, and even her mother-in-law's name was Juana.) To honour the debt incurred the day of her birth, Eva needed a long memory, and indeed she was a woman who never forgot a thing. She stored the good and the bad in her soul forever. An Indian woman had risen at the crack of dawn to bring her into the world. The Indians were therefore good.

❖

Don Juan Duarte was originally from the small neighbouring

village of Chivilcoy. It was said that he had rented ... from Mayor Malcolm, a conservative who elected Don Jua... the position of magistrate. But according to Father Meinrado Hux, a Swiss Benedictine who had become the region's historian, things were not as clear-cut as they appeared. First of all, it seemed that Duarte had bought, not rented, the *estancia*. (This fiction was necessary in order to avoid paying taxes on the land.) He was also fired from his post in 1915 by Malcolm himself, accused of having misappropriated funds. Duarte was a small-time conservative caudillo with personal ambitions, a 'duartist' conservative. At *La Unión* he ran the show. Playing the role of a feudal lord, Duarte skimped on nothing. For one of his parties, he even hired the entire village orchestra. Don Juan promised the pack of gauchos who voted for him – those who wore black hats, silver belt buckles, and pantaloons – that they would never go hungry; Duarte the magnificent would offer them mountains of fresh-baked empanadas. In fact, behind Don Juan's curtain of magical extravagance was Juana, who dutifully played the dual role of cook and mistress without batting an eyelid as her blistered hands kneaded the dough and stuffed it with beef.

The main course, the *pièce de résistance*, was always an entire cow roasted in its skin. Such lavishness was not limited to holidays. Anyone who arrived at *La Unión* any day of the week was guaranteed to eat and drink to the health of Don Juan, an ingenuous man, jovial and patently crooked, for all these opulent celebrations were funded by the oblivious community.

✢

'Your mother was traded for a horse and buggy.' Eva could not remember if the drunk who had said that awful thing to her had been one of her father's guests or if he had come stumbling out of the Los Toldos bar, but she would never forget the words he had whispered in her ear: 'Your mother was traded for a horse and buggy. That is the price your father paid Doña Petrona, your grandmother.'

The Los Toldos square was not reserved exclusively for heroes with moustaches. You could easily find nooks and hiding places there to call your own: the rock-formed 'caverns,' the orchestra's rotunda with a railing with thick columns and romantic garlands, and finally the ombu, the giant tree of the pampas whose thick and overflowing roots seemed to have streamed rather than grown down. The ombu pours out its guts into the earth. Argentines complain about not having roots, but they forget about the ombu roots where they used to play, as if in their own mother's womb.

Evita hid among the caverns, the rotunda, and the inviting ombu, thinking about all the spoken and unspoken words and about the absent father who had abandoned them to return to his wife and his legitimate children in Chivilcoy. Yet no one could accuse her three sisters – Elisa, Blanca, and Erminda – and her brother Juan of not being Duartes. She thought about her female family with only one boy, a boy who was teased relentlessly due to his jet black hair and his long, velvety eyelashes. Eva's sole weakness, he would grow up to be an irresistible Don Juan. It did not take much for a family to become a tribe when it was tightly huddled around a chief as strong and crafty as Doña Juana, a methodical woman with hard-and-fast rules that included forbidding the children to play with girls of 'dubious morality' or follow them down the muddy and dusty roads, whispering their grandmother's words to them. This is how you form a permanent bond between children and their families. But even within her tribe of women, Evita isolated herself. Like all humiliated souls, she was torn between solidarity with her clan and the shame of belonging to it. Her temperament was also torn: joyful and whimsical at home, withdrawn as soon as she crossed its threshold. A woman with such a mercurial disposition was also prone to

tantrums, and often her own rage would shake her, e.
her. It was a wonder such a sickly body could contain suc.
storms of emotion.

The Nuñezes, Evita's mother's family, lived on the outskirts
of the village. They lived also on the edge of society, so much
so that 'honest' folk would point at them with a gesture that
seemed to shoo them far away, keeping them out of the centre
of village life.

The Nuñezes represented the other face of Los Toldos. They
had always been different, even in the days when Don Electo
Urquizo founded the town in 1892. Actually, the founder of
Los Toldos was named Urquiza, like the general who had
vanquished Rosas, the tyrant. But Don Electo believed that
such a man as he should not have a woman's name, so he
changed Urquiza to Urquizo.

Urquizo opened a general store on exactly the same site
as the Coliqueo tribe had previously attempted to establish a
village. When Urquizo discovered that the railroad tracks were
to pass right through this same place, he bought the land. He
hired a surveyor and had him outline the square where San
Martín would rest, which Urquizo considered the centre of the
universe. Urquizo also ordered the first church to be built on
the square.

A town, however, needs townspeople. The Coliqueos were
too discouraged to try again to inhabit a town, so they stayed
in their huts. So Urquizo arranged for the *criollos* to come to
town. These were the mulatto Argentines, half-Indian, half-
Spanish or black or simply natives of the country. The *criollos*
were immediately followed by a crowd of Italians, Spaniards,
Basques, and French. In 1895, the Franco-Spanish Toldos
Association was formed, and by 1903 it became the French
Association. Suddenly, Europeans were flocking to Argentina.
They came daily, by the hundreds. No matter what their
country of origin, they all wore the same look of wonder.
They all cried for the loss of a land, a home, a fiancée, a dog,

and in the midst of this loss, of this absence that weighed heavily on all, the tango was born.

Juana's father, Ibarguren, was among the Basques. He was the charioteer for his state and, out of respect for history's symmetry, should also have been named Juan, but his name was Joaquín. Instead of speaking to Don Urquizo, the charioteer took a detour and stumbled upon the other founding father of the village, Espíritu Nuñez, an even more prestigious name and one that fortunately was neutral and not in need of change.

Espíritu Nuñez was the patriarch of those 'Nuñezes from the outskirts.' Petrona Nuñez, Evita's grandmother, might have been one of his illegitimate daughters. According to Olelo Borroni and Roberto Vacca in their biography of Eva Perón, Petrona was a descendant of those 'ambulatory, semi-human saleswomen who satisfied the passions of the soldiers of the Desert.' Was this a quirk of Petrona's, or did she carry this defect in her blood – an ancestral defect, an aptitude to survive by 'satisfying passions' – that Evita would later inherit?

Ibarguren, the Basque with a preference for eccentric villages, loved Petrona. Together they had two girls: Juana Ibarguren, who, according to a drunkard's story, was traded for a horse and buggy, and Liberta Nuñez, the wife of Valenti.

In keeping with family tradition, in her official history Eva would erase the village of Los Toldos from the map. Her sister Erminda recalls in her memoirs that when Petrona Nuñez died in 1927, Evita, who was still a child, had cried desperately. The description of this image of Evita overwhelmed by grief is grippingly real. And yet, the drunkard's theory that this tribe of women hid the old Petrona in her ranch of misery, and that they even faked her death twenty years before it happened, is believable. Father Hux insists that Petrona enjoyed a happy longevity and did not die until May 29, 1953, not long after her famous granddaughter. In that case, who is the Petrona Nuñez who died in 1927 and whose tomb lies in Los Toldos cemetery? It remains the mystery of a foggy collective memory, one that will surprise us often throughout this story, as if, by selecting one version over another, each of Evita's biographers and each witness to her life retells his or her own biography. Indeed, Eva's entire life was one of secrets, of forbidden words. The families suppressed names and dates, hid illnesses and lovers.

One needed courage to live as Juana did. When she was abandoned by Juan Duarte, she took her five children and rented a brick house in Los Toldos. It was a single room, divided by a partition, with a kitchen floor made of clay. Juana was poor, but she did own a sewing machine, a Singer, and she made pantaloons for a store that sent her the patterns. She spent so many hours sitting hunched over the sewing machine that the veins in her legs were bursting. Her daughters had to lift her by the armpits to help her get out of bed. Only then would the rhythm of the needle that measured her time in centimetres resume.

Nevertheless, in spite of her weight, her varicose veins, and her children, Juana managed to please. She needed a protector, and she found many. The most important one was Don Carlos Rosset, a landowner who financed Dr Heubert's mayoral campaign in the 1920s. Rosset was the landlord of the brick house on Francia Street, and although there is no evidence that he helped Doña Juana financially, he must have forgiven the months of unpaid rent. Through Heubert, he also procured a job at the town post office for Elisa and one for Juancito, the only son, as office boy at the educational council. (Blanca had gone to Bragado to continue her studies and become a teacher.)

However, in Evita's eyes, Don Carlos Rosset did much more for the family. For instance, on rainy days he would send his chauffeur to pick up Juana's children to take them to school. What a wonderful adventure it was to climb into the Chevrolet that smelled of leather! Evita would sing for the entire trip, all the while caressing the shiny seat. She would wait impatiently for the rain to come, as this gave her the chance to feel like a princess.

A few residents of Los Toldos, who wish to remain anonymous, insist that Don Carlos died in Doña Juana's bed. At that time, the tribe of women lived in Junín. Rosset's son Alfredo came to recover the body. Doña Juana would always protect Alfredo and would appoint him municipal inspector when she gained power through Eva Perón. Eva, on the other hand, was merciless to Don Carlos's daughter. Once she became Perón's wife, Eva went so far as to prevent Lina Rosset, a soprano, from singing in the Colón Theater in Buenos Aires.

Whether such action was just one of Evita's whims, or whether darker motives were at work, is unknown. The anonymous storytellers go so far as to suggest an astonishing resemblance between Lina (who established an international singing career and even sang at La Scala in Milan) and Evita. As for Eva's titled half-sisters, the legitimate Duartes, she entertained them and even helped them from time to time, if only perhaps to legitimise herself.

Their first meeting was not one to forget. The legitimate and illegitimate children met at their father's funeral in 1926. Juan Duarte died in a car accident; thus, at least as Evita saw it, abandoning his tribe of women a second time. A little girl never forgives a father who abandons her; it was even worse in this case because he did not wait for her to grow up. In dying, the father shattered Evita's dream of one day, glowing with beauty and dressed like a queen, going to find him. Although the traitor would get down on his knees, crying in repentance, she would be loyal to her mother and haughty, like a marble statue.

The date on which he left them is willfully ignored. Opinions are divided, but the fact that Evita later searched for a man surrounded by masses of supporters, much like Juan Duarte, leads us to believe that she was drawn by what her father had been – a leader of men.

It is believed that Duarte's legitimate wife died in 1922, three years after Eva's birth. That is why, when she married Colonel

Perón, Eva hid her real birth certificate and substituted a false document stating that she was born in 1922 instead of in 1919. One biographer considered this female vanity. Another biographer, Fermín Chávez, explains it differently. While her father's wife was alive, according to Argentinean law Evita was considered not only an illegitimate child, but worse yet, a child born of adultery. Under no circumstance could a man of the military marry the product of adultery. She had to erase this from her past, by changing her birthdate so that it was after Señora Duarte's death. In this way, the false document legitimised her.

Upon the death of this legitimate wife, Doña Juana would have gone to Chivilcoy to wear the crown, but it does not seem that she was honourably received. Her attitude is born of a challenge and reveals her pain. Had the dead wife ever been aware of Juana's existence during her life? If so, she must have feigned ignorance, or perhaps she told herself that a husband who works far from his family needs a woman and she had better close her eyes in order to keep her marriage vows sacred. Señora Duarte sometimes went to La Unión to see Don Juan and to reinforce these ties. At these times the official wife was discreet; she hid her children and appeared only in her role of cook.

Duarte's wife's maiden name was close to that of her husband and for good reason. It was originally the same name. That her name was officially D'Huart and not Duarte was the fault of the officers of the port of Buenos Aires who mixed everything up due to the large flow of immigrants. When this Basque family – Duarte, D'Huart, Diuart, or Douarte – docked on Argentina's muddy shores, arriving from Pau, its name was at the mercy of the officer who changed it as he saw fit.

The fatigue of the voyage also played a role here. When confronted with incomprehension, it is easy for the immigrant to give up. D'Huart? Duarte? What was the difference? A bed to sleep on was really all that mattered to them.

Juana's father, the Spanish Basque, was lucky. In Buenos Aires, the spelling of his name had not been touched since the days of the Conquest: half of the conquistadores were Basque. To this, add that Juan Duarte's mother was named María Echegoyen, also Basque, and we can conclude that Evita had three Basque ancestors. Even her godfather and godmother belonged to this stubborn people: the names of Don Antonio Ochotorena and Doña Paz Michotorena, took up an entire line in her baptism record, the only one she did not falsify.

Don Juan died a widower, and on that day in 1926, Juana took her Basque stubbornness to extremes. Contrary to public opinion, she considered herself a widow. So she dressed in black and quickly sewed four dresses plus a black suit for her son, and the tribe went to Chivilcoy.

She knew exactly what she was up against, and she met it straight on. It was not love of humiliation, but, on the contrary, bravery, showing the world that she was dutiful and that this was her place. She succeeded in her mission by holding her head high as she faced the legitimate clan. At least Juana did; her children were refused entrance into the home by one of their half-sisters.

In Los Toldos, Juana's children were used to being insulted. There were those who refused to greet them, others who wore a conspicuous smile when Elisa or Blanca passed by. 'Like mother, like daughter,' they would say. In small doses, affronts such as these reinforce one's will. In big doses, they weaken it, and unfortunately this was often the case for little Evita.

Evita was seven when the expedition to Chivilcoy took place. Her mother had dragged her there to reaffirm her dignity, worrying little about the slap she would receive. There is no doubt that Evita must have hated them all: the legitimate children who stared at her as if she were an alien and also her mother who did not belong to this other world.

The five Ibargurens who wanted to call themselves Duarte

would finally kiss the cheek of the figure in state with the long, slim nose and follow their mother, walking behind the legitimate family. The cemetery seemed far, that January 8, in the heart of the summer, and Eva, the youngest, was last in line. This was the moment when Eva swore to herself that, one day, she would be first.

✜

Given the literal and figurative dust that was blowing in the streets of Los Toldos, what could they do but close the shutters? The Ibarguren-Duartes lived in a withdrawn state unto themselves. Doña Juana sacrificed herself for the family. When asked to stop sewing, her reply was always, 'I do not have time to stop.' These were words that Eva would later repeat, maybe without even realising their origin. The residents of Los Toldos still say today, 'All that she did, she did for her children; she was driven by need.' They describe her as a 'true lioness defending her young.' 'All that she did' refers to the lovers she took, presumably for the sake of her children.

Doña Juana wanted her daughters to be beautiful, immaculate, respectable, and to marry well. These were big dreams. Her children were not to be traded for a horse and buggy. On the other hand, Juancito had begun to worry her. He was a hooligan, who had managed to find himself a shiny blue car, a Ruby, in an era when only the rich owned cars. But if Juancito's dreams of easy money and laziness worried her, Doña Juana did not harshly oppose them, for the truth is that she could all too easily imagine herself somewhere else beyond the poor brick house.

Nor were Eva and Erminda deprived. They depended on Juancito, who had helped them make a piano out of a wood crate, a piano that produced real sounds. He made kites for them, which Evita let fly away freely but Erminda held back fearfully, and little houses in the back of the garden, where, on rainy days, Evita settled and listened to the raindrops on the corrugated iron. They had built a circus where Evita pretended to be a tightrope walker; one would have sworn that the wire that stretched between the weeping willow and the paradise tree was her true land. Elisa, their eldest sister, made clown costumes and carnival robes for them. One memorable year, Erminda dressed up like a gypsy, while Evita, in a fairy costume, was followed by a long sky-blue tulle train scattered with stars.

None of this was expensive. With two pieces of chiffon and some gold paper, their agile hands created miracles – that is, until the day when Evita revealed her true ambition. It was Kings Day, the day when Caspar, Melchior, and Balthazar brought presents to the children. She had asked for a doll, but not just any doll: she wanted the *big* one. Doña Juana had gone to the general store and after having searched for what seemed like an eternity, unearthed a big doll that, unfortunately, had one broken leg. She paid two cents for it due to the defect. The night of January 5, as Evita lay sleeping, she laid the doll on Evita's shoes (or were they espadrilles?). In the morning, the little girl took the doll in her arms and studied it thoughtfully. Her mother, who had been watching Evita carefully, took this moment to explain that the doll had had an accident, she had fallen from Caspar's camel! That is why, she added, Evita had to love her very, very much. Indeed, Evita tenderly loved this broken creature that, like her, was missing something vital in her life.

Juana Ibarguren had a vivid imagination. An austere mother would have bought a tiny doll and taken advantage of the occasion to lecture her offspring on life's difficulties. The clan's reaction was to push the game farther. They tried to help Evita's lame doll 'walk,' so that it would not fall and hurt itself. The family entertained the illusion with warmth. Elisa made a long dress that hid the doll's injury because, of course, defects, want, and shame had to be hidden.

Evita had chestnut coloured hair that her mother cut short for practical reasons. But the sisters had always dreamed of long, golden, curly manes, and from the moment she discovered her freedom, Eva turned this feminine dream into reality. Indeed, Eva's entire life history finds expression in her hairstyles. This insight demands, perhaps, more attention than it has been given by biographers or psychologists in the past. The journey from the timid straight hair to audacious curls to her tight chignon tells much about Eva Perón.

Her skin was mat with an ivory, yellowish tint. It had not a trace of pink. It was also naturally translucent, perhaps the result of a childhood accident. Her sister Erminda's memoirs tell of a day when Evita was in the kitchen, watching the blue flames dance on the polished bronze stove. The stove had a beautiful name, a prestigious name whose Latin consonants reminded one of mass: 'Primus, it was called.' When Evita moved in closer to get a good whiff of the sweet smell of gas, which reminded her of winter's pleasures, the frying pan that was sitting on the burner flipped onto her face. After an initial scream, she fell quiet. The stinging of the burn must have numbed her. Her wide eyes glistened in the black crust that gradually covered her face like a mask. As the days went on, the mask dried out and became stiff and wrinkled. When it finally fell off, Eva's skin was perfect, too perfect. It was so smooth and so pretty that it looked like a mermaid's, or a corpse's.

❖

Politics and her relationship with Rosset had enabled Doña Juana to get jobs for both Elisa and Juancito, but it was also politics that would demolish this fragile situation.

Dr Heubert had been replaced by a radical mayor, Pascual Lettieri. Lettieri's own testimony reveals much about Doña Juana. He describes her as a courageous and wily woman who could anticipate and manipulate events. Shortly after Lettieri's victory, the heavy but always beautiful lady appeared at the town hall. One of the rare villagers who wore perfume, she smelled lovely. Lettieri was waiting for her, but to play it safe, he asked a certain Castagnino and a certain Azcárate to come along. He expected and feared a scene. She got straight to the point: 'And now,' she said, hands on her hips, 'are you planning to fire my Elisa?' 'I'm afraid so,' said the new mayor. She began to cry. Faced with the abundant rolls of flesh covered by a flowered dress and shaking from the sobs, he did not know what to do. This was flesh that had sinned, troubling flesh that a few of his friends had told him about in detail, for in a small village, conservative and radical men alike frequented the same cafés. 'Well I could transfer her,' he proposed in a weak voice. Juana lifted her head. She squinted her sparkling and shrewd eyes, as if she were threading a needle, and said too quickly, in a triumphant and eager tone that betrayed her, 'Yes, to Junín.' 'That little devil planned the whole thing ahead of time,' he would later say. He who, in the end, enjoyed his newfound power by displaying severity at first and then magnanimity, he who had armed himself with two human boars to protect himself from Doña Juana because she frightened him so – or rather excited him so – he understood it all. But it was too late. By playing the victim, she had manipulated him. It was she who had wanted to leave Los Toldos, and she got her own way.

The trible left the village at night, leaving behind many unpaid debts. Evita left behind one friend, Emma Vinuesa, her schoolmate, one of the few whose parents had not forbidden her from playing with Evita. She was also leaving behind the sick lady whose life Evita had brightened by singing to her, by dancing for her, and by dressing up like a clown, as well as the lonely woman who had an altar with baby Jesus right in her home. Every Sunday, after church, this woman would call the children over to show them the altar, and every time she would tremble with emotion as if it were the first time she'd laid eyes on the baby Jesus. The children trembled too because they liked to relive that emotion.

We are not sure what mode of transportation the family used to leave, but we do know that they went deep into the pampas, from Los Toldos to Junín. The pampas were created for that reason, to leave 'just as we lose our blood,' according to the final words of *Don Segundo Sombra* by Ricardo Güiraldes. The past and the future of the people who leave are lost in the earth on the infinite horizon. The pampas are flat, yet the tribe felt as if they were climbing. Leaving Los Toldos for Junín represented an ascension. In Junín, Doña Juana was not as well known as she was in the village, at least that's what they hoped. No one would ever again talk behind their backs about the horse and buggy. The worst had passed.

A CRISIS UNFURLS ITSELF ON THE TANGO

It is said that the true Argentines are the ones who own land. In 1930, a stretch of land in Argentina equal in size to Belgium, the Netherlands, and Switzerland combined, was owned by 1,804 landowners. These 1,804 happy Argentines had inherited the land; their ancestors had either taken it from the Indians or won it as the spoils of civil wars. The government surely owed them as much, as a reward for the tattooed ear of each and every Indian they killed during their fierce combat.

Before this partitioning, the pampas belonged to no one. It was a land of nomads, and the immensity of it all prompted men to continue on their treks without settling. The farther they delved into the pampas, the more it appeared to continue ad infinitum. The Indians strode across it liberally. Born of a union between Indians and Spaniards, the gauchos perpetuated this constant movement across the terrain, but there was one big difference – their souls were torn apart by the interbreeding from which they were born and, therefore, they never felt an allegiance as members of a group. Whenever they had the chance they would leave the women who bore their children. The gaucho of long ago was aggressive and proud, he felt entitled to whatever he wished for. If he was hungry, he would lasso a cow from one of the many herds that blackened the interminable plain. He would dismount his horse, cut the cow's throat with his knife, slice off its tongue, roast this choice slab on the coals, then go, leaving the entire beast to the birds of prey that circled overhead waiting their turn.

The country had certainly changed. Now only the oligarchs – those 1,804 happy landowners – lived extravagantly. Six months were spent at the *estancia*, six in Paris. The two and a half million Argentines who did not holiday in Paris floated in unreality, not knowing what their fortune might be. Since they did not own land, they did not feel like true Argentines. They were still immigrants in their own country, as their ancestors had been. A few of them had rented land and invented Argentinean agriculture. But for the most part they had regrouped on Argentina's surface, the 'foam of days' that is Buenos Aires and a few minor cities. European immigrants were still arriving in 1930, but an exodus was forming in the deep country. The landless were packing their bags and heading for Buenos Aires or Junín.

The world financial crisis of 1929 did not spare Argentina. The country depended on its agricultural exports. Its currency, the peso, displayed the two emblems of its prosperity: a bovine head and a sheaf of wheat. But the peso was linked to the pound sterling. Argentina had profited from World War I. Its neutrality was only a formality; from an economic standpoint, it belonged to the Commonwealth. It had enriched itself by feeding and clothing the English. The 1920s were its golden years. Buenos Aires was the largest Latin American city and the third largest city in the hemisphere after New York and Chicago. Argentina had achieved an economic status equivalent to Canada's. The oligarchy, who professed a lay liberalism, always encouraged European immigration, all the while mocking the new arrivals. Those sentimental Neapolitans who sold their wares while singing, those Spaniards from Galicia with those crazy eyebrows – oh, were they ludicrous!

Meanwhile, headed by their leader Yrigoyen, the radicals won the elections in 1916 and again in 1928, and the oligarchy began to worry. These radicals represented the middle classes whose ancestors were the Neapolitans and Galicians. 'Do they think they can run the country?' the traditional Argentinean landowners asked. On top of all this, the world stock market crashed.

The landowners decided to take things into their own hands by supporting General Uriburu's coup in 1930. He was Yrigoyen's adversary and conqueror. The select group of 1,804 were not unaware of the changes arising from the change of power in the heart of the army. The era of spoiled soldiers who were satisfied with holding parades during patriotic ceremonies and combing their thick moustaches was over. Now, military men were made in the Germanic mould – they even wore the Prussian helmets trimmed with a spear's arrow. Until now, they had never dared disobey the Anglophile and Francophile oligarchy, which in fact had had no problem deploying them. But in 1932, the oligarchy became aware of the military's Germanophilia and its thirst for power, and the oligarchs dismissed the soldiers just as one would dismiss a maid, thus remaining in power for another decade through electoral fraud.

To combat the crash that had exploded elsewhere, the oligarchs in power moved from a pure form of liberalism to protectionist politics. This progression resulted in an accelerated rate of industrialisation because the products that were previously bought in Europe now had to be produced at home. The majority of new factories were built in Buenos Aires. The workforce, too quickly rushed in from the provinces, was introduced to progress – unemployment and housing shortages. It is these frustrations that are revealed through the emotional music of the tango.

All of the tangos from the 1930s speak of a young girl from the outskirts, dressed in percale, and of an evil woman swathed in a mink coat. The tango also tells of *conventillos*, the dilapidated houses shared by many families who, since the start of the century, met or argued in a common courtyard. Each family spoke Spanish in its own way. In fact, Argentinean theatre was born in these courtyards. It was a meeting between Moustafa, Giuseppe, Manolito, Itzjak, Heinrich, Dimitri, Clemencio, and others. The poor souls had nothing, but they did have salt and thus the uproarious theatre they inspired was called *sainete*.

But tango speaks not of famine or of 'popular soups' that nourished the victims of the crash in the streets of Buenos Aires. Much like the Argentine of a bygone age, the tango is modest, and it complains as an aristocrat complains. It never cries for its own, those who are hungry; the wife and children do not exist within the tango's realms, just as they did not exist for the gaucho. Fathers do not exist either. Only mothers (saintly women!) exist. The man of the tango weeps for her as well as for the woman in the mink coat. Whether a descendant of immigrants or of gauchos, he is the solitary spirit who abandoned the cow and left it for the birds of prey. In *El hombre que está solo y espera* by Raúl Scalibrini Ortiz, the *porteño*, an inhabitant of Buenos Aires, is the man leaning against the wall on a street in the centre of town, a lone man waiting, for what? This man who is in love with his mother and with death, who hates women and the future, and whose mind is always on a past that will never return, is he really waiting for something, or is he indulging his spite, the spite that comes from not being able to spend one's winters in Paris?

Junín was, of course, bigger than Los Toldos, but it was still a small town. However, it had become a railroad centre. Hence, Junín took in workers from everywhere and was a breeding ground for pure and austere anarchists and for socialists with a rhetoric at once pompous and candid who were moved by the highest ideals. The Argentinean labour movement was alive and well. If Perónism had not come and given hope to the workers, the story told would be quite different.

NORMA SHEARER IN JUNÍN

Luck had smiled on Doña Juana more often than it had on other unfortunate souls. Elisa had her job at the post office, Blanca was a teacher, and Juancito was employed by a company called Jabón Federal. Thanks to all this, the tribe did not have to suffer living on the other side of the railroad tracks, in the makeshift neighbourhoods that were built for the new arrivals. The Ibarguren-Duartes were poor but not desperate. The poor can live in a real house built out of adequate materials and survive since the house sustains them as can an adobe ranch built from mud dried by the sun. But as soon as the poor lose their home and seek shelter under the hastily erected sheet metal, their souls unravel.

Doña Juana's tribe never came unravelled. They found shelter in a small house with a courtyard and potted geraniums. However, their foreign status stuck to them like glue, and they would move three more times, always in the centre of Junín. They did not have land and they had no male head of the family. In fact, their description mirrored Gardel's famous tango: '*Eran cinco hermanos / y ella era una santa*' (they were five children / and the mother was a saint). This image was quite close to reality in terms of her happiness and the contentment of her children, but Doña Juana did not wear a halo. Despite everything, they were finally brushing up against a new social class, and this is when Doña Juana, the only one who had not been able to find work, came up with a brilliant idea: she would cook for gentlemen.

The Ibarguren house in Junín was not big enough to host couples. Doña Juana parked her family in the kitchen and saved a little room for the dining room to entertain three quality lodgers: Major Alfredo Arrieta, leader of the military district; Don José Alvarez Rodríguez, rector of the National College; and his brother, the attorney Justo Alvarez Rodríguez. Sometimes these three guests were visited by Dr Moisés Lebensohn, the famous journalist and radical leader.

The three men ate together the plentiful and rustic meals that Doña Juana served. They spoke of politics in low and distinguished voices, all the while wiping the corners of their lips with napkins that they then swiftly placed on their knees. Evita would spy on them from the kitchen, curious as to what one had to do to be considered 'classy.'

In contrast, over coffee, Elisa and Blanca were allowed to look at these men face to face. They were clean, neatly dressed, and discreetly dolled up. In addition to the suffering they had endured, the young women now had to take every precaution to behave appropriately, and this mixture gave them an interesting air. Elisa later revealed an ambition equal to Evita's. Blanca, much like Erminda, was softer and more self-effacing. But all three of them obeyed their mother, and Doña Juana surely told them to greet these polite gentlemen with warm smiles. They must have been charming, since Elisa ended up marrying (some say by cohabiting with) Major Arrieta, and Blanca married Alvarez Rodríguez, the attorney.

God had fulfilled Doña Juana's dreams (even if Erminda entered into a shadier marriage, to an elevator operator named Bertolini whom she later divorced using the excuse of Juancito Duarte's suicide – or murder – in 1953). In the 1930s Juancito was employed at Jabón Federal. He wore a linen suit and greeted one and all by tipping his panama. He drove a Packard that had been given to him by Elisa's lover, Major Arrieta. A charmer, Juancito knew how to take care of himself, and his moustache drove the girls mad.

As for Evita, she wanted to be somebody else. Like her brothers and sisters, she was, by birth, divided into two different people. According to the sociologist Juan José Sebreli, she had a dual membership. She was a descendant of landowners – her father – and at the same time a descendant of the homeless poor – her mother. Such a fate was typical of a 'mulatto' country, a mirror country, torn by its desire to be something else, to find itself elsewhere.

In families as in nations, there is always someone chosen to feel what the others prefer to forget. That is how Evita's personality became more and more contradictory. Her schoolmates thought she was soft but with the soul of a leader. One of her friends, Elsa Sabella, recalled that Evita always wanted to order others around. She was the boss because, since she had been left behind, she finished elementary school when she was fourteen and her schoolmates were twelve. Evita is remembered as a mixture of charm and fear, distrusted by students with less cunning. 'The boss' had therefore divided up her class according to the choice of gift that the students would give to their teacher at the end of the year. Half the students were leaning toward a missal, the other half, the one that followed Eva, wanted to give her a rosary, and they were sticking to their guns. Eva was tender yet authoritarian. She had dreamy and piercing eyes, serene and nervous gestures. She would later evoke whole litanies of opposite terms. Saint and whore, adventurer and militant, frivolous and martyr, the 'white myth' and the 'black myth.'

Yes, she was always somebody else and wanted it that way. She observed her mother's and her sisters' efforts with a suspicious eye and chose to conform to her own rules. She was too proud to bend in this adaptation crusade, which she knew was bound to fail. Doña Juana's reputation had followed them to Junín. Here, just as in Los Toldos, her schoolmates were not allowed to play with her. Despite the women's vain efforts, Evita immensely preferred Juancito's defiance; his elegance imposed a certain style. To be somebody means to become untouchable due to one's beauty or personality, to carry an air of being somewhere else. That is how she remained faithful to the other person she was. She hated the town of Junín and had only one fear: that Doña Juana would one day want to marry her off to one of the boring dinner guests.

Evita knew that white telephones and heart-shaped beds with satin sheets existed in a world beyond her own. She often told Erminda that she would marry only a prince or a president, although in certain states of despair, the only solution was to shoot for the stars. Evita would run off to the movies where she dreamed of being Norma Shearer in the role of Marie Antoinette. Rarely is a wish ever realised to such a great extent. Evita would never have escaped her flat life without Hollywood films, music magazines that related the gossip about the stars, fashion magazines, and radio soap operas.

In school, Evita was always last in maths and first in poetry. She always waited for the rain to fall, because on these days the teachers were less strict since so few students came to school. Evita took advantage of this to embark on a journey from class to class to recite 'poetries.' (Even as an adult, Eva never said 'poem,' she said 'poetries' or, worse yet, 'verses.' The oligarchs laughed at her because Eva never possessed the keys to the language which opened the door for the chosen.)

Her teacher, Palmira Repetto, would leave her be, and even the boys would listen to her with a distracted ear. But the girls sighed at the teary verses that Evita unearthed in textbooks and recited with much emotion but catastrophic diction. Even as a radio actress, Eva still said *ojepto* instead of *objeto* and *amigos del écter* instead of *amigos del éter* (friends of the ether, a common expression in Argentina that reflects the bodies of Argentines and, even more so, their souls). The sound waves were sometimes named after this word that poetic tradition reserved for the highest and most spiritual motives, thus establishing an unexpected link between radio and the sky. She would correct these errors only when she became Eva Perón, as if, by the grace of power, her tongue had finally been untied. The possession of language, like land, is a birthright. Once she had climbed to the apex of glory, Evita, who had been deprived of this right, thought of the other dispossessed and ordered that diction classes be given to her *muchachas Perónistas*, her loyal followers, the girls of her party who, like her, had been born deprived of correct diction.

On Sundays she could not go to the movies. This was the day for new releases, and the tickets were expensive. So on Sundays, Evita like the other girls, took walks up and down Rivadavia Avenue. She was eleven, then she was twelve, then thirteen – the time when each year seems to last a century. When they walked past the boys who were lined up against the wall, or huddled on the street corners, Erminda would squeeze her arm. Girls learned to fear boys at this early age. The boys would yell out obscenities to prove that they were capable of doing so. And, after all, the girls were excuses for a game that would stay, at least for the time being, male-dominated. The girls had to walk past them pretending to be deaf, their eyes glued to the ground, speechless.

Evita and Erminda licked their ice cream, waved to school-mates who would not approach them for fear of being seen with them, and at dusk, they would go home. From the end of the street they could smell the sweet aroma of *milanesas*. Revolted, Evita would pout. Every time Doña Juana placed a piece on her plate, she felt threatened. Could a girl chosen to become the next Norma Shearer be chubby? Throughout her life, she refused to eat, so that she would not become like her mother. She forged for herself a body that would reject her mother's roundness.

Movie day was Tuesday, when tickets cost only thirty cents. Evita would come home at noon (there were no afternoon classes) and pick at her lunch, with knots in her stomach, under the reproachful watch of Doña Juana who felt rejected by this refusal to eat. Then she would leave for the Roxy or the Crystal Palace, dragging along the loyal Erminda.

There was a moment, when the lights of the theatre went out, that reminded Evita of the fear instilled by the boys. In the dark, waiting for the lion on the screen who softly roars and is surrounded by a ring of stars, Evita, at fourteen, already knew what the strongest emotion of her life would be. It would not be waiting for love, but rather the anticipation of a show about to begin. The young audience tapped their feet to the rhythm of a military march that they called, for reasons no one knew, 'French bread, English cho-co-late.' Then, finally, illumination! Hollywood overflowed onto the children of Junín. The theatres never showed fewer than three films, so Evita could escape far from herself for the whole afternoon.

She did not limit herself to enjoying the film simply as a spectator. At an early age she already brought a 'professional' eye to the screen. All the other girls had read Norma Shearer's biography, too. They knew that Evita's idol had been born, poor and obscure, in Montreal, and that she had tried her luck in Hollywood, where Irving Thalberg had hired her at MGM, the company with the exquisite lion. They all knew this, but Evita knew it in a different way. She would go home, her face imprinted with a profound seriousness. She would wave away the annoying aroma of the *milanesas* and announce, 'I am going to be an actress.' Her mother, who at fourteen had not had the luxury of imagining her future as it had already been clearly drawn out in her own mother's mind, felt betrayed. 'What! So much work to be like everyone else and then the princess decides to throw it all away?'

If Juana dreamed of a respectable life, her bed did not always correspond to her dreams. It opened from time to time to some greying friend. This was a contradiction that Evita could exploit, for she knew this subject inside out. Her mother could be as authoritarian as she wanted, but she had neither rigid principles nor definitive ideas. Her generous nature engendered a laid-back attitude. So Doña Juana hesitated. What if the little one had talent after all? She had not been so bad when she acted in that school play. And Don Pepe Alvarez Rodríguez had gotten her into the National College's acting troupe when she was only in sixth grade. After that, didn't Evaristo Tello Sueyro, the family hairdresser, encourage her to perform with him in the amateur clubs? And hadn't she recited poetries on a real microphone in that music store? The owner had placed a speaker on the street because he wanted to bring life to this sleepy town. Through this instrument, Evita's little voice took on a strange tone and her voice glided over the town. 'Doña Juana,' said Don Pepe, 'we cannot tear down a child's vision of her vocation. Let her be. If she fails, she will not be marred. If she succeeds, then good for her.'

During this time, Eva had dated Ricardo, a conscript into the Junín military. Eva began asking herself a bold question, 'Can social barriers be overcome? Must it be my fate to live my life among nonlandowners when I am so beautiful?' It was thanks to their beauty that Elisa and Blanca had found fiancés, boring ones perhaps, but very much above their condition. The four sisters were pretty. And Juancito was the perfect image of the Latin lover. So why not take a chance? the devil murmured to her. The radio soaps that she passionately listened to told of the love between a poor young girl and an aristocrat.

That is how she came to accept, with a friend, an invitation by two young 'oligarchs' (she didn't know the word then, but later she would often use it). The boys invited the two girls from an inferior social caste to a day trip to Mar del Plata, the 'Pearl of the Atlantic,' a luxurious and boisterous seaside resort. In Junín during the 1930s there were more than enough naive souls to go around. Eva and her friend honestly believed that they were en route to a game of beach Ping-Pong and a nice dip in the ocean. Maybe they even imagined a kiss under the stars, but not for one second did they imagine that the car would stop at an isolated *estancia*, that the two 'aristocrats' would try to rape them, and that, to exact revenge for their stubborn refusals, they would throw them naked onto the side of the road. A trucker driving by with his family picked them up and covered them with a blanket. Years later, Eva must have been remembering this painful scene when she railed against the oligarchy before the crowds that came to see her in May Square.

In a crazy love letter to Perón in 1947, Eva dispelled the rumours that had been spread about her life in Junín. Rudi Freude, a very blond and very handsome German who was good friends with Perón, had brought gossip to the President. 'I was thirteen when I left Junín!' she writes in the letter, forgetting in her despair that she was fifteen. 'What an indignity to imagine a little girl capable of such lowliness!' In light of the rape episode, this clumsy message manages to touch us. Eva, at the apex of power, still had to explain herself to men.

❖

Her attempt to get close to high society had failed. In order to become something different from her mother and her sisters, in order simply to become someone else, to do something else, to be an actress, Evita had one choice: leave Junín. There are so many versions of the story of her departure that most biographers, exasperated, agree to tell only the essential fact – that she left. This pattern of uncertainty about Eva's life returns again and again. The slightest detail always seems to be mirrored by its opposite or followed by many facts that are similar but not completely the same, like a stone that shines under the water, broken and fractured by the light's refractions. It seems that many of the trails were intentionally muddied by Eva herself.

In the first version of her departure, the one according to Erminda Duarte, Evita asked her mother to accompany her to

Buenos Aires to audition for the National Radio. After much hesitation, Doña Juana finally agreed. Evita recited Amado Nervo's poem '*Adónde van los muertos*' (Where are the dead going?), and the radio director, Pablo Osvaldo Valle, offered her a small contract. The young actress settled in Buenos Aires at her mother's friends' house.

The second version is from biographer Fermín Chávez. Evita asked her mother to accompany her to Buenos Aires for an audition at Radio Belgrano. With the help of Palmira Repetto, the teacher whom she loved so, she had rehearsed three 'poetries' for a month, one of which was Nervo's '*Muerta.*' Mother and daughter went to Buenos Aires, Evita auditioned, and they returned to Junín. But the radio station's response took a long time. Even so, Evita announced to her teacher, 'With or without a response, I am leaving.' Juancito, who was completing his military service in Buenos Aires, would protect his little sister from the perils of the big city.

The third version, the one adopted by journalists Jorge Capsitski and Rodolfo Tettamanti among others, is that the tango singer Agustín Magaldi appeared at a theatre in Junín. Juancito approached him to talk about his sister who wanted to be an actress. Eva visited the singer in his dressing room and begged him to take her with him to Buenos Aires. Magaldi agreed, the trip wrapped in an exemplary decency since his wife was travelling with him.

The fourth version, this one from Mary Main, the most ferocious and unforgiving of her biographers, is that Evita sneaked into the singer's dressing room, became his mistress, and that is how she got to Buenos Aires, with him, to live a life of debauchery.

Within this succession of possible scenarios there is only mystery. These refractions can be explained only by the era's prudishness, to which Evita was forced to adhere, or by certain political reasons. The first version, the family's version, tends to present things conventionally. The second emphasises a very real element – a teacher's testimony – but the trip itself leaves us wondering. The fourth enjoys its salacious suggestion.

Agustín Magaldi was nicknamed 'the Carlos Gardel of the provinces' (Gardel was a famous tango singer). He was a pale man with a high tenor voice. To highlight his voice's poignant melancholy, he would sing with his hand on his heart and lift his eyes to the sky as if he were looking at a saintly Madonna. In fact, he was married, and he was generally considered too gloomy to chase skirts.

In terms of beauty, Evita was a little thing who was pale, skinny, and poorly dressed. She could act audaciously, but her cold and clammy hands always gave her away. She had no breasts, no hips, and no shapely calves. Her only assets were her transparent skin and her vivid eyes. Her beauty had not yet been born. Evita did everything by herself, she invented it all – her life, her beauty, even her death. During that time, when she looked in the mirror she saw her future image. It is impossible to say that this future image was seen by others or that the melancholy Magaldi glimpsed it.

Among the four versions, let us choose the third, the one where Magaldi and his wife drove this poor young girl in her maroon pleated skirt and white blouse (Evita would later describe her travel outfit to her designer, Paco Jamandreu) to Buenos Aires. Or better yet, Magaldi gave her his address so that Evita could visit when she arrived in Buenos Aires, and she took the train. One thing is certain: Magaldi met Evita. It is he who introduced her to the theatre critic Edmundo Guibourg, a serious intellectual whose recollections, quoted by Jorge Capsitski, leave no ambiguities.

Let us then embrace the most convincing scenario. On January 2, 1935, at fifteen years of age, Evita left her mother and her sisters and took the train to Buenos Aires. Clutched in her hand was a scrap of paper on which Magaldi had scribbled his address. Juancito picked her up at the station and took care of her as best he could within his means. Eva left behind a flat land and a flat existence. Of course, Buenos Aires is built on the same flatness. It just tries to trick us by erecting tall buildings like the thirty-three-floor Kavanagh, the highest building in all of Latin America. It was with the Kavanagh that Evita secretly identified in her heart. She would do whatever was necessary to rise higher than all the others.

Chapter 2

❖

THE ACTRESS

The sense of grandeur that Buenos Aires inspired in 1935 was not just a little provincial girl's illusion. In the nineteenth century, Argentina's capital was imposing. The port of Buenos Aires, which faced Europe, had become a gigantic and cosmopolitan head that rested on an immense but unpopulated body. Buenos Aires was the railroad hub, the slaughterhouse where the cattle were sacrificed, the dead centre of the country.

But its heart was divided. Its architecture represented the entire world. After all, the whole world had ended up on its muddy shores. It was as if every architect had played a child's game of Pretend. Pretend we are England. Or Pretend we are Spain. Or, better yet, Pretend we are gothic and from the Middle Ages, or baroque, or the Moors. As often happens when children imitate their parents, Buenos Aires surpassed its models. In 1931, the American writer Waldo Frank wrote: 'There is no other place where the Italian confectioner's style appears in such a spectacular fashion; there is no other place where hospitals, clubs, and private and public "mansions" attain such a high level of expressiveness.'

However, the jigsaw city lived its plurality in anguish. Even during this period of expansion and pride, it was hard to find New York's optimism and joie de vivre. The crash had had its impact, but there was also a strange regret and a nostalgia for the past that northern cities never knew, since they were facing the future. Buenos Aires's tragic soul prevented it from understanding its own identity. Although it was frantically searched for elsewhere, it resided in the exacerbation and the explosion of imitation. And it questioned itself, questions inherited from Europe – 'who am I?' – as if its identity had to be undeniably unique and therefore linear, when all the while the answer was in the joy of its fragmentation.

Evita had been to the capital before, and Buenos Aires had already disappointed her. The white telephones and the satin sheets from her fantasies were nowhere to be found. But the visits had been brief, and her mother's solid mass at her side was enough to reassure her of her own solidity. But now there was only Evita on earth, Evita and her light weight. These are the moments when you feel your own existence like never before. Where would she go? Where *did* she go?

One version has Evita lodging at the actress Maruja Gil Quesada's cousin's house; Magaldi had introduced them. An eyewitness, Eduardo del Castillo, described the cousin's apartment on Sarmiento Street as having 'very high ceilings, with a crescent-shaped balcony.' But according to other witnesses, Evita found herself in a sordid boarding house and never knew the comfort of that rounded and maternal balcony. The two stories do coincide, however, on the neighbourhood. Both the cousin's place and the sordid boarding house were next to the Congressional Palace.

Evita was steps away from the square that contained a monumental structure of an interesting person: Rodin's *The Thinker*. The porteños always hastened to add that it was 'the real one, not a copy,' though of course the 'real one' is in Paris. The sculpture's influence without a doubt transformed the Plaza Congreso into the perfect place for thinking. Retired folk came here to feed the pigeons as they watched life pass them by, like philosophers. Life streamed up and down the Avenida de Mayo, where all political events took place and which led straight to the house of government, the Casa Rosada.

The Avenida de Mayo also had a less solemn facet. It was nicknamed the 'Avenue of the Spaniards,' a tribute to the nationals of the Mother Homeland, and was populated by emigrants from the peninsula who lingered to drink the thick hot chocolate in which they dipped cinnamon doughnuts covered with sugar. Evita definitely walked here. At the end of the avenue, the light pink colour of the president's house appeared like a distant dream; no one at the time could have imagined that one day it would be covered with bullet holes. Nor could anyone – not even Evita herself – have imagined that one day she would walk along this avenue in triumph and settle into the balcony of power.

Benigno Acossano, one of Evita's biographers who believes the boarding house theory, tells of Giovannoni or Giovannone, a friend of Doña Juana and the owner of a restaurant. Giovannoni's boarding house was the meeting place for visitors to Buenos Aires from Junín. It is possible that, at the very beginning of her trip, Evita ate at this restaurant. But not for long. She attained the austere goal she had set for herself when she was being threatened by her mother's *milanesas*. She went hungry.

In such circumstances, there is no better remedy than *maté cocido*, a kind of hot tea. The *maté* that one drinks from the gourd, with a silver or white metal straw, requires a very delicate ceremony. But when one is alone and desperate just to put something in one's stomach, it is necessary only to boil a little water in a pot with three or four spoonfuls of this blessed herb. In case of a shortage, one can reuse yesterday's herbs and congratulate oneself. Just like the lyrics of a tango: *'Cuando no tengas ni yerba de ayer secándose al sol'* (when you don't even have yesterday's herbs drying in the sun). Then drink the greenish liquid, which leaves a harsh aftertaste, a pasty residue in the mug and comfort in one's heart, in big, greedy gulps. The people had good reason to call it *maté cocido* 'green *milanesa*,' for it is true that this infusion replaces food and drink.

Later, Perónism would find a name for Evita's misery. The years between 1930 and 1940, the years of the popular soup and of electoral fraud, were called 'the infamous decade.' If she had known this at the time, she would have taken comfort in drinking her *maté*, for one must only name reality to begin feeling better. But she lived the infamy day to day and did not have time to put it into words. That is why, when she met Perón, who had found the words for humiliation and hunger, she fervently seized these words, tirelessly saying them again and again, like a mantra.

But at fifteen she cruelly lacked these magic words. She had neither the adequate vocabulary, nor the correct pronunciation, nor striking, clear beauty that would have replaced the eloquence. A street urchin, she did not have the spare time to study acting. And anyway, is that what she wanted? Few actresses had gone to the Conservatory, which had recently been formed. From the minute she arrived in Buenos Aires, Evita learned the only thing that seemed vital to her, the acting network: whom to approach and where, in which downtown café, she could find contacts.

It might have been Magaldi who gave her the crucial push by introducing her to Joaquín de Vedia, the director, and to José Franco, the actor. Later, when her elongated and tight face became familiar in that circle, she knocked directly on the theatre doors. But it is logical to think that someone helped her out the first time. Her first theatrical experience taught her that directors, famous actors, and critics often used the proverbial casting couch. Eva had entered a vindictive world that ran much like that in Junín but with a sharper pettiness. It was déjà vu, and she took refuge in silence. Here it was no longer Doña Juana, but Eva herself, whom people found insignificant. They watched her with a saccharin smile, waiting for one wrong step, for a fall, as if this fate were written in the lines of her palms.

José Franco and Joaquín de Vedia gave her her first role in

a play called *La señora de Pérez*. Eva played the maid who had to announce, 'Lunch is served.' These three words were simple, and she seems to have pronounced them correctly. Other roles followed, silent ones in plays with tempting titles such as *Cada casa es un mundo* (Each home is a world unto itself) and *La dama, el caballero y el ladrón* (The lady, the knight and the thief). The premiere of *La dama*, on January 2, 1936, coincided with the anniversary of her departure from Junín. Already a year had passed! The era of each year lasting a century had ended. She now moved to the rhythm of her lively and nervous heart. Admittedly, the only word the critics used to describe her, if at all, was 'discreet.' But at least they did not use the word 'bad.' And although she worked for peanuts, she worked nonstop. The future seemed positive. But when the curtain fell on *La dama*, Evita fell into a rut. There was no work, no hope on the horizon. As poverty dragged along, Eva fell into a pattern of wandering from place to place.

This wandering lasted until May, and for four months, to keep her spirits up, she constantly had to remind herself of the most brilliant point in her career so far. It was also the riskiest, the one where the beginner played one of Napoleon's sisters in *Madame Sans-Gêne* (Mrs Cool Customer), by Moreau and Sardou. She wore an Empire dress that clung to her alabaster skin. 'An important person's dress, for someone with power, someone who likes to command,' Eva Franco, the director's daughter, would prophetically say. The high waist was supposed to accentuate the small chest and Evita cheated on the volume with the help of a pair of balled up socks.

One member of the audience, who must have been fooled by this false advertising, sent Eva flowers. They were sent to Eva, no last name. Eva Franco, the star of the company, innocently accepted the delivery, for who could imagine that the other Eva would receive flowers? To her surprise, within the arrangement she found a gilded visiting card addressed to Eva Duarte. Following the receipt of these unfortunate flowers, the relationship between the two Evas quickly deteriorated, and Eva Duarte performed only one more time for the company.

During the rehearsals for *Madame Sans-Gêne*, and prior to the flower incident, the teenager was the butt of a joke. Her friends had persuaded her to climb on top of a table with a candle on her head to show off her progress in the theatrical arts. 'Balance is essential for an actor,' they had said. Poor Evita, who wildly recited her 'poetries' whenever she found an ear that would listen, climbed onto the table with the candle on her head. Once she got up there, she saw their smiles and heard the mean cackles. Was it possible that the sound, so linked to her childhood memories, was now resonating in the 'artists' circle? – All she wanted now was to descend graciously from the table, but her hopes were in vain. Grace forgets the humiliated. The crowd did all they could to prevent the fire carrier from coming down, and she was left to fall with a loud clunk.

✢

In May, Argentina's autumn, Eva was finally hired again, this time by Pepita Muñoz, Eloy Alfaro, and the same José Franco's troupe. The plays to which Evita lent her slight presence and, less frequently, her voice were naive comedies of manners of the 'digestive' genre, so called because they were after-dinner plays. These were not the disturbing 'theme' plays of the period, which later enabled the young actress to go on tour. In Loïc Le Gouradiec's *El beso mortal* (The deathly kiss), Eva was always part of the troupe when father Franco headlined. She portrayed the role of a nurse, and the 'deathly kiss' was that of syphilis, a titillating theme for an audience not used to subjects of a sexual nature.

At the time, a theatrical tour was a harrowing adventure. If the play was panned, and most were, each actor had to make his or her own way back to Buenos Aires. No one was paid for rehearsals, and the actresses had to provide their own costumes.

But no one complained. There were two performances per day, three on Sunday and on holidays. The writer, David Viñas, perfectly described the situation: 'It was in the midst of the days when the Republic was ruled by landowners. A theatre was managed like an *estancia*. . . . Eva performed either silent parts or the one of "neighbour #2." She represented the anonymous and voiceless entity that we call the womb of the people.'

According to Fanny Cúneo, the company was in Mendoza on the day when José Franco entered Evita's dressing room and demanded with an authoritarian attitude as if he were a landowner: 'Sleep with me or you're fired.' If she had only known that a handsome captain of the mountain troops by the name of Juan Domingo Perón was at the Royal, the same hotel, at the same time!

She took the advice of the company's prompter, who had become her confidant and dispenser of practical advice. She was not fired. Then Franco's wife joined the troupe in Rosario and threw a fit. She threatened her husband, but she terrorised Eva. Just as the tango says, the guilty are always women. Back in Buenos Aires, Eva had to leave the company.

According to Carmen Llorca, many years later Evita would give Franco an important job in her Foundation for Social Aid. It was a delicious vengeance to be able to shower the enemy with favours. Wasn't it you who gave me my first part? Did you not force me to sleep with you? Didn't you throw me out on the street in fear of your wife? Now that you are old and poor, here, take this gift. I am the queen and this is my bidding.

Before Eva left Franco's family, the troupe was in Mendoza, a town where everything is possible, including all perils. An actor fell ill. It was not syphilis, but it was contagious. The director forbade any visits to the hospital, but Eva felt sorry for the man and furtively visited him. She gave him the 'mortal kiss' and caught his illness. Years later, she would receive hundreds of destitute folk daily and would be incapable of seeing a leper, a woman whose face was eaten by God knows what horrible wounds, or simply a flea-infested child, without hugging, kissing, and caressing them. She worried more about not offending than about protecting herself from the danger of contact.

The director of the company who hired Eva on her return to Buenos Aires was Pablo Suero, nicknamed 'the Toad.' The writer César Tiempo called him 'the super-hetero-harmless, slanderous, and to top it all off, Spanish, scorpion.' Suero was obese and had bulging eyes. He spent his time sitting at a table of the café Real on Corrientes Avenue, the main artery for theatres and lights. It had just been widened and was proudly nicknamed 'the street that never sleeps.' One after the other, starlets searching for jobs would approach his table. And one after the other, they allowed the man with the shiny nose, the greasy double chin, and the hairy hands to touch their buttocks while he officiated over their applications. Evita had to clench her jaw and grit her teeth. After her tour, she shared her boarding room and her *maté cocido* with two other unlucky girls, Fina Bustamante and Anita Jordán. Anything was better than returning to her mother. In December 1936, she got the part of Catalina in Lillian Hellman's *Las inocentes*. In the play, Evita, who had not yet ended her battle with her mother tongue, had to exclaim in Latin, '*Ferebant!*' Then, 'You are so stubborn!' That was her only line, but according to another young actress, Eva did not have to act in order to play the role of a candid schoolgirl. 'She had,' this other actress remembered, 'chestnut eyes, very red lips, transparent and colourless skin, and the softness of a magnolia. She was the image of innocence itself. And it was true, for Eva was very pure deep inside.'

For once, in order to cast his company of innocent girls, the hetero-harmless director had called on the students of the Conservatory, middle-class girls who did not use their heels to chase down a cup of creamy coffee. Eva was arm in arm with Suero when she showed up for her first rehearsal. She was dressed in a modest blue cotton dress. Unfortunately, silk was in style. Flowery dresses and 'smoky' stockings had to be silk, and Evita's stockings were unforgivably opaque. However, one specific detail made a lasting impression on the young innocents who watched open-mouthed as the Toad and his protégé entered the room – the Basque espadrilles that were laced high around her ankles in the rustic fashion. It goes without saying that Evita did not wear these to honour her roots. She was greeted with an uncomfortable silence, which she rejected by immersing herself in her own eternal silence. She was already intimate with humiliation.

[It was Benigno Acossano who told the story of the espadrilles. Witnesses, such as the actor Raúl Rossi, indignantly rejected it. Rossi confirmed that even at the beginning of her career, Evita dressed in a classic style.] It is not difficult to understand this indignation and to feel it too. These types of detail were too often used by vicious anti-Perónists in order that they be considered innocent. Benigno Acossano was known to be Evita's detractor. Among this abundance of tendentious details, it might be possible to distinguish those based on imagination and those based on observation.

The troupe left on tour for Montevideo, Uruguay. While the other girls travelled with their mothers, Eva lugged her suitcase and her stage fright by herself. Still, the walks on this charming city's half-sea half-river beach soothed her. Her guides were young Uruguayans from good families, much nicer looking than the Toad, although equally obtuse. One of them later formulated this revealing declaration: 'Eva was attractive, but ordinary: she was neither too intelligent, nor too dumb. The type of girl that comes by the dozen. Besides, you know, she was from a very inferior class.'

It is Acossano who tells an amusing anecdote that reveals in him an involuntary tenderness. One night in Montevideo, Eva returned to her hotel in a silk dress, silk stockings, high platform shoes, a large patent leather purse, and a little cape with a rose pinned on it. She undressed in her room, where the others had followed, with a distracted air, pretending not to notice her companions' astonishment. The others played along and ignored her too, content to watch the figure in her lace bra and satin skin-coloured slip. At that moment someone knocked on the door, and an enormous bouquet for Miss Eva Durante (no one knows why she changed her name, although it was not for long) invaded the room. A gigantic bouquet was the sign of success. The girls rushed to her side, shook her, kissed her, and questioned her. Eva came out of her silence, the colour returned to her cheeks and the words to her mouth, her hands became less clammy, and she told stories, laughed, felt alive, human, surrounded, like a dream.

Back in Buenos Aires, she did not wear a silk dress to go to visit Suero. The amphibian was getting ready to stage a new play at the Astral theatre. Eva arrived in a white printed dress with a big green flower on her cleavage. Luckily, her face was partially hidden by the brim of her hat and she could not see the looks that followed her. The waiting room was swarming with actors who had come to pitch their talent, just as she had. She was announced. The Toad opened his office door and screamed, consumed with rage, 'Stop bothering me! I'm married!' This announcement was followed by a stream of insults. Eva calmly responded that she was only looking for work. And this man responded, 'Just because I slept with you doesn't mean that I have to give you work.' Everyone froze. 'Eva,' said one actress who was there, 'was barely able to articulate a word, with even the softest voice; her face went white.'

After this, the demanding nature that she had always adopted took a respite. Eva had the honour of performing in Luigi Pirandello's *La nueva colonia*, directed by Armando Discépolo who was anything but a toad. He was an excellent writer of fine plays such as *Mateo*, *Hombres de honor*, and *Mustafá*. Evita had only three words in the play, which lasted just six days, but no one humiliated her here, and for once in her life the theatre critic Augusto A. Guibourg found her to be not 'discreet' but 'gracious.'

The premiere of *La nueva colonia* took place on March 5, 1937. Between the scene with Suero and this play, she had endured a period of inactivity. However, it was shorter than the one she was about to experience. 1937 was the worst year of her life.

ONE PRINCE CAN HIDE ANOTHER

Eva met the type of 'lost' woman about which the tango sings in either a moaning or an enraged, but always insistent, tone. In the 1920s, the Parisian prostitutes worked their way up within the 'Buenos Aires network.' They dreamt of the slick *estanciero* who would take them away from it all, the very rich *estanciero* they saw in Paris once a year and whose elegance they adored, a dark, handsome man with pale skin and charcoal eyes. The other kind of rich Argentines who visited Paris, all dressed in leather, they called 'rastaquouères.' Some girls went to Buenos Aires, including Polish Jews who were swayed with promises of marriage by the Migdal, an organisation of Jewish pimps. They disembarked with thoughts of marrying a nice Jewish doctor but soon found themselves locked up in a bordello. The tango never spoke of them, but it did address the French prostitute who arrived in the twenties and who, after ten years, still had not found her *estanciero*. The tango never stopped sympathising with her cruel fate. How could a chauvinist and misogynist complaint like the tango capture the pain of a Parisian woman overcome with homesickness? But the tango did not forget the porteña who was 'hurt by men' either. It spoke of her often and with surprising understanding. The misery of the twenties was so intense that the tango's male instantly forgot his mother and his hurt ego, and instead was so moved by a woman's heart that he shared her tears.

Eva was certainly not like all these women. It is true that she had been hurt by men, but she had a pursuit and a career that took priority in her life. She was passionate and willing to sacrifice everything in order to reach her goal. During her artistic period, each one of her lovers was chosen with one specific objective, to get a part. The others, the ones she had to find when she had no prospects of work, served only to allow her enough time to find a new play or a new film. All her life she was incapable of settling for one man who would protect her without helping her to succeed. To Eva, men were not an end, they were a necessary means. How could one do without them? Evita waited outside the radio station's headquarters, with the singer Juanita Larrauri, for a man, any man, to ask her out. She had even accepted an invitation to go to an island in the Delta with another girl and two strangers for the weekend. One of these men did not want her, for he found her vulgar. 'To have her as a mistress was expensive,' said a third. 'She was always sick, and you had to pay for her medicines,' medicines such as calcium for malnutrition.

The man who found her vulgar had been shocked by her language. It was a 'filthy' language that only prostitutes used at the time. Eva was a pioneer even on this front. From the moment she gained power, Eva began furiously to insult ministers and ambassadors with words that had never resonated off the red carpets and the austere panelling. However, she insulted only important men; she was perfectly courteous with her *cabecitas negras*, (little black heads). She chose her targets from the world's most powerful. Her split personality appeared according to the social status of the person to whom she was speaking. Only the humble had the right to call her Evita to her face. On the other hand, if she spoke harshly to the delicate stranger who meant no harm to her, it was because for her he represented a detested image. She therefore fought her desire for revenge and behaved like the prostitute that he saw in her.

When her sister Erminda had a serious bout of pleurisy, Eva went to Junín and settled in at her bedside. Her mother and her sisters took advantage of this opportunity to beg her to come home and to abandon her foolish illusions. Eva remained unshakable. From the day of her departure, this stubborn Basque had not budged an inch. 'I will come back later,' she said, 'but only after I succeed.'

Throughout most of 1937 Eva was without work. She had gone back to wandering on an empty stomach and with holes in her shoes. *No hay suegra como la mía* (There's no mother-in-law like mine) fascinated the audiences from November 1937 through March 1938. It was also broadcast by Splendid Radio, but this was not very rewarding for Evita since she had a silent part. Nevertheless, she had work, and she knew how to cast the demons away. Then in the beginning of March 1938, a radio competition organised by the magazine *Sintonía* gave her the opportunity to meet Chilean journalist and former race car driver Emilio Kartulowicz, editor of the magazine.

Besides Perón, Kartulowicz was the only important man in her life, and this has much to do with what *Sintonía* meant to her. *Sintonía* was the magazine she read in *Junín*, the one that published Norma Shearer's biography and had therefore lit a sacred fire in her soul. It was the reading of this magazine that had, years later, driven her to enter this competition. To enter, one had to apply for a part in *la gruta de la fortuna* (The grotto of fortune), a comedy that Pierina Dealessi's company was soon going to put on in the Liceo theatre. Evita could have introduced herself to Kartulowicz by saying, 'If I am here, it is because of you.' What she really said is not known, but we do know that she fell in love with him on the spot.

Finally, a true feeling, perhaps an illusory one, but at least it warms the heart. This feeling was also inspired by the man's power. Even while loving him, she searched for support, a recommendation, a photo in the pages of his magazine. However, this should not take anything away from her feelings for Kartulowicz. Evita loved the Chilean. He was big, muscular, warm, and powerful. He was athletic, well built, and capable of helping her. This was her model of prince charming, a model that would appear later in her life in another man who was just as accomplished and athletic. In fact, this love served as a dress rehearsal. If she had been involved solely in sordid love affairs, Perón's love would not have sounded an echo in her. But everything in life is an echo, 'a forest of symbols where smells, colours and sounds' – but also loves – 'respond to each other.'

Kartulowicz published Evita's photo. That is how he paid, with his money, for a love that soon began to annoy him. Eva was too passionate to be wise, and she knew nothing about coquetry. Mauricio Rubinstein once saw Evita wait in the halls of the magazine's offices for Kartulowicz for twelve hours, filing her nails. The actress Juanita Quesada, who worked with Eva at Radio Belgrano, elaborated: 'Evita was not lucky with men. She exhausted them, she was clingy. Kartulowicz would go to the Delta for the weekend with other girls, and she would follow him all the way there.' She was honest and direct, she had an ardent heart and body, and she was ahead of her time in her refusal or incapacity to use detours.

There is no doubt that the photo in *Sintonía* helped her. Kartulowicz published more of them after their breakup, and he continued to talk about her at opportune moments. Kartulowicz was therefore not the worst of her lovers. When Evita became the wife of the President, she gave him the gift of paper for his magazine during a period where the Argentinean press was suffering a shortage.

However, for the first time, it is due to a woman's protection that Evita owes her relative success of 1938. It all started with a part in *La gruta de la fortuna*. She won the competition and was admitted into Pierina Dealessi's troupe. The Italian actress had noticed the pale creature who had waited her turn, and she had been moved. She said, 'Evita was a little transparent thing, she was very skinny, very fine, with black hair and an elongated face. We hired her for a pitiful salary. We worked seven days a week, and on Sundays we performed four times in a row. In the afternoon we would meet in the dressing rooms to have a drink. Evita would have *maté*, but her health was fragile, I added some milk. She was so thin, you would have thought she was a draft. . . . Her hands were always cold and clammy due to her hunger, to her sadness and to a certain neglect. Indeed she was cold even in her acting work: a real ice cube. She was not a girl who could show emotion. She was very subdued and very shy. She was a sad girl who was devoted to the Virgin of Itatí. She ate very little. It seemed as though she never ate. When the poverty ended, she deprived herself of food for lack of time. The only love of her life was her brother Juan, an adorable scoundrel.'

Pierina Dealessi, who was single and lived with her mother, often told Eva with a tender solicitude; 'Sweetheart, after the theatre, come sleep at my house. It's dangerous to go home at three in the morning.' She would set up a makeshift bed for her inside her old immigrant's travelling chest.

Navarro and Fraser maintain that at one time, Evita lived with a young actor who was close to marrying her. He had moved her into an apartment where she led a 'decent and normal' life. However, one evening when she came home to their love nest, she found the apartment empty. The actor had left and taken everything, the furniture and even the pots. Evita had to return to the sordid boarding houses.

John Barnes and Jorge Capsitski relate a similar story of a lost apartment. Juancito, the charming little devil, had completed his military service in Buenos Aires. He had always remained close to Evita. Indeed, brother and sister were such accomplices that they finished each other's sentences. Juancito understood everything, even the things she could not admit. The bad boy of the family made common cause with the adventurer. Evita moved into an apartment (Capsitski says it was the Savoy, a luxurious hotel) with a rich industrialist. Then she heard the news: that her dear Juancito had embezzled funds from the savings bank where he worked. She sold everything to pay off her brother's debt and found herself back in a boarding house once again. Capsitski goes farther still, confirming that Evita ended up in a *convent*.

RADIO TEARS

Suddenly, on May 1, 1939 (one of the dates that Perónism will use as its symbol), an abrupt turn took place in her career. The Air Theater company began to broadcast a series of soap operas written by Hector P. Blomberg. The headliners were Evita Duarte and Pascual Pelliciotta. And this is how Evita became part of a company while a writer wrote custom-made scenes for her.

That same month, the magazine *Antena* published her photo twice: one black and white, the other in colour and on the cover. One side of her dark chestnut hair was elevated with the help of hairpieces to frame her face, and the other side fell over her shoulders. It was a middle-of-the-road hairstyle, the hairstyle of an Eva who had not yet taken control of it all. Later, when she forced her hair to obey her, taming it into a tight chignon, it would be clear that she held her destiny in her fist.

Hector P. Blomberg was almost forty. He was a novelist and a poet, famous for historical plays which were often set during the time of Rosas's dictatorship. Blomberg belonged to a nationalist current that included the nineteenth-century dictator and Argentina's popular culture. At the time, Evita was far from having an ideology, and she successfully threw herself into her radio career by allying herself with a writer whose ideas foreshadowed those of Perónism.

Writers from the other side of the spectrum made things difficult for them. The Argentinean culture of the thirties was first French, then English, but always universal. On the left, antinationalism displayed the same disdain for 'populace' culture that Evita personified. Radio soaps, which were more emotional than ideological, could therefore be compared to Rosism. Indeed, the gulf between Perónism and its adversaries was aesthetic in nature. Evita had been Perónist well before Perón himself was, and all as a matter of taste. From social resentment to the aesthetics of tango and of radio soaps, she had a thousand reasons to get along with Perón.

One evening, in a bar in Buenos Aires, the famous novelist Roberto Arlt, author of *Seven Lunatics*, was fervently speaking, making big gestures with his hands. At his table, a pale young girl was sipping her café au lait. She was so fragile and coughed so much that she seemed to have jumped out of one of his novels. The girl was Eva, and due to his extravagant gestures, the writer ended up spilling a cup on the girl's skirt. To ask her forgiveness, he got down on one knee with his hand on his heart, at which point Evita got up and ran to the restroom. When she returned, her eyes were red. She calmly sat back down and simply said, 'I am going to die soon.' 'Don't worry, gorgeous,' he reassured her, 'I will die before you.' In fact, he died July 26, 1942, and she followed ten years later, also on July 26.

Her photo was appearing regularly in magazines, her dark curly hair tumbling down over her frail shoulders. In fact, Eva's photo appeared so frequently that the public was beginning to recognise her smile. She had a slight overbite, so that her retracted lower lip, bitten by her canines, gave her a candid, almost silly look. But she was finally becoming 'visible.' She existed. However, dissatisfaction seemed to be her nature. If before she had lived alone due to poverty, she now had to remain so in order to preserve her acquisitions. Her relationships, her liaisons existed to advance her career. At the radio station, she taped her broadcasts without speaking to anyone and went home as soon as she was done. Pablo Raccioppi, an actor who worked with Eva, mentioned the rancour that men inspired in her. 'It's all they think about,' he admitted to her. When Raccioppi, who was married, spoke to Evita of his wife and his children, 'she kept up a scowling silence.' This corroborates other accounts of Evita as a tense, ambitious, and frigid woman. In short, she lacked sex appeal. It was a time when the definition of femininity was specified by a famous bolero: '*La mujer que al amor no se asoma/no merece llamarse mujer*' (A woman who does not love/does not deserve to be called a woman).

Eva performed a second series of Blomberg's soaps broadcast by Radio Prieto, then she began a third. She also acted in a historical film on the Patagonia, *La carga de los valientes* (The heroic duty), and made her last two forays into theatre in *Corazón de manteca* (Heart of butter) and *La plata hay que repartirla* (The money must be divided up). Theatre parts did not help her very much. They paid next to nothing, and almost all her parts were silent. In 1941, Evita appeared in two films, *El más infeliz del pueblo* (The town's unhappiest one), with the famous actor Luis Sandrini, and *Una novia en apuros* (Bride in a jam) by the American John Reinhardt. However, these roles were not memorable, and radio was still her bread and butter. There's no doubt that Eva was aware of this. Her confessor, Father Hernán Benítez, says that she often admitted, 'In the theatre, I was awful; the movies, I managed; but if I was good at something, it was radio.'

The broadcast system that would carry shows throughout the entire country had not been invented yet, but radio manufacturers sent trucks equipped with loudspeakers to towns still without electricity. Every day at five o'clock, the house mistresses, the maids, and, if the noise permitted it, the women factory workers would experience a moment of magic. The themes of the soaps were always the same. It was the story of Cinderella over and over again. A young, poor, pretty, tender, pure, and unfortunate girl was in love with the boss's son. For months she suffered and cried at half-hour stretches. In the end, due to her beauty, but more so to her kindness, she overcame the social barriers. This was a dream role for Evita. Her voice was high-pitched and trembling, painful and honest. It was childish, clumsy, and unrehearsed, a plain voice that resembled her listeners' voices. For these women, this was their favourite moment, a moment that belonged only to them. It was also *maté* time, and while they sipped the last drop, the murmur of the straw seemed to imitate Evita's sighs.

Between 1939 and 1940, Evita's name was linked to one or two soaps. That means she was associated with the companies that sponsored them. Mauricio Rubinstein confided that her new relationships allowed her to later find the job for her brother at the savings bank from which he ended up embezzling funds. Cocinero oil sponsored Evita's broadcasts on Radio El Mundo. These companies used Evita's radio theatre for commercial purposes with guaranteed success. This is not surprising, nor is it surprising that she made a promotional film with Linter Publicity, *La luna de miel de Inés* (Inés's honeymoon), and posed for publicity shots. Rather it was the era that was surprising. When she visited Paris in 1947, *France-Dimanche* published one of these old photographs. The Bembergs, a very wealthy and anti-Perónist Argentinean family, had obtained the photo for the newspaper in order to reveal to the French Evita's true nature. In the photo, the Argentinean president's wife, who at this point was on an official tour, was draped in a fabric that she held in one hand on her chest and in the other on her stomach, as if to prevent it from falling. Her foot peeked out of a very high-heeled slipper, and finally, horribly, you could see her entire leg.

Nothing but quick tears and improvised sighs were cried and delivered on the hour in those years, until 1943. The scenes were written by Martinelli Massa, or by her always faithful Blomberg. Every day, a half hour before taping, the writer would read the dialogue he had just written to the actors. Did Evita's tongue still slip? Did she still say *ojepto* instead of *objeto* and *écter* instead of *éter*? Raúl Rossi refused to admit it. 'It is true that she would ask the scriptwriter to change a word, which she found unpronounceable, to an easier one, but we all did the same thing: what actor didn't? Except when Evita became friendly with Perón, we waited for her at the taping, and we would never reproach her.'

Gloria Alcorta's version is different, but it must be pointed out that this author belonged to a much higher social class than Evita's and that her testimony refers to a later period in her career – which in terms of voice and delivery does not change a thing. 'We began to listen to the radio at a time when my husband, Alberto Girondo, was ill. It was a new experience for us: we had never heard it before. And, randomly, we stumbled upon a certain Eva Duarte playing the part of Catherine of Russia. She was completely unknown to us. But what a revelation! And what a daily pleasure, this nasal voice that played the empress with rural tango accents! It was hilarious. We always anxiously awaited the start of the soap opera, and we even talked about it with our friends. I think we contributed a great deal to her stardom.'

However, those who did not live in Gloria Alcorta's world listened to Eva without laughing; even better, they cried. Thanks to these women, and to their tears, Evita left the mouldy boarding house in 1942 and moved into an apartment on Carlos Pellegrini Street near Libertador Avenue, a very chic neighbourhood. But Pablo Raccioppi adds a disturbing detail to his account: 'The people in the world of entertainment used to say that this apartment was Colonel Aníbal Imbert's bachelor pad.' This comment is perplexing, for almost everyone agrees that Evita did not meet Colonel Imbert until after the Revolution of June 4, 1943. There are two exceptions: Silvano Santander and Carmen Llorca.

The first, a radical deputy, was the author of *Técnica de una traición* (The techniques of betrayal), published in 1955, after Perón was overthrown. Santander did not pull any punches and accused Evita of having worked for the German Embassy beginning in 1941. It would have been by involving herself in espionage for the Germans that she might have met the Argentinean soldiers who were the pro-Nazi craftsmen of the Revolution. He mentions Perón but not Imbert, and yet they were both members of the same group, the GOU (Group of United Officers). Santander based his theory on supposed photocopies of cheques made out to Eva Duarte from the German ambassador, Edmund von Thermann. While Santander's claims are basically true, the documents he refers to are gross falsifications, and this honest but excessively passionate writer abused them.

As far as Carmen Llorca goes, she relies only on her own intuition, which tells her that Perón and Eva met long before June 1943, although the official date of their meeting is January 22, 1944. Since Evita disappeared from the radio waves in the first few months of 1943, Llorca deduced that she had begun to work for the Perónist movement. In fact, most writers are surprised by Eva's disappearance just when success was knocking at her door. Some suspect an illness. Others accept the explanation she herself gave to the magazine *Antena* on May 27, 1943: 'Lately, I have not received interesting enough offers for an artist at my level.'

It is hard to imagine Evita involved so early on in a political cause, and even harder that she was Mata Hari in 1941. Her political persona was formed over time and in a visible way perceivable by all. Everyone noted her blunders and laughed at her mistakes. She lacked finesse and tact until 1946, when a trip to Europe transformed her. How can one imagine that, in the middle of a war, the German ambassador would risk hiring a twenty-two-year-old girl with a loose tongue? At her low level, she got along. Befriending a sponsor of a broadcast is one thing, becoming a spy for a Nazi count is another.

It is true that Evita was a young and ambitious actress in 1942. She wanted revenge, and she had a natural predisposition to nationalism and an interest in social problems. As she confirmed in her autobiography, *La razón de mi vida* (My mission in life), she was enraged by injustice throughout her life. The feeling was so violent that it suffocated her. There is no one who confirms Llorca's – or Santander's – hypothesis. If Evita did meet Colonel Imbert before the Revolution in 1943, their relationship certainly had nothing to do with 'the cause.'

So why did Evita disappear at the beginning of 1943? The only believable hypothesis is that she was ill. She was so pale, that they diagnosed anaemia and even leukaemia. If she had disappeared to devote herself to a political endeavour, then how can we explain the fact that, once she became Perón's official mistress, she did not retire and in fact recorded a plethora of radio broadcasts?

Another story concerning Evita's feelings toward injustice, anchored in her heart since before 1944, is more convincing. One rainy night, in a poor neighbourhood far from the centre of town, a desperate woman was frantically searching for transportation to take her husband to the hospital. A taxi stopped, and out came a beautiful young woman who offered her help. She said that she knew a good doctor at the hospital, and she asked the driver to take them there. This beautiful young woman was Eva. She spent the night at the man's bedside and later continued to visit him to assure herself of his recovery.

On that distressing night, however, an anarchist worker also visited the ailing man. The author Libertad Demitrópulo tells this story and adds the following: 'Eva Duarte and the worker became friends. They talked at length about the country's politics about which Evita had very precise ideas. Life, which had initiated their relationship, launched them into action during critical circumstances for the two of them and for the Homeland, until the day when, eleven years later, Eva's death separated them.' Farther on, this Perónist author – who came from an anarchist family, at least according to his first name, which was very common among libertarians – took a risk by venturing a name. This mysterious worker was none other than Isaías Santín, a member of the CGT, a workers' resistance movement, which collaborated with Eva until the end. Evita can plausibly be associated with both the Nazis and anarchism. Perónism is a hodgepodge that allows all sorts of interpretations. Indeed, it favours them.

It very much appears that Raccioppi was misguided as to the dates but not in his description of a glacial, selfish, and tense Evita (as real as the Samaritan Evita from the preceding story). She had succeeded, or so she could believe. The same person who was capable of staying up all night at a sick man's bedside did not hesitate to say about other actors: 'Pablo, you and I are headliners now. We can no longer frequent the same cafés they do. Let us keep our distance, and go to a more expensive place.'

She was moving in the direction of hierarchies, motivated by a desire to shake off the life she had deserted. She spat at an actress who had requested permission to arrive late so that she could give her baby its bottle, 'This is not a home. If you can't come in on time like everyone else, then find another line of work.' However, in conclusion, Raccioppi grudgingly admitted, 'Evita always said what she was thinking.'

Chapter 3

❖

THE LOVER

On June 4, 1943, a coup d'état fomented by General Arturo Rawson overthrew President Ramón S. Castillo and replaced him with General Pedro Pablo Ramírez.

When the preceding military revolution of 1930 had broken out, Evita had just moved to Junín with her matriarchal tribe. When she heard gunshots, she showed her sister Erminda the bolted door and said, 'No need to panic, we are safe.' Did she know what this new revolution was about? Was she familiar with the events that had occurred in her country since 1930? She knew the headlines. She was certainly not unaware of the existence of a conservative social class that owned the land, a middle class that often claimed immigrants as their ancestors and supported the radicals (old Yrigoyen had been the well-liked caudillo), an emerging working class, and the army. Among the unionised workers, there was a Socialist, Communist, or anarchist minority; the rest of the population let destiny take its course. In 1930, the army had attempted to overthrow Hipólito 'The Tattoo' Yrigoyen, who was becoming increasingly incoherent.

Yrigoyen had always used obscure language. But as he got

older, his cryptic tendencies worsened. What should one think of his famous '*efectividades conducentes*' (appropriate effectivities), an Yrigoyenish expression that his decoders translated as 'that which brings effectiveness'? One had to heed the evidence that no one listened to Yrigoyen anymore. The army had taken advantage of this to launch the first military coup in Argentinean history. Its stated mission was for the army to settle things down, to 'stabilise' the country by giving it back its forces, its morale, and its Christian and national values. The hidden agenda was to take control.

Uriburu and his followers were bogged down in confusion. They had been fed by Maurras, Mussolini and Primo de Rivera, and they had ideas from the extreme right that they dared not yet admit. Their movement had very naturally fallen into the hands of the oligarchy, Argentina's traditional ruling class that was no longer nationalist and Germanophile as it used to be, but liberal and Anglophile instead. The oligarchy had replaced the slightly shocking Uriburu with a more classic general, Augustín P. Justo.

That is when a 'democratic' ('infamous' to Perón's followers) decade began. It was placed under the sign of electoral fraud and was going to transform Argentina into an exporter of raw materials destined for the English. The crash of 1929 had been exacerbated by an accelerated industrialisation, and in 1939, the war in Europe had forced Argentina to industrialise itself farther. The manufactured products and the workforce were no longer arriving from Europe. Consequently, internal migration was accentuated and workers rushed in from the provinces.

That is why the working class grew and why it changed colours. The *criollos* or *cabecitas negras* that Evita always treated tenderly and courteously were invading Buenos Aires like a charcoal dust, and the city which was white and proud to be so, attempted to shake them off. They had mocked the Neapolitan with the carnation and the Galician's face. Now, no one laughed at the *cabecitas negras*, but no one could stand to see them, or rather to see *oneself* in this unflattering mirror. Their presence alone revealed the national wound: Argentines were not as white as they thought they were. Rather than laugh at their expense, they would have preferred to conceal them. Couldn't they at least be polite enough to stay in their distant suburbs? The *porteños* could continue to ignore them, continue to believe that they were still European. But for how long?

When faced with the European war, Castillo's government was torn by a dilemma that would be inherited by the revolutionaries of 1943: Argentina's neutrality. The English 'understood' their friend's position and did not force them to declare war against the Germans. They were so understanding because they wanted to avoid a situation where Argentina would be influenced by the United States and give in to the pressure of this power that was an ally, but that was also a competitor in the realm of expansionism. Nor did they not want Argentines to profit from this piece of good fortune that would allow them to play in the winner's circle, even in the case of an Axis victory.

The sinking of the German battleship *Admiral Graf von Spee*, the mystery of which took a long time to clear up, introduced a fluctuating game. In December 1939, the *Graf Spee* was attacked by English ships in the Río de la Plata. The Germans were winning the naval battle, when Hans Langsdorff, commander of the *Graf Spee*, turned his back on the aggressors, penetrated the Río de la Plata, and headed for Buenos Aires, straight into the trap.

In his book *Los nazis en la Argentina*, Jorge Camarasa explained that Hitler himself had authorised this procedure, for he knew that Léon Scasso, the Minister of Defence, was a 'partisan of the Axis.' There thus appear to have been pro-Nazi sympathies at the very heart of an otherwise liberal government. With England's blessing, Argentina slipped into this war story, much to America's indignation, since the United States had insisted that Argentina choose a side.

The detonator that set off the Revolution of 1943 was the Castillo government's nomination of a candidate preselected to win the next 'free' elections, Robustiano Patrón Costas, a man who had made billions in the sugar cane industry. The moralising army or, specifically, the GOU, which spoke of modernising the country and giving it 'structure' and 'order,' could not tolerate the revelation of this latest fraud, the most scandalous yet. Besides, the Revolution of 1943, which was also proposing to 'stabilise' the country by giving it back its force and its values, had a much clearer objective than that of its big sister of 1930. The objective was to seize power. The army had become a social class unto itself, one country within another. This revolution had clear ideas. Uriburu had lacked a leader who knew what he wanted and who understood it all, having lived in Mussolini's Italy. In short, he had lacked Colonel Juan Domingo Perón.

However, Eva didn't know any of this yet. Her acting work would be affected by a revolution that spoke of stability and values. Colonel Aníbal Imbert, named Director of Postal and Telecommunications, distributed a harsh communiqué. It was forbidden to broadcast certain 'negative tangos' (those that twist the knife in the wound by repeating words of a lost youth that vanished forever). Preference would be given to the more innocent, more 'national,' and therefore more positive and more martial provincial folklore. More important, the radio scriptwriters would have to submit their scripts to him for review and approval. Eva and all her colleagues had been called by a state employee, Celedonio Galván Moreno, to report to the Postal Bureau. He had taken over an entire floor for the purpose of leisurely examining the scenes to ascertain their 'decency.' However, at the height of luck, right there next to Galván Moreno was none other than Oscar Nicolini, the old Nicolini from Junín whom Eva knew well. This employee of the Buenos Aires central post office, who had worked at the Junín post office, had just been charged with investigating a complaint against a coworker by a certain Elisa Duarte. On such an occasion the plaintiff would have introduced the greying man to her greying mother. But perhaps this would not be necessary. A neighbour of the Nicolini family confided,

'The entire neighbourhood knew that Nicolini had a mistress in Junín. We knew because we heard his wife screaming at the top of her lungs in the courtyard: "You're going to Juana's again, aren't you?"'

Whether it was a love affair or not, Nicolini played an important role in this part of Eva's history. He was a simple and boring man, but a man who was always in the right place at the right time. Had he not been close to Galván Moreno, and especially to Colonel Imbert, and had Evita not already known him through Doña Juana, she would have had a hard time introducing herself so quickly to the new director. (This hypothesis suggests that she did not yet know Colonel Imbert, thus casting doubt on Pablo Raccioppi's statement about the colonel's 'bachelor pad' where he has her living from 1942 on.) She also would not have become Imbert's mistress, and he would not have helped her get better roles than those in the tearjerker soaps – and she might never have met Colonel Perón. On top of all this, if Evita had not named Nicolini Director of Postal and Telecommunications in 1945, the army would not have participated in an uprising against Perón and the events that led the latter to the nation's presidency would not have taken place.

This string of hypotheticals reformulates the problem of chance and destiny. Chance puts you in a situation. Destiny depends on how you take advantage of the situation. Even if Evita was in cahoots with her mother's friend, someone else might not have been as swift. That first day she displayed a curious look of triumph on her face when she left Colonel Imbert's office. It was a look of both irritation and determination, a distinctive look that would be seen again in Evita's first photo as the first lady, barely two years later. It was a look that quickly alerted the other actors who were assembled in the hallway and in the waiting room that Eva had beaten them. She was the fastest one of all.

No one had to wait long for the results. The Revolution took place in June. In September, *Antena* magazine announced that the 'famous actress Evita Duarte' would star in a series of Radio Belgrano broadcasts devoted to women who were equally famous, such as Empress Charlotte, England's Elizabeth I, Sarah Bernhardt, Alexandra Feodorevna, Empress Josephine, Isadora Duncan, Mrs Chiang Kai-shek, Eleonora Duse, Eugenie de Montijo, Lady Hamilton, Anne of Austria, Catherine of Russia. The scriptwriters would be Alberto Insúa and Francisco Muñoz Azpiri, a nationalist writer and future speechwriter for Evita. Certain writers, like Marysa Navarro, who like to stick to the facts, maintain that one must not draw conclusions about the distinctiveness of these roles. For her and for others, it is more important to isolate each biographical element without taking into consideration the 'connections' that link them, the echoes that bounce one off the other. The Perónist circles tend to refrain from giving any significance to those historical roles, or to any event that preceded the meeting of Eva and Perón: Eva would be born of Perón (just as her biblical namesake was born of Adam).

Eva was born in 1919. Each moment of her life before meeting Perón illuminated, if not announced, what would happen next. Other actresses, like Mecha Ortiz, had already portrayed famous women. It is possible that Colonel Imbert, with his penchant for the grandiose, had considered the theme of historical and artistic heroines extremely noble and appropriate. But beyond these two truths, a third, less simple, less substantiated, and more poignant truth seems to stare us right in the eyes, a truth that was seized in a surge of brief and intense joy. As a teenager, Evita dreamed of being Norma Shearer playing the part of Marie Antoinette. During her trip to Europe in 1947, as she was entering the Cathedral of Notre-Dame, Monsignor Roncalli, the Italian priest who would later become Pope John XXIII, exclaimed: 'E tornata l'Imperatrice Eugenia!' (The Empress Eugenie has returned!). We all have within us a gallery of personalities, and one of them ends up dominant. In Evita, the queen co-existed with more impoverished personalities, but was there nonetheless; it always had been. If Perón guaranteed her victory, it was not he who conceived it.

The fabulous contract that she signed with the director of

Radio Belgrano, Jaime Yankelevich, with whom she would have a strained relationship, allowed her finally to rent her own apartment at 1567 Posadas Street, an address that remains in the country's history. Her ties to Colonel Imbert also helped her. She had always been aware of her particular intelligence, a survival instinct of wild animals and warring humans. Imbert held his position because the GOU (which counted Perón as a member) considered radio a very powerful and influential vehicle. Evita was only sensing the atmosphere of the era. While at Imbert's place, she surely heard snatches of conversation. On August 3, 1943, she was among the founders of the Radio Association of Argentina (ARA), whose goal was to 'defend the interests of Argentinean radio's workers.' This event was a perfect harmony of both Eva's own anger (the theatrical impresario Francisco López said that in Mendoza, she often argued with theatre folk 'because there were certain humiliations she would not accept') and the new ideas she was already seizing in midair.

During this period, from the end of 1943 to the beginning of 1944, it seems that Evita and Perón played hide-and-seek. They passed each other but did not meet. But they were looking for each other. If the Argentinean press of that period had published personal ads, they could have both benefited. Perón was looking for a young, cute woman who would look good on his arm. Since there were no personals, he depended on others to introduce him to his dream date, for he had neither the experience nor the time required for the business of seduction. For other reasons, he was also looking for someone who was affiliated with radio; how sweet if one unique woman possessed both criteria. More than ever, Eva was looking for a man with power, and in Argentina in 1943, this could mean only someone in the military. It wasn't Colonel Imbert, with his severe looks. He was not made for her, and she was not made for him. Carmelo Santiago states flatly, 'Imbert could not stand Evita's indomitable personality, so he introduced her to his friend, Colonel Perón.' He adds, 'Evita's friend, Dorita Norvi had been Colonel Imbert's mistress. . . . Eva knew Imbert's entourage since she had attended his parties.'

One of the many confusing and contradictory accounts of Eva and Perón's first meeting comes from Sarita Romero, a 'Perónist of the first hour,' who heard it from none other than Dorita Norvi (or Norby). Sarita Romero provides this version: 'Perón needed a girlfriend. Dorita Norby was asked to throw a party and invite actresses to introduce him to. Díaz, the owner of a public relations agency, came up with this plan. First we thought about Zully Moreno, who was very well known, but too pretentious. Then, when Díaz saw Evita, he found her to be simpler and more feline than Zully. He introduced them and voilà, it worked.'

As we have already seen, Perón frequented the radio circles for reasons that were far from sentimental. And, even if the party organised by Díaz Public Relations had never taken place, it is certain that before he met Evita (or at least before their official meeting), he visited Radio Belgrano at least twice to greet the actors and to distribute smiles and handshakes. If Evita was present at either one of these visits, there are no photographs to prove it. Did Perón know Evita before the earthquake of 1944 that represents the official date of their first meeting? He may have seen her at one of the parties thrown in his honour or during one of his visits to Radio Belgrano. Or maybe Colonel Imbert introduced them, in which case they might have looked at each other, stared each other down, flirted with the idea of the triangle they could form with Imbert. In any case, the fact remains that on December 25, 1943, Perón showed up at the radio station to deliver a Christmas address to the people of Argentina accompanied by a girl he introduced as his daughter. If he had already met Evita – the exclusive, possessive, and jealous Evita – he had not yet tied a true knot of a relationship with her. For then he could not have appeared in public with his child-mistress, a teenager whose father, a peasant from Mendoza, had entrusted her upbringing to Perón. Of course Perón did not have a daughter. He was a forty-eight-year-old widower who loved young girls. Evita, who was twenty-four, could still be mistaken for a doll, and Perón was accomplished in the role of the paternal male. Now they were both ready to err, ready to fall into a misunderstanding that nature uses to form history, a misunderstanding that mixes human error with indifference.

AN EARTHQUAKE SHAKES HISTORY

On January 15, 1944, the town of San Juan (situated in the Cuyo region, like Mendoza, and also famous for its wine, which spawns the Argentinean expression for drunkenness 'to be between San Juan and Mendoza') was destroyed by an earthquake. Ten thousand people died, and the scenes that were shown at the movies – since there was no television in Argentina until 1951 – brought tears to the entire country's eyes by showing orphans, whose black eyes seemed huge in their small olive faces. Very few families did not consider adopting one. The Argentinean Radio Association was among the victims' aid committees that offered to help organise an artistic festival to benefit the homeless.

The festival took place on January 22 at the Luna Park stadium. The actors began to meet in the offices of Colonel Juan Domingo Perón, Secretary of Labour and Social Affairs, who was accompanied by his deputy, Lieutenant Colonel Domingo Mercante, and a few students from the Military Academy that morning. Perón welcomed the theatre folk by shaking their hands, as if each person were unique. And each one felt in her hand the vibration of an energy that seemed emitted exclusively for her, and in his eyes, a warmth that was initiated by her alone. Each person felt like she was the chosen one.

He was tall, massive, and square. He wore a white uniform, a black cap, and boots. He also wore the gleaming 'Perón smile' that he seemed to be able to turn on by pushing a button. It was a smile that gave the illusion that his heart was far more accessible than other people's, so accessible and so big that his good, warm, rough, and virile – very virile – face was split in great detail. A certain stoutness, just enough to make the women swoon, carefully enveloped his well-kept muscles and contributed to this reassuring image; one felt sure that poor Argentines would no longer have to sleep in the streets. The immaculate uniform went hand in hand with the splendour of that radiant smile. He would later tell one of his biographers: 'In the army's photos, it is easy to recognise me by my uniform, mine never had wrinkles.' His boots were shined with the same zeal – or with the same anger. Did this obsession with cleanliness remind Eva of Doña Juana scrubbing her daughters' pinafores? For now, she saw in him only the absence of any imprecisions, wrinkles, or doubts. She did not see the short arms, or the wide hips, or the way he tilted his head when he smiled like a choirboy. She saw only the image of man, the Argentinean man par excellence, with the allure of Carlos Gardel and a resemblance to San Martín (he had even been asked to portray the hero in a film) all in one package. A man whose contours were neat and polished, a clear, honest man who was easy to understand.

When he lifted his cap for a second, she was able to appreciate his hair's perfection; it was black, slicked back, and carefully flattened, which prolonged the oblique line of his forehead. The laboriously tamed thick hair and the aquiline nose betrayed his Indian origins: did not Perón look like Patoruzú the Indian, the hero of a famous Argentinean comic strip? In fact, psoriasis caused the virile, rough patches on his cheeks that he treated and camouflaged with ointment. That is why he had Gardel's excessively photogenic mask. But for those who ignored all this, these bumps spoke of the Patagonian desert, that is, of a certain hardness, a masculine bitterness.

In *My Mission in Life*, Evita writes that that was an 'incredible day.' It is easy to believe her, to imagine her excited, attentive, treading softly, and shaking her money box like a bell to benefit the victims. Evita and the other actresses followed Colonel Perón along Calle Florida, the commercial avenue lined with the city's biggest stores. One could not fail to notice him. Oh, that wide back! That sure step! Who wouldn't have followed such a man? It was one of those heavy and humid days of the porteño summer that makes one's ankles swell, and Evita's had this unfortunate tendency even though her legs were thin. Still, she followed him effortlessly, like a sparrow dancing around a bull.

Evita would have never imagined walking the Calle Florida without window shopping. Because of the war, the windows of Harrods and Gath and Chaves were no longer overflowing with the subtle-tasting teas or the soft mint candy that elegant ladies savoured with respect, almost unction, as if receiving Hosts just because they came from England. But despite the disgraceful return to the vulgarity of the hard lozenges, made in a working suburb of Buenos Aires, the Calle Florida retained its human tide that passed every now and again, with curiosity and sympathy, to deposit a few pesos into the money boxes of the pretty girls whose faces had become famous through *Antena* or *Sintonía*, and in the soldier's who was cordial, human, and familiar, despite all the badges that proved his importance.

Had she been able to get his attention during the meeting in the *Secretaría?* If so, how? Was it a word? A speech? Had she really said to him, 'If your cause is the people's, then I will be at your side, no matter what I have to sacrifice for it,' as she claims? (And did she put words into action by hurrying to walk at his side, so that he would see and hear her: 'Please help the San Juan orphans! Ladies and gentlemen, please help!') Or had he gravely explained to her, as he relates in his memoirs, that in order to give money to the poor, they had to take it from those who had it? Or, as the ex-deputy Angel Miel Asquía reports, did she throw him this curveball: 'Colonel, will being seen with actresses harm your image?' And seeing that she was so determined, lucid, and committed to the cause, did he put her in charge of it all?

Nothing is certain. Perón's memoirs simplify events by taking shortcuts, moving too fast, and drawing a portrait of Evita that would not be accurate until later in her life. They are the memoirs of a distracted man who easily forgets details. Thus, he says that Evita was blonde when they met ('a long blonde mane that fell over her shoulders') when in fact she had not yet begun to dye her hair. In this portrait that Perón traced twenty years after Evita's death, there is only one interesting observation: 'Eva's skin was white, but when she spoke, she would get flushed. She would intertwine her fingers and her hands would get red. She had guts.' He describes Evita's 'fragility' and her 'ardent eyes,' but we get the feeling that he could have used these words to describe millions of women. On the other hand, the red hands have the weight and consistency of reality, and, oddly enough, it is not a sensual observation. The words he uses to describe Eva's beauty are abstract or else they reveal a cold evaluation. Was this a professional distortion? One would think he were testing a soldier's suitability. 'Is he gutsy?' 'Yes, sir.' 'Very good then, enroll him.'

One day, in his old age, looking back on all this from Madrid, his city of exile, he would tell Tomás Eloy Martínez that Evita had been his work of art and that he had polished her like a diamond. He would add that it had been a difficult task, for Evita was indomitable. He would speak again of her long hair, her piercing eyes, her hands – this time they were 'slender' – and her 'little feet that looked like filigree.' But he would also frankly admit, 'Her body wasn't all that bad. It was the typical body of a thin *criolla* – skinny legs and thick ankles. I was not attracted by her looks. It was her kindness.'

Kindness is an unexpected quality for an ambitious soldier to look for. But one must not define it as 'A penchant to do good, to be soft and indulgent' as the dictionary does. For if Evita had this tendency, and she did, he was not yet aware of it, and it is hard to believe in any case that he would have been attracted to her for it. One must instead use the tango's definition, the macho definition whereby a good woman is a loyal woman who does not betray her man. In brief, Perón went beyond Evita's body. He only spoke concretely of her hands and her feet (Tomás Eloy Martínez went so far as to say that Perón had a fetish for women's feet), but he immediately seized this kindness in an intuitive flash, and it was this kindness that he would use as his instrument.

This was Perón's great contradiction and his most sympathetic feature. By loving teenagers, that is, girls who were incapable of 'penetrating his non-feelings,' to use Tomás Eloy Martínez's expression, he let a woman fill him with wonder. The wonder and fascination he felt when he realised Eva was an instrument endowed with a certain look no doubt equalled the wonder that the protagonist from Milan Kundera's *The Book of Laughter and Forgetting* felt when his eyes met those of the 'woman-object' he was making love to. This is when he experienced the feeling you get when you are hammering and suddenly discover that the hammer is looking at you.

However, Perón did not run off screaming as the character in Kundera's novel did. On the contrary, he gave wings to her feminine existence. And by doing this, he demonstrated a unique form of courage (one could even say with a certain meanness that this was his only form of courage). Admittedly, he spent the rest of his life obstinately repeating, as if to convince himself, 'Eva is my shadow.' Many men think of their wives as shadows and appear 'impatient' when faced with concrete details. Floating in abstraction has its advantages. It allows one to be somewhere else and it prevents one from committing oneself. Until now, this might have been a trite story. However, when we consider a woman who became a man's light, who willingly transformed herself into his shadow, and who, guessing that the light was disturbing him, decided to turn herself off and die, the story loses all banality.

✛

The festival at Luna Park started at four thirty in the afternoon, but Perón arrived at ten thirty that night, accompanied by President Pedro Pablo Ramírez and the first lady. They both gave speeches, but it was Perón who aroused the crowd's enthusiasm by highlighting the contrast between 'the worker's suffering' and 'many of the ruling party's good life.' Then Ramírez and the first lady left. There were two empty seats next to Perón and Imbert. This was a decisive instant for two lives and for the life of Argentina. It was so crucial that the many versions of the way Evita managed to find her way to the empty seat are infinitely varied. The truth about who holds responsibility for having engineered Evita's meeting with Perón remains a state secret. Among the candidates for this distinguished honour are Homero Manzi, the famous tango lyricist who related his adventure to the nationalist writer Arturo Jauretche, Roberto Galán, the television host, and Lieutenant Colonel Mercante.

According to Manzi, Evita and the actress Rita Molina were trying in vain to find their way to Luna Park's entrance past the guards who blocked their path. One of Manzi's cousins asked that the two women be let into the stadium, as the actress was recognised and held a slight prestige. Once inside, Eva exclaimed, 'Look at all these people! We'll never be able to sit down.' 'Yes we will,' responded Manzi, pointing to the empty seats next to the colonels, 'there are two empty seats.' And Evita, followed by Rita, made her way through the crowd and sat down.

In Galán's version, Evita was already in the stadium. But instead of sitting down, she stood beneath the stage, tugged on Galán's pant cuffs (he was in charge of organising the event), and pleaded with him, 'Galancito darling, introduce me. I want to recite a poetry.' Galán, who was new to the business and did not have the power to insert the starlet into the lineup of big artists – the tango singers Libertad Lamarque and Hugo del Carril, the Canaro and D'Arienzo orchestras – asked her to wait. So Evita stood there, waiting for her moment of glory.

Meanwhile, Perón had arrived with a few other colonels. They were all sitting in wicker chairs (twenty to be exact) that Galán had placed next to the presidential podium. By the stroke of midnight, Ramírez had left and a few seats had opened up. That is when Galán had a brilliant idea. He called Evita, who was ready for anything, and three other actresses – Rita Molina, Chola Luna, and Dorita Norby – and told them, 'There are a few colonels who came alone. I will introduce you to them and tell them that you are part of the women's welcoming committee.' That is how Evita found herself sitting next to Perón. From that moment on, everyone could see that the strapping colonel had eyes only for her. He seemed entranced by this woman who talked and talked, though no one could be sure what she was talking about.

However, Domingo Mercante's son said, 'When I was a teenager, I would go with my father to Perón's country house in San Vicente every weekend. And, at the table, in front of everyone, I heard Evita tell him a thousand times: "Mercante, do you remember when you led me to Luna Park by the hand and let me sit next to Perón? I was so scared! But, you were truly inspired that night!"'

However it happened, Evita and Rita did indeed manage to fill the two seats next to Perón and Imbert. As we already know, one of them was already an 'acquaintance' of Imbert's. Hugo Gambini, the journalist and author of *The History of Perónism*, has confirmed that Imbert was responsible for the meeting between Perón and Evita. One of the men quoted above must have given Eva the opportunity to find herself face to face with her lover. When he saw her he must have incredulously exclaimed, 'What are you doing here?' and then introduced her to Perón.

But beyond the more or less discordant or simultaneously

plausible details (all the versions taken together could indeed hold the truth), the underlying history is clear: despite her success in radio, her activity with the union, her relationship with Imbert, and her walk along Calle Florida that very morning, Evita had not been able to get herself invited to the festival or to be recognised at the entrance gate. Whether she requested she be let in to 'recite a poetry' or whether an inspired Mercante, who ran into her en route and randomly or compassionately decided to choose her out of the many, the image is the same – desperate applicant who stomped her feet and pleaded with the well connected. Two soldiers saw her in the middle of the crowd, moving heaven and earth to get up to the front, and it is only then that they thought to offer her a seat. From that day on, she would never be forced to knock on others' doors – except for the very narrow and inaccessible door to Perón's heart.

What did Evita say that night that made Perón leave this squeaky and rusty-hinged door ajar? Did she find herself in that state of perfect happiness when the right word just comes to one? We know only that at the beginning Evita was speaking with Imbert and Rita with Perón. But afterward, she was neither tense nor nervous, and while she was looking at the crowd very far below her from her coveted position, she slipped away from Imbert and turned toward Perón. Did she really utter the decisive words that the old exiled colonel would later confide to his biographer: 'Thank you for existing'? *Se non è vero, è bene trovato*. These brief words were a summary of the life that they were about to begin. By saying 'You exist,' Eva implied 'I do not exist, I mean nothing.' (In fact, according to Perón, she also said, 'Oh, I am not an artist, I am good for nothing.') 'I am nothing,' a voice inside whispered to Perón, an expert on abandonment and emptiness, 'but I can be you, become you, and serve you.'

In a photo that shows the two of them, fascinated by each other, sitting on the wicker chairs, they are attentively looking at each other. Two powerful profiles, two strong aquiline noses face to face – these are impossible to compare to the brief effigies that were in then style. She was wearing a black dress, black elbow-length gloves, and a black hat with a white feather. After the show, Perón was to have a drink with the festival organisers, but he called them over and excused himself: 'Sorry, boys, we are going to have dinner with these young ladies. This way, there'll be more for you to drink.' So the four left, two by two. One of the couples was headed for oblivion, the other toward a history that has never stopped haunting us.

✣

At this time, Perón was living with his child-mistress in a small apartment on the corner of Arenales and Colonel Díaz streets, in the northern neighbourhood. They must have gone to Evita's, on Posadas Street, during their first night of love. However, once the white uniform, the hat, the feather, the gloves, and the black dress were off, they must have been shocked. A colonel's uniform and ceremonial dress hold a rank that no naked body can attain, especially if the desire is not intense. This was a moment of total nudity, without illusions, though it was probably not the worst way to become a couple. By seeing each other as they truly were, they were saving themselves the task of reconstructing a different relationship based on a different concept two years down the road when the passion evaporated.

It is a mistake to think that they were deprived of all sensuality and imagination due to the fact that she was frigid and he lethargic. Of the two, Evita was more experienced, and she no doubt quickly understood that the colonel's love fed on diminutives. Denying in his heart the existence of another, man or woman, Perón could love only by diminishing and minimising. Therefore, it was not despite her puny body that he chose Eva, but because of the barely sexy skin that he could laugh at, cuddle, and belittle. A buxom actress with generous lips and heavy, sugary eyes that looked like they were filled with Turkish pastries, such as Zully Moreno, was not made for Perón. Admittedly, Evita had an aquiline nose that gave away her power, but as for the rest, she was not yet fully formed. She was twenty-four, and her lazy beauty was slow in its birth. Her face was waiting, malleable, like clay, which was also the colour of her skin. Pygmalion's tragedy seems to be knocking on the door. Did not Pygmalion love his creation to the point that he became jealous of it?

At first, Perón found his student funny. He treated her like the doll he dreamed about, and that night, when they became a couple, they were like two children, for the master liked to slip into a childhood he had never known. Indeed, when they later lived in the Unzué (the republic's presidential palace, which is now demolished), President Perón and his wife would descend the majestic staircase by sliding down the rails.

Slightly grudgingly, Evita forced herself to play the part of the doll. The childish games tired her almost as much as sex did. She had lived a true childhood, with lame dolls, admittedly, but they were crowned with dreams. Those who remain children are the ones whose childhoods were thwarted. Eva had been a little girl at that age, and now she was a woman. Blinded by his fantasies, Perón scorned this fact.

In his memoirs, the writer and politician Bonifacio del Carril describes the first time he met Eva in Perón's apartment on Arenales Street. Perón had introduced Eva by saying, 'It is incredible how well she knows people. She has a nose for politics.' He then took her adult nose and squeezed it, the power of this gesture rendering her nose childlike. He then asked Evita to bring them some wine. During her absence, he explained that he would not let himself 'fall for a woman'; after all, he was the only master of his persona. Finally, when del Carril jokingly said that they had called a doctor to come take care of him, Perón quickly sat up in his bed and uttered the following extraordinary statement: 'Evita is very capable. No one knows how to use the cupping glass the way she does.' Politicians read between the lines: 'Mind your own business. I've found my confidant.'

And how did she feel, faced with a massive body she first took for a bull, but which on closer acquaintance reminded her more of a calf? She was delighted. She had known older men, known them well; she had loved 'old Kartulowicz,' *Sintonía*'s editor. She was looking for a father, a father who wore boots, who would form one entity with his horse, a *caudillo* of a father who would be surrounded by a crowd of partisans. Power and politics excited her much more than sex did. And like many women, she was able to feel an enormous amount of tenderness for this deceptively macho build, which she alone knew to be less virile than it appeared to be. Moreover, by being the only one to know this, she had a hold on him. And, by telling del Carril that he was his own master, Perón was admitting, in the end, his fear of falling under her power.

As far as love goes, there are a thousand and one ways to love a man's body, to feel protected by his mass, to sleep enveloped by his virile heat and smell. And whether he was ardent or cold, a man who was this big and solid had to feel like a manly man. To humour him a little, to alleviate the weaknesses of his age that she discovered, that is, to lavish him with tickles and cupping glasses, gave her the right to snuggle up to him at night. She finally found her roof, her paternal home. After all, the right to expect shelter from a man can be traced back to the bible and the story of Ruth. When she became a widow, she followed her mother-in-law's advice and conquered the protective Boaz by sleeping at his feet. This was the same advice that Doña Juana had given to her daughters.

Perón's singular sexuality liberated her. She could easily move onto more serious issues, to politics. In del Carril's story, Perón had already noticed Evita's political flair. Arturo Jauretche echoes the idea: 'I ran into Eva a month after the day she was united with Perón. Although she was obsessed by the theatre, Eva was asexual. That was her affinity with Perón, for he too was not very sexual. This marriage united two wills, two passions for power. It was not a marriage for love.'

❖

Evita followed Perón like a shadow (clearly, this metaphor comes from the colonel himself). Evita would listen to the compromising political conversations that took place in front of her in the Arenales apartment; she was always on the lookout. This would stun the outraged politicians and soldiers, who asked themselves how Perón could stand it.

It is said that when Perón came home one day, he found Evita there. Her dresses were hanging in the closet and her beauty creams had replaced the psoriasis ointments in the bathroom. Before he even had time to ask what she had done with his girlfriend, Eva announced, with a challenging air that hid an intimate trembling, 'I sent her back to Mendoza.' Perón was quiet. Without raising his eyebrows, he accepted the decision of a woman imposing her authority on him. Perón's own version differs only slightly. He told Tomás Eloy Martínez that Evita had invaded him little by little, placing her beauty creams on the shelves one by one. Perón's version seems more convincing. Eva had her own apartment on Posadas Street, and even in the heat of passion, how could a bohemian always in search of a roof over her head leave the apartment that she had worked so hard for? It is more probable that she pursued Perón gradually. Sometimes, when he came home late, he found Eva waiting for him on the landing, falling back into the excesses that had driven Kartulowicz, and who knows how many others, away. However, this time she felt she could take the initiative. Such tenacity could only sway Perón. But where did the influence that she had over him, that astounded politicians and soldiers alike, come from?

It was more than the tickles and the cupping glass. Evita possessed a human experience that Perón lacked. He had always lived within the army's cocoon. He had known women only as prostitutes (or as temporary play things), and men only as soldiers. If his ideas about Argentina and about himself as a leader of this country were clear, the rest remained theoretical. Eva knew people. This talent allowed her to survive the theatrical jungle. She was able to probe hearts, to recognise true loyalty or the temptation to betray. She also carried her own unique trump card: her version of the tango's 'kindness.' She was loyal no matter what. Perón was abstract and found in Eva an alert companion who was always able to warn him, 'Watch out for that guy.' However, Perón was not completely abstract. Along with his military rigidity and his ideas imported from Italy and Germany, there was a *criollo* wisdom, a wisdom built on concrete knowledge, a pragmatic wisdom that Evita recognised after having seen it shine in the Indian eyes of the Núñezes in Los Toldos. This was Perón's duality or labyrinth that Evita began to understand by listening to his story.

PERÓN'S LIFE

Little by little he no doubt told his story to her, first modestly, then with confidence. He would tell it when he found an attentive ear and unwavering support, support that was almost frightening, since it was so upright and faultless. Perón was a loner, and for the first time he had someone beside him. How could he, who had experienced emptiness in its purest form, not let Eva fill him up, all the while believing that he had created her? The void within him came from the desert, from Patagonia, where he grew up. He was raised by a father who was a dreamer and a mother who was as round and powerful as the earth itself. He was also raised by the army.

He was born on October 8, 1895, in Lobos, a little town

in the province of Buenos Aires. 'Just like Junín,' Evita must have said, proudly noting a coincidence that made them, if not equals (Never! He was the superior being, and she was the subordinate, privileged just to listen), at least vaguely similar. She would soon discover other similarities – troubling ones – in Perón's life.

His father, Mario Tomás Perón was the son of Tomás Liberato Perón, a doctor, chemist, and senator who was sent to Paris by President Sarmiento (the originator of the students' white pinafores) for services rendered during the yellow fever epidemic that had decimated Buenos Aires's population – mostly the black population – around 1870. The famous grandfather, the son of a Sardinian merchant who had arrived in Argentina in 1830 and a Scottish mother, Ana Hughes Mackenzie, had married a Uruguayan woman, Dominga Dutey, the daughter of Basques from Bayonne. In a fit of happiness, Evita must have exclaimed, 'Oh! You have Basque blood in you just like I do!' Then she must have added, 'There are Basques on my mother's side too.'

For the doctor's son had chosen a path different from his father's. He tired of the medical studies he had begun only so that he wouldn't disappoint his father. After his father's death, he left Buenos Aires for Lobos, where he managed the property he had just inherited. He had no experience in the pampas. To choose this lost place was to flee. Was he trying to escape the ghost of his ever-present, intrusive father? (His brother, Tomás Hilario, chose a different escape route. Instead of burying himself in the desert, he committed suicide.) When he arrived in Lobos, Mario Tomás met a young *criolla* servant and got her pregnant. The child, Mario Avelino Perón, was Juan Domingo's brother. The woman's name was Juana Sosa Toledo, and her parents, Juan Ireneo Sosa, the local mason, and Mercedes Toledo, lived in an adobe ranch in the vicinity of Lobos. 'Just like the Núñezes,' Evita might have murmured, more troubled than enchanted.

In fact, they were real *criollos* just like the Núñezes. What is a 'real *criollo*'? The *criollo*'s father was the Spaniard, who himself was a mixture of Arabs, white or dark, Hebrews, and one hundred other savoury spices. The truth of the *criollo* condition is to not be real. Or, according to Tomás Eloy Martínez, the only Perón biographer who dared delve into the corners of this past life, Juana Sosa Toledo readily admitted that her paternal grandparents had pure Indian blood. To which Basque, lost in the night, did these Indians owe the name Sosa? Did Perón explain to Evita where his slit eyes and his Patoruzú nose came from? Or did he instead insist that his Basque origins came from his mother in order to impress her? After all, this is what he said to others: he told Italians that his name was really Peroni and the French that it was Perron. The *criollo* condition is a shattered mirror. Those who understood this would know how to charm, with their multiple fragments, a disparate and diverse crowd. Had Eva been Jewish, he would no doubt honestly have declared that Toledo was a Jewish name. The geographic map of Perón's bloodlines was typically Argentine in that it was vast, extending throughout the entire planet and depicting imaginary countries and bordering other worlds. In Argentina, the feeling of absence and its resulting love of the fantastic arose from the emptiness of the pampas and an overabundance of origins.

After Mario Tomás Perón had given Juana Sosa Toledo her first child, he promised his family and the well-wishers of Lobos that he would cut all ties with the overweight servant whose thick blue hair, brassy skin, oblique eyes, wide face, and pronounced cheekbones revealed the Indian blood. But he did nothing of the kind, partly because he was lazy, and partly because Juana played the part of the ombu in the pampas in his empty life. By taking cover under this vast, dark body, and by hanging on, this pale and feeble citizen who was lost in his theories on nature and in his foggy speeches was less afraid to fly away. Four years later, still unmarried, they conceived another son, Juan Domingo. The

Toledos could not believe it. They wanted a girl! Grandmother Mercedes had even sewed beautiful diapers trimmed with pink ribbon. And Aunt Honoria, who was going to give her niece silver earrings, prayed and asked that God fix his mistake and change the newborn's sex.

Juan Domingo was three when his family moved to another town within the province of Buenos Aires. Later, when his father was hired by some landowners to be the caretaker of their land in the Chubut province, in the middle of Patagonia, the wandering Mario Tomás headed for the desert. Alone, he was shepherd to five hundred sheep. During that time, Juana lived in Buenos Aires at the home of Doña Dominga Dutey, Mario Tomás' mother. In 1901, one year later, when Juan Domingo was six, the father returned to marry Juana and to acknowledge his two sons. The whole family then left for Puerto Madryn, a southern port.

From Puerto Madryn, they continued in a buggy, making their way through the dunes. They travelled in the midst of storms and under the Patagonian sky, which is even heavier than the sky over the pampas for its reversed colours oppress one's heart. Here, the earth is an almost blue-grey, and the sky is green. The *estancia La Maciega* was waiting for them at the end of the road. There was nothing around them, nothing but space. That is where Perón learned to talk to himself, to imitate animals, to ignore the cold, hunger, and emotions. That is also where he taught himself the art of strategy – military and political – by chasing guanacos. These creatures have the annoyed expression of llamas and camels and they spit at your face with a very accurate aim. Perón had to entrap these proud beasts by making false signals, a skill he used later with people.

La Maciega would be only one stage of this frantic journey. A few years later, the family would move again, this time to Chankaike, which seems to be the end of the world, the extreme south of all hope. It is a harsh and acrid region where being a woman is impossible. Doña Juana knew this, and like Evita's mother, she did all she could to survive. She rode horses, tamed animals, cured the sick, helped women give birth. She had built a relationship with her sons. Her husband being what he was, she had to be able to speak in code with them, to wink at them behind his back – a malicious wink, carrying the same feminine and *criollo* weight that Perón always did. (The colonel's wink of an eye, that flash in the middle ,of a conversation that allowed the speaker to believe that he alone was the recipient, was in fact a tic, but a revealing one, a nervous joke that subconsciously imitated his mother.) 'My mother was a friend, a counsellor,' Perón would say on the rare occasion when he spoke about her. In his adjectives, he used the masculine endings to accentuate his praise, as if the feminine was not strong enough.

Actually, Perón's official biography, *Perón: Destiny's Man*, attributes feminine virtues to his mother and a harsh virility to his father. According to these biographers, Mario Tomás was a strict teacher, jealously watching over his sons' education. There is nothing wrong in this, but it does not explain the way the father, who was always fleeing farther away, seemed to dissolve, to unravel in space. And what could a strong woman do, in the middle of the desert, when the man who dragged her there became inconsistent, when he vanished in his dream of an endless departure? In *La novela de Perón*, Tomás Eloy Martínez tells us. One day, when Juan Domingo returned from Buenos Aires (where his parents had 'abandoned' him, leaving him with his grandmother Dominga and his aunts so that he could learn to read and write and so that he could forget the guanacos and become human again), Perón found his mother in bed with one of the *estancia*'s workers. He left immediately, without saying good-bye, and never forgave her. He walked for days in complete solitude, in a type of communion with his betrayed father. When he reached Puerto Madryn, he boarded a ship for Buenos Aires.

From that point on, his life and his father's seem to bifurcate. Mario Tomás left again and settled in with his last one hundred sheep, which were all sick, on a new desert stretch under green skies. Ironically, he baptised this place *El Porvenir* (The future). Meanwhile, Juan Domingo enrolled in the Military Academy. The more the father wandered, the more the son constructed his own life around rigid discipline, an *esprit de corps*. Were they really all that different? Juan Domingo was a fair student, a good rider, a good boxer, and an excellent fencer. The perfect son's discipline hid the same vacuousness that propelled the father, haunted by ghosts, to flee. Did he not join the army somehow to escape from everything that goes beyond neat and clear outlines, to escape life's dissolution, or rather the dissolution that is life? Leaving his family to join the army was just another form of exile. Eva must have recognised her own exile and her own uprooting in this story. She understood, without any possible confusion, Perón's marginality, his condition as a 'double child' who came from two different social environments and who, at least for the first few years of his life, was also an illegitimate child.

Juan Domingo's existence was now on a permanent course. He would never be lost. The widest plain with its mirages could not lead him astray. In fact, he would become a master at planting trouble in others' minds. Hardened by his Patagonian childhood, he survived the army's initiation tortures and cruel methods of breaking a trainee's will. It was a string of manoeuvres, exercises, sadistic jousts during which Perón would not let up in front of his classmates. The tango says it best: '*La patota me miraba y no era del hombre el aflojar*' (the entire group was looking at me, and a true man could not falter). He was now prepared for a life that showed others he was not a weakling.

He became sublieutenant for the infantry in 1915, lieutenant in 1919, and captain in 1924. Early on, he wrote army training manuals on gymnastics, hygiene, and morale. In 1917, the workers of *La Forestal* went on strike. He was able to defuse the situation by simply speaking to the workers who were surprised to find such an understanding military man with such a radiant smile. He would later write studies on the liberation wars in Peru and about the Eastern Front during World War I. He taught subofficers at the Academy and at the High Academy of War. In 1929, soon after he received the diploma for a state officer as the first in his class, he married Aurelia Tizón. 'That's enough!' Evita exclaimed. (During an electoral campaign trip, she would have to leave the room because a folkloric band was playing the samba, poor Aurelia's favourite, for Perón.)

There is nothing about Aurelia to incite such jealousy. Efficient as always, Perón had met her at the exact time in his life when his soul and his conscience told him it was time to marry. Until then, the lieutenant's love life had been simple. From time to time – less frequently than his buddies – he went to the bordello. The rarity of his escapades had been noticed, and he needed a woman to show that he was a man, just as he had earlier proven his endurance.

It goes without saying that the versions of his first encounter with Aurelia are as numerous and different as the ones that relate the story of that night in Luna Park. She was introduced by friends and he spoke to her at the movies; she was the daughter of a friend; he met her at Francia Square in front of the Museum of Fine Arts, where she was taking an art class. . . . The young girl's age generates less debate; let us just say that she was somewhere between seventeen and twenty, when her fiancé was easily over thirty. She played the guitar and the piano and painted with watercolours. She was neither pretty nor homely. In Perón's eyes, her greatest asset was that she would not bother him or distract him when he was working. Save her artistic talents, Aurelia was self-effacing. General Lonardi's wife (the general who lead the *Revolución Libertadora* against Perón in 1955) met Aurelia in Chile in 1936 when Perón was the military attaché for the Argentinean Embassy. She described her to Tomás Eloy

Martínez as an insignificant genius, a little thing dressed like a schoolteacher.

Aurelia greatly respected her husband, whom she never called by his surname but only 'Commander.' As for her, she was so young and insignificant that she did not even have the right to a name. People knew her only by her childhood nickname, Potota (a childlike way of saying *preciosa*). We will later see the long and painful process through which Evita secured the right to use her own name, albeit tenderly belittled by the diminutive.

In their large, dark, majestic apartment (visitors described it as a 'true mausoleum'), Perón read and wrote his military manuals, while Potota, whose presence was further diminished by the huge marble and black wood furniture, knitted booties on a large couch that almost swallowed her up. She wasn't pregnant, but she placed all her hope in the day when she would feel a new movement. So she knitted constantly, until the day the doctor told her she was not sterile. But how can you tell a husband whose name does not escape from your lips, 'You're to blame'? Instead, Aurelia quietly picked up her needles and her wool and continued to knit. One evening, in 1938, when the family was together celebrating Perón's patron saint day, Aurelia fainted. Soon after, she died of uterine cancer.

The year 1930 inaugurated a decisive stage for the country. We have already seen that Argentina's history divides itself into two periods: pre- and post-1930. Before, it was a liberal country, founded in 1810 on the French Revolution's sacred principles. After, although the army had not acquired absolute power, Argentina had to admit the existence of a nationalist military force. There is no doubt that Perón participated in the Revolution of 1930 which overthrew Yrigoyen. He was reticent about this, but the reticence was formal, based not on ideological content but rather on the coup's lack of organisation, a coup whose ideas he approved of and whose leader, Uriburu, he respected. He endlessly repeated that

Uriburu was 'an honest, good and brave man.' However, these words did not prevent him from contradicting himself later on. After having declared that he basically agreed with the uprising of 1930, he clarified that by participating in Yrigoyen's overthrow he was only following his superiors' orders. This was a conscious ambiguity. His readings in military strategy linked with his own childhood experience of being a guanaco hunter. Perón liked to divert the truth, often multiplying the versions, the positions, the ideas of a story. The more theories generated, the easier it was to find someone who would adhere to one or another. Perón seduced by accumulating uncertainties.

In 1931, he was promoted to the rank of major and was a member of the committee in charge of defining the borders between Argentina and Bolivia. In 1936, he was named military attaché to Chile, and he climbed to the rank of lieutenant colonel. It was in Chile that he became the protagonist in a strange story told to Tomás Eloy Martínez by Lonardi's widow. Perón made contact with a Chilean officer, Leopoldo Haniez, who was to provide him with secret documents about his country. This was not unusual, for espionage was a part of normal diplomatic activities. But the story becomes strange when we learn that Perón, after having brought Lonardi on this perilous journey, let him go the moment Chilean counter-espionage agencies surprised Lonardi with Haniez, a rendez-vous that only Perón knew about. Finally, in 1939, Perón left for Italy.

Evita had surely seen a photo that showed him skiing in Chieti for the Fourteenth Mountain Regiment. The photo is comical. He is wearing knickerbockers, thick wool socks, and a visor cap on his head (a foreshadowing of the famous cap he would later wear, after Eva's death, when he forced young students to call him 'Pochito,' a time when he was able publicly to reveal an aspect of himself that until then he had carefully kept hidden). The man in the photograph is a smiling and energetic athlete, but there is something false about him, as if he were in disguise. Did the Italian influence turn him into an actor? Or was he liberated of all constraints in a foreign land and finally able to reveal his true colours?

In any case, Perón, a recent widower who was sent to Europe by the Minister of Defence to study the situation, was living the good life in Italy. He was fascinated by Mussolini and by fascism, which he considered the most extraordinary and revolutionary social experience in all history. The fascist art of having others obey you and the notion of complete authority amazed him. In 1965, Perón would tell writer and journalist Eduardo Galeano, that, 'To manipulate people is a technique, a leader's technique. An art that requires military precision. I learned this in Italy in 1940. Those people knew how to command!' He also admired Hitler and had read *Mein Kampf* over and over again. The perfect order of German Nazism fascinated him, and later he regretted only a few 'excesses' committed in the camps, much like other Perónists.

Perón spoke perfect Italian, so he chose Italy over Germany. He wanted to bathe in the public baths, speak with the people, share their tremendous enthusiasm for this stimulating renewal that was going to change the face of the world. From Perón's point of view, the Italian people were similar to Argentines, and, in June 1940, the Italians fanatically followed their duce's preparations to win the world conflict. Perón was among the united masses that cried when Mussolini, from the heights of the balcony of the Palazzo Venezia, announced his decision to enter the war. His own fervour was so strong that, although he was usually physically repulsed by physical contact – he was a cordial man who would embrace others but never let anyone touch him – he hugged the healthy and strong workers whose eyes were sunny and whose skin smelled like olive oil. This is the day when his dream of a strong and healthy Argentina that would recapture the torch of the 'third position' took shape. In 1968, Perón told historian Félix Luna, 'When faced with a world divided by two imperialisms, the Italians responded: we are with neither side, we represent a third position between Soviet socialism and Yankee imperialism.' We need look no farther for the origins of the expression 'third position' that became the definition of Perónism.

This was a dream that came from deep inside him. Despite Perón's emotional frigidity and the Machiavellianism of the old guanaco hunter, he would remain loyal to fascism. When journalist Valentín Thiébault informed Perón of Mussolini's death and said, 'We will have to erect a monument for him someday,' an unusually passionate Perón responded, 'One monument? Only one? Please say you mean one on every street corner!' It is uncertain whether he had really met Mussolini as he said so many times. It may have been his desire to see him up close that fooled him into believing that he had. Perón did insist that he met Mussolini privately on July 3, 1940 and that he saluted him in the fascist way, with his arm raised. True or false, this gesture dwelled in Perón's imagination.

Previously, Perón had been named the foreign auxiliary commander of the Tridentina alpine division and of the mountain infantry division of Pinerolo. He had devoted himself to strengthening his muscles with a maniacal rigour and would expend his energy through vigorous exercises that soothed the brain and ironed out the soul. He got drunk on harsh, salutary, and joyously virile mountain songs and on pure snow where his childhood ambiguities disappeared like a bad dream. On the white mountain, all of nature was a well-ironed uniform. He had learned the secrets of mountain war at the mountain climbing school of Aosta and the Sestriere ski school. Then, in Turin, he attended theoretical science classes, and in Milan, applied science classes. That is where it all came together for him. Capitalism and communism were cosmopolitan, but the real novelty was national socialism. He had finally penetrated the internal functions and the traps of a capitalist economy, the methods of capturing power through trade unionism and propaganda. Just before the war broke out, he took the train to Berlin. A few officers of the Wehrmacht amiably welcomed him. He felt comforted by his idea of a working German people who formed a block around their führer. When he visited the Loebtzen line in Eastern Prussia and the Russian Kovno-Grodno line, the Soviet officers, who were very friendly with the Germans, showed him around their country. He also visited Hungary, Yugoslavia, Albania, Spain, Austria, and France.

However, when he returned to Argentina in 1941, his ideas were not understood by the Argentinean officers with whom he tried to share his experiences. They thought he was a communist, and in order to get rid of him, they sent him to the immaculate snow of the Andes, to Mendoza where he ran the centre for mountain instruction. He accepted his removal philosophically and did not lose hope. Perón believed Argentina was sinking into corruption and rot, just waiting for something to happen. This anticipation was perceived by the Spanish writer Ortega y Gasset when he visited Argentina in 1939: 'Argentines beware or you will have a dictator!' This anticipation did not escape the shrewd eyes of certain observers. According to Juan José Sebreli, on May 3, 1942, Goebbels wrote in his journal, 'Argentina could become very important in the ultimate evolution of the Latin American situation.' One year later, and one month before the revolution of June 1943, General Wilhelm von Faupel, the German espionage chief in Spain, went to Buenos Aires where he met with the nationalist leader Ibarguren and three members of the GOU: von der Becke, Perine and Perón.

Let us talk about the GOU for a moment. Did the phonetic resonance of Perón's name influence the choice of the young nationalist colonels who came looking for him in the half-melted snow in the summer of 1941? In politics, nothing is negligible. It is true that the Argentinean masses, in need of a father, would have difficulty chanting a name that ended in a fish tail like Perine. On the other hand, the Spanish suffix -ón suggests an increase. To chant 'Perón, Perón' would awaken a feeling of grandeur in the masses.

But the young colonels were not yet envisioning this. They were in search of Perón because they knew and shared his ideas about fascist Italy, Nazi Germany, and the future of Argentina. The GOU was a secret military lodge whose members planned on becoming the Latin American gauleiters after Germany's triumph, which they thought was certain. Argentinean nationalism was an already ancient tradition. Among its ranks were intellectuals like Diego Luis Molinari, Manuel Gálvez, Leonardo Castellani, Carlos Ibarguren, and many others who were partisans of Perónism and of German national socialism, which financed the journals *Pampero* and *Clarinada*. The writer, Raúl Scalabrini Ortiz, did not openly adhere to Nazism. He had gone to Berlin and had supported Hitler with the 'pragmatic' arguments that were so dear to Perón. 'What Hitler is doing in Germany does not interest us,' he said. 'Or at least only to the extent to which it favours Argentina, Peru or Venezuela. If he is against England, as he appears to be, we have to take full advantage by scorning the Hitlerian ideology and methods.'

Therefore, the movement's key and its most positive aspect was the rejection of English colonialism. We can also add in his defence that, at the time, Scalabrini Ortiz was not aware of the details of Hitler's practices. As for Perón, he rejoined the GOU. It had no head, but its most active members besides him were Colonel Eduardo Avalos, Colonel Enrique González, and Colonel Emilio Ramírez. He became the thinking teacher for the officers who dreamed of a nation as white as snow.

The Perónist snow-whiteness tolerated nuances. However, the secret manifesto of the GOU of March 13, 1943, which Carlos Ibarguren assures us is authentic, was very clear: 'Germany is making a titanic effort to unify the European continent. The biggest and best prepared nation will be in charge of governing the continent's fate within its new configuration. In

Europe, that will be Germany. . . . Today, Germany is giving life a historic direction. We must follow this example. . . . Hitler's fight, in times of peace and in times of war, will have to guide us from now on.' Perón, who was loyal to this document's principles, visited von Faupel and became not only Ambassador Edmund von Thermann's friend but also the friend of two German billionaires who had settled in Argentina, Ludwig Freude (whom he had already met in Italy) and Fritz Mandl.

When Evita met Perón, she already knew the rest of the story, including the Revolution of 1943, Perón's nomination as Secretary of the Minister of Defence, and later to the *Secretería* of Labour. The first position carried more prestige than power. President Ramírez had named General Edelmiro Farrell Minister of Defence and Farrell and Perón were great friends. It was clear that Perón was waiting for a much higher future position and that he was already using his power by means of Farrell. But what about the second position? Evita no doubt asked herself the same question that his friends at the GOU had pondered: why was he chosen? We can almost imagine Perón's wink and his response, 'They think it is a secondary job, but actually, true power lies within the unions.' He would add, 'And on the radio,' just as his left eye winked again. This reflex would transform him into Gardel's *Viejo Vizcacha*, Old Vizcacha, the malicious gaucho from José Hernandez's *Martín Fierro*, who lavished astute and cynical advice. He was the exact opposite of the noble and proud gaucho who was tragically doomed.

FITS OF ANGER

A few days after their first encounter, Perón went with his colleague from the *Secretaría*, Domingo Mercante, to Evita's broadcast. It was the first time that Perón and Evita would be

seen together. Evidently, he wanted to support her. Nevertheless, that week was not an easy one for him or other government
members. From the outset, the subject of Argentina's neutrality
had seriously divided the GOU. On January 26, President
Ramírez succumbed to the increasing American pressure and
broke off all ties with the Axis. In this way, he revealed the
weakness, if not cowardice, of a country that made a decision
at the last minute when Germany was almost defeated.

The Americans had been insulted by an odd story of selling
arms. In August 1943, the Ramírez government had requested
arms from Washington. According to Jorge Camarasa, the reply
from the United States was, 'How can we give arms to a country
that has a relationship with Germany?' Ramírez then sent a
commission to Germany to acquire the weapons that they
could not get elsewhere. The ship carrying the Argentinean
consul who was in charge of this mission was seized en route to
Barcelona by the English. They intercepted the compromising
documents on board and sent them to the Americans. Some
American ships were on their way to the Río de la Plata,
and the American banks obstructed the Argentinean funds.
The Argentinean government was forced to break off from
the Axis. As for Perón, he accepted his superior's decision.
However, he had participated in this strange episode that
revealed the stubbornness of the Argentinean soldiers who
still believed in a German victory. Be that as it may, the crisis
had already been triggered. On February 24, 1944, General
Farrell replaced Ramírez as the republic's President. Two days
later, Perón became Minister of War.

Throughout all this tumult, he did not neglect Evita's career.
The day he was elected to the head of the cabinet, he showed
up at Radio Belgrano. A photographer who was present but
not aware of their liaison told this revealing story. He was
preparing to shoot the scene before his eyes: Perón and Imbert
were sitting and Evita was standing in between them with
one elbow resting on each chair back. Perón noticed the

photographer, whom he took for a kind of spy, and angrily screamed, 'What are you doing? Stop that!' At which point two police officers seized the photographer and ripped the film out of his camera.

This incongruous and angry action was Perón's last masculine stab at independence. That same month, Jaime Yankelevich proved that he knew the motive for Perón's visits. He created much publicity around the new broadcast of the famous women series. This time, it was devoted to Elizabeth of England. He entered into a year-long contract with Evita and paid her a salary that prompted her to boast, during an interview with the radio magazine *Radiolandia* on April 7, 1945, that it was 'the highest salary ever paid by Argentinean radio.' The lack of elegance and modesty is excusable, for she was a woman who had come a long way – from the *maté cocido* to the gold bridge – and her employer was bowing at her feet as a bonus. By now, there was not a photographer who didn't know that she was the Minister of War's mistress. Perón openly stuck up for her and was happy to use his authority to grant her respect in the workplace.

In his memoirs, Bonifacio del Carril relates a picturesque scene in which Evita enters the radio station, trembling with rage. She complains bitterly about Yankelevich. Perón is annoyed and tries to reason with her, finally promising that he will take care of the problem. This was a new characteristic to their relationship. Perón skirted around Evita's outbursts without ever facing them head-on. Was this the attitude of a mature man faced with a young woman's childish tantrums which, as a good macho, he attributed to ovarian irregularities? Or was he scared of her? He confided in Tomás Eloy Martinez that Evita was maladjusted but that he never feared her eruptions because she eventually always became docile for him. Perhaps this was simply Perón, in his old age, trying to regild his personal image of her. Evita treated Perón like a coward when he was impassive.

According to a friend of the Duarte sisters, one of Eva's tantrums took place around April or May 1944 at the dinner table of the Machinandearenas, the owners of the San Miguel movie studios who had just hired Evita to star in *La cabalgata del circo* (The circus rider). The topic was marriage. Perón was avoiding eye contact and conversation. Evita, who was not at all like a guanaco, was not going to back down, so she furiously barked at him, 'You'd better marry me, or I'll tell the world everything I know about you!' It was not clear what compromising information she had. Was it sexual (Perón the impotent) or political (Perón's friendships at the German Embassy)? Whatever it was, Perón listened to these words in silence and certainly seemed caught in a trap. There was either some terrible secret that she threatened to divulge, or else this man who had never belonged to anyone, who had never depended on a woman – not even to wash his uniforms or his laundry – needed her.

It must have been his need for her that terrified Perón the most. Evita's supposed 'threat' seems naive, for no one in Argentina would have taken seriously a radio starlet's denunciation of the Minister of War as impotent or a fascist. On the other hand, the quiet man who would stop at nothing to calm her down needed this woman. He needed her for numerous reasons, not least of which were tickles, affection, loyalty, political flair, and radio propaganda. Soon he would add gratitude to this list. The line between need and love is often blurred. At the time, Perón certainly loved Eva, at least within the limits of his capacity to love. It wasn't flawless, but he had feelings for her that were close to love. She may have thought that he would marry her only out of desperation, to avoid a scandal. But she was wrong. Marrying her was the worst scandal, for he risked the army's hostility, and in the end, the army would in fact turn against him because of Eva. Given this, he surprised his male comrades but he also surprised himself. Fortunately, as always, there was a tango that described his situation and that made him feel less lonely. The *compadrito*, shunned by his *patota*, lays his woes out to the woman who dominated him: '*No me has dejao ni el pucho en la oreja / de aquel pasao malevo y feroz*' (You didn't even leave me with a cigarette butt in my ear / as a souvenir of my days as a bad boy').

THE BLONDE MADONNA

La cabalgata del circo, starring Libertad Lamarque and Hugo del Carril and directed by Mario Soffici, began filming in March. Evita became a blonde for her role. She would remain a loyal customer of Pedro Alcaraz, the stylist who dyed her hair, for the rest of her life. He accompanied her on her trip to Europe, created the gold chignon that would become legendary, and even styled her corpse's hair. There were no secrets between Eva and Pedro. In fact, his hair salon would become her favourite rendezvous spot when she suspected ears in the walls of the presidential palace or in her office.

On June 1, a photo of her, newly blonde, appeared in *Antena* magazine. The golden locks transformed the pale brunette, though her pallor now seemed strange and her future illness would render her supernatural. Her skin's transparency was accentuated by the contrast with the obviously artificial golden colour. Since hair dyes had not yet been perfected, the colour's ambition was, in fact, not to appear natural. It was a theatrical and symbolic gold, a gold that imitated the effect of the golden halos and backgrounds of the religious paintings of the Middle Ages. This art isolated holy bodies, distanced them from the earth, from heaviness and from density, and from the opaque skin that occupies space and projects shadows. Blondness was – and is – a sign of wealth and social ascent. Once Evita was blonde, she discovered that it exalted her beauty. In fact, it finally let her blossom. The morning fog that once hid her had been lifted. Evita had been put on this earth to radiate light. Just as brown had entombed her, gold liberated her. From now on, Evita would would wear the virtual halo so often evoked by Perónist propaganda. With the birth of Evita the beauty came the birth of Evita the Madonna. From then on, she would polish and refine her personality by gradually eliminating all excessive ornaments: first the banana earrings, then the flowered dresses. Meanwhile, the gold in her hair, which was pulled back tighter and tighter, would become the saintly halo that penetrated even the deepest realms of her own self-perception. In fact, she would so literally incarnate the role of the saint that her skin would seem to become not just flesh and blood, but mortified flesh.

THE ANARCHIST SLAP

The new flamboyant hair of Perón's mistress was not the only intriguing topic of discussion for the cast of *La cabalgata del circo*. The highlight of the film was to be a slap, a slap that the film's star, Libertad Lamarque, would give to Evita. Libertad Lamarque was already an indisputable star. In fact, it was Lamarque who was singing in Luna Park at the moment when Perón and Eva exchanged glances for the first time. One story even places her sitting next to Perón first that night. When she got up to sing, Eva reportedly took her chair. The story, true or not, certainly reveals a rivalry between the two women.

Libertad was a plump, short, and stocky brunette who had a large lower jaw, heart-shaped lips, and big dreamy eyes that looked up toward the sky when she sang, much like Augustin Magaldi. The magazines had noticed a similarity between Libertad and Evita's idol, Norma Shearer. Both the Argentinean singer and the Canadian actress were slightly cross-eyed. Thus, Evita should have felt tender pity for Libertad, but this was not the case. Libertad's roles consisted mostly of young ingenues.

Her face was framed by jet black ringlets (in certain very particular situations, ingenues with natural hair were tolerated), she wore a dress with laced-trimmed flounces, and she sang like a nightingale, all the while fleeing from the advances of a dark, handsome, and slick man with a thin moustache. Those who accuse Evita of being a bad actress should see some of Lamarque's films.

However, Evita did not even have the strength to be ridiculous as an actress. She was too stiff and frigid for that, and no doubt too timid. Her voice could inspire laughter, though, according to Gloria Alcorta. But in *La pródiga* (The extravagant), the only film in which she could actually be seen, Evita deserves the unique adjective that her critics always granted her, 'discreet.'

In her memoirs, Libertad Lamarque relates her version of the episode that made ink flow and tongues wag. Libertad was a star when Evita, almost unknown to movie audiences, got her part thanks to Perón. Libertad was also a democrat who feared the rise of a fascist army, while Eva was on the road to being a militarist. Nevertheless, Libertad maintains that the real reason for their quarrel was professional. Evita was never on time. She would come to the set in the afternoon for a scene that was supposed to have been shot in the morning. Libertad would wait in costume in her dressing room, uncomfortable in her corset, and hungry, for she would not eat lunch, fearing that the diva might show up any minute. Finally, around four thirty in the afternoon, Evita would arrive in a gleaming black car. The Minister of War's chauffeur would rush to open the door for the blonde Evita. Libertad must have ground her teeth, for she had risen early to apply her own makeup (in order to save time), had taken the train to San Miguel (a distant suburb of Buenos Aires), and had walked along the dirt road to get to the film studios from the train station.

According to Sergia Machinandearena, the slapping scene, or the lively argument between the true star and the star with connections, took place during a rehearsal of a *pericón*, a folkloric dance that did not require any talent and that all schoolchildren knew. But Evita's feet would not obey her. Libertad, who danced like a charm, exploded, not by slapping her, according to her own story, but by telling her everything – she was sick of her ridiculous work hours and sick of this unfortunate *pericón* for which they had to hire a dance instructor. While she spoke, a very pale Evita, who was strangely calm, just smiled, as she had during the scene with the Toad.

On the other hand, Mario Soffici considered Evita a very conscientious actress. However, this contradiction does not mean much. She was a good colleague to those who did not treat her high-handedly, and she could certainly have enjoyed provoking the singer who looked down at Evita. When she was late, she radiated the nonchalance of a spoiled woman, her eyes lost in an eloquent dream that was extremely irritating to other women. She constantly spoke about Perón – passionately, candidly, and with no holds barred. Her words always revealed their intimacy. At the San Miguel studios, it was not unusual for her to complain about indigestion, pat her stomach and say, 'Who knows? Maybe there is a little Perón in there.' Did she really believe this? The actress, Fanny Navarro, told photographer Anne-Marie Heinrich that Evita had miscarried Perón's child. This story is upheld by Fermín Chávez (who did not reveal his source). Finally, two women supported the theory of Perón's fertility: Isabel, his third wife, who says that she also had miscarriages, and a woman who claims that she is the former President's daughter. Tomás Eloy Martínez, on the other hand, always maintained that Perón was sterile. Of course, some find this idea unbearable, for a leader must be virile and fertile. Sexuality, the capacity to procreate or not, became political topics.

It was the flaunting of her happiness that infuriated Eva's colleagues, including Libertad Lamarque. Was it ingenuous?

One can be simultaneously candid and 'prudent' – that was Christ's advice. She really did feel happy, and letting it show was her revenge. It is easy to imagine her arrival on the set in her official car as the apologies for her lateness flowed. Meanwhile, the famous star was miserable in her corset, and her makeup was all dusty. When Libertad finally exploded, it is easy to detect the idea that began to germinate in Evita's head, an idea that was reflected in her pallor and in her strange smile: 'Just you wait, just you wait a little while longer, and you'll see what I'll do to your professionalism and your jet black ringlets.'

In fact, seemingly from the moment Evita gained power, Libertad was unemployed and left for Mexico, where she was already famous and where she would go on to become a national monument. In Argentina, no one would have dared give a part to an actress whom Eva had cursed.

However, Roberto Galán and Pedro Maratea assert that the supposed curse did not exist, and that Libertad even requested a meeting with Evita once she became the President's wife. According to one version, it was Libertad's daughter who requested the meeting, for she was worried about her mother who was in Colombia during the bloody revolts. Eva helped find Libertad and return her to Mexico, safe and sound. In a second version, Libertad went to see Evita herself and requested permission to work in Argentina. Eva smiled ironically and said, 'Go ahead and work, who's preventing you from working?' And when Libertad babbled about not being able to sign a contract, Eva's smile would broaden, 'Maybe no one here is interested in your films anymore.' Whether or not the singer requested an interview with the all-powerful Evita, the bottom line is the same – the story contains a slap and revenge. The slap may have been metaphoric. The revenge was subtle, and poor Libertad must have felt constrained to negotiate with her rival.

Another actress, Nelly Ayllon, may have also slapped Evita during the filming of *El cura de Santa Clara* (The priest of Santa Clara). This woman's argument had a significant economic and political motive, the need for film reels. Argentinean cinema had flourished in 1939, but during the war, it had entered a decline due to the difficult ties between Argentina and the United States. Americans manufactured cellulose acetate, and most manufacturers refused to sell it to a neutral country. In 1944, the Argentinean executive power signed a dictatorial decree that allowed it to raid all imported cellulose and to distribute it as it saw fit. Perón and Evita were already beginning to present themselves as the major communication manipulators they would become. The image of the colonel giving his girlfriend the film reels he monopolised presaged the future image of the President and his wife becoming masters of the press through their possession of paper.

Not too much later, in September 1945, *Sintonía* magazine published a cartoon of a man with a bouquet of flowers in his hand being jilted by his fiancée. A maid shows him to the door and says, 'Madame does not want to hear a peep from you again. She received some film and she's going to become a star.' Thus 'Old Kartulowicz' was settling the score with Eva, who would later furnish him with paper for his magazine. Argentina was a society of 'favours.' Rightful owners did not exist, and only friends were worth anything. This was inscribed in Evita's soul even before she met her colonel, for Mauricio Rubinstcin related that during her artistic period, Evita would often say, 'I do not see my friends' faults just as I do not see my enemies' virtues.'

A HOUNDSTOOTH SUIT FOR A BETTER WORLD

In 1944, it was Perón who was packing his suitcases instead of Evita. This was a first. An apartment was vacated in Evita's building on Posadas Street and Perón moved in. This allowed the two lovers to live together but separately. It was a comfortable arrangement rather than an attempt at concealment, for their relationship was already public. However, that time, a minimum of discretion had to be taken. It would not have been acceptable to advertise their cohabitation, and Evita was preparing herself for a life of performances, not theatrical, but official instead.

Paco Jamandreu, her designer who met her at Arenales Street shortly before Perón's move, gives a clear image of Evita's mental attitude at the time. Jamandreu was a chubby homosexual who loved to be photographed dressed in feathers, with lips puckered and shoulders bare. He had a sharp, malicious, and prolific tongue, but, he gives more justice to reality than either Evita's idolaters or detractors.

'Do not think of me the way you think of your other clients,' she would tell him. 'From now on, I will have a dual personality. On the one side, I am the actress to whom you can give her poufs, lamé, feathers, sequins. On the other, I am what the Big Shot wants me to be, a political figure. On May 1, I must accompany him to a demonstration. People will gossip, it will be the first appearance of the Duarte-Perón couple. What will you create for the occasion?'

'A suit,' the designer replied, 'a double-breasted houndstooth suit with a velvet collar.'

Thus, Eva Perón was born. This was the first in an uninterrupted series of little suits with the same look, which Evita loved. Perón would complain, believing that she was always wearing the same one, and suffer, for he longed to dress her up like a princess. This became Evita's work 'uniform,' and it was almost as much a trademark as was her chignon. Perón was clearly the 'big shot' who wanted to prepare her for political life, and he would grumble from the adjoining room about Jamandreu's presence in their house. 'Come on,' Evita would say, 'he wants to meet you and he has no patience. He is the most anxious man! He exasperates me.'

When the designer entered the room, he saw the colonel lying on a bed that was as modest as the rest of the apartment.

He was eating a chorizo sandwich and drinking cheap red wine. He looked curiously at Jamandreu, as if 'he were looking at something he had never seen in his life,' and the designer looked back at him. Two worlds were face to face, the nut with the pins and the rough and tough leader whose massive body took up the entire bed. Between them was Eva.

From their first conversation, Evita revealed to Jamandreu a few aspects of the complex framework of her relationship with Perón. She stressed that Perón wanted to push her and exhibit her: 'That lunatic wants me to go with him to the Colón theatre for a gala on May 24th' or 'I have to visit a shanty town to see if I am ready to assume the duties that I am called upon to perform, according to Perón.' We now see that after being briefly surprised by Eva's flair, he went on to exploit the raw political animal that she was, the charismatic image of tenderness and kindness that she was capable of projecting. Admittedly, she did disclose a slight irritation toward her man in saying that he exasperated her, in calling him crazy, in criticizing his chorizo sandwich. But there was a certain coquetry in skinning him alive, and she was very careful about not flaunting her joy, afraid that it would evaporate. Nevertheless, the real Perón, the daily Perón, had begun to annoy her.

The more the real Perón irritated her, the more the ideal Perón claimed her heart. This is the Perón she loved to the point of adoration and sacrifice. It is her gratitude to this Perón, the redeemer who had chosen, purified, and saved her, that drove Evita to a cancerous self-destruction, all the while singing canticles. 'She would not stop thanking me,' Perón told Tomás Eloy Martínez. It is possible that the mystical love that he had inspired annoyed him just as much. Was he willing to accept that Evita loved him superficially and not for his thick body and his chorizo sandwich? That she loved his image more than she loved him?

But who was the 'true' Perón? And how could this question

have an answer when they were both consciously and calculatingly determined to define their public image? The day would come when she would naively admit, in *My Mission in Life*, that Perón was jealous of Perón. Who wouldn't have been in his place? To cheat on her husband with himself was the biggest sin of this Madeleine, who by becoming blonde, and by choosing a transfigured image over the real one, had also fooled herself.

Time would help Evita find the answers, the fatal answers. For the time being, she began to sketch a movement that would temporarily distance her from Perón but eventually get her closer to him.

In June 1944, Evita threw herself into a series of broadcasts called 'Toward a Better Future,' the goal of which was to reveal the colonel's ideal image to the audience. Francisco Muñoz Azpiri, her nationalist director, had just been named Director of Propaganda under the administration's Information Subsecretary. 'Toward a Better Future' was his work, and Evita played the part of a woman of the people who exalted the June Revolution and most of all exalted Colonel Perón. He was not yet a candidate for the presidency, but this broadcast unequivocally presented him as the true leader of the Argentinean people.

A few excerpts of this text deserve to be quoted. Their vitalistic rhetoric is fascist, to be sure, but, curiously, one cannot ignore in it the leftist revolutionary poetry that flourished in the forties and was most popular in the fifties and sixties, a poetry that always spoke of 'viscera' and of 'sap,' that is, badly digested Pablo Neruda. As for the symbolic character of Juan Laguna (John Lagoon, a poetic way of saying John Smith, but representing a Smith that was elevated to the rank of an ideal worker), a character we will meet later, the coincidence is even more troubling. This is how the Communist painter Antonio Berni later baptised one of his characters, a character who took on the same meaning: the man of the people, the real man blessed with all virtues. This was not done randomly. At Perónism's outset, the Communist Party divided itself into pro-Perónists and anti-Perónists. In the seventies, young leftist bourgeois adhered to Perónism primarily due to certain shared tastes of rhetorical and aesthetic orders.

Here is an excerpt from the broadcast. Imagine military music in the background, drums and bugles. A man with a clear and virile voice says, 'Here, among the mysterious bustling in the street, where a new will is gestating and is preparing to be born ... Here among the anonymous mass of the working, silent, suffering, and thinking populace ... Here in the pupils of fatigue, of hope, of justice or in those of fraud ... Here among this shapeless caravan that is the motor of a major capital, the nerve centre, and the motor of a giant American nation in motion ... Here is THE WOMAN who defines our movement through her intuition as a mother, a wife, a sister or a fiancée. . . . Listen to her! ... It is she!' Eva would then say, 'Do you remember June fourth? It was a steel dawn, harsh and bloody! No one will ever forget it, because from it was born a wave of new emotion, as violent as an orangutan who does not spare a single soul! ... The Revolution was born of something anguishing and hard that sprouted within, in the depths of the viscera ... where hatred and passion reside and a sense of injustice make the blood flow on one's hands. . . . The June Revolution was made for Juan Laguna who returned to his native province. . . . A man who would give his work a notion of redemption; a dignified soldier said those who saw Juan Laguna return home saw him bearing a cross of famine; a soldier of the people who felt the flame of social justice burn in his heart, who decisively contributed to the dawning of this people's revolution. This is his voice and his confession.'

Perón's speech followed. His voice was set off by the speaker's stereotyped virility and by Evita's nervous voice that was like a hoarse bird (her voice would become deeper and more intense over the years). Perón's voice was earthy and reminded one of his smile. Little or no hysteria, no rhetoric. It was a voice that was barely veiled; at this time, Perón had not yet found his final tone, the tone of *criollo* wisdom. Yet this wisdom was felt or believed to be felt, and its effect was reassuring without being icy. On the one hand, the drums, the bugles, and the shrill or nervous voices elated the audience. On the other, this man who spoke of truth as a 'dignified soldier of the people' inspired their confidence.

A certain truth can often slide into the emptiest rhetoric, as if smuggled in. And within this script are words that poignantly express Eva's truth. She speaks of 'something anguishing and hard that sprouted within, in the depths of the viscera.' Indeed, this nucleus of suffering was the beginning of her death.

✜

When Jamandreu saw Evita for the first time in 1944, he found her faded, colourless, and very poorly dressed. The apartment on Posadas Street was a marvel of bad taste. However, even then the new Eva existed, and she was getting ready to leap out toward herself. One day, she asked Jamandreu to accompany her to a shanty town to see if she was 'able.' Among the poor who welcomed her, a few recognised her radio voice, though many did not. But they all recognised a sincere woman who was offering her help. They knew that she was indeed sincere because they saw her bite her lower lip each time she received an answer to her repeated and almost obsessive question, 'Where is this child's father?' The mothers responded that the children were fatherless, illegitimate thus sealing a silent pact with this stranger.

Another Evita was born of Jamandreu's hands. Perón the 'lunatic' wanted her to look like Cinderella at the ball at the Colón theatre gala on May 24. May 25 is the biggest patriotic holiday in Argentina, which, with July 9, celebrates the liberation of the former Spanish colonies. 'What kind of dress are you going to make for me?' she asked anxiously (though she had neither the pumpkin-coach problem nor the horse-mouse problem, for she would go to the ball in an official car with the Minister of Defence as her escort).

Jamandreu created a black silk gown with an enormous skirt narrowly cinched at the waist. The bodice and the long, close-fitting sleeves formed a braid of velvet ribbons. A jet pearl shone at each intertwine. When Perón saw the gown, he exclaimed, 'You must pose for a picture. We'll have it published in a magazine, yes, in *El Hogar*!'

Old Vizcacha amused himself by attacking the oligarchy's vulnerable spots: *El Hogar* published only social chronicles. Never had an actress appeared on its pages, and never had the mistress of a minister attented a gala at the Colón theatre, in the official box. Perón laughed until he cried. Even the gown seemed to enjoy this provocation. It was a malicious gown that spread itself in the box whose thousands of jet beads sparkled as if they enjoyed being scrutinised by the legitimate wives' binoculars, by so many eyes contorted in horror. It was a battle of looks, a multitude of gloomy pupils staring at Evita's chest and arms.

Part Two

Chapter 4

❖

GRATEFUL

La pródiga! For some mysterious reason, this movie, which was in the early stages of filming, fascinated Eva. Suddenly, all her energy was concentrated on one thing – she was the Extravagant. It was useless to argue that the San Miguel Studios had already chosen Mecha Ortiz, a well-known actress, as their star. Mecha Ortiz had played the parts of the famous women long before Evita had, and the Extravagant's character – a mature woman – fitted her like a glove. Ortiz was at the age when women cease to be beautiful and become interesting. Evita had just begun to find beauty, but she possessed the rare strength of knowing what she wanted. Hers was a naked and raw desire that moved mountains, and it had nothing to do with nostalgia and tango. Eva was not prone to the longing for some other time that was characteristically Argentinean. She wanted the here, the now, the immediate. Tact and remorse would not get in her way. She had been a victim of injustice, and she knew she had the right to an ardent desire. Life had to be assaulted just like on those little multicolour Porteño buses that were always jam-packed. You needed good legs and sharp elbows to hang on. Later, Evita would insert this message when addressing the underprivileged. She used other words, but everyone understood what she was really saying: 'Do as I did! Desire! Request the most expensive, the most beautiful, luxury, happiness! It is all yours! Take it fearlessly!' For the time being, the violent desire that quickened the beat of her heart had the face of the Extravagant.

Perón was a man of ambiguous feelings, so he could only admire Evita's clarity, her wishes, her loves, her hatreds. He ended up giving in or, rather, he established a game that would become their way of life. The rules were, push Evita to act, then pretend to give in so that she believes it was her influence. The roles in this game would always be confused, for which was the master and which the slave? By 'submitting' to his master's wishes, adopting the half-clever, half-resigned facial expression of the male who obeys, and winking to suggest the opposite, Perón made it clear to the owner of the San Miguel Studios that he would deliver film reels for the shooting of *La pródiga* on one condition, that the starring role go to Evita. And so it did.

Eva wanted this role so much it seemed her life depended on it. The Extravagant, a character created by the Spanish novelist, Pedro Alcarón, is a repentant sinner who devotes herself to charitable acts. The little people consider her to be semidivine and call her '*la Señora*,' 'the mother of the poor,' 'the sister of the afflicted.' At the time, perhaps Evita could have imagined that she would one day soon become '*la Señora*.' Was the power of her desire so strong that it could transform reality? As suspicious as we should be of premonitions, coincidence continues to surprise us, for here was an actress who would eventually play, in life, the part that she had on the screen. Let us suppose, however, that when Eva founded her Foundation for Social Aid, she asked Raúl Apold, who was in charge of propaganda, to designate her as '*la Señora*' or as 'the Lady of Hope.' So much will was not surprising. It was exerted by a woman of the theatre who simultaneously became the character and the director.

Yet *La pródiga* was never released in Argentina. It is difficult to obtain a copy even today, for the film was, to a certain extent, cursed. Few Argentines were able to see Evita in her premonitory role. Those who did see her all agree that her performance was insipid. It was a harsh criticism. She did have a monotonous but actually rather touching voice. Her face expressed only an eternal melancholy, which did not, however, lack nobility. Perhaps she was too young for the role. It would have been impossible to tell this on the screen since her hair was made up in a fin de siècle style and was reconsidered and corrected by 1940s fashion. It was one of those hairstyles that seek not to rejuvenate but to emphasise importance, dignity, and majesty. Despite her skin's freshness, she appeared older than she was. In this role she had wanted so badly, she looked like a girl wearing her mother's clothes. As for the film, it was rife with incongruous details, for example, when the populace carries the drowned Extravagant, her long, golden, carefully waved, and perfectly dry mane drags on the ground. However, to be fair, the history of world film is rich with incongruities, especially hair-related ones. It is easy to recall the hairstyles of 1950s American film in which every strand of hair was always in place, even if the scene took place in a spiny bush. Yet it is not a question of combs and brushes that kept *La pródiga* out of circulation. The truth was, it was not tolerable for the President's companion to show herself on a movie screen, no matter how touching she was. By ousting Mecha Ortiz from the film, Eva thought she had her own life, her life as an actress, under control. She would never have imagined that this would be her last role – at least in the cinematic realm.

She did not imagine this on April 7, 1945, when she was interviewed by *Radiolandia* magazine. She did not discuss her theatrical experience. This time, the novelty was that she admitted with charming candour that she owned a house. Not the apartment on Posadas Street. No, even better, a real house on Teodoro García Street in the Belgrano neighbourhood, where English and Germans lived in noble, Englishstyle residences. In fact, it was a German – Ludwig Freude, the billionaire whom Perón had met first in Italy and then at the home of Ambassador von Thermann – who, according to two sources, had given it to her. Fifteen months after the night at Luna Park, Evita had made great strides. If this businessman considered it appropriate to flatter her in this manner, then it must have meant that she was already considered Perón's wife. Still, we must ask why the German billionaire used the device of a 'corporate gift' to Eva in order to flatter Perón.

THE NAZI MECCA

In order to answer the question, it is necessary to look back to August 10, 1944, and leave Argentina to go to Strasbourg in occupied France. On that day, according to Jorge Camarasa in *Los Nazis en la Argentina,* seventy-seven men were assembled in a building called the Red House on Kleber Square. Two months earlier, the Allies had landed at Normandy. The seventy-seven conspirators, the crème de la crème of the Nazi hierarchy, knew that their days in government were numbered. They had only one thought in mind, to save their assets. All the infamous powers were present, including Martin Bormann, Albert Speer, Admiral Wilhelm Canaris, the big industrialists of the regime (the Krupps, the Thyssens, the Messerschmitts, the Siemenses), the bankers, the financiers, in short, all those who owned something and feared losing it. It was Martin Bormann, or maybe it was his representative, who summarised the group's final proposal: 'The hierarchy of the Party assumes that a few of its members will be condemned. . . . The Party is prepared to substantially fund the industrialists' endeavours in organising post-war activity abroad. In exchange, we request control of the funds that are transferred overseas in order to build the future of the new and powerful Reich, once this one is brought down.'

This project of banking on the future did not take into account only industrial revenues, but the Red House's guests did not realise this. According to Glenn B. Infield, in *Skorzeny: Leader of Hitler's Commandos*, at the end of 1943, Martin Bormann discovered 'the existence of a substantial gold mine which was stored in Berlin's Reichsbank. It was mostly composed of silver, gold and jewels, stolen from the Jews in the concentration camps' and deposited by 'Max Heilger' under the care of Dr Walther Funk, president of Reichsbank. Bormann dipped into this treasure, and with the help of his collaborator, Dr Helmut von Hummel, as well as Otto Skorzeny (whom we will encounter again later), he dispatched his booty on board a submarine. Destination: Argentina.

Furthermore, the Red House's guests planned two possible itineraries for the future Nazi fugitives. They would leave Munich, travel across Austria, and end up in Madrid; or they would travel to Genoa in order to sail to Egypt, Lebanon, Syria, or Buenos Aires. In every case, the voyage would be organised by something called the 'Roman network' or the 'road of the monastery.' The heart of this network would be the Vatican. Its soul would be the Austrian bishop Alois Hudal, assisted by twenty-one other members of the Vatican, among them the Italian cardinal Umberto Siri and the Croat archbishop Kronislav Draganovic. According to the May 29, 1994, issue of *La Republica*, Hudal was part of a Vatican organisation, the Pontificia Commissione di Assistenza. Monsignor Ferdinando Baldelli presided over the section that obtained passports for the fugitives.

Soon after the Red House meeting, another friend of Martin Bormann's, Walter Rauff, moved to Milan. He offered to rid Italian partisans of their fascist archives. They were his, on one condition: he had to force the Nazis to leave through Genoa. It seems that this favour was granted.

Elsewhere, German industrialists and Nazi leaders transferred their assets abroad where they either established new enterprises or financed existing ones. The example for this option was first presented by Propaganda Minister Joseph Goebbels, who had deposited substantial funds in an Argentinean bank in 1942. Switzerland headed the list of countries selected for this reinvestment, followed by Franco's Spain and Perónist Argentina. The latter welcomed ninety-eight companies. Many Nazi leaders imitated the Minister of Foreign Affairs, Joachim von Ribbentrop, who transferred his personal funds to Banco Alemán Transatlántico Banco Germánico, Banco Strupp, and Banco Tornquist in Buenos Aires.

Argentina had long been entangled in a love affair with Germany. It was a love-hate relationship that President Sarmiento had been the first to speak about. According to Luis V. Sommi in *Los capitales alemanes en Argentina*, Sarmiento denounced an article in the magazine *Deutsche Rundschau* in 1882, that described the southern regions of Brazil, Argentina, Uruguay, and Paraguay as 'German provinces.' The expansionism that incensed Sarmiento was accompanied by the usual theories of German superiority. So many German companies had settled in Argentina during the nineteenth century that the ground was well prepared for the rise of Nazism. The vast majority of the German community supported the Nazi movement, to the point that in 1938, the radical deputy Raúl Damonte Taborda and the Socialist deputy Enrique Dickmann created a commission to investigate anti-Argentinean activity. Their investigations were quite fruitful.

During this time, Perón was happy to have found Nelson Rockefeller, who became coordinator of the Office of Inter-American Affairs in 1940. What pushed Argentina's government to declare war on Germany and Japan on March 27, 1945, only five weeks before the German surrender? Simply an exchange of winks between the two individuals. Rockefeller and Perón were both astute in their own ways. Rockefeller offered Perón diplomatic recognition and membership in the United Nations, among other privileges, on the condition that Argentina join the Allies against Germany.

In 1970, Perón would admit to Tomás Eloy Martínez that,

'We had begun to prepare ourselves for post-war long before the end of the war. Germany had been beaten and we knew it. But the victors wanted to appropriate the immense techno-logical advances made by the Germans over the last ten years. The machines had been destroyed, but manpower remained. So, we let the Germans know that we were going to declare war against them to save lives.' Salazar of Portugal and Franco of Spain sent this message to the Germans, and according to Perón, they proved to be very useful after the war.

The victors, especially the Americans, were not interested in the German 'machine.' Did they appreciate Perón's position, the position of an ambitious leader who wanted to take over the vanquished giant's technological knowledge? Did they not contemplate the notion that science and ideology were strangers and that, in fact, German scientists were very useful? Until then, nothing in Perón's attitude went beyond the pragmatism and cynicism every politician is supposed to practice. However, the story (or legend according to some) of the two submarines filled with gold by a phantom Martin Bormann may have surpassed standard political practice.

On July 10, 1945, a German submarine aimed its periscope toward Mar del Plata's coast, the luxurious and rowdy resort town to which two young oligarchs from Junín had invited Evita ten years earlier. The captain introduced himself to the Argentinean authorities as Lieutenant Commander Otto Vermouth. The Argentines were fascinated by this apparition, and they nicknamed Captain Vermouth 'Cinzano.' A second submarine, led by Lieutenant Commander Heinz Shaeffer, appeared in Mar del Plata, demonstrating that the first had in fact been an appetiser. But what more succulent meal were they announcing?

The two submarines excited the Argentines' imaginations. They were suddenly propelled into a scene of world conflict, much like the *Graf Spee* affair, and they finally felt they were at the heart of the action. Argentina was a country of children, European progeny. The Europeans were adults who had real wars, while Argentines watched life happen to others far away. Now life was literally emerging on its shores! The entire country abandoned itself to the most whimsical, exasperating, and delicious conjectures.

'Cinzano' and Shaeffer's declarations satisfied no one. They claimed to have learned of the surrender of the Third Reich on May 8, 1945, while they were out at sea. Despite the recent break of ties between Argentina and Germany, they said they preferred to surrender to the Argentines and their natural kindness rather than to such unpleasant adversaries as the English. No one believed them, that is, no one except the Argentinean government, which turned these declarations into evangelical words. Thus the government rushed to announce that the two submarines were transporting nothing and no one suspect, and that, for example, Hitler – yes, modestly Hitler – was not on board. But perhaps the mere mention of this frightening name provided a smoke screen to hide Martin Bormann, or maybe even his treasure?

The sociologist and intellectual Perónist Juan José Miguens provides a version that is diametrically opposed to history. According to him, the submarines never existed. Instead, at the end of the war, the English broadcast demoralising radio messages to the German soldiers, including one announcing that their submarines were leaking. The Americans intercepted this message and believed it. But the British 'forgot' to refute the rumour and Americans believe it to this day . . .

Alain Pujol's description, which painstakingly details the submarines' contents, leaves us wondering. Pujol, a member of the French information agency the Second Bureau, mentioned two landings that occurred on the incredible nights of February 7 and July 18, 1945.

The action took place on the beaches of San Clemente del Tuyú, not far from Mar del Plata. A few mysterious men unloaded enormous trunks on the beach. With a lantern, one could read the following words on the trunks: *'Geheime Reichssache'* (State Secret). The man with the commanding build who gave instructions to the truck drivers lined up by the road on the edge of the beach was none other than Ernst Kaltenbrunner, the Third Reich's chief of the Secret Police. The trucks, packed with the extremely heavy trunks, were going to the nearby *estancia* Lahusen. There were three witnesses from the *Graf Spee*: Brennecke, Detelmann and Achotz. The trunks collectively contained 187,692,400 marks, 17,576,500 dollars, 4,682,500 pounds sterling, 24,976,500 Swiss francs, 8,379,000 Dutch florins, 54,963,000 French francs, 17,280,000 Belgian francs, 2,511 kilograms of gold, and 4,638 carats of diamonds and precious gems. Who then would be responsible for depositing these funds in the Alemán Transatlántico, Germánico, Tornquist, and Strupp banks? It was none other than Ludwig Freude, the German undercover agent in Buenos Aires. And in whose name would they be deposited? In the names of Juan Domingo Perón and Eva Duarte.

These figures appear identically in Ladislas Farago's *Aftermath: Martin Bormann and the Fourth Reich*, published in 1974. This book, which not everyone believes, is filled with disturbingly precise details. Farago confirms Perón's role in the placement of the Nazi spoils in Argentina, especially those of the Krupp family. He insists that Martin Bormann was in Buenos Aires, confirming the story of a member of the American Embassy, John Griffiths (whom we will come back to). Farago adds that Bormann had been 'extremely frugal' all his life, and he treated Argentinean Nazis with the same frugal spirit. In brief, he did not generously share the gold mine, which displeased Ludwig Freude and his three associates, Heinrich Dörge, Ricardo von Leute, and Ricardo Staudt. This all ended tragically, with an assassination, a 'suicide,' and a mysterious disappearance. We will see this later, when we examine another equally suspect 'suicide', that of Eva's brother Juancito Duarte, in 1953.

Before the end of the war, Perón had given the military attaché to the German Embassy, von Leers, eight thousand Argentinean passports and one hundred thousand Argentinean identification cards that were signed and sealed by the police, without photos or fingerprints. On August 8, 1944, that is, two days before the meeting at the Red House, Heinrich Himmler received his set of documents in Strasbourg. The passport gift must have been the beginning of Perón and Evita's famous Swiss bank account that launched a steady stream of ink. Von Leers had also bought a house for Perón, in Cairo, where he himself lived in 1960, the year Adolf Eichmann was arrested in Buenos Aires. This is how, according to Juan José Sebreli, Argentina's capital became 'the Nazi Mecca.' A report issued by the International Committee for the Study of European Issues estimates that in 1947, ninety thousand German Nazis were spending happy retirement in Argentina. Among them was the group of officers from the Luftwaffe whom Perón jovially called the 'justices of the air': Kurt Tank, the engineer who built the *Pulqui II*, the first Latin American jet plane; Lieutenant General Adolf Galland and Hans Ulrich Rudel; and Otto Behrens and Werner Baumbach, the aviators.

Curiously, Israeli and other Jewish researchers were responsible for dispelling the stories of the Nazi treasure, which were much used by anti-Perónists of the 1950s. Simon Wiesenthal, the famous war criminal hunter, was fascinated by Bormann and followed his many worldwide 'sightings' and his many 'deaths' (his 'graves' were found all over the place). In 1972 he finally accepted the West German government's confirmation that Bormann's death took place on the night of May 2, 1945. He was apparently attempting to flee the chancellor's bunker. Wiesenthal declared, 'The Nazis used Bormann like a flag. After the war, they repeated: *He is alive. We will return.* . . . Today, we know that he committed suicide. There is no doubt about it.'

No doubt? Not according to Paul Manning, who confirmed; 'Wiesenthal ceased to investigate the Bormann affair due to pressure from Jewish leaders. The Bormann organisation was not only an organisation of former Nazis. It was a very powerful economic group whose interests go far beyond ideology today.'

Was it a coincidence that Wiesenthal himself declared in an infuriated tone that revealed years of useless research and effort, when he was consulted during a congress on anti-Semitism held at the United Nations in 1992, 'I have no proof on Perón! None! I implore the Argentines to leave me alone'?

However, in 1992, when President Carlos Menem visited the United States, Gerald Posner, author of *Hitler's Children*, published an article in *The New York Times* that struck like a bomb. In this article, entitled 'The Bormann File,' he stated that he had written many letters to President Menem asking him to make public the police files concerning the Nazis, but he never got a response. He asked the following question: 'Why would Menem protect the files of war criminals forty-six years after the end of the war?' Then he answered the question: 'Argentina has a lot to hide in the Bormann affair.'

This time Argentinean authorities did respond, but only to deny the existence of a Bormann file in the Federal Police Bureau. Posner was angered by this response, and on December 7, 1992, he countered in a letter to *The New York Times*, 'I saw the Bormann files with my own eyes in 1984. The file was more than twelve inches thick. And besides, if these files did not exist, then why did the Federal Police Bureau respond to my letter in September 1991, refusing to let me see them?'

Posner finally won the case. The files were released to the press and to the representatives of the Simon Wiesenthal Center and the World Jewish Congress. They concerned five war criminals: Josef Mengele, Josef Franz Schwamberger,

Walter Kutschmann, Eduard Roschmann ('the Riga butcher'), and Martin Bormann.

These very thin files confirmed a Nazi presence in Argentina but did not satisfy expectations. However, this was proof enough that the rumours had not been as fanciful as many had believed. According to one file, Roschmann, who was guilty of exterminating forty thousand Jews in Latvia, had lived in Argentina since 1948 under the alias Wagener.

The extreme thinness of the Bormann files prompted Gerald Posner to say during an interview with Alberto Oliva for *Somos* magazine, 'A file that is less than 12 inches thick is a tampered document.' 'What do you think was the "hottest" item within these files?' Oliva asked. 'The logistics and the content of the five submarines that anchored on the Argentinean coast,' Posner responded. 'The Nazi files indicate that these vessels unloaded 550 ounces of gold, 3,500 ounces of platinum and 4,638 ounces of diamonds, as well as hundreds of works of art, millions of gold marks, dollars, and Swiss francs.'

What remains in the files suggests what is missing, and it is the biographer or historian who must find the links between these. According to this file, in September 1950, an Italian, Dr Pino Frezza, recognised Bormann in the ABC, a bar on Lavalle Street. A report dated October 14, 1952, issued by the directors of the Federal Coordination and marked 'strictly confidential and secret', discusses a house that was bought in the Ascochinga region in the Córdoba province by an ex-officer from one of the submarines that landed in Mar del Plata. The text confirms meetings in Ascochinga among such Nazi leaders as Heinrich Dörge and Ricardo von Leute. The latter, who was president of the German Transatlantic Bank of Buenos Aires, had established a rapport with 'Martin Borman.' And in 1944 he had organised the routing of gold and valuables to Argentina. The text alludes to the *estancia* Lahusen, to Patagonia, and even to Josef Mengele.

At first, the Congress on Nazism that was organised in

Buenos Aires in September 1993 by the Delegation of Israeli Argentine Associations (DAIA) and by the Torcuato Di Tella University did not clear up the problem. The goal of this meeting was to study the files. Among its participants, only the Argentine Jorge Camarasa, the Canadian Ronald Newton, and the German Holger Medin focused on the concrete problem of Nazis in Argentina. The congress concluded that Martin Bormann had in fact lived in Argentina but that there was no proof that the treasure existed.

Let us now return to the attitude, which was not very vindictive, that was adopted by certain Jews toward Perón. The first Israeli ambassador to Argentina, Iaacov Tsur, initiated the devilification of the Argentinean leader. The legendary ambassador, who lived in Argentina during Perón's regime, found this devil to be much less contemptible than he was widely believed to be, or at least than he pretended to. Indeed, what good would it do to accuse a regime that had recognised the State of Israel since 1948 and that had left the Jews to live in peace?

It is by closely examining Perón that we grasp the true reason behind this geniality. The February 1992 issue of *Humor* magazine published a transcript of Perón's surprising words: 'I consider what happened at Nuremberg to be a base infamy on the part of the victors. That is when I realised that they should have lost the war. Nuremberg was an atrocity that History will never forgive! As far as the Jews go, I remember when one German, who had arrived in Argentina after the defeat, broached this subject to me. "How could you even think that I would get bogged down by this problem," I said, "knowing that Hitler and his one hundred million Germans were not able to resolve it? If the Jews are living here, I can neither kill them nor chase them away. The only solution is to let them work within our community."'

It goes without saying that the desatanising of Perón was due to more than the refusal to scrutinise his character. Thus, Professor

Leonardo Senkman, a researcher from the Hebrew University of Jerusalem, insists on throwing the heaviest responsibility in this Nazi affair on the Vatican and on the Americans.

We should remember Klaus Barbie, who was used by the American information agencies that later got rid of him by sending him to Bolivia, via Argentina. We should also remember Paperclip, the space project on which the Germans were collaborating. And finally we should not forget that the Americans, the English, and the Soviets were rivals in their ambitions to appropriate the most sought-after Nazi scientists and technicians. According to Senkman, Argentina picked up the crumbs of this feast. A good example is that of General Walter Schreiber. This war criminal and Nazi scientist was used for many years by the U.S. Air Force's School of Aviation Medicine. Then the Americans placed him in Argentina, much like Barbie.

Let us add to this that, according to a documentary broadcast by Arte, the Franco-German station, in May 1994, the Croat war criminal Ante Pavelic, who was aided by the Vatican's Archbishop Draganovic, had previously been protected by the English. Pavelic, who was reputed to have been even more ferocious than Hitler, had fled to a British zone in Austria in 1945. In 1946, he was at the San Girolamo School in Rome, which had become the centre of the exiled Croatian government. The Americans knew that he was there and, just like the English, did not arrest him. Postwar times were as much devoted to anti-Communist struggles as to the anti-Nazi revenge. Moreover, many Nazis were welcomed.

One question still remains: why would tainting the Vatican, the United States, and England purify Perón?

The latest findings show that the files of Alfredo Stroessner, the Paraguayan dictator, which were accidentally discovered, reveal that Bormann lived in a town on the Argentinean-Paraguyan border. He had stomach cancer. His doctor, Josef Mengele, was unable to save his life. This was the Mengele who lived in Argentina under his real name until the 1960s, the Mengele who, as was recently revealed by the mayor of La Coruña, Francisco Vázquez, had landed in Argentina in 1949 or 1950 at Vigo, aided by 'a Spanish pro-Nazi organisation, *La Araña*.'

According to Stroessner's documents, Bormann died in 1959 and was buried in an unmarked grave that no one has found.

Allow me to give in to the temptation to transcribe a personal conversation between the people who were close to the Mossad, the Israeli information agency, in Buenos Aires in September 1993, shortly after the DAIA congress.

To begin with, I was surprised and troubled by declarations by Shimon Samuels, the representative from the Simon Wiesenthal Center, that appeared in the Argentinean newspaper *Página 12*. Samuels announced that Israel was stopping all research on Nazi criminals developed by the Center, which somehow tallied with Paul Manning's suspicions.

My interlocutors let it be known, in a clearly ironic tone, that the Simon Wiesenthal Center was not considered the expert Nazi hunter. Who then was the most qualified in this field of research? The Mossad, of course. The Mossad that had captured Adolf Eichmann in Buenos Aires in 1960, under President Arturo Frondizi's government.

Then why was the Mossad not able to locate Martin Bormann?

An even more surprising response. Israel, which was too isolated on the world scene, could not allow itself to carry out two similar trials simultaneously.

'In other words, the Mossad was about to capture Bormann but let him get away because they were listening to the State?'

A long silence, then nods.

'What about the treasure, then?'

A smile appeared. 'In Madrid, they asked Perón the same question, and he responded, "Go ask Jorge Antonio."'

Jorge Antonio was the Syrian-born billionaire who hit the jackpot after Perón's exile in 1955. Today, Jorge Antonio is still the businessman closest to the Argentinean government and to President Carlos Menem, also of Syrian descent.

'So Jorge Antonio seized the treasure?'

'Let's just say that he managed it well. Very well.'

'Is he still managing it?'

There was silence.

'And what was Eva's role in this scenario?'

'She had nothing to do with the Nazis, except that she would offer them coffee when they came to visit her husband.'

'And she also accepted their gifts. . . .'

There was more silence and the shrugging of shoulders, since the subject was obviously not important to them.

'But do we have proof, any proof, that the treasure existed?'

'I will only speak of what I saw,' my interlocutor said. 'In 1955, among Perón and Evita's personal belongings – which were exorbitantly luxurious and were exhibited at the Revolución Libertadora – I noticed a sumptuous inlaid box. The box held silverware. On the cover, there was a mother of pearl star, a Star of David. I was still a child, and I called my father over to show it to him. My father had come to Argentina after the war; he was a German Jew. His entire face was altered. "Maybe it was a gift from the State of Israel or from the OIA," the Jewish Peronist Organisation, I said, so that he would not have the same thought that was already in my head. But he answered that neither of these would have given an object for the home with a Star of David to a Christian head of state. The donor could not have been a Jew. This object had to have belonged to a rich Jewish family that was no longer in any condition to use it. Its presence among all these things – jewellery, clothing, shoes, hats by the hundreds – testified to the donor's vileness and to the receiver's large indifference.'

This conversation occurred in September 1993. On December 28, the newspaper *L'Humanité* published a small news item in a corner of a page: 'Mengele was spared by the Mossad. Zvi Aharoni, a former Mossad agent (the Israeli Secret Service), confirmed that his superiors ordered him to let Josef Mengele, the Nazi war criminal whose nickname was "the angel of death" at Auschwitz concentration camp, get away. In an interview with the Israeli newspaper, *Maariv*, the former Israeli spy says that he had found Mengele in an isolated farm in Brazil, but that Isser Harel, the Mossad leader, had told him to "forget about it."'

On July 18, 1994, a bomb went off in Buenos Aires, killing more than one hundred people. The target had been the AMIA, an institute that manages Jewish life in Argentina. It was a symbolic target. After the murderous attempt on the Israeli Embassy in Buenos Aires in 1992 – which was concurrent with President Menem's release of the Nazi files – the pro-Iranian Hezbollah, which was considered to be responsible for both incidents, aimed at the heart of this community. With its immigration files reduced to ashes, the memory of Argentinean Jews had just disappeared.

There was more. On the fifth floor of the AMIA at 633 Pasteur Street, the *Testimonio* group had been working on finalising the definitive conclusions reached by DAIA Congress on Nazism in Argentina that had taken place in September 1993. Three months before the bombing, the *Testimonio* researchers had finally found a number of leads on Bormann and others. These had been leads that the international neo-Nazis wanted to erase.

BUFFALOES, MUSKETEERS, AND FURIOUS SOLDIERS

In 1945, Evita possessed a noble home on Teodoro García

Street. 'The Extravagant' was the object of a grand extravagance. And Ludwig Freude, considered to be the front man for managing Nazi funds, with the help of his four companies that had been established in Argentina since 1942, was financing Perón's electoral campaign.

The shooting of *La pródiga* ended in September. A few days later, before the film premiered, a crisis erupted. On October 5, Evita, who wanted to gain power within the world of art, had named her old friend Oscar Nicolini to the post of General Director of the Post Office and Telecommunications. It was an innocent move that she never imagined would cost her and her lover dearly.

At the time, Perón held three positions: Secretary of Labour, Minister of War, and Vice President of Argentina. The series of popular steps (demagogic to his adversaries) taken by this sui generis soldier had assured him the loyalty of the poor. The Communists, the Socialists, and the anarchists had never taken power and thus had never gotten the chance to prove the validity of their intentions to the workers. Perón was the only one who took care of the workers. Already in 1943, the June Revolution had lowered, then frozen, the rent. Then Perón hiked up the salaries, created labour courts, and improved welfare systems. These were actions that the Socialists had long before voted for, but until now they had been disregarded. The agricultural worker statute of 1944 transformed the peón, who was exploited by the big landowner, into a full-time worker with a minimum salary, paid vacation, severance pay, and Sunday rest. This did not hurt the *estancieros* much, though it did ruin many a little farmer. But this was not the worst of it. In the eyes of the army, the worst was the loyalty that the people vowed to Perón. This was a dangerous gratitude, which made him dangerous.

Then there was Evita. The soldiers were formal on this subject. She dared to rest her arm on the back of the presidential chair on the day of a minister's nomination.

The legitimate wives cried scandal. That arm, which was too white, too bare, too adorned with jewels, was the serpent that had to be quashed before it was too late. Eva and the serpent. It did not take long for the chair of Bernardino Rivadavia, the first President of the Argentines, to be compared to the tree of good and evil knowledge. That leaves us with Adam's part. For who but Perón encouraged the serpent to slyly wrap herself around the sacred trunk?

Perón's attitude was incompatable with military and virile honour. He was fascinated and amused by the satanic, climbing creature. Everyone could see the malice sparkling in 'his' eyes when he officially introduced an unworthy woman. What was he laughing about? Did he get the foretaste of absolute power when he imposed Evita on others? Did he think that he could take the liberty of exacting revenge on level-headed people, on well-wishers, just as his father had done by marrying a mulatto servant? When his army colleagues, with quivering moustaches and severe brows, explained to him that his liaison with an actress was not highly regarded, Perón opened his penguin arms and responded, 'What, would you prefer that I have a relationship with an actor?'

Perón had an odd sense of humour, which was often less than wise, and a laugh that could never hide his secrets. His disdain for others, and a self-destructive urge were often unintentionally revealed. The day would come when Perón could no longer control his laughter or his nervous wink. Then his sense of humour would turn against him, just as the ambition to hold everything in her hands would turn against Evita.

The democratic opposition shared the army's disdain for the actress, but it had another reason to hate Perón. He was a Nazi (and worse, he was cunning). To them, military meant Fascist. The anti-clerical liberals looked down on the institution of religious teachings in schools in 1943. As for Communists, they had been outlawed since the military coup. The entire central committee of the PC, including my own father, lived in a dismal prison in Neuquén, in the middle of Patagonia, from 1943 to 1945. And all the books from the Communist library were burned. It is otiose to describe the Communists' feelings toward the 'boots.'

That is when Spruille Braden, the new United States ambassador, arrived. Braden personified good conscience. He seemed to have escaped from a combination of a Sinclair Lewis novel and a western, a cocktail party whose guests were Babbitt and John Wayne. He was big, ruddy, euphoric, and sure he was right and on the right side. But his good intentions were not entirely naive. According to Ignacio Klinch, Braden had been taken over by the anxiety of the American Jews, who believed that their Argentinean brothers were in danger, and so he had become their messenger. It was a profitable anxiety that he could use to his advantage. For as we have seen, the shrewd Perón had studied the German example and, ironically, did not intend to disturb the Argentinean Jews in the least.

Either Braden did not understand this or he had no interest in understanding it. But had he at least noticed Rockefeller's leanings? And did he realise that, despite his anti-American declarations, Perón could become an ally in the fight against communism, number-one enemy of the United States? There is nothing in his attitude that leads to this interpretation. He arrived in Buenos Aires as fresh as a rose and ready to intervene without any restraint. He was welcomed by the entire democratic coalition – oligarchs, radicals, Socialists, and confused Communists. In the face of the dangers of Nazism, this ruddy Mr Clean played the part of the Messiah.

As he played this part, his beneficiaries were not the coalition but Perón. Braden openly interfered in Argentina's affairs, with what he thought was good reason. The pure and hard nationalists, those who dreamed of a Fourth Reich in Argentina, considered Perón to be a traitor since he had broken off all diplomatic ties to Germany. But now they were face to face with a cowboy, and they decided to strengthen their ties to Perón. Perón used them or pushed them away, according to the situation. When he did find them useful, he treated them as *piantavotos* (a slang expression meaning 'bastard votes').

Let's come back to the cowboy. Many times had Perón enjoyed saying that if he owed his electoral victory to anyone, it was to Braden. The rosy-cheeked American paid him a visit in June. Faced with Perón who displayed a choirboy's candour, Braden evoked 'the German and Japanese assets' that the Argentinean government could seize. He added, with raised eyebrows inspired by Groucho Marx: 'But, Colonel Perón, you know that if we work these affairs out, the U.S. will not get in the way of your future presidential candidacy.' 'Alas!' Perón cried, opening his arms, 'There is still a problem.' 'What problem?' 'In this country, he who enters into this type of scheme with a foreign power is a son of a bitch.'

Braden turned livid with rage and left without even a good-bye, in his haste forgetting his hat. Perón burst out laughing and threw the hat to 'his boys' for a little game of soccer. 'Braden is a buffalo,' he would later say. 'I was provoking him, and when he was hopping mad, he charged at the walls with his head down. . . . This was to my benefit: it was exactly the reaction I was looking for.' A buffalo. Why not a guanaco? This former hunter knew how to adapt his speech so well that, by dreaming of American films, he had changed breeds, although in his heart he was certainly still trapping the Patagonian beasts.

The elections were imminent. President Farrell, who was sensitive to the critics of the democratic opposition just as the military feared Perón's increasingly strong power, announced to the Argentinean people that they would have the opportunity to choose their governors before the end of the year. On August 4, 1945, Farrell raised the state of siege. The exiled Argentines, who had taken refuge in Montevideo following an old tradition that had started in the age of Rosas, returned to Buenos Aires. And on September 19, the democrats defied the speech that Perón had uttered the night before, in which he complained about 'the combination of foreign elements, reactionary spirits, hopeless politicians, and selfish plutocrats,' and paraded in the city's streets.

This March of Constitution and Liberty brought together two hundred thousand people. Spruille Braden led the crowd, elbow to elbow with Communist, conservative, Socialist, and radical leaders. It was indeed a daunting combination, but the one thing that united all these disparate people was their hatred of the military and the Nazis, and the love of culture. Later, Perónists and leftists (the New Left of the sixties) alike would joke about these cultured demonstrators who marched and sang '*La Marseillaise*.' When they shouted at the top of their lungs, these elevated people who loved the French Revolution thought they were right, just as Braden did. 'Books yes, boots no!' When you hear the Perónist response, which would soon come ('Espadrilles yes, books no!'), it is easy to understand the fears of the cultivated folk. They dreaded an ignorant Argentina, the Argentina of radio soaps, Evita's Argentina. The humour was also dated. At the time, these well-to-do people who feared this Argentina also found it ridiculous.

There is one last visual observation about this Liberty March: all its participants were white. Braden's florid tint certainly contrasted with the romantic pallor of Alfredo Palacios, the Socialist leader with a big moustache. There was no *cabecita negra* there to sing '*The Marseillaise*.' You could call one side or the other ridiculous, but is was impossible to mistake the skin colour.

That is when Evita appointed Nicolini on October 5. The military, who had heard the antimilitarist message from the ladies and gentlemen during the Liberty March loud and clear, said *basta*, enough of this all-powerful whore who's giving the well-to-do a reason to scorn the army. The officers of the Campo de Mayo on the outskirts of Buenos Aires, the location of the country's most important garrison, were angered for the last time. The commander, General Eduardo Avalos, was chosen to deliver the message of his colleagues' discontent to Perón. Early in the morning of October 6, Avalos went to see his friend, the Minister of War. He displayed a jovial mood and asked Perón to retract the unfortunate appointment and replace Nicolini with the army's candidate, Lieutenant Colonel Francisco Rocco.

Perón was surely cunning, but no one is always at his best. After all, the appointment of poor Nicolini was only a detail. He could have given in, for he had recently shown the extent of his flexibility by proclaiming his high regard and admiration for President Yrigoyen, to whom he would later consider himself a successor (forgetting about his participation in Uriburu's revolution when he was overthrown).

And, in the same vein, he had named the radical leader Hortensio Jazmín Quijano to the post of Minister of the Interior on August 2.

So why was Perón not flexible now, faced with Avalos? He may have felt that the army's demand had more to do with Evita than with Nicolini. And Evita was becoming more and more important to him. Perón was tired of being only cunning. To enrage Braden was to set a trap, for an angry Braden was much more useful than a calm Braden. But what was the advantage in angering the army? It seems as if he wanted to precipitate things by treating his own colleagues like swine. By dismissing General Avalos, Perón was not playing the part of the guanaco hunter but simply that of a man. An ambivalent man like all others, malleable and rigid, winking and letting himself be blinded by pride, a man who started to discourage himself.

There were too many struggles, too many enemies, too many disparate partisans. What did it mean to be on Perón's side in 1945? His 'party' was made up of a good sprinkling of Marxists, a pinch of nationalists, a few ounces of Yrigoyenists. The people loved Perón and everyone knew it, but these people had not yet materialised as skin and bones; they were still far off in the distance, abstract, a simple idea. The Liberty March had been very successful, so successful in fact that General Rawson thought that it was the perfect time to lead a coup, supported by the democratic opposition, notably the Socialist Alfredo Palacios, the one with the big rimmed hat and the d'Artagnan moustache. The only result of this attempt was that Rawson and his colleagues were quickly arrested, and order was immediately reestablished in the state.

But the country was lodged in a climate of war. On October 6, while General Avalos was chatting with Perón, then with Farrell, then again with Perón, the funeral procession for Aarón Salmún Feijoo, a student who was shot by the 'boys' of the *Alianza Libertadora Nacionalista* for having refused to shout 'Viva Perón!' was parading down the streets of Buenos Aires. The funeral ceremony turned into a violent anti-Perónist demonstration, and all the Argentinean universities were there. A few days prior to this, Perón had delivered a pompous and insincere speech. For once, this great seducer who usually could put himself in others' shoes, could not remember his words. The students booed him. Twenty years later, the children of those students would judge Perón's language – which was improved by time, of course – to be immensely sensible. That is how two generations erred; one through hatred, the other through love.

While Avalos tried to convince Perón, who was becoming

increasingly irritated, Evita was coming and going at Posadas Street, paler than ever. For some time now, there had been rumours of an assassination attempt on Perón. According to the photographer Anne-Marie Heinrich, Evita even cooked and tasted all his food in order to protect her man. Other witnesses say that Perón's food was tasted even at the Machinandearenas. In both cases, poison plots were in the air, and Evita's weakness was apparent.

The dialogue became heated at Posadas Street. At least twice Evita exclaimed, 'Don't give in! You're the boss!' Finally, exhausted and at the end of her tether, she said, 'What you should do is drop everyone once and for all and leave; you need rest. Let them take care of themselves!' Avalos could not stand this woman's presence. Everything about her bothered him: her gestures, her voice, her hysterics, her vulgarity, her badly dyed hair (due to the tension over the last few weeks, she had not had time to colour her dark roots, and to Avalos, she looked like a maid). He was at least able to convince the spell-bound Perón to meet the leaders of the military units. Perón was not the same person, either. He seemed bewitched.

Colonel Domingo Mercante, Perón's right-hand man, came to the apartment on Posadas Street that evening. He had never seen his friend in such a state. Perón went from anger to weakness. The next morning in the car, the leader ripped his cap off and hurled it to the floor. Childishly, he repeated, 'I am sick of this, sick of it.' It was his fiftieth birthday.

The meeting at the War Ministry was wrapped in confusion. On the one hand, the ministry's subofficers had prepared lunch to celebrate Perón's birthday. On the other, Perón was not weakened to the point that he forgot his strategies. He had invited forty servicemen who were still loyal to him. The talks lasted all day. That night, the Campo de Mayo contingency had decided to march into Buenos Aires and overthrow Perón, who knew it. Some proposed that he use air power to suppress the troops, but he refused. Morning came, and he waited at the ministry for events to unfold, still surrounded by his followers. He cancelled a planned visit to the War School. It was a wise choice, for the students had come together to kill him.

What was he waiting for? He was waiting only for the results of the meeting between Farrell and the Campo de Mayo insurgents. During the meeting, Avalos summarised his and his colleagues' sentiments. They had had enough of Juan Domingo Perón, they wanted to get rid of him. Perón would immediately have to vacate the nation's vice presidency, the Defence Ministry and the labour post. 'Everything?' a stunned Farrell echoed. 'Everything.' Obviously the Nicolini appointment had been forgotten. Now the goal was altogether different, to oust Perón and to designate Avalos as his successor. Almost apologetically, Farrell offered to resign his post as the nations's President (the only thing that made him happy was playing the guitar in the bordellos in Mendoza), but they asked him to stay. So he called Perón on the telephone and said, 'Unfortunately, you will have to resign.'

One hour later, Perón wrote a signed document ('so that everyone would notice that my hand did not shake'), and then went home.

A DISTRESSED COUPLE

Evita was waiting for him.

She had mixed emotions. She felt guilty for having started the drama, proud that her man had defended her blow by blow, and anxious about the future. She helped Perón out of his white uniform, which was tight at the waist, and helped him into his robe. The red robe highlighted his skin's almost green pallor (surely his liver) and aged him. One could easily tell he was fifty.

When evening fell, their friends came to visit. They whispered as if at the bedside of a dying man. Perón, however, had

not lost his appetite, and he quickly devoured a cold dinner
served by Evita. She watched him eat his Russian salad. She
felt like his daughter, and she hated food because of Doña
Juana. For his part, Perón hated mothers. But that evening
she had to mollycoddle him, approving of every bite with a
nod. In a couple's life, there is always an instant, sometimes
imperceptible, where all the chips are out on the table, and if
one person doesn't notice what the other needs, that person
loses. Evita perceived this, and she won – at least for now.
She understood that this man, who had been alone since his
childhood, wanted someone to say, 'Good, that's right, eat.'

✛

The news threw Argentines into a state of shock. A few union
leaders hurried to visit their disgraced leader to assure him
of their loyalty. The democratic opposition demanded that
the government be transferred to the Supreme Court. Farrell
risked being alone in heading the country. Just as a tree loses
its leaves, he was losing his ministers one by one. So Perón
took off the red robe that did not flatter his complexion, and on
October 10, he went to the labour office to say his good-byes.
Fifteen thousand workers had gathered in the street in front of
the ministry where they had often been received by the only
man in power who ever thought about them.

What could be more natural than to speak to them? And
what could be more normal than the radio broadcasting his
speech? Argentina heard Perón utter words that in no way
evoked defeat. He would resume the work that he had
accomplished, and most of all, he announced, before he left
the labour ministry he had signed two decrees: a salary raise
and the introduction of a 'fluctuating, vital and minimum'
wage that would be fixed to the cost of living. He advised
the workers to remain calm, but he concluded, 'I ask you
to respect public order so that we may follow our triumphant

march; but, if one day it becomes necessary, I will ask you to fight.'

Evita was in the street among the workers. It was the first time she felt the heat of the crowd admiring Perón. There was the Perón she loved, a man vibrating with energy like a beehive. But now that Perón was emerging from his shell to challenge the army, Eva was scared. Yankelevich had already called to say that he was cancelling all her broadcasts on Radio Belgrano. Evita's career had just come to a halt. Too bad, it was too late to retreat. Perhaps she had picked the short end of the straw when she chose Perón. In the past, she would have undoubtedly asked herself this question using the same analogy. She was now living a novel that transformed her character. The action was becoming too dizzying for her not to be swept along by the current. How could she dwell on petty issues? Her lover's life was hanging by a thread. With this speech, Perón had signed his death sentence.

It was midnight when they left the apartment on Posadas Street. Mercante was there. He was distraught that Perón was abandoning his fight. But the leader reassured him and took the driver's seat just to show him that he was still in command. Evita was by his side. Juan Duarte and Rudi Freude, the son of the Nazi billionaire who had given Evita the house on Teodoro García Street, were in the backseat. Each was young and handsome in his own way, one through his pallor high-lighted by the striking black, the other in gold, pink, and blue. It was as if they were two pages escorting the royal couple.

They expected to find a refuge in San Nicolas, a little town in the pampas, at their friend Dr Román Subiza's home. But en route, Rudi suggested a different destination, why not hide out on his father's island in the delta? The idea seemed like a good one. Although it was a little port on the Paraná River, San Nicolas was situated on a vast plateau of open land. How could one hide there? The pampas have no corners. He who is fleeing remains visible long before disappearing into the horizon. Mountains and forests were very far from Buenos Aires. Since the beginning of time, fugitives from the law had chosen the thick undergrowth and the muddied and shady streams of the delta of the same Paraná River on the outskirts of the city. During the preceding centuries, the fugitives' skin was blackened by nature and by the coal made out of the island's wood. The delta also had an erotic aspect due to its many inns where one could enjoy a one-night stand. Many French prostitutes, who had taken 'the road to Buenos Aires' in the twenties, had spent time in the delta. But now, after the war, another group of white runaways had replaced the blacks and the 'white girls.' Pretty Swiss-German chalets were sprouting up in the delta's folds. The disorienting place where the couple ended up was a wood house that seemed to grow out of the Black Forest, surrounded by tropical vegetation and water mirages. The couple walked in the earliest morning, looking at the earth that was water and the water that was earth. Three streams converged, thus its name, Tres Bocas (Three Mouths). Three embouchements, three directions: power, exile, death. They were dazed, for the delta sent them confusing images. Their destiny was obscure like the waters.

This is how Mercante and Mittelbach, the police chief, found them.

ORPHAN EVITA

While Perón and Evita contemplated the water that constructed and deconstructed destinies, the pandemonium in Buenos Aires was in full swing. The radical leader Sabattini, who had just left his hometown of Santa María in the province of Córdoba, was there. Perón had dreamed of recruiting him to his party, but, alas, this hope was lost. The night of his hurried departure, he had said in a bitter tone, 'Everything that is happening to me is due to that *little macaroni* from

Villa María.' He was right. If Sabattini had only agreed to support Perón! Once again we have the ambiguous charm of the conditional tense. In fact, Sabattini was an intelligent, well-respected man with legitimate presidential ambitions. And he now thought that his time had arrived. Perón had disappeared, and he could now negotiate with the 'democratic' or at least less Nazi militarists, Avalos, for example. Was this a mistake? Surely it was, but one of those mistakes that become as necessary as they are inevitable.

The day after Perón's departure, a second group filled Plaza San Martín. Now the people from the Liberty March had been joined by students from the left. The civilised democrats lined up along the shore, just as they were used to, and distanced themselves from the hot heart of a barbaric Argentina. Meanwhile, they could not have imagined that other waves, brown ones, were advancing onto them, at their backs.

In the meantime, Mercante spoke with the workers, who asked him, 'Where is Perón?'

Mercante decided to seek out the fugitive. But when he went to the house where he expected to find him, he found only Rudi Freude and Juan Duarte, who were able to provide him with news, although the police had already interrogated them. That is when Mercante called Mittelbach, the police chief, to ask him to help him find the colonel. It was an odd decision, but it seems as if there was a link between this choice and the concern that he had communicated to Perón the night before. He feared that his leader would give the movement the slip. He went to look for him to request that he return to being Perón no matter what (aware of the risk he was asking him to take). Such anti-Perónist authors as Benigno Acossano always attributed this part to Evita and succumbed to caricature by describing her as 'trying to push Perón forward by kicking him in the rear' in order to summon him to appear in front of the people on the night of October 17. That scenario ignores Mercante, the son of a worker who would later pay for his 'crime' of loyalty. Just like Eva, and for the same reasons, the loyal Mercante was condemned to fall from grace.

The motorboat approached Tres Bocas. Two silhouettes emerged in the distance, one big and square, the other frail. Soon their forms became clearer in the fog, as if they were emerging from memory, even though Mercante had seen them the night before. This was a decisive moment. Perón and Evita were arm in arm. She was wearing trousers and was very beautiful. The humid air gave her un-made-up skin its pearly quality. But her long hair, which tumbled down her shoulders, retained the fold of the hairpiece and of the absent curls, as if doubting liberty. Two pins lightly held the traces of a tight hairstyle.

Mittelbach docked first. He told Perón that President Farrell had called for his arrest to save him, for there were plans to kill him. 'Where are you taking me?' Perón asked. 'Maybe on a Navy ship, maybe to Martin García Island.' 'I am a soldier and only the army can arrest me!' Perón cried. Mittelbach promised to speak to Farrell, so Perón boarded the boat, followed by Evita.

When they arrived on solid land, they got into Mercante's car. It was raining. It would rain during every sad moment of their lives, just as it was beautiful during every joyful moment. The people would notice this and say, 'The sun is Perónist.' Eva, who had cried so little in her life, did not hold back now. She let the streams of tears drown her. Evita's sobs took on a life of their own, replacing the 'real' problems and becoming the only reality. Perón, Mercante, and every male in the car listened to her in silence. Eva blew her nose, sighed, and murmured, 'My God.'

On Posadas Street, twelve black cars were waiting for Perón, parked and anonymous as if in uniform. Perón took one look at the dark cars – each with its four passengers dressed in street clothes but who also seemed to be in uniform – shrugged his shoulders, and went upstairs to shave.

One hour later, President Farrell announced his decision. He rejected Perón's demand to be arrested by the army. Evita, red-eyed, stormed into the room. When she learned the news, she screamed with pain and begged Perón not to get into any of the cars. When Perón left, followed by Mercante and a police officer, she grabbed onto his arm and held the elevator door with a strained hand, until the policeman pulled her away. Her tense hand remained in space like a bird's little claw.

It was already two in the morning.

Eva stayed in her apartment alone. The silence that followed the voices was a deathly silence, and Evita could not stand solitude. She had never known it. First surrounded by her family, she later lived a life of an actress in which she had to share everything, the rooms, the *maté*, the dresses. When she became the wife of the President, she would always request a companion, even late at night, and she chose her guests just as a queen chooses her courtesans, with an imperious attitude that would never quite hide her sorrow. She needed company to think, to act, and even to feel. Isolation prevented her from thinking of anything but her own abandonment. She loved Perón, the last few events made her understand this, but she was incapable of imagining what was happening to him.

Perón arrived at the port, rolled up his vest's collar while trembling, hugged Mercante, and said, 'Take care of Evita.' He then climbed, with a feigned nonchalance, aboard the gunboat *Independencia*, which was to take him to Martin García, while tears rolled down the cheeks of a sailor who stood guard.

Mercante would later tell Evita this. He would tell her that when he saw those tears, he was filled with an immense certainty, for the sailor was the portrait of the people, and the people were crying for Perón. But on this night Evita knew none of this. Solitude turned her into an orphan. Perón's departure was a premonition of Juan Duarte's death.

A LOVE LETTER

What did Eva do during Perón's imprisonment? According to some, everything; according to others, nothing at all. To the former, Eva was the heroine behind the October events that brought Perón to power. To the latter, she wanted only to save her man and to tremble with fear.

The two hypotheses did not necessarily coincide with Perónism or anti-Perónism. On the contrary, to the visceral anti-Perónists, the thought of Eva as a mistress, capable of forcing a cowardly and faint-hearted Perón to take power was an absurd argument, for women are not courageous. As for Perónists, it was not until after his death that they transformed Evita into the Pasionaria from October 17, 1945. Until then, no one, and certainly not Eva herself, had enhanced her portrait with this additional aura. It was only after her death that Perón sanctified her, praised her memory to the heavens in order to safeguard his own declining prestige. That is how two different motivations (to disparage and exalt Evita) lead into the same legend that turned her into the factotum of the Perónist revolution. The 'black myth' and the 'white myth' fed off identical elements. Denigration and exaltation were complementary in that each rejected the reality of the other.

Nevertheless, these legends that would call her domineering or intrepid do not come from nothing. Evita could have had a heroine's calibre, and it is not impossible that she could have said, 'When Perón gets deflated, I pick him up with a kick in the balls.' Yes, she was brave, but during Perón's absence, her bravery did not prevent her from hiding out at Pierina Dealessi's one night, all the while sobbing in her arms. It is easy to tremble at night, then wake up at dawn, fresh and ready to walk like a martyr. The need for coherence that historians have toward a famous individual allowed us to consider Dealessi's account proof of Evita's weakness. Why not say that Evita was weak in front of Pierina and strong in front of the union workers who were prepared to listen to her? Why not say that the weakness displayed to one made possible the strength displayed to the others? And finally, why not say that both the fear and the courage were real?

From the moment he arrived in Martin García (an island smack in the middle of Río de la Plata, which was deserted by the soldiers who took it over), Perón wrote two letters; one to Mercante and the other to Evita.

In the first letter, written in a bombastic tone, he said about his enemies, 'I have what they do not: a loyal friend and a woman who loves me and whom I adore.' He added, 'Take care of Evita. The poor thing is a wreck and I am worried about her health. As soon as I retire, I will marry her and I will go away, no matter where.'

The letter to Eva deserves to be reproduced almost in full:

My adored treasure,

It is only in being apart from loved ones that we can measure our affection. From the day I left you, with the deepest pain you could imagine, I have not been able to calm my sad heart. I now know how much I love you, and I cannot live without you. My immense solitude is full of your memory.

Today I wrote to Farrell to ask him to accelerate my retirement. The second it is granted, we will marry and we will go away, anywhere, to live in peace.

I am sending you a letter in the mail and one for Mercante. But this one, I am sending to you via a messenger, for I fear that my mail will be intercepted.

Here I am on Martin García. I don't know why and no one has given me an explanation. What do you think of Farrell and Avalos now? What shameless cads, to behave this way towards a friend! That's life.

From the moment I arrived, the first thing I did was write to you. I don't know if you have received my letter. I sent it certified.

I ask you to please tell Mercante to ask Farrell to leave me alone, so that you and I can go to Chubut.

I have also told myself that we should start some legal proceedings. Ask Dr Gache Pirán, the federal judge to find an answer, he is a good friend. Tell Mercante to contact him immediately and do as he says . . .

You must remain calm and watch your health while I am away, and wait for my return. I will feel better knowing that you are not in danger and that you are well.

While I was writing this letter, they informed me that Mazza will come to see me today which makes me very happy for that is how I shall contact you, albeit indirectly.

Be calm. Mazza will tell you how it's going. Somehow or another, I will try to go to Buenos Aires, so you can wait for me quietly and watch your health. If I am successful in retiring, we can get married the next day. If not, I will arrange things differently, but we will resolve this situation of abandonment in which you currently live.

My little one, my soul, I have your little portraits in my room and I look at them all day long with tears in my eyes. Nothing can happen to you, or my life would be over. Take care of yourself and don't worry about me; but love me very much for I need it more than ever.

My treasure, be calm and learn to wait. This will all be over soon, and then life will be ours. I am justified in history's eyes for what I have already done and I know that time will tell me that I was right.

I will begin to write a book on all this and I will publish it as quickly as possible. Then we'll see who was right.

Dumb people are our era's and mostly our country's problems, and you know a dumb person is worse than a mean person.

My soul, I would like to continue writing to you all day,

*but Mazza will tell you all this better than I. The boat will
be here in a half-hour.*

*I devote the last words of this letter to advise you to be
calm, to stay put. I send you a big, big kiss. All my love to
my dear little* chinita.

Perón

Perón's words were taken from boleros, from tangos, but what
other words could this distressed military officer have found,
if not those that he held in his ear after having heard them
on the radio, those that by nature moved Eva?

Perón worried about Evita's nervous state of mind. He
promised to protect her and to marry her; he offered his
shoulder and his hand. It was a letter from a weary man
who wanted nothing more than to run away with his loyal
girlfriend to his land of childhood memories, to the south.

In his biography of Evita, the Perónist author Fermín
Chávez tries to explain this letter in order to reassure his
fellow Perónists. Perón wrote this letter for the benefit of the
soldiers who, he knew, would certainly intercept it. He was
taking advantage of their curiosity to make them believe that
he was abandoning the party. Chávez needed this explanation
to protect himself from doubt, for he could hardly admit that
the revolution's leader was tempted to let it all go.

Alas, Perón certainly was tempted to let go. His letter
says as much. The letter is too leftist and too sad to be an
indirect message addressed to any guanaco. Argentina would
stop being a country with authoritarian tendencies the day it
would admit the truth that a leader is not a father always in
full command.

Why did Perón call Evita *chinita*, which means 'little Indian
girl'? This word is a sign of affection. He is again playing the
diminutive chord: little, feeble, unfortunate, poor, abandoned
thing. Only a woman of the people could be all this. The
lover does not allow himself to be deceived by his sweetheart's

golden hair. Eva was a *chinita* in the roots of her soul just as she was in the roots of her hair, and he liked that. Later, however, in Madrid, he would act irritated when a journalist asked him if it was true that he used to call Eva '*mi negrita*.' 'How could that be?' he would say. 'You know damn well that she was blonde!' Was it a distracted old man's forgetfulness? Or was it a negation born of a social wound that never healed? In any case, when it came time to confide and to be intimate, in his eyes, Evita had black hair.

According to Perón's letter, Dr Angel Mazza was to play the part of the messenger. He was a medical captain and a friend of the colonel's. His visit took place on October 14 and was reassuring to Perón, both because he learned that a few unions and a few soldiers still supported him and because he exchanged a wink of complicity with Mazza. In fact, the doctor led him to believe that he would return to Buenos Aires with the troubling message that the prisoner was ill! Subsequently, Vice Admiral Vernengo Lima, a ferocious anti-Perónist and a member of the new cabinet, sent two doctors to Martín García Island to find out the nature of this illness.

It was a lost cause. Perón refused to take his shirt off in front of them and refused to repeat 'thirty-three' while one of the two glued a vexed red ear to his back. The two doctors looked at each other, hesitating. Was Perón really that sick? He certainly did not look well. They could not risk having him become a martyr, so Vernengo Lima ordered his admission to the military hospital in Buenos Aires. It was October 16.

Since his imprisonment four days earlier, Perón's supporters had mobilised, led by the loyal Mercante. They were followed by other workers from the Office of the Secretary of Labour. Isabel Ernst, a secretary and intimate friend of Mercante's was among them.

A little while later, this tall, blonde daughter of Germans would become Evita's assistant. Evita would then suddenly realise that of the two blondes, only one was natural, and, moreover, one was excessively so. But Isabel's natural blondness was not Evita's only source of jealousy. After she was married and became 'Mrs President,' she turned to prudishness (she preferred the legitimate Mrs Mercante's friendship to Isabel's, who played the part of Mercante's mistress). Eva was not unaware that Isabel had been the Pasionaria of the revolution of October 17. In 1945, Evita knew few union leaders, whereas Isabel had known them for a while through her work. Helping Mercante coordinate the unions' actions, between October 12 and 17, was as natural for her as her blonde hair. That is how she efficiently accomplished the work that Perónist propaganda would later attribute to Eva after her death.

Isabel Ernst was all about grey suits, linen-coloured hair, and discreet makeup. This was the image that Evita would coopt, and that time would help, by making her more theatrical and exquisite. Isabel was simple, calm, sure of herself. She had a serene and distinguished beauty about her. She unequivocally clashed with the 'actress' who had cascading curls, flowered dresses, a strained voice, and tense hands. The union leaders, such as Cipriano Reyes, Libertario Ferrari, Luis Gay, Montiel, and José Argaña, were in a hurry to save Perón, so they voluntarily parleyed with the natural blonde. Later, many of them would be fired, if not tortured.

This was not a time for subtractions, but rather additions to Perón's group of supporters, as disparate as they were. In Berisso and Avellaneda, two proletarian neighbourhoods, these worker-leaders who came from different horizons had organised 'spontaneous' demonstrations to support Perón. The reigning chaos lent itself to these demonstrations. The public had not even been informed of their leader's imprisonment. On the contrary, after the press published an open letter addressed to Avalos from Perón, the government denied that he had been in prison. Who could trust him now? Argentina felt as if no one was governing it.

On October 16, the CGT met to deliberate about announcing a general strike to demand the colonel's immediate liberation. As was proposed by Libertario Ferrari, would they
support Avalos, who was more of an ally to Perón, in order
to get rid of Vernengo Lima, who hated him? They decided
on a twenty-four-hour strike on October 18. Its goal was
to defend 'the social rights, which had been acquired and
would be acquired, and which were now threatened by the
capital's and the oligarchy's political takeover.' Perón's name
was not mentioned on the paper on which they had printed
this laborious statement. It was not that its content lacked
truth or that its union leaders were distanced from the 'base,'
as the Communists would have said in their usual jargon. It
was that people, simple people, had come to a point where
they made fun of statements, just as they made fun of the
fixed date to strike. They had been saturated. They had been
galvanised into action. On October 17, they followed no one's
orders to strike. Instead, they started a revolution.

VENUS CONTRACTS A DEBT

It was heavy and grey on October 17 at seven in the morning
when the workers were to report to work. A few raindrops fell,
but it was the sky's perspiration rather than rain, not enough
to put out the spark. In the working suburbs of Berisso,
Lanús, Quilmes, and Mataderos, someone shouted, 'Perón is
at the military hospital! Let's go free him!' In Avellaneda, a
brown-skinned populace who came from the provinces and
who, until now, had never dared wander into the centre of
town – the kingdom of white-skinned Argentines – began to
cross the Riachuelo bridge.

It was a muddy stream whose pearly oil surface was indeed
a border. Farther away, especially toward Maciel de la Boca
Island, the poverty was dire. Children were nourished only by

bread and *maté*. Women lay down to give birth alone, a bucket of hot water within arm's reach; stillborns were wrapped in newspaper and thrown out, for there was nowhere to bury them. Nauseating odours flew over the oily, multicoloured water whose morbid rainbows sometimes crowned a swollen cadaver that only the horses discovered while passing, with a frightened jump. It was a border that ceased to exist on that day.

So they crossed the Riachuelo to liberate Perón. And when the bridge was raised in order to stop them, they took dilapidated boats or joined wood planks with rope and made rafts out of them. Then, just as mysteriously as it was lifted, the bridge was lowered to let them cross. They already knew, instinctively, that the new chief of police Filomeno Velasco, was with Perón, and they sensed a friendship. The police officers did not arrest them, but instead smiled with an accomplice's grin, and their lips mouthed for the first time, '*Viva Perón.*'

Around ten in the morning, the first contingents had already reached the Plaza de Mayo. When the dirty troupe arrived, scared store owners quickly pulled down their metal gates. Two Argentinas were face to face: one on the street, the other (the one that belonged to the European ancestors) staring out the windows. This was not the ideal people evoked in the Argentinean Constitution's preamble, nor was it the odourless, colourless, and insipid people that Alfredo Palacios dreamed of. This was a mass of swimming skins and straight hair. The whole was as dark as the unknown and as black as fear. The air smelled of perspiration, of dirt, of alcohol, and the people screamed obscenities, laughed too loudly, pissed on walls, and washed their hands and feet in the fountains of the historic square.

The dirty ones were jubilant. For the first time, they were biting into the city's juicy apple, and their desire and their pleasure were stronger than revenge. They wanted Perón – to see him, to have him to themselves, to own him. In the chants they sang with famous melodies, the colonel's name rang 'like a cannon's explosion,' according to Leopoldo Marechal. To scream the name Peeeeróóóón, an enlargement of the masculinity, appeased all the rage. Someone who had such a name had to be a man, a *macho*.

Evita was not as absent from their thoughts. Although the people did not think of her as a revolutionary, they did think of her. They even had created this rhyme: '*Oligarcas a otra par-te/Viva el macho de Eva Duar-te*' (Oligarchs, stay away/Long live Eva Duarte's man'). She was already becoming a necessary element in the Perónist ritual. Her existence proved Perón's manliness. Destiny had been decided, and they would make her dance like an erotic standard. If Evita had not existed, they would have invented her. She was the queen bee in the people's unconscious.

But the opulence of these images lies in their contradiction. The poor Evita who was first protected then used by Perón, who was himself contradictory, was not an image that could take the place of the queen bee; instead she completed it, enriched it. Somehow, despite all she had experienced before October 17, and despite her feminine power to which the people devoted a rhyme, Eva was 'born' on that day, 'like Venus from the sea,' as one of her courtesans would later say. The simile made sense. Its primary objective was certainly to erase her past as an actress by identifying Eva with the Botticellian young lady who covered her sex with a golden curl. But there was also something else to it. If Eva had been 'born' on that day in 1945, it was thanks to the people who, by saving her man, saved her too. To an illegitimate daughter, this meant being reborn. She whispered the words that she had never before uttered, 'Thank you.'

In *My Mission in Life*, Eva relates that she had felt 'small and insignificant' the week before the seventeenth. When Perón was imprisoned, his mistress had become more annoying than useful to his friends and allies. She pretended to be the only one to save her lover's life, to make him leave the country. For now, her cause was love, and she felt like a man's heroine rather than the people's. She was always so nimble and so quick, yet her intuition was now betraying her by preventing her from feeling what History, with a capital H, was cooking up for both her and Perón. So, she asked Atilio Bramuglia (a future minister of the Perónist regime) to present a habeas corpus appeal that would allow Perón to go far away – with her, of course. She would never forgive Bramuglia's response: 'All you want to do is save your man! You don't get it!'

He was right. A revolution was about to explode, and Eva, blinded by emotions, thought only of the beating of her heart. But Perón had committed himself to her. He was writing to her of marriage and of a trip beyond a popular uprising. The Perónists felt that their leader was ready to pack his bags. Besides, the more Evita insisted on the habeas corpus, the more they were suspicious, for she was sending them an image of a weakening Perón that they did not want to see. On the seventeenth, Evita would understand her mistake. She had not counted on the people's power, and she had been deluded by her feelings and had believed that the only solution was to leave. So why did she not forgive Bramuglia? Because, unfortunately, he had witnessed Eva's blindness. You must destroy the enemy who has seen you fail.

Once again she felt like the victim and was unable to understand why a man like Bramuglia 'mistreated' her. Her old feeling of humiliation came back in full force. But this time it was worse. Thanks to Perón, she had enjoyed a certain power, but, a feeling of nakedness overcame her. Before she met her colonel, she had at least held the power that all young women hold within. Now she was surrounded only by indifference. The prisoner's mistress no longer existed. She had become nothing, no one. She was invisible. At night, she cried in Pierina's Dealessi's arms and tried to describe this feeling of loss. The Italian would smile indulgently and say, 'That's exactly what you feel when you get older.'

The union leaders like Cipriano Reyes, Luis Gay or Luis Monzalvo, who consider themselves among the true authors of October 17, emphatically deny that Evita participated at all in the movement's preparations. Others are less severe. The metal industry leader Angel Perelman said that the morning of the seventeenth, Evita drove through the populist neighbourhoods and called for the workers to strike. Meanwhile, the textile industry leader Mariano Tedesco said that Evita had contacted the workers in her union throughout the entire week, setting 'strange meeting places and times.' But where is the truth? In life, as in dreams, it is often found in feelings. We should not dismiss Eva's abstract memories, which are purely sentimental.

After Perón's arrest, Evita took a taxi to Román Subiza's place in San Nicolas. So, she was running away. As they were passing by the fake medieval building that was the Engineering School on Las Heras Avenue, the taxi driver denounced her to the students, crying, 'My passenger is Eva Duarte!' The future workers punched her face so violently that later, when she took another taxi to leave town, still headed to Subiza's, the highway patrol did not recognise her.

Those are the facts. As far as the feelings go, she described them in clearly religious terms: 'I thought I would die with each blow, yet, I felt myself being born with each blow. This baptism of pain was both rough and ineffable. It purified all cowardice in me.'

To die, to be born, purification – that is what baptism is all about, when the new man is born out of the ashes of the old. What an obscure joy when baptism involves blows rather than water. She certainly had the impression of paying for all her mistakes, as well as the ones she inherited from her mother. The accepted martyrdom was delightfully experienced. Her skin was thrilled to have suffered for Perón's love and for that of the people.

✣

Around noon, they had stopped counting the thousands of workers who were looking for Perón in the vicinity of the port, at the Villa Devoto prison, at the *Casa Rosada*, and, for the well informed, at the military hospital. That is where a delegation of railroad workers finally saw him.

Perón was in his pyjamas, calmly having lunch. He told them that he was forbidden to leave the hospital, but he was lying. Neither Avalos nor Vernengo Lima had the right to forbid him from doing anything. The stunned President Farrell and cabinet members were at the *Casa Rosada*. They contemplated the crowd that had filled the Plaza de Mayo and were so filled with wonder by this spectacle that they almost forgot their defeat. In Argentina's history, there had never been such a crowd.

A human sea streamed in hour by hour. Were there two hundred thousand, three hundred thousand? A million as the Perónists claimed? In any case, the entire mass of workers from the capital and its suburbs was there. Some of them had brought their *bombos*, the drums that gave the scene a deep throbbing of hearts and entrails, chills of an ancient memory. Perched on the lampposts and on the trees, throngs of men were swinging, arms raised. It was as if they were imitating the movement of palm trees, recalling a colonial age when Buenos Aires was still very tropical, before Sarmiento had Parisian plantain trees planted in an attempt to show the world that Argentines were indeed civilised.

But on that October 17, time was heavy and was in charge of contradicting that image of days gone by. Under a red hot sky, the sweaty men had removed their shirts. That is where the condescending *descamisados* (literally 'shirtless,' but also meaning 'ragamuffin') came from. It was used by *La Prensa* and became the sacred word that would, from now on, designate the Perónist people, just as *sansculotte* had referred to the French revolutionaries long ago. *Bombos, descamisados*, human clusters – it would seem that the people were aware that they were inaugurating a ritual that day, a theatrical and religious ceremony in which one could discover oneself, once and for all inventing the signs of complicity that would continue to be useful year after year during the celebration of their Mass, until the end of Perónism.

As for Perón, he was still waiting in his pyjamas. He did not change out of his bedclothes until later that night. At the time, men would go out in the street in their pyjamas to run an errand or to chat with neighbours. Then, living in one's pyjamas did not mean the same thing it does today. Therefore, pyjamas symbolised Perón's doubts. He wanted to say, 'For now, I will remain huddled in my nest with my *chinita's* photos. We'll see about later.' He was more stunned than anxious when he asked at second intervals, 'Is it true that there are so many people out there?' He was a surprised seducer, a Don Juan who loved to conquer, who seemed jealous that he evoked a love he would never be able to feel but embarrassed by the fact that he could enjoy it. The emptier, icier, and more paralysed he was, the more eagerly he awaited the arrival of a growing crowd capable of filling him, pushing him, heating him up.

For anti-Perónist authors such as Mary Main or Benigno Acossano, it was Evita who violently forced Perón to get dressed before his appearance on the balcony of the Red House. Of the three angles of the triangle, only the people did not hesitate. They possessed a certain instinct that the couple lacked. The people were not content to give birth to Evita from their muddy waves, so they took Perón and forced him, by dint of love, to become himself. Of course, by doing this, didn't the people create an illusory Perón? Did they invent him, or did they simply discover the true Perón, the luminous being in whom he himself did not believe, and who, besides the people, was believed only by Evita? But every act of love arouses the eternal question: are we imagining the loved one or perceiving his light, sometimes despite himself?

Finally at 9:30 P.M., after many phone calls and trips back and forth between the Red House and the military hospital, Perón spoke to Eva on the phone. She had spent the day wandering the streets, from the hospital to Plaza de Mayo, contemplating the crowds. These men and women from the suburbs had certainly reminded her of the Nuñezes, her grandmother's family. Thousands and thousands of Doña Petronas, and Juana Guaquils, and Coliqueos all returned from the edges of her memory and her blood, all present. Of course she tried to see Perón at the military hospital, but she did not insist on it, not wanting to cause a scene in what was an already electrifying mood. Later, wisely and discreetly, she went home to Posadas Street.

We don't know what words they exchanged over the phone. But when he hung up, he got dressed. He was now awake. Still quiet – he had not uttered a word all day – he seemed to accept his destiny with a lighter heart.

At 11:10 P.M. he appeared on the balcony of the Red House, welcomed by a passionate roar. The Buenos Aires night was illuminated by flaming torches. Each arm raised toward him represented a pact of fire.

Alone at home, sitting in front of her radio, Evita listened. The announcer was hoarse from introducing Perón's speech, which had not started. One could smell the crowd's excitement in the 'ether.' Their cries and pleadings of love became louder and louder. Perón had to speak.

Let us imagine the anxiety of this woman who hated to be alone but who, on this night, chose to go home, to miss the show, and to not be a part of it. Was this a choice? Let's just say that she got the order, and for once, the voice of reason took over. But the loneliness she felt on this day was different from the loneliness she felt the night Perón left for Martin García. The radio made the difference. It was warm, and its rough canvas square vibrated when one put one's ear on it so as not to miss a beat, or a sound, or the most imperceptible screech, or Perón clearing his throat, although he still had not uttered a word.

What could she be thinking while she was waiting for her man to speak? She said it a thousand times, in her speeches and her memoirs. It was simple, strong, definitive: she was thinking that she owed everything to Perón and to the crowds that saved him. She acknowledged this debt and vowed to repay it.

What about Perón? In order to buy some time, those who surrounded him on the balcony asked the crowd to sing the national anthem, '*Oíd mortales el grito sagrado.*' The anthem was almost over, the last verse that speaks of 'eternal laurels' was sung. Why couldn't Perón decide what to do?

Finally, after what seemed an eternity, he said: 'Workers!'

The crowd roared.

He continued, but the crowd interrupted him: 'Where were you?'

He did not want to answer, but the crowd insisted: 'Where were you? Where did they take you?'

He ducked the question and spoke of the people. The crowd echoed: 'Yes, the people are here, we are the people.'

It's not that the crowd did not want to listen. They tried everything to entice him to speak. But until now, throughout history, they had stayed quiet. Now, finally, they had a voice, they could converse with him, their father, their son, their lover, roles that were all jumbled. It was this dialogue that mattered, the originality of the ritual that they were now inaugurating. In political history, there are few examples of dialogue, of an authoritarian leader speaking publicly with his people.

Moulded, 'swept away by the crowd,' Perón ended up saying the cursed word he would never again say: 'Mother.' When his real mother, Doña Juana, died a few years later, he did not go to the wake but sent an aide in his place. The mother he invoked in his speech was someone else. 'As I stand here in the midst of these sweaty masses,' he said, 'I would like to hug you all from the depths of my heart just as I would my mother.' Then: 'I have just said that I would embrace you as I would embrace my mother, because, in the last few days, I believe you have felt the same pain and the same emotions that she . . .' The crowd approved: Perón had just complied with an imperative. He had to invoke his mother, just as a soccer player or a tango singer must tell himself on the day of his triumph, 'I owe everything to my poor dear mother who suffered so.'

After the speech, the crowd joyfully dispersed, although there was some violence. Gunshots were exchanged between the journalists of the newspaper *Crítica* and the 'guys' from the nationalist *Alianza*. Perón would not find this out until later. This is not why he had a solemn look on his face. 'I have a headache,' he said. His mood led one to believe that it was good to win. But for the time being, enough. He sullenly asked for two aspirin and went home.

He had not seen Eva since October 12.

We can deduce that after he kissed her, he saw the black and blue marks on her face. These were the signs of the 'baptism of pain' to which the students had submitted her. This is all she did for October 17, this is all she received. She had been scared. She had wanted to run away. She had tried to save Perón in order to leave with him. She had fruitlessly tried to imitate Isabel Ernst, and she had harvested a few black and blue marks. For a distracted look, that's not a lot. But her spirit was not distracted, and if she highlights the 'baptism' episode in her autobiography, it is because she was simply getting ready to honour a debt that could never be settled. She was becoming a martyr.

Chapter 5

❖

WIFE

Five days later, in Junín, Doña Juana and her daughters were ironing embroidered tablecloths for Evita's wedding. Suddenly the phone rang, and the four women ran to answer it, pushing one another out of the way. It was Eva, calling from the small town of Luján in the province of Buenos Aires. 'That's it, girls!' she triumphantly announced. 'I caught him. We just got married.'

Dora Dana, a neighbour in Junín and widow of the journalist Moisés Lebensohn, describes this family scene. Her story, confirmed by Roberto Carlos Dimarco, a local historian, challenges the official version that has Perón and Evita marrying in Junín in the presence of the 'girls.' But let's go back in time to examine another 'ironing' story that took place in early 1945, when Elisa Duarte had tried to remove the wrinkles from Evita's identity.

She had gone to the Los Toldos town hall to request Eva María Duarte's birth certificate. It must have been coincidence, or curiosity or both, for a town hall employee had just made a discovery. While glancing at the files to look for Duarte, a name that was quickly becoming a hot topic, he found nothing, so he looked to Ibarguren. That was it: Doña Juana's tribe was under that name. So when the oldest daughter showed up, he already had an answer for her. Eva María Duarte did not exist.

Elisa did not admit that she was an illegitimate child. This was not at all acceptable. The attitude was so strong that a demonstration of anti-Perónist women had chosen the slogan 'Perón's mother is single.' Where justice failed, the Mafia-like methods ruled. In fact, Elisa had the strongest temper in the family; Evita's tantrums were a joke compared to hers. Thus her peremptory order to the employee, 'I *must* have this document, no matter what! My sister is about to marry Colonel Perón who will be President.' Shocked by the authority that pierced her voice (this was a foreshadowing of the vengeful *caudilla* she would later become), the employee asked his brother, the state attorney, and his general manager for advice. They both advised him to do nothing and not to falsify any documents as Elisa was suggesting.

On October 18, certain sleepless inhabitants of Los Toldos were surprised to see the light of a lantern zigzag through the darkness toward the town hall. They would later understand that it was that night that Eva María Ibarguren's birth certificate disappeared. The trail of the thief shows great haste, even though the stolen document was replaced by a false one. A few years later, Juan Duarte's death would be similarly camouflaged. Such effort has only one explanation, that the respect for public opinion was so poor that one did not even bother with the details to fool it.

The forged birth certificate presented by Evita on her wedding day stated that she had been born in Junín on May 7, 1922. Someone was born then and there: Juan José Uzqueda, a stillborn child that the forgers had crossed out of the registry in order to insert Evita. How did Eva react when she learned that she was replacing a dead child? In dreams, the image is too strong for it not to have, sooner or later, haunted a woman who never existed under her true name and who never had a child of her own.

The forged document did not simply swap Ibarguren for Duarte. It also reversed the order of the names to María. The virginal name would now precede that of the world's first sinner. Now that she was legitimised, Eva was supposed to behave appropriately. Only a woman from the fringes, like Doña Juana, could allow herself the fantasy of naming her daughter Eva María. For the well-to-do girls, the norm was María Rosa, María Clara, María Elena. There is no doubt that María Eva was more Christian than Eva María, and, in fact, twenty years later, nothing would change. Perón's second wife, whose 'war name' was Isabelita, recorded as Estela in the state records, took on the name María Estela to assume her duties as first lady.

Evita's history is formed by her names as much as her hairstyles. Her name was Eva María Ibarguren, but her mother introduced her as Eva María Duarte. When she was an actress, her name was Eva Duarte (or Durante). After she was married, she became Doña María Eva Duarte de Perón. On her return from Europe, she was Eva Perón. She wanted the people to call her Evita.

She died before anyone knew her real name.

✢

According to the official version, the civil marriage ceremony took place on October 22 in Junín. This version was accepted and even embellished by other townspeople who guaranteed that they saw Doña Juana ironing not tablecloths but curtains. It is normal that the mother was hurrying to prepare her home on 171 Arias Street for the big event. Notary Hernán Ordiales would have married them across the street in his study, and after the ceremony, the couple, the family, and the guests would have crossed the street to have a drink at Doña Juana's. We can imagine that the 'girls' were also expecting to celebrate the event at their mother's, but the couple surprised them by choosing a more secret location. Perón was an expert in ploys and might have led them to believe in the family party in order to divert attention. The more they ironed, the more the conspirators believed that the marriage would take place in Junín. After the fall of Perónism, other versions confirmed that Hernán Ordiales had broken the law by taking the town hall registers to Buenos Aires in order to marry the couple. The fog that surrounds one fact or another throughout this story is sometimes explained by the hypothesis of a sham. But not always.

For example, it is easy to understand why, on her forged birth certificate, Eva is twenty-three instead of her true age of twenty-six. As we have seen, this lie was intended not to make her younger but rather to hide her illegitimacy. But why did Perón appear as a bachelor when he was a widower? For obvious reasons, Doña Juana was presented as Juan Duarte's legitimate wife. But the necessary marriage certificate was not there. Why? More awkwardness, accompanied by the disdain for public opinion.

Many years after the wedding, notary Ordiales furnished details on the event to the writers of *Historia del perónismo*. He stated the ceremony took place in Junín. He said that Perón and Eva were so moved, they almost looked sad. The groom wore a 'greyish' suit. The bride wore an ivory suit that 'contrasted with her long blonde hair.' In fact, Evita's locks must have blended with her suit's ivory colour and not stood out. She was in ivory from head to toe. The bleached silhouette, which followed the laws of discretion if not mystery, was the image the couple wanted to project throughout the ceremony. Are there more details that escape us? Was Junín not really Junín, but Luján instead? Or Buenos Aires? Ordiales refused to reveal more information. 'I am writing a book where I will tell all,' he said.

The same sobriety surrounded the religious ceremony. It was scheduled for November 26 in La Plata, and only a few close friends knew about it. Despite the well-guarded secret, though, a crowd appeared at the church and prevented the groom from getting in. So the date was pushed back to December 10. On that day, once again, a crowd encircled the Church of San Francisco, and the newlyweds had to sneak out through a back door.

That is all we know of the wedding. There is no photo of the bride. The only one who spoke of this ceremony was father Hernán Benítez, the ex-Jesuit who would become Eva's legendary confessor, but the only information he revealed was the name of the priest who officiated the ceremony. But we do know this: Evita's wedding was at 8:25 P.M. This would be an insignificant detail if the time did not correspond to the time of her 'official' death, which, according to some, is not the time of her real death.

Benítez and Eva had met when they were both at Radio Belgrano, where Benítez conducted a religious broadcast. Eva was impressed by his eloquence and had requested a meeting, but he never showed up. Years later, Perón introduced this priest who had become his friend to his wife. 'I know you,' she said, smiling. 'I wanted to meet you a long time ago. But you stood me up. Obviously, I was not an Anchorena girl, I was just a small insignificant actress!' Father Benítez struck his chest, remembering that, at that time he was the priest for the elite, surrounded by aristocratic daughters and women. He did not even remember the face of the poor actress who was in spiritual trouble.

The newly formed couple spent a few days in San Nicolas, at Ramón Subiza's home, and in San Vicente, at Perón's country house. It was an austere military house, with a Spartan simplicity and walls decorated with weapons and harnesses. The photographs portray them smiling and relaxed on the stone porch. Perón is wearing boots and britches, Eva is wearing trousers, with her hair almost loose. Were they happy? Perón, who loved barbecues, gardening, horseback riding, poodles, and doves, adored San Vicente. Evita hated the forced rest of the country Sundays. Perón's naps especially drove her crazy. During these endless hours, she would roam the house while in the bedroom he snored serenely. In time, sleep would become as anguishing as eating. And she increasingly fled from the slowness and dampness of their shared bed.

For the time being, the couple was still united by an emotion close to love. They quickly returned home and officially moved to Evita's apartment on Posadas Street. They had lived there for a year already, but Perón had pretended to live in the apartment across the hall. The marriage allowed them to use Perón's apartment as an office and to live in the other in plain view. The serious Perón found himself again in a starlet's bedroom where his boots wreaked havoc on the raised satin stitched bedspread decorated with flounces and blue ribbons.

For Evita, her bedroom's decor – an intimate place fluctuating between the childlike and the erotic – was not a problem. She had created it with no complexes and had not even debated over placing a doll in the middle of the bed. On the other hand, her living room, the social room par excellence, revealed her doubts, an anguish that is unknown to those who are born with an innate sense of taste. 'It was as if Laurel and Hardy had decorated it,' writes Paco Jamandreu. 'She had prized pieces of furniture, but they were so oddly arranged, that one felt as if one was both at Mrs Récamier's on a brocade couch, then at Milonguita's [the heroine of a famous tango] in front of the enormous piano that Evita opened only to have cleaned, playing it very rarely. On the piano, there was a big wood wheelbarrow . . . with a zinc planter inside, the water overflowed from it and dripped onto the piano keys.' ('But it's a present!' she would say about the wheelbarrow, half mad, half smiling, to defend herself from the designer's critiques.) Also on the piano was a parrot flanked by two doves, all three afflicted with wire-rimmed glasses. 'Yes, these are also presents!' she would say angrily. 'Oh, Perón the imbecile puts anything on my piano!'

Paco Jamandreu had introduced Eva to a certain Mrs Artayeta, a friend of the Uruguayan ambassador, who had advised her to decorate the walls with miniatures suspended by velvet ribbons. Apparently this was the latest style. But Evita could do nothing in moderation. The phrase that Perón uttered a thousand times in his old age, 'Everything in just measure and harmony,' seemed to be directed at her even after her death. If miniatures were in vogue, then Eva wanted them. She placed them everywhere from the ceiling to the floor. 'One had to lie flat on one's stomach to see the ones closest to the floor,' Jamandreu complained.

After the wedding, the most important task was to eliminate the old Eva. The radio recordings, films, and publicity photos all had to disappear. Yankelevich and Machinandearena gave her what they had. A private screening of *La pródiga* was shown at Ramón Subiza's, while all other copies were destroyed. Eva fell in love with this film, the nostalgia, regret, and a secret rage that she used to her advantage in order to transform herself. But this screening was the first and the last. No one would ever see *La pródiga* again. Deep inside, she knew only too well that Argentina's most triumphant woman was a failed actress.

Nonetheless, she continued to observe herself with a critical and narcissistic eye, just as a good actress should. She worried about the roundness that the screen pitilessly revealed. 'You made me too plump,' she complained to Mario Soffici. The director responded that at the time of the movie's filming, she was a bit chubby. This was a white lie, for by 1946, the young newlywed's cheeks had puffed out a bit. Later, when she became 'masculine,' she would not allow herself to simper, but in 1946 she was still 'feminine.' Her florets, her curls, her smile, and her shape testified to this. Add to this that this feminine model was that of the little bourgeois starlet. When the high-society ladies spoke of Evita, they rolled their *R*'s to pronounce the insult: '*Gorrrrrrda!*' (Fffffatty).

ON THE TRAIN

The presidential campaign worried Perón more than his wife's roundness, although he did criticise her in front of Jamandreu, insisting that she exercise. In 1946, he was faced with a problem that would characterise his movement: the disparity of his supporters. The seducer seemed to agree with each person who approached him. Leftists, rightists, and all those in the middle who believed, in good faith, they were 'married' to him, came to him to show him their wedding band and demand their due. The working party founded by Cipriano Reyes and Luis Gay, among others; the renovationist junta, an offshoot of the radical party; the nationalists; a few conservatives and Communists like Rodolfo Puiggrós – all asked him to keep his promises.

Most annoying were the workers. They were pure and innocent unionists who had found nothing better to do than choose Mercante as a candidate for the vice presidency. This bothered Perón, who would have preferred a wily *caudillo* such as Quijano. Mercante was too honest and ran the risk of offending him. He was certainly loyal, but Perón was in no position to evaluate this, since he did not believe in loyalty. He saw only baseness in men. Since he understood base people, he could easily dominate them. But 'the best thing you can do with a loyal friend,' he said, 'is watch him like a hawk.'

In order to unify all these factions, Perón abolished the working party and the renovationist junta. The too-small offshoots dissolved themselves. In place of these he formed one revolution party, which was soon called the Perónist party. As for Mercante, Perón promised to name him governor of the province of Buenos Aires, so Mercante withdrew from the race.

Perón did not use his wife to get rid of Mercante as he would later do. Instead, he manipulated her in order to dismiss Cipriano Reyes, who talks about it in his memoirs. One day, Reyes was talking with Perón at the apartment on Posadas Street, when Evita stormed into the room. 'I want more radicals on the lists,' she angrily demanded, 'for I am very radical.' Reyes had been aggressively self-taught by an inferiority complex and was a Savonarola of the union battle. He turned pale. How could an actress of dubious morality, dressed in an almost transparent red negligee, dare interrupt their very virile conversation to give him, Cipriano Reyes, the austere and hardened fighter, orders? He turned to Perón, hoping to find the man in him. Alas, head bowed, displaying an annoyance that he was far from feeling, the leader weakly said, 'I agree with her.'

Perón used Eva. He would complain about an ally or an adversary, always with a wounded attitude, as if he had been betrayed. He had measured the acoustic phenomenon that amplified his words when they passed by her. An acoustic and therefore thermal phenomenon, Eva became white hot and thus attacked the object of his complaints (Cipriano, in this case). Then Perón would shake his head, half reproachful, half touched, and exclaim in a fatherly tone, 'Oh, that Evita! What a girl! She'll never change.'

In his speeches of the time, Perón declared that his doctrine issued from papal encyclicals. In substance it was simply social Christian doctrine. (Father Benítez swears that he was behind these speeches, which seems probable.) It was a simple doctrine, easy to retain, and conceived to seduce the people without terrifying the bourgeois. He did, after all, tell the workers that, at the end of the day, there were also good bosses. With his elementary speech disguised under a banner, he left for his electoral campaign. On December 26, he took a train that he baptised *El Descamisado* (the No-Shirt) to travel to the north of the country. His opponents took another train called Victory. In their minds, victory identified itself with the symbol of the anti-Nazi struggle that consisted of forming a

V with the index and middle fingers. Both the No-shirt and the democratic Victory trains were objects of assassination attempts. This violence was unusual for a presidential campaign and attributed a feeling of importance to the choice.

But the biggest novelty of these trips was the presence of a woman on board. Until then, no wife had accompanied her husband on this type of tour. Evita was there, silent, but there nonetheless. It was immediately evident that the people were content just to see her and touch her.

She did not leave with Perón but joined him in Santiago del Estero on December 31. Around that time, the news of the marriage was finally published in the Perónist newspaper *La Epoca* owned by Eduardo Colom. Why was it not announced immediately in the big newspapers? Clearly, the couple did not want to attract attention to a marriage that was plagued by forged documents.

The *Descamisado's* itinerary seemed to be the exact opposite of Evita's former acting tour. They passed through Junín, Rosario, Córdoba, and Mendoza, but she was now exuberantly acclaimed. Did she now think about José Franco: 'Sleep with me or you're fired'? Or did she decide to shoo this unfortunate memory away just as she would a fly? The idea of revenge on all the Toads of the world must have occurred to her. But not often, because the present worried her so. The photographs of this train ride depict a happiness with no past. Life is so just and simple that once our wildest dreams come true, it is as if a ripe fruit is placed in our mouth. We accept this as if we have never tasted another, at least not one this delicious. She would, however, seek revenge – but later, when she felt less happy. For now, on the train, she behaved with natural perfection as if this were all very normal.

Her head was at the train window. Her smile. Her blondness that seemed otherworldly. The brown crowds that hurried to see Perón discovered Eva, who embodied a total presence, body and soul. This was the exact opposite of her husband who, quickly tired by the climate's heat, had a stand-in replace him. Once he delivered his speech, he sneaked out. Another Perón stood at the door, smiling the Perón smile and waving the Perón wave, with the same short outstretched arms, like those of a Patagonian penguin.

Eva did not flee. The province of Córdoba's dry pampa where, in the January heat, each clump of earth burned like embers, threw an ardent dust that grated between her teeth. And Santiago del Estero! The white sun lay heavily on the spiny plants. To lean out was like putting one's head in an oven, at the risk of seeing one's skin become scaly just like the earth. But she had not come here to care for her skin. Faced with the fleshy women who smelled of perspiration and took care of their children, only one desire moved her fingers, she wanted to caress them. She needed them to feel her as well, to put her to the test, to be recognised by these dark beings who were like blind men looking to ascertain her existence. Perón hated their rugged palms grazing him. Perón, whose skin was reddened and gnawed at by psoriasis, was obsessed with his rejection of caresses while Eva and her mother-of-pearl skin poured herself onto them, arms open wide. These naked and white arms. To touch was to conclude a pact. The farther the train advanced into the hostile, charred regions with their minuscule ranches made of mud and straw, lost in the fire's vacuousness, the more she was confirming her intent to settle her 'debt' in her own way.

As the train continued northwest, the faces became increasingly Indian. To Perón it may have seemed as if the same face was multiplied a hundred fold at each station, but not to Eva. She was incapable of melting these faces into one abstract entity called 'people'; she had to identify each one. She would never abandon this right. To pay was also to remember, to store each trait in her memory. She had a surprising memory that would allow her to store thousands of faces. Later, on the balcony of the *Casa Rosada*, she would watch the enormous crowd blacken the Plaza de Mayo and force herself to recognise a majority of them, to count them, and scrutinise them, while he who was beside her would turn on his automatic seductive smile, arms raised, like a boxing champion, waving to the amorphous and ordinary masses.

The photos of the first trip, like the ones that would follow, showed her dressed in blouses and bell skirts, with a kerchief on her head tied in the 'Portuguese style.' She was as fresh as a rose even though it was one hundred degrees in the shade. Beside her springlike freshness, it was her softness and kindness that attracted the attention of others. It was no doubt the gesture of an actress, a fairy, or a princess, which she considered the most appropriate for the occasion, but it also was the real Eva. The two faces of Eva – soft and dreamy or nervous and sharp. The first was often displayed during this journey. The joy of being there, of being loved, expunged the need to control everything.

The second trip subjected her to less harsh conditions. On the ship *París*, the couple crossed the Paraná to visit the coastal provinces of Entre Ríos and Corrientes. Here, the wetness and shine replaced the dryness. The *París* coursed through the middle of river, a river so wide, that one could barely see the banks, high in the muddy ravines that announced the town of Paraná, where the fervent gestures of the dazzling palm trees seemed to applaud the couple's arrival. Sometimes it was hands instead of branches. In Rosario, the crowd waited for them on the riverbanks, waving to them from afar, handkerchiefs in the wind. It's amazing that this was the same river and labyrinth of deltas from a few months back. Once again, the Paraná was an image of their lives – and of their souls. Evita's, in a straight line, and Perón's, one thousand times split.

Until now, Evita had never delivered a speech. The Miss Radio part of her must have suffered. Finally, on February 4, she made her first début – with disastrous results. The location – Luna Park – must have inspired her. An association of women

Perónists had organised a rally to support the Perón-Quijano ticket. The women were waiting for Perón, but the leader was ill. So he decided to send Evita instead in order to put her to the test. However, he made this decision at the last minute, and Eva got to Luna Park two hours late with only enough time to ask her old director, Muñoz Azpiri, to write a speech for her that she would memorise.

Two hours of waiting had heated up the atmosphere. The crowd was impatient, chanting 'French bread, English cho-co-late' with their hands and feet. These women wanted Perón, and they were not the type to keep quiet when the colonel's wife tried to 'deliver a message' in her best soap opera style. Evita tried to raise her soft voice above the racket, but it was useless. Later her voice would become rough, violent, and authoritarian, but for now, she was a little bird going hoarse just asking for silence. The female audience had pegged this insipid blonde for a rival. It was the rise of political eroticism. It was only later that Perónist women would identify with Eva and make love to Perón through her. But on that day, they were enraged. On their way out, they lifted their skirts to show off their panties and said, 'We want Perón's son.' They assaulted the passersbys, especially the men in ties, the 'oligarchs.' The police had to disperse them with tear gas.

❖

Perón's campaign was bolstered by two unexpected sources of support. Spruille Braden, the American ambassador, had gone home. He was the originator of the *Blue Book*, published by the State Department, which denounced Perón's Nazism. This was a profitable accusation, and the leader transformed it into an electoral slogan: 'Braden or Perón.' This labyrinthine man was conveniently becoming a Manichaean. He was telling the people that their vote had to resolve an intolerable dilemma existing in the patriot's heart. There was not an honest Argentine who could hesitate between an American who was interfering in Argentina's affairs and a good old boy from home. Later, Perónism would take the taste of the disjunctive proposition to worrisome heights. And Braden became death in this new simplification. For a long time, the cry 'Perón or death' disheartened many more inclined to subtlety, who would never have chosen one or the other. Only Evita the Manichaean believed in this choice. Perón made fun of it.

The second supporter was the Church. This support did not rest on an accusation turned upside down but rather on hypocrisy. One had to know how to read between the lines. The Church proclaimed its neutrality loud and clear, all the while forbidding the pious to vote for a party that supported divorce, which was upheld by all other parties, whether they were liberal or leftist. More irony was to come, for after Evita's death, Perón put the law of divorce up for a vote. But for now, he supposedly supported a Catholic programme, and the well-off Catholic families struggled to come to terms with this new dilemma: how could they listen to their priests without betraying their social class, which commanded them to despise the populist leader? By displaying his faith, which in reality he believed in as he would a superstition (limiting himself to keeping the image of a saint in one corner), Perón differentiated himself from the Fascists, pagan by nature, all the while enjoying the division of his adversaries. There was not a fascism that highlighted his contradictory position between anti-Christian paganism and the consideration of Christian hierarchy.

There was simplification on one side, confusion on the other, plus the massive support of the popular strata. This was the equation that on February 24, 1946, resulted in a Perónist victory. The Perón-Quijano combination won 56 percent of the vote.

THE WOMAN PRESIDENT WITH THE BARE SHOULDER

Four months passed between the electoral triumph and the official inauguration ceremony, four months in which Evita led an intermediate existence between her past and her future. By virtue of her origins, the intermediate state suited her well. These were the only months in which she felt young. At fifteen, she had struggled to earn her bread. At twenty-six, she could finally be fickle, frivolous, and charming. At a time when informal language was not common, she used the *tu* form instead of *usted* when speaking to important men. She didn't care what they thought. Her life belonged to her since she was still purely a project. And since she knew this could not last for long, she hurried to take advantage of it, swaggering a little to hide her anguish.

A symbolic death ruined her happiness. Anita Jordán, an old friend from her destitute times, died of cancer. Evita and Anita had shared a room at the boarding house, the *maté cocido*, as well as clothes. On the evenings when one of them went out with their only presentable dress, the other stayed in bed.

Cancer was the illness one spoke of only in euphemisms. It was the illness that Eva had followed closely since 1945. In that year, she had harassed Anne-Marie Heinrich with very specific questions, for the photographer's mother was dying of the disease. She confided in Anne-Marie that Doña Juana suffered the same symptoms. And the famous German photographer, author of many photos of Eva, whom she had already met when she was a pale teenage actress just landed in Junín, was surprised that she knew so much about the subject.

For Eva, Anita represented much more than a destitute past. She also represented the type of woman with whom Evita would never again be able to spend time. Eva was used to a certain female solidarity born of solitude, and she looked for replacements, women of another circle who could guide her in her new incarnation. She found two: Isabel Ernst, whom we already know, and Lilian Lagomarsino de Guardo.

We must look to Perón, busy building his team, to understand Eva's choice of Lilian. In the early days, Perón feared his eventual rivals less than he would later. He called appropriate personalities to his side, and his first cabinet was his best. But his tendency, supported by Eva, was to select collaborators on the basis of loyalty (she said) and malleability (he said) rather than intelligence. Among the appointments that most obviously revealed this tendency were Rudi Freude and Juan Duarte. The latter was named to the post of private secretary to the President, which simply increased his wife's power.

However, Evita was isolated. Deprived of a suitable social circle, she had to unearth her future friends from Perón's circle. And alas, Rudi was not a big hit with the women (the slanderous opposition going so far as to suggest that the too handsome German was indeed the President's lover). As for her brother, he had too many women, among them the actresses Fanny Navarro and Elina Colomer whom Evita knew well, though the poor girls were not in a position to teach her good manners. Evita appreciated Mrs Mercante, the legitimate wife of the future governor of the province. Unfortunately, it was Isabel Ernst, Mercante's mistress, whom they prescribed as her mentor. And although she was a distinguished person, Isabel could not and did not want to be Eva's adviser in the realm of fashion and social graces.

One of Perón's other collaborators, Alberto Dodero, whose importance was growing, had become close to Evita. He was invited to San Vicente every weekend. She relied on his company to play rummy while Perón napped. His wife, Betty Sundmark, was an American from Chicago, an ex-vaudeville dancer. This was more reason for her to befriend Eva. But the opposite occurred. Evita would spend the rest of her life jealously stating that 'in government, one actress is enough.'

Finally, there was Ricardo Guardo. He was a dentist from a good family who had supported Perón from the start and, before being disgraced, would become the president of the House of Deputies. And it was his wife, Lilian, who was chosen as Eva's companion.

Lilian was a traditional house mother. She came from a good family. She was elegant and cultured. She had four children and was interested in nothing but them. Her appointment was dropped on Eva like a bomb. One weekend her husband took her to San Vicente to introduce her to the President and his wife. Lilian had led such a discreet life until then that Perón hadn't even known Guardo was married. We can imagine that on that day, she was dressed simply in country attire. As for Evita, she was wearing her favourite outfit: Perón's pyjamas knotted at the waist and two cute little braids. At dinnertime, Perón asked her to make something to eat. Eva answered, 'I'm not in the mood. I'll just open a few cans.'

This anecdote comes from Guardo himself. Perón, Lilian, and Guardo stayed in the living room, pretending to take this repartee as a charming frivolity, when Evita's voice came from the kitchen. She was calling for Guardo at the top of her lungs. He ran to her and found her busily opening the canned goods. That is when, as if everything was fine, she told him what was bothering her. It was the dress she would wear to the June 4 ceremony where Perón would speak. 'I talked about it with Betty Sundmark,' she said. 'She wants to lend me one of her dresses. But I don't know. After all she is a foreigner! Would she really know how to advise me on what to wear here for this type of occasion?' She handled the can opener as if it were the key that would give her the answer. Finally, she blurted something out. She hardly knew Guardo, but she asked an astonishing favour. 'Say, would you come with me to an haute couture boutique to help me pick something out?'

More startling than the question was the response. Guardo

accepted the invitation on the spot, not even guessing what was obvious. The insecurity Evita felt when faced with a proper woman explained this offhandedness. She found it easier to turn to a man, even a distinguished one. She had known these men and knew how to handle them. Their wives remained a mystery to her.

So it was Guardo, not Lilian, who went to Bernada. The idea of Evita visiting the store did not thrill the owner, who said bluntly, 'This is not my type of client.' But the second reaction, more thought out, was, 'Well, after all, she is the President's wife.' Guardo sighed and hurried to the phone to relay the good news that Argentina's first lady had been reprieved by the designer.

On the day of the fitting, Eva passed up every dress. She was not at ease and had no idea what she wanted. She finally settled on a suit with gold buttons and military epaulettes. Guardo bit his lip, drummed up all his courage, and told her that the June 4 ceremony would be full of true servicemen with real epaulettes showing ranks. This time Eva bit her lip. She avoided the saleswoman's eyes and selected a silver silk evening gown that revealed a bare shoulder, togastyle, and a black suit with a hip-hugging fur overskirt.

On the eve of June 4, she tried on her silver dress for the official banquet. The bare shoulder would not have created such a scandal had she not had the bad luck of grazing a cardinal. As the President's wife, Evita was placed at the head of the table. To her left, the side of the bare shoulder, sat Cardinal Santiago Coppello.

The contrast between the two seemed to have been planned to evoke a comical effect. Coppello was sitting up straight with his hands crossed. Pouting, he was bald and had small eyeglasses, the spitting image of a prudish and petty being. Evita displayed a too conspicuous beauty, thanks more to her makeup than her clothes. Of course, there was this troublingly perfect goddess's shoulder. But most of all there was a mouth, a large mouth that was not her own, that she had painted by going outside her lip lines. No one had advised her on the lipstick issue. Later, her key adviser on all these matters would be Father Benítez. He forbade her to paint her eyes or cheeks, and by doing so he made her eternal, if not in her soul at least in the image of her body that has stayed with us. Many years later, Evita would remain beautiful thanks to the absence of makeup in the post-1947 photos. Without an indicator of the times on her eyelids and her skin, with just a touch of lipstick to highlight the contours of her mouth, she continues to smile at us like today's woman. Eternally contemporary.

Soon after the banquet, Sofía Bozán, a popular vaudeville actress, appeared on stage dressed in a grey dress with a slanted cut. Glued to her bare shoulder was a sequined bird. Not just any bird, a cardinal.

For Congress's ceremony, Eva was perfect in her black suit with fur overskirt and under her discreet hat. A very suitable wife for a President. But in the photos, her irritation is evident, her look is too focused. She is tightly grasping the arm of a robust, solid, and protective matron, Mrs Quijano, the Vice President's wife. Rather than Evita's clothes, it is this provincial woman's attire that attracts attention. Her massiveness is covered by a shapeless coat, and the whole is overhung by an enormous hat, tall rather than wide, and draped with cloth that falls over her shoulder. Eva looks like a sparrow next to her, a determined sparrow. Even with her habit of biting the inside of her cheek, she had charisma.

As for Perón, they had removed three silver suns from his uniform and replaced them with a gold button. He had just been named general.

After the ceremony, the President and his wife went to rest at the Unzué palace.

THE PALACE

One has to imagine a French-style palace at the turn of the century, with 283 rooms, 282 more than Evita had settled for throughout her life. It stood in the middle of a hilly park, between Austria Street and the wide avenue now called Libertador but at the time called Alvear. The Unzué family belonged to the cattle aristocracy that Sarmiento believed stunk of manure. They had sold the palace to the state in 1930. Since then, every Argentinean president had lived there.

If this palace, with its gold and ivory walls, had had a soul, and with this soul, a gift of prophecy, it would have trembled from the moment Perón and Eva set foot in it. Their presence symbolised a death wish for the Unzué palace. In 1955, when the Perónist regime fell, the *Revolución Libertadora* knocked down this noble dwelling and erased all traces of it, so that in the future, no Argentinean president would sleep under a roof that had housed such shame. The righters of wrongs chose to build the modern National Library in its place to replace the old one, the one on Mexico Street that Paul Groussac, then Jorge Luis Borges, had run. The message was clear: to erect a symbol of culture in a place where ignorance had taken refuge. And yet, it would seem that this new library was cursed by the old palace. Although construction began in 1964, it was not inaugurated until 1994. For decades, it remained naked, steel and cement exposed. Its construction materials were heavy and menacing. Its shape, with its sharp angles, retains some of the violence that engendered it. A library cannot be born of an irrational act of blind destruction. José Cabrera Infante would say in *Mea Cuba* (forgetting the quotation marks, for it is Borges's phrase quoted from G. K. Chesterton: 'There are buildings whose architecture is cunning.').

Ricardo and Lilian Guardo had come with Perón and Eva to their new home. Their friendship was progressing (in the photo of the inauguration, Lilian's head can be seen in the background, just between Evita's and Mrs Quijano's). As they were climbing the stairs, Perón stopped to contemplate the marble staircase with the forged iron rail that opened at the bottom like the train of a princess's dress. It was so wide, so solemn, that suddenly he felt the need to mock it. The oligarchy had placed one of its most beautiful treasures at his feet. But it was not his taste. In fact, he had no taste. He chose austere objects. As for the miniatures hanging on the walls or the flounces of his wife's bedspread, they amused him and heightened his self-image of virile simplicity.

But in his home, amusement often went hand in hand with vengeance, a childish vengeance. They would see what he would do with their nobility. 'Let's go,' he said to Guardo, who tells this story. 'Let's race down the railing. You take the left and I'll take the right.' The two men ran up the stairs, straddled the railing, and slid down.

THE FIRST WEAPONS

Would Eva now play the ornamental role of the President's wife? Would she also preside over the Charity Society, an honorary role that all first ladies were asked to assume? Let's say that this combination of water and oil could not and did not mix in this way.

There were many reasons for this. The Charity Society was, to use the populist language, a 'bastion of the oligarchy.' It had been created by President Rivadavia in 1823 to protect orphans and take care of the 'public and hidden births.' The original direction of the organisation dwindled away over the years. The charitable, very Catholic women were now dripping with pearls. They dressed the orphans in black or grey uniforms and shaved their heads. They left them in the middle of the street, flanked by posters that read 'Sick child' and described each child's misfortune. In 1946, their President was the wealthy Guillermina Bunge de Moreno, and when it was time to officially appoint Evita, the ladies responded that she was too young. At least that is the response attributed to them. Accordingly, Evita supposedly said, 'In that case, pick my mother!'

In reality, it is likely that there was agreement within the disagreement on both sides. As much as she was outraged by this affront, Evita was relieved that she would not have to put up with the contempt of these women in the flesh. Besides, her skin was already pearly; she had no need to wear pearls. And as for the orphans, her plans did not include uniforms.

However, a sigh of relief did not mean that she forgot about it. Instead, the Charity Society would be dissolved by the government on September 6, 1946, through Dr Armando Méndez San Martín who would have a disastrous influence on Perón during the 1950s. Was this Evita's revenge, as the women claimed? The nationalist senator Diego Luis Molinari, who requested this action of the Senate, claimed that the government was simply proposing a social action that would invalidate the ladies' efforts. From now on, the numerous hospitals they ran would be a part of the Health Department. This made sense, since the Charity Society was mostly subsidised by the state. Besides, there were rumours that the organisation was being blamed for embezzling funds raised by its lottery, and that the orphans and the teenage mothers were yielding healthy dividends.

Perón stepped in and more or less planned Eva's future activities as he was planning his own. I say 'more or less,' because it is a typical Argentinean expression that goes hand in hand with a sleight of hand. One of the criticisms of Perónism is that it was constantly fluctuating, or rather being improvised. And Perón himself would defend this with a phrase typical of the Argentinean countryside, '*Andando se acomodan los melones,*' an elliptical expression that can be

translated as, 'The melons find their place with the movement
of the cart.'

The Perónist party was still in the crib, but once it came
to power, it took off like lightning. In November 1946, Perón
presented his five year plan to a crowd of workers. In an
allusion to his party's popular condition as *descamisados*, he
wore an undershirt which was mocked with a childish logic
by the anti-Perónists who hastened to exclaim, 'So it's not the
vest, but the shirt they should take off!'

From a theatrical point of view, the symbol was extremely
powerful, especially within the decor of the Colón theatre, the
place for the cultural elite. It was known and appreciated by
world-famous orchestras, operas, and ballets. And in a confused
way, the workers knew this. When Perón decided to have the
folkloric bands play in this classical music sanctuary, a joke was
created. They would yell 'To the Colón, to the Colón!' to any
street musician or singer. But the people had not yet imagined
the Indian *bombos* amplified by this theatre's acoustics. On
November 26, the people contemplated the Colón theatre's
interior for the first time – the blue dome, the scarlet velvet,
the golden mouldings, and the crystal chandeliers that inspired
an endless respect. To see one's President surrounded by such
decor, sleeves rolled up, pronouncing himself the 'first worker,'
and announcing the nationalisation of the railroads on top
of a string of social measures was enough to assure sweet
dreams.

But on every stage – and Perónism certainly was one – there
is room for improvisation. So for Perón, Eva was one of those
melons that one throws into a disorganised cart that once on
its way rolls into its proper place. That would soon happen.

Right after June 4, the situation became embarrassing. The
workers at the Bureau of labour were used to seeing Perón in the
flesh and did not think this would change. Perón had become
who he was thanks to these people who had torn him away
from the military's claws and who had voted for him. They felt

him to be close and accessible, to the point that they could easily ring his doorbell to see if he was there. Clearly, the demands of his new task prevented the President from offering coffee to each one of these workers. To offer this post to another was to hand him power on a silver platter. It would be better to assign a shadow, that is, a woman to this post. The only one who would not overshadow him in this position was Eva. Or so he thought.

Oscar Nicolini, a grateful man, took care of everything. Let's not forget, his nomination as Minister of the Post Office and Telecommunications had triggered the military crisis that was settled by the Perónist triumph on October 17. He had the brilliant idea of moving Eva's office close to his, in the central post office, an old building on Corrientes Street that evoked a railroad station, even with all its British implications in the eyes of Argentines. Once settled in her office, she would receive delegations of workers, immerse herself in their problems, and later relate them to her husband.

At least that is the generally accepted version of the story. But Raúl Salinas, who was then Secretary of Culture for the municipality of Buenos Aires and who knew Evita before she knew Perón, adds a nuance to this story. According to Salinas, Evita had formed her own team, a team of Evitists, immediately after her husband's election. Besides him, the members were Nicolini, Guardo, and Vicente Sierra, another civil servant. Evita's goal was not (at least not yet) to have an independent political agenda, but she wanted to form her circle of power. One day, Perón asked Salinas, who came to see him every morning at 6:40 A.M., 'What's going on at the Post Office? I saw a number of official cars parked outside. Is Nico [Nicolini] celebrating something?' Juan Duarte, Colonel Juan Francisco Castro, and José Figuerola (a Spaniard from the extreme right who had collaborated with Perón at the *Secretaría*) were there. Salinas had to admit that Evita was meeting with her team. 'Perón thought it was great,' he reported later. 'Or at least, if he had reservations, he did not reveal them.'

Certain hardened unionists like Cipriano Reyes did not like Evita, but the simple workers did not share his animosity. So their requests ended up with Perón. Eva was turning out to be a good mediator, and her effectiveness was rewarded. On September 23, Evita did not go to her office at the post office. Her car drove around the *Casa Rosada* and stopped on a little street behind the Cabildo. It was the Labour *Secretaría*, and it was in the spot where the old Deliberation Council had been.

Eva walked into the sacred enclosure, the place where Perón had once officiated as Labour Secretary. It was one of the most solemn moments of her life. She was going to have the same office he had occupied. She was not the new Labour Secretary. She had no title. She was there only to represent Perón. Later, she would want to exist in a more official way, to be named to a real post, to become, for example, Vice President of Argentina. And she would hide this ambition as one would hide a disgrace. The extraordinary thing was that her power would grow without being based on any actual accomplishments. Once again, she could not claim any legal title or authority except for that of wife, and that is what allowed her to be free in her work. This liberty would cost her dearly.

Here she was, sitting at her dark desk, in the big room with dismal panelling. Once again, the style leaned toward British: melancholic, virile, and deeply serious. But besides placing a few flower arrangements in the room, Evita did not do anything to liven the place up. On the contrary, she religiously respected Perón's old office, an office of the man she blindly admired (and she preferred to follow him as little as possible in order to retain her blindness). No, light did not pertain to a change in decor, but rather to her. Although Eva was dressed more and more often in her legendary outfit, a houndstooth suit with black velvet cuffs, she was often overcome by the desire to come to the office wearing lots of jewellery. Her hats and her hair always introduced a luminous note to this temple that had been conceived to shelter only severe faces.

Only two steps behind Evita was her shadow, always discreet but firm, the shadow of a shadow, Isabel Elfride Constancia Ernst, Isabel who dictated all responses to Evita in whispers. Isabel's main purpose was to protect Evita from blunders. She was the indispensable, or inevitable, adviser from whom Evita would try to flee and would finally get rid of when she returned from Europe. It is difficult to say whether Isabel was an example to or an imitator of Eva. But it was a constant question for those who saw them together, one behind the other, identical in everything: same suit and sometimes same hat (the only difference was that the German woman was four inches taller than Eva). Or for those who witnessed Eva's annoyance when she harshly put Isabel in her place. Had she forgotten about their double dates with Perón and Mercante when the women used the *tu* form to address each other? Now, when Isabel had attempted to use *tu* with Evita, Evita had made it clear that she should quickly lose that habit.

And yet in the letter she would write to Perón shortly before her departure for Europe, Eva asked him to consider raising Isabel's salary. Maybe there was no real tension between them, but the German was forced to play the objective role that Eva found unbearable. Luckily, Isabel had a weakness in Eva's eyes. She was relegated to the role of mistress, while Eva was a legitimate spouse. However, this was not apparent to all at work and mistress or not, Isabel was overwhelmingly perfect. Even someone less sensitive than Evita would have suffered from a 'narcissistic wound,' an expression widely used among Argentines rendered experts in psychoanalysis by the aftereffects of Perónism, twenty years later.

A fine example of Isabel's role was seen when a central junta delegation of women Perónists paid a visit to Evita. They brought her a present, a missal, the work of Argentinean workers and blessed by Monsignor Andrés Calcagno. The

President's wife received hundreds of gifts, but on that day she decided not to accept the gift. 'I cannot accept this gift,' she said. 'For General Perón has put an end to the activities of all factions and proclaimed one single Party of the Revolution.' She said this with such an unpleasant tone that the women left outraged. Isabel ran after them, took the unfortunate gift, and excused herself on Evita's behalf. But was this really a blunder? Yes, if it is framed within the period in which it occurred. No, if we consider that Evita would form her own Woman's Perónist Party in 1949, thus dissolving all the other groups of Perónist women in one blow to incorporate them into her own. Her tone revealed that she was already thinking about this.

Eva was timid in her gestures, but more so in her language, of which she seemed almost afraid, ending every other sentence, 'Do you understand what I mean?' Her anguish over not mastering words became so poignant that it prevented her from both speaking and understanding. Emptiness was setting in. But she would not give up and would repeat the same thing over and over again. And that is when, suddenly, she understood, and she would give the workers an unexpected solution. A small, concrete, efficient, and luminous solution no one had thought of.

Let's return to psychoanalysis in order to examine Evita's 'small solution.' In his book about Perón, Dr León Rozichner studies one of the leader's texts, which relates his thinking on the role of the woman leader: 'Big things always consist of little things that must not be neglected. As a leader, one of a woman's essential talents is to use small means extremely powerfully, a tactic unknown to us men.' According to Rozichner, the 'small female' was an enormously important characteristic in Perón's personality. The popular mother with a malicious knowledge and the astute wink of an eye thwarted the father's domineering temper, he who was superior to the mother but deep down was truly weak. By identifying himself with both, Perón hid his 'smallness,' appearing before the people as a dominating father. He did all this without believing a word, knowing his own and his father's weakness. He needed Evita, who helped him conceal the fact that he identified with his mother. She was in charge of representing the 'small thing' and was there to certify Perón's virility.

We will spare the reader Evita's many comings and goings, her frequent visits to factories, schools, hospitals, unions, athletic and cultural clubs. Her energy was superhuman. However, it is worth discussing Eva's debut as an impromptu public speaker. Although Muñoz Azpiri was still around to lend his pen to her cause, since her first encounter with the workers, the first time a little girl gave her a bouquet, one thing was clear: she would have to improvise. She came out on May 31 at the Astral Theatre during a demonstration organised by the Confederation of Commercial Employees. First Perón spoke, then a minister, after which the assistants asked Evita to take the podium. This expression says it all in terms of the domination Eva exerted, for she took hold not only of her listeners but also of all space around her. It was a virile hold. In Argentina at that time, only a few women grasped language. Most only gave in to it.

Evita threw herself into her speech. She spoke too quickly, as if she were being pursued by a mob of official and titled speakers. Her voice was shrill. She was a happy little girl when she was complimented at the end of the speech and was even rewarded with a wink from Perón. Her words were but a mea culpa, and she did not stop justifying herself, repeating the sentence she would dwell on until her death: 'I am but a woman.' No matter, for the trigger had been pulled. She had spoken, and while she did so, she understood the workings of a 'speech.' All she had to do was repeat her leader's words and the words of those around her. She had no other words, but with these words she would weave miracles. She would take these words and make them her own, and she would succeed in hypnotising the crowds with extremely poor and unusually vapid verbal baggage. Her secret was to reiterate, to rehash the same thing in order to evoke the expectation of familiar words that never took long to come and that reassured the people. The litany-speech. Out of her mouth, this passionate hammering would become fascinating and throbbing like a savage rhythm.

The name Perón was highlighted by the insistent cadence of African music that is the tango. This word was obsessively sprinkled throughout her speech. The more she distanced herself from her husband's body, the more she savoured his essence contained in these two syllables. Here is part of her Christmas address to Argentinean women: 'I come from the people, this red heart that bleeds and cries and covers itself with roses when it sings. I come from the people, like General Perón, and I am happy, on this Christmas of Perón's *pan dulce* [fruit cake] and Perón's good cider, to enter the homes that Perón has reestablished within their Christian dimensions.' (The anti-Perónists would laugh until they were blue in the face. In Argentinean slang, *pan dulce* means ass.)

When Eva spoke again to the Argentines on January 27, 1947, to announce that the women's vote project was close to being accepted, the Socialist women reacted badly. They had fought for this cause for decades, but it was an entirely different thing to have the vote awarded to such a vulgar person. Alicia Moreau de Justo, their role model, had graduated as a doctor at a time when for a woman to study was quite an achievement. She was a dignified, lucid, and independent woman, who had not been moulded by her husband. Just as Communists and anarchists, the Socialist elitism went hand in hand with a certain prudishness, and, for them, repentant prostitutes existed only in novels by Andreïev or Tolstoy, not in reality.

On the other side, the aristocrat side, the writer Victoria Ocampo had predicted in 1945 that Evita would succeed in having the law passed. And she had stomped her foot: No! This was not her vote. This friend of André Gide, Roger

Caillois, Drieu La Rochelle, Paul Valéry, Igor Stravinsky, and Rabindranath Tagore could not accept this from such ordinary hands. However, she was finally able to see her mistake and had the courage to admit it. The Argentines voted, no longer asking themselves if this right was any less precious because it came from an ignorant actress.

While Evita improvised her speeches, clutching at words with both hands, and each time squeezing them so tightly against her heart, Isabel Ernst was always there, the undesired adviser. But sometimes, for other reasons, Lilian Guardo was there too.

BITTEN JEWELS

Evita's fascination with Lilian remains a mystery. It is true that to quiet the gossip, she needed a Catholic friend who was an irreproachable wife and mother. It is also true that Lilian could help her choose her dresses, now that Evita dared ask her to her face. But whether she loved or hated, Evita was forever incapable of putting limits on her emotions, and Lilian endured her love just as one would endure a natural catastrophe.

A few months after the Peróns moved into the palace, the telephone rang at the Guardo household. Eva requested that Lilian come to see her in her office. Lilian liked the President's wife. She found her 'charming, young and pretty.' At the Labour Ministry, she witnessed a surprising scene. The Labour Minister, José Maria Freyre, a union leader nominated by Perón because of his mediocrity, was bustling around Eva. Didn't he recall the Chinese proverb: 'When a sheaf of wheat gets taller than the field of wheat, cut its head off'? Also present was the administrator of the residence, Atilio Renzi, who, with Eva, would be the pillar of the Eva Perón Foundation, the inimitable ever-present Isabel Ernst, plus a swarm of obsequious workers. In examining the photographs from that period, one can only sadly linger on all these anonymous characters with small moustaches who were smiling subserviently.

Luckily, on the other side of the desk, the faces were more noble. They were also workers, but there were more and more women, children, elderly. Evita had not yet started her true task which would be the direct redistribution of riches, but the idea of a foundation was germinating in her head. People were already coming to her to request jobs, shelter, a few pesos – and to touch her skin. In a flash, she was already finding small solutions for each one.

From time to time, Evita would interrupt her meetings with the poor or with the ministers to chat with Lilian about frivolous topics, feminine chitchat for which she thirsted. When it got late, Lilian would attempt to leave, but Eva would plead with her, 'Please stay. It is so reassuring for me to see you here.'

Lilian would fruitlessly insist that her four children were waiting for her at home. Evita acted as if she had found a better role for her than that of a housewife. The telephone invitations followed. A veritable pursuit, friendly, no doubt, but arising from Evita's manipulative spirit, and even a touch sadistic. It was as if, while admiring the aura of domestic tranquillity that haloed her friend, Eva wanted to distance her from her family. (We will see how she chose the leaders of the Women's Perónist Party and prevented them from leading private lives by setting the standard with a mother superior's fanaticism.)

The pressures on Lilian were relieved only on Friday evenings when, finally, she took a train that to the country house where her family was waiting for her to spend the weekend together. The rest of the time, she was at Eva's disposal, and Eva wanted her to stay seated and immobile: a monument to the woman with no ambition or history. The kind of woman that Eva could not have been and did not want to be.

Besides remaining seated to evoke this peace that reassured Evita, Lilian had other talents her boss required. She knew how to distinguish one porcelain from another, and ivory from plastic. She helped Evita evaluate the gifts given to her by ambassadors or unionists. And she would accompany her to Ricciardi, the famous jeweller, who on their arrival would hide his most valuable pieces.

Doña Juana often joined them on these visits. Since Eva had met Perón, and since the couple had moved to Posadas Street, she was champing at the bit in far off Junín to settle in Buenos Aires. Jamandreu heard Eva yell at her mother over the phone, 'Wait! Don't come now! Not yet! My situation here is still not very stable!' For a long time, she held her mother and sisters at a distance. However, they were still a tribe, and Evita would never betray this connection, even if it irritated her (which only proved how strong the emotion was). The nominations of Juan Duarte as secretary to the President; Orlando Bertolini, Erminda's husband, as Director of Customs, an interesting job in terms of her import issues; Major Arrieta, Elisa's husband, as senator; Alvarez Rodríguez, Blanca's husband, as member of the Supreme Court; and Blanca as director of the lower and middle schools, say a lot about her faithfulness, if not her nepotism.

In the meantime, Doña Juana had become a very hefty matron whose roundness was sensual (no similarity to Mrs Quijano's one lump of virtuous morality). She wore a chignon and glasses, but not just any chignon or just any glasses. Behind the lenses adorned by clinking chains, there shone an astute look that sparkled with greed. Her daughter's success had awakened certain desires in her. Of course, power seduced her just as it seduced Elisa (Blanca and Erminda remained discreet), but most of all she had concrete desires for tangible, sparkly things and jewels.

When Paco Jamandreu came to Eva's for the first time, he was surprised by the fur coats and the small jewels, 'a prudent and thrifty schoolteacher's jewels.' This proved that Evita thought about life's realities, but also that in 1945, Martin Bormann's jewels were not in her possession. Was this fabulous or phantom treasure locked up at her far away *estancia* San

Clemente del Tuyú? If she had something to dwell on, then why did she raid Ricciardi's?

She was insatiable, and by 1946, her jewels, wherever they came from, were no longer those of a schoolteacher. Dodero, who knew her weakness, had given her splendid jewels. Perón thought this was wonderful. 'For Dodero,' he would say, 'giving jewellery is like giving flowers would be to someone else.' Doña Juana's shameless bargaining with Ricciardi, and her requests for rebates, forced the jeweller to hide his most beautiful pieces when he saw Evita. 'Señor Ricciardi!' Eva would complain. 'This is not a jewellery store you have here, it's a hardware store!'

Lilian was shocked by these scenes and by the greed of her powerful friend – powerful, but so fragile and unsure of herself. Lilian concluded that for Evita, jewellery was reassurance, visible proof that she was loved. Jewels calmed her as food calms others. Since she could not eat for fear that she would get fat, she binged on shiny candy: mint emeralds, strawberry rubies. Thanks to Jamandreu, we know that Evita tasted her jewels; she actually sucked on them and bit them.

Ricardo Guardo had suggested to Evita that she wear fewer diamonds on her next visit to Congress. Evita responded with the same argument that she would later use with Franco, the dictator who was shocked by the gold and precious stones she wore to go meet the Spanish workers. 'The poor like to see me be beautiful,' she stated. 'They do not want to be protected by a poorly dressed woman. You see, they dream about me. How can I let them down?' According to Carmen Llorca, Franco took this so seriously that he consulted Perón on the phone. Imagine the scene: two aging tyrants talking fashion across the ocean. Much to the Spaniard's surprise, his Argentinean counterpart, a Spartan military man, approved of his wife. Eva had to shine. She had explained to him the mysteries of identification that she knew only too well, for she had wanted to be Norma Shearer when she was a young girl.

So Guardo got the same answer. But, in Eva's spirit, the advice to wear less jewellery started to sink in. Soon, Perón would be decorated by the Spanish government at a party at the Spanish Embassy. She ordered Jamandreu to find a simple necklace to wear with the green and brown dress he had just made for her. 'All the other women will come decorated like Christmas trees,' she added to justify this newfound modesty. 'I want to surprise them by doing the exact opposite.' And across the street Jamandreu saw a green and brown necklace. Just as he was triumphantly returning to the residence, he ran into Perón who said, 'Phew! Luckily you're here! My head is spinning.'

Evita wore the dress and the necklace for the famed ceremony. She was moved and nervous and could not stop putting her necklace in her mouth and nibbling on it to calm herself. That night she called Paco and spewed a stream of abuse in which the word 'fag' was blurted most often. One could hear Perón laughing next to her. The tailor finally understood that the necklace was made of painted noodles. As she had listened to the speeches, clapped, and sung the national anthem, she had not noticed that her tongue and lips had turned green and brown.

HAIR FULL OF FLIES

A series of different Evitas, innumerable Evitas began to emerge, one after another – frivolous Evita, greedy Evita, manipulative Evita, Evita who dreads blunders, insolent Evita who shows off to hide her fear, sensitive Evita, the protagonist of a beautiful story. One day she visited Villa Soldati, a shantytown in the Flores 'marsh.' This was not the first *villa miseria* she had seen, but it was the worst. Many families sought shelter in the steel frames of old cars. Others assembled pieces of wood or cardboard to build shacks, which fell down before being finished. In extreme destitution, despair prevents one from solidly hammering the uncertain materials that act as a roof or from discarding the pile of refuse in front of the entrance.

That is when one loses one's appetite for life. One forgets to fight and even to eat, for the less one has to eat, the less one is hungry.

Eva knew this, she felt it. The sense of abandon that she read on these faces was familiar to her. So, little by little, she came up with the idea to heal them, like a psychologist, by awakening their desire. Her foundation would rest solely on this principle: to give luxury to the poor so that they would learn to desire. 'You must want!' she would say. 'You have the right to ask!' That is the fundamental reason for the hatred she would arouse. Throwing meagre things to the poor like the patron ladies did was fine, but filling them with desire was not.

One shack of Villa Soldati attracted her attention. Without knowing why, she moved the tattered jute bag that hid the entrance. In a corner, there was a mound of rags. Eva leaned over and discovered it was a small child, his thick hair falling over his face. As Eva approached, what she thought was hair flew into the air. Eva ran out, struggling to shoo the hundreds of flies that were chasing her and that she had confused for jet black hair.

She could not sleep, remembering the horrible burst that had hit her in the face. Three days later, she returned to the shantytown with the mayor of Buenos Aires and the Minister of Health. Before the residents, she announced that at least they would have decent lodging, starting now. But she insisted on one point: 'Do not take anything with you, just what you need for the night, or a souvenir, nothing more.' They did not have anything anyway. No furniture, only crates that read 'apples from Río Negro,' 'grapes from Mendoza.' Soon there would be nothing more than pieces of cardboard, and an immense solitude.

Eva had the whole place burned, but she did not leave. The fire was raging when the mayor came to tell her that she would catch a cold in the dampness (she had been there for eight hours). 'No,' she said. 'I want to see it through to the end. I need to know that it is gone. Did you know that these people were born in the mud? Tonight, when they are under the clean sheets, they will miss the earth's odour. I know them, they will want to come back. If they found a roof or anything still standing, I bet they would want to stay.'

This sensitive Evita revealed an infinitely patient woman who, when her poor were accused of ripping the wooden flooring out of the aristocrats' brand-new apartments to make barbecues, would respond, 'Lay down another floor. And then a third. To convince oneself that one has the right to live decently takes time.' She also revealed a woman obsessed by the idea that she personally had to monitor everything, like the passengers travelling on a mountain road who cannot take their eyes off the heater, persuaded that if they look away, the car will fall into an abyss.

JOKES AND GOOD ADVICE

The much hated *La Señora*'s activities evoked disproportionate reactions from the opposition. Silvano Santander, the radical deputy whose *Técnica de una traición* accuses Evita of having been a spy for the Germans, presented a legislative bill to 'prevent public, civil or military workers' wives from enjoying the same honours as their husbands, and from representing them at public demonstrations.' The majority in the Chamber of Deputies was Perónist and the bill was not approved. However, Evita did not sway the senators the same way. The United States ambassador George Messersmith told Spruille Braden, always eager to learn Argentinean news, that Evita detonated in the Senate room, in the middle of closed-door deliberations. (The word 'detonate' was often used to describe her behaviour, as if everything about her was explosive.) The Senate president asked her to leave the premises, and Evita left in tears, which reveals the extent to which she felt wounded. Eva never cried. This characteristic caused Father Benítez once to say, 'Eva was the woman with no tears.'

On that day, Perón became angry. How could they have kicked his wife out, even if it had been a private session. A half century later, his anger perplexes us. Where was the astute pragmatist, the one who liked to say with the wink of an eye, 'You must pluck the hen without letting it scream'? Where was he that day? Instead of calmly plucking the Senate, Perón exploded. Did he lose his temper, or was he actually showing his power by feigning a crisis? In either case, the message was clear: he and Evita were the two faces of one coin. Whoever offended Eva offended him. He agreed with her because she was him. (Cabrera Infante defined him differently: 'Perón, the man who Evita was.') He had hailed the Senate president screaming like a banshee. During the next session, Evita was there. She attended the deliberations, standing haughtily with her hand on the president's chair.

If commenting on Evita had become the Argentinean anti-Perónists' favourite pastime, the Americans had a lot to say, too. In May 1946, *Newsweek* published an article that designated Evita the 'woman behind the throne.' Not long after that, the same publication nicknamed her the 'woman President.' As for Braden, he seemed as obsessed by Evita as his Argentinean friends were. In his memoirs, he tells many jokes that she had the talent to inspire. (An entire generation of Argentines grew up with these jokes that occupied an enormous place in family conversations. During every celebration, whether it was Christmas, an anniversary, or a birthday, people succumbed to the passion of telling these stories that replaced a lost tradition, the forgotten folklore, and without meaning to, created an Argentinean memory.) The following is one of the most famous (for the most part, the others cannot be translated): Eva takes the elevator with a retired general. The elevator boy looks at her out of the corner of his eye and whispers under his breath,

'Whore!' When Eva gets off the elevator, she complains to the general, who responds, 'Pay no attention. It's been ten years since I retired, and they still call me general.'

It goes without saying that Argentinean newspapers did not dare call her 'the woman behind the throne,' the woman President, or much less, a whore. However, in 1946, the press still enjoyed a certain independence. The regime had not put its repressive machine in gear. *La Nación* made sure it said everything, but not clearly. As for *La Prensa*, it often took risks and ended up paying for them. Besides Eduardo Colom's *La Epoca*, Perónists did not have a newspaper. The government decided to purchase *Democracia*, a rag with a small audience. Evita became the owner of the paper. This is a curious detail. Since she did not have enough money to buy it, the National Bank, which had just been nationalised, lent her the funds.

While she did not become the director of the paper, her presence was felt and seen. On days when photos of Evita in a ball gown appeared, the print run was quickly exhausted. The director of *Democracia*, Valentín Thiébault, had to recognise the obvious: Evita sold copies. The prettier she was in the photos, the more readers he had, especially women, anxious to cut out her radiant picture to mount on the armoire door, next to the Indian saint Ceferino Namuncurá.

If Evita was more than present in these pages, Atilio Bramuglia, the Minister of Foreign Affairs, the same one who, in 1945, shouted at her, 'All you care about is saving your man!' had become invisible, anonymous. Evita was taking revenge by erasing his picture and his name from the paper, which now referred to him only as 'the minister' and never published his photo. If he appeared in a group shot, they either cut out or erased his silhouette. If he was among others, the photographer used strange contortions in order to cut off his head. Certain people bought *Democracia* only to see a decapitated Bramuglia. Just desert or double injustice: after the fall of the regime, it was Evita's image that was wiped out, and her name that was banned by journalists. They were both erased, cut up, scratched out, broken, unsewn, burnt, according to the material that served to support them, bronze or marble in most cases.

How did she see herself in May 1947 when she was preparing for her trip to Europe, invited by the Spanish, Italian, French, Swiss, Portuguese, and to a lesser degree British governments?

Valentín Thiébault tells us. Thiébault showed us the giant photograph that Evita had given him in 1947 while writing for the newspaper. She was already the President's wife, worked three days a week at the *Secretaría*, and had announced women's right to vote over the radio. Yet she had not yet thought of having official photos taken. The photo in question is the one that in 1945 had been used for the promotion of her radio broadcasts. A big, juicy rose was placed on her head. Under the rose, and of about the same dimensions, was a child's round and sleepy face (an effect created by the shadow on her lids) that held a disarming candour.

'Look at her signature,' Thiébault said.

On the bottom right hand corner of the photo, Evita had neatly written: María Eva Duarte de Perón. María Eva Duarte de was written in small letters, without pressing too hard on the pen and respecting the horizontal line. PERON was traced in an ascending impulse in capital letters.

'At the time,' Thiébault said, 'we, Perónist men, did not believe in it too much: frankly, the idea that Evita would represent us in Europe made us smile. At the paper we called her "the Lady of Hope" and "Argentina's First Samaritan," a title that the Association of Hospitals and Clinics had given her. But that was only between us . . . until the day when a group of women came to the editorial office. They had read the news of Evita's trip and they wanted to meet her. We told them Evita did not come to the paper. So they asked to see me.'

Thiébault met with them. They were humble women of a dark complexion and poorly dressed. They had come a long way to say the following: 'This is what brings us here, sir. Evita is going to represent Argentinean women in Europe. And we want her to be very, very beautiful. So we have come to advise her to wear her hair in a chignon. The chignon suits her best. Will you tell her that, on our behalf?'

That day the journalist understood that Evita lived within these women. They accompanied her in thought, just as a mother and aunts accompany a young girl who climbs onto the stage for a school graduation. They would have given anything to touch up her chignon, to add a bit of blush to her cheeks, to sew up a hem, kneeling in front of her, their mouths full of pins.

We're not sure Evita ever got this message. It is true, however, that although she left Buenos Aires with her hair in layered curls, she returned with a chignon. Messages do not travel in a straight line, but one always ends up hearing them, believing to have discovered them instantly, though for some time those obscure voices may have been whispering in our ears what road we ought to follow.

Chapter 6

❖

THE MESSENGER

Eva boarded the plane to Spain on June 6, 1947, a year and two days after the memorable June 4 when she slept at the Unzué palace for the first time. Franco had invited Perón. It never occurred to him that his wife would represent him instead. Spain was isolated on the world scene and was bent on thanking the only nation that had supported it in the UN. Perón's Argentina had not only maintained excellent diplomatic relations with one of the last Fascist regimes still standing but had also extended it a loan for the purchase of meat and cereal. The Spaniards began to dream about the Argentinean Eldorado where almost every one of them had an uncle or a cousin who had emigrated long ago. There was a kind of Marshall Plan in the air, this time from Argentina.

These dreams can seem surprising if we think of Argentina as a country in crisis, but in 1947, that was no longer – and not yet – the case. Argentina had grown richer with the war and now was among the most prosperous countries in the world. Europe needed its raw materials. The European industrialised products had become rare, national industry was flourishing, and Argentina was becoming a land of immigration again. But the new Europeans it accommodated were no longer illiterate peasants like the uncle or the cousin from Lugo or Pontevedra had been before. They were qualified professionals of all origins and all types (as much the victims of Nazism as the executioners themselves.) For a leader, the Argentina that Perón had just inherited was a true gift. But what was in it for him to stay on such good terms with Spain?

Argentina had just reestablished its diplomatic and commercial relations with the USSR, it was a UN member, and the United States was beginning to associate with its regime more than they had originally thought possible. And at that time, Perón was giving Franco a substantial helping hand. Certain leftist Perónists, like the union leader Isaías Santín, a Spaniard who was very close to Evita, said that they were unable to understand his actions. But in fact, the contradiction was typical of Perón and came from a miscalculation, which for once was aroused by an emotion. The fascism coiled in his heart prodded him to bet on a third war. He was a disconcerted Machiavellian and based the Argentinean economy on an illusory foundation. This mistake would cost him dearly, for during his second presidential term, when Argentina was becoming less and less opulent, a European war was becoming less and less probable.

Perón could not accept the Spaniards' invitation in person. It was unthinkable to believe that all his efforts to make a good impression would have failed. On the other hand, Evita could replace him. Even if we do not know who suggested this idea to him, we do know that Evita jumped at the chance. She dreamed of Europe. She had often said so to journalists when she was an actress. To return to the source, to accomplish an inner pilgrimage while displaying the tangible proof of success. Franco's guest abandoned herself to a sudden nostalgia for Spain, which was founded in her Basque origins. And Hispanic nostalgia has a particular rhetoric, so Evita prepared herself once again to incarnate an aesthetic that was close to being mistaken for a nationalist soap opera.

Once the idea of sending a substitute was accepted, the next step was realising that a trip only to Spain could be misinterpreted. In order to disguise the trip's objective, other countries had to invite her as well. Father Benítez went to Rome to ask the Vatican to receive the 'Argentinean Mary Magdalene,' her nickname behind the scenes, and soon thereafter, the Argentinean government decided it would be wise to announce that, besides Spain, Doña María Eva Duarte de Perón would visit Italy on an extra-official visit and France in the most official way. The following ambiguous reply came from the perfidious Albion: Evita would be 'well received' in England.

Ambiguity and treachery ruled. On the Argentinean side, one could refer to a poetic image: Evita was going to Europe to 'hang a rainbow of beauty' between the two continents. The image was syrupy, but it confirmed her constant role of an intermediary. Later, she would define this role herself through a stronger image: 'I am a bridge connecting Perón to the people. Cross over me!' A rainbow or a bridge, two ways of stretching between different worlds that only a being with a split identity could join together. On the Argentinean side, the ambiguity explained itself by a psychogical fluctuation that gave Perónism its multiple nuances. On the European side, it had first an economic origin. Europe was hungry, and Argentina had surplus livestock and wheat. Evita and her multicolour pomp suggested a contradictory idea: fascism and rump steak. Each of the implicated governments treated the former with a gradation of nuances that went from sympathy to courteous rejection, so as not to deprive itself of the latter.

In Buenos Aires, the preparations for the tour had reached a frenetic pace. Mrs Perón had to look ravishingly beautiful and rich. This ostentation was possibly used to hide a treasure that was a thousand times more fabulous than the one she displayed. Whatever the case, wearing too beautiful feathers to visit countries that had been ravaged by the war was a faux pas. However, the moral of the story is something else altogether. Whether she was nouveaux riche or a true queen, Eva was right. They would not still remember her in Europe today if she had travelled there enveloped by simplicity in an attempt not to offend the naked and the poor. Few people would have understood that kind of elegance. Evita was dazzling, and the people ravenously devoured her with their eyes.

Lilian was the first chosen victim. Among the available women, none would be a better companion for the dazzling messenger. The entourage was formed accordingly: Juan Duarte, less disposed to visit the grandiose monuments than the women of little virtue; Muñoz Azpiri, who stopped by the airport to say good-bye to his favourite actress and was spontaneously recruited; Julio Alcaraz, a silent Figaro and trustworthy man in charge of carrying the pig leather suitcase that enclosed the jewels; Dr Alsina, a doctor, two seamstresses; Alberto Dodero, who, according to Eva, was financing this entire trip; a journalist from *Democracia*; the marquis of Chinchilla and Count Foxá from the Spanish Embassy; two aides from the presidential camp; and chambermaids. As for Lilian, she played the role of French interpreter, who was qualified in good manners and as a scapegoat.

When Evita had brought up the subject of the trip, Lilian initially refused to leave her husband and children, so Eva called unsuccessfully on Guardo. In the end, Perón even invited the couple over in order to convince them. At the end of dinner, he took Lilian aside and said to her with a tremor in his voice, 'Please say yes, Lilian! It's important for the country! She will cancel her trip if you don't go with her!' When faced with emotional bribery, the Guardos both sighed submissively and agreed. Evita was as happy as a child and managed to obtain a nice cash reward for Lilian from the Minister of Foreign Affairs, which, in bad taste, Guardo refused. It was Eva's turn to sigh. How annoying these complicated people are! Was it so difficult to comply with her whims?

The jewels in the suitcase were carefully chosen. These were far from the jewels of a 'thrifty schoolteacher.' Whether they were gifts from Dodero, Evita's acquisitions from Ricciardi, or phantom treasures, the result was extraordinary. According to Jamandreu, there was a set of black pearls that was the only one in the world.

There was also a big bracelet with pearls and diamonds, pearl teardrop earrings, and a necklace with many rows of pearls and a diamond pendant.

As for the planned wardrobe for the trip, the designer Ana de Pombo says that Eva requested a dress that was 'even more beautiful than the queen's,' and with a monumental cape, to climb the stairs of Madrid's royal palace. Ana understood, and she created for Evita a sky blue lace dress embroidered with rhinestones. The cape was made of blue ostrich feathers, and it had a six-foot-long fairy train. (When she returned, Eva commissioned a full-length portrait by the Spanish painter Sotomayor. She provided him with many photos of her face and the blue dress on a mannequin. Sotomayor was to perpetuate the celestial image.)

Three days before her departure, Evita christened the first of her 'transit homes,' which was probably named 'María Eva Duarte de Perón.' (The next ones would be called 'Eva Perón,' 'Evita,' and other similar variations.) It was located in the southern neighbourhood, and the plan was for it to shelter forty-six young women from the provinces who were looking for work. For Evita, it was a symbol. She remembered arriving in Buenos Aires with nowhere to sleep. Now other young girls like her, 'immigrants from the interior,' would have what she did not: the roof, the food, the company.

She had decorated the home. Who else would have chosen the provincial cloth patterns with garish flowers? But who else had ever given a moment's thought for the well-being of these girls? Eva's adversaries jokingly said that she was very good at doing bad and very bad at doing good. This was an acknowledgement that she had done things, that she was proactive. In fact, the printed cloth patterns had a meaning: Eva did not want her guests to live in a sad place. She wanted to surround them with luxury and joy. To have the blue fairy dress, one must first dream it. But in order to pluck up the courage to imagine, one must first see it. Evita was there to tell them that fairies existed.

THE GOOD-BYES

That same evening, the Spanish ambassador, José María de Areilza, count of Motrico, held a reception for her at the embassy. The photograph that captures this evening is the type a propaganda expert should have burned immediately. In the photo, a trio of Areilza, Perón, and Evita gleefully look at us, drinks in hand, which explains the happiness on the three faces.

The ambassador, with the well-bred nose and the raised eyebrow of a vain, ambitious *señorito* with a biting spirit, had just shown Perón his letters of credit during a magnificent ceremony. He had been the Francoist diplomat chosen above all others to sign the Franco-Perón protocol in which Argentina agreed to extend a credit in *pesetas* to Spain in order to buy wheat. Areilza, the father of a little girl Evita adored, quickly became an intimate friend of the presidential couple.

Later, this friendship would progressively deteriorate. Well after her return from Europe, Mrs President was told that she was the butt of many jokes at the Spanish Embassy's dinner table. One day when he was waiting in a room in the Unzué palace, Areilza heard her yell: '*Ese gallego de mierda que se espere*' (That shitty Galician? Let him wait!). In Argentina, no matter what region a Spaniard was from, he was considered a *gallego*. Areilza picked up his hat and yelled back to all present, 'Tell your mistress that the Galician is leaving, but that the shit stays.'

In the photo in question, Areilza's face is friendly if a tad ironic and does not hide the high opinion that its owner had of himself and his noble lineage. In the middle, in the background, Perón affects a smile that is not his own. This time, he had not turned it on to welcome the crowd with open arms. He is standing in the shadow of his own 'shadow.' To say that his face is that of a lecher seems easy today, like reading a book when one already knows how it ends. Meanwhile, the shrewdness that screws up his small slanting eyes and the joyless sensuality of his wet lips could not fool anyone, neither then nor now. He is letting his hand with the drink in it fall onto Evita's mink stole, as if to confirm – but so weakly – his ownership of the stole and the woman. Of Areilza and Perón, the first seems to say, 'Look how noble I am. I visit these nouveaux riches from the antipodes for their cereals, but I despise them.' And the second, 'See how shrewd I am. I am playing the game I like most, imposing my wife on them. I am keeping the true reasons for this trip to myself. And we'll see about the wheat later.' Both of them express this subtly, one twisting his eyebrow, the other his mouth. Although she is disguised like never before, with her white hat placed like a plate on her head, her curls enhanced by a hairpiece on her forehead, and all her emeralds, only Evita does not seem to play. Pretty, unrefined, innocent, she radiates a simple and direct happiness. Here, the actress is the only candid soul.

In the chapter of good-byes, Argentina did not prove itself unworthy. During an evening in Eva's honour, José María Freyre, the Labour Minister, lyrically declared that Evita was the 'most accomplished representative' one could have dreamed of and the 'archetype of the Argentinean woman, who shows her personality not with a peacock's vanity, but as the incarnation of an exquisite femininity.' At the end of the speech, with the rough tone she reserved exclusively for important men, Evita retorted, 'Stop that! Do you want me to bring you back a present or what?' However, she was starting to get accustomed to servile flattery. Had they not just come out with a song entitled *The Lady of Hope?* Still, she retained the freshness of a 'muddy flower from the slums,' as the tango says. Between the satisfaction of being worshipped and of humiliating someone of a certain rank, she chose the latter.

Eva was not the only one to react to the minister's speech. The Conference of Socialist Women published the following communiqué: '1) Socialist women do not feel represented by this woman. 2) They deplore and object to the honorary degree awarded to her by the University of La Plata. 3) They regret that the French government, made up in large part by socialist collegues, officially invited her to France.' (Other countries could invite 'this woman' with impunity. But France could not. Coming from France, a truly intelligent country, the invitation was a betrayal.)

The most significant good-byes, from a political point of view, took place on June 5 at the Rural Society of Argentina, another bastion of the livestock aristocracy. There, each year, the landowners exhibited (and still do), their cows and bulls. The conservative newspapers always published the photos of the Shorthorn or the Aberdeen Angus on the front page, next to the photos of the military service men. At the time of Evita's trip, the Sunday crowds of this lofty place had already been tainted. The *cabecitas negras* had come to get some air across the street, on the lawn of the Plaza Italic, before going to see the elephant in its Hindu-style palace at the zoo next door. This sight had never been seen before Perónism: dark-skinned people, shining from pomade, in their Sunday best, workers and maids, born in the tropics and in the dry lands, all wearing sunglasses. To pretend to have delicate eyes, as if they had come from foggy lands, was the supreme sign of success. At least that is what the fat cattle exhibitors would say under their breath, while scornfully looking toward the meagre lawn of the square.

That is where the union workers said good-bye to their good fairy who was ready to fly away. One hundred thousand workers had come to send her off. Beside her, Domingo Mercante beamed. Evita repeated the word that had never left her lips: *corazón*, heart. 'I am leaving, but I leave you my heart.'

June 6 finally arrived. At 4 P.M. the Morón airport, west of the capital, was overcome by crowds. Eva was familiar with these crowds, their heat, their dangers. During her last trip to Tucumán, the human avalanche took seven lives, left many injured, and caused two premature births. Eva went to the hospital to visit the wounded. She even insisted on seeing the dead. And when she left the morgue, she fainted into the arms of Lilian who was concerned about her health and the state of her nerves. Luckily, on June 6 the scene was different. No one pushed, her feelings were respected; she seemed touched. She kissed Perón and hesitated before boarding the plane – it was such a long trip! Then she climbed onto the Iberia DC-4, like a queen on the scaffold.

The members of Eva's entourage travelled with her, but the suitcases were sent in an Argentinean aircraft. The moment the DC-4 took off, she cleared her throat and said, 'Listen up boys: starting right now, we have to be careful. The whole world is watching us. So, don't screw up! And watch out if you give them the tiniest reason to laugh at us!' She was obviously not worried about the two noble Spaniards or Lilian, who was listening to her, open-mouthed. She was worried about her brother. Her intuition was far from wrong. When they arrived in Spain, with Dodero as an accomplice Juan Duarte ditched the official ceremonies in order to run off to see the Sacromonte gypsies in Granada. Later, in Rome, Father Benítez would have a hard time justifying the 'adorable scoundrel's' scandalous behaviour.

This said, Evita was not nervous only about Juancito. She was nervous about her own awkwardness, too. And her stage fright was intensified by the fear of death. The plane was definitely going to crash. Besides, her past was following her. At midnight, she picked up a pen and wrote the following letter to Perón:

My dear Juan,

I am leaving on this trip with much sadness, because I cannot live far away from you, I love you so that I idolise you. I may not be able to show you all that I feel, but I assure you that I have fought many hardships in my life for my ambition to be somebody. I suffered a great deal, but then you came along and you made me so happy that I feel like I am dreaming. And since I had nothing to give to you other than my heart and my soul, I gave it to you entirely. But it is certain that during these years when happiness grew by the second, I never stopped adoring you, not even for a minute, nor thanking the heavens for the kindness that God showed towards me by rewarding me with your love, that I tried to deserve every minute by doing everything I could to make you happy. I do not know if I succeeded, but I can assure you that no one in this world respected you and loved you more than I did. I am so faithful to you that if God no longer wanted this happiness, and took me with Him, even after death I would be faithful and adore you from up there. My darling, forgive me for these confessions, but you must know, at the moment of my departure and when I am in God's hands, not knowing if I will be in an accident, that your wife with all her faults has been purified by you, because I live for you, I feel for you, and I think for you. Take good care of yourself. You are right, to govern is a thankless job. God willing and if we finish all this well, we will retire to live our life, and I will try to make you the happiest man possible because your joys are mine. Juan, if I die, please take care of mom, she is alone and has suffered a great deal. Give her 100,000 pesos; for Isabelita, who has always been loyal, 20,000 pesos and a better salary. And I will watch over you from up there. Keep my jewels for yourself. Same thing for San Vicente and Teodoro García so you will remember your Chinita who loved you so. It's useless for me to ask you to look out for Doña Juana because I know you love her as much as I do. But, since we live in our eternal honeymoon, we do not show our affection for the family, though we love them very much. Juan, stay friends with Mercante who adores you, and keep him as a collaborator because he is loyal. Watch out for Rudi, he is very fond of business deals. Castro told me this and it could harm you. I want to see your name as clean as you are

yourself; I know it's painful, but you have to know what Rudi
did in Junín. Castro knows. I swear to you, it's an infamy (my
past belongs to me, but when I die, you must know it is not
true), it is painful to love one's friends and to have them pay
you back in this way. I left Junín when I was thirteen. How
cruel to imagine such baseness in a little girl, it's completely
wrong. I cannot leave without telling you all this; I didn't tell
you when I left because I was too saddened by having to be
separated from you, and I did not want to deepen my pain,
but you can be proud of your wife, because I looked after your
name and I adored you. Kiss, kiss, one thousand kisses . . .

Evita

The Castro in question is Colonel Juan Francisco Castro, the
future Secretary of Transportation. Rudi is Rudi Freude, Perón's
secretary who was in charge of receiving the Nazi refugees
who were welcomed to Argentina. And what had the German
billionaire's son uncovered in Junín? We cannot help but bring
up the two aristocrats who had abandoned Eva and her friend
on the side of a road. But why would Rudi try to discredit her
in her husband's mind? That is an obscure question, as is the
question of why Evita was leaving the house in San Vicente
to her husband when, by all accounts, it had been his since
before their wedding.

MRS. FRANCO'S SMILE

It was June 8, at 8:35 P.M., a clear and balmy summer night,
when the plane landed at Barajas airport, escorted by forty-
one fighter planes. Eva descended the stairs, and there, on
the esplanade, she saw Generalissimo Franco, flanked by two
women dressed in black: his wife, Doña Carmen Polo de
Franco, and their daughter, Carmen Franco Polo. The three of
them walked toward Evita, surrounded by countless uniforms

and cassocks. A bit farther away, a colourful group of young girls from the Falange, in folkloric costumes, waved their handkerchiefs. On the ground, the red carpet stretched on for miles. There were flowers and Spanish red-yellow-red and Argentinean blue-white-blue flags everywhere. And all around the airport, three hundred thousand delirious Madrilenians called out her name.

As she stepped off the last step, just as she grazed Spanish soil, Evita's body gave a barely noticeable hint of a contortion. Just like all the other photos, one, which appeared in the Spanish newspapers of the time, depicts a smiling but tense Eva, her right shoulder raised and her left foot crooked. Eva's right arm, which is as rigid as if it were in a cast, is separated from her body, while her left arm holds her handbag close to her waist, as if in this Spain, Catholic and corseted by a dictatorship, she were afraid of being robbed.

Her outfit, much like her body, reveals neither grace nor agility. Her advisers had probably decided that she should look serious. The result was stiff, but not without humour. Her hair was styled in a French twist that went around the nape of her neck and made her look as if she had no neck. Her square hat was pinned in place on the back of her head and was decorated with a big ribbon that stood up stiffly. Her suit had a long vest that was hardly waisted, with big shoulder pads, and a straight skirt with flat pleats in the front. It was made of a thick fabric that gave her silhouette a massive appearance.

Just when her body played the trick on her of twisting itself like a gaucho, always oblique, Evita smiled timidly. (Later she would be more careful to control her foot, and she would respond to Franco's bowings and scrapings with a sweet closed-lip pout.) The *gallego* dictator (he was truly both of these) bowed to kiss her hand. So she too bowed slightly, in a gesture borrowed from the nobility, a gesture she would later repeat before numerous other European personalities, and each time it would be more successful. In Argentina, hand kissing was not part of the protocol.

Eva walked by the troops with Franco. Here, her stiffness and her seriousness are justified. She transformed these into a haughty attitude, and into hurtful words when the unlucky Argentinean ambassador, Dr Pedro Radío, arrived late. Running, his jacket half-ripped and his tie crooked, he was bathed in sweat.

He apologised: the crowd had prevented him from being on time. But instead of forgiving him, or laughing it off, Evita humiliated him. The woman who had let her foot go found in him a perfect scapegoat.

Calmed by this fit of anger, she climbed into the car with the three Francos, and the long caravan rolled into town. The mild climate began to relax her. She was coming from the winter, and her body retained the cold of Buenos Aires in June. The crowd's warmth was also working miracles. The Madrilenians knew how to obey their *caudillo*, who had suggested they decorate their balconies all along the Calle de Alcalá where the motorcade was to pass. It was Sunday, which is why the people were able to come to Barajas, and why they lined the streets, the terraces, and their windows. Tomorrow they would have the day off in order to welcome Evita in the Orient Plaza.

The procession followed the Calle de Alcalá and led into Plaza de Cibelas. It was a dazzling spectacle: The Alcalá door, the *Espartero* statue, and the Gran Vía were flooded with light! The Madrilenians had long since got used to seeing their city in a half-light. This light let them imagine many a crazy illusion. If the generalissimo was giving in to extravagance, it was because he was counting on the result of this visit and on the visitor whose wheat-coloured hair seemed to bring a gentle confirmation of their hopes.

The trip ended at the Pardo, the palace where Evita and her entourage would stay during their visit. That is where the Franco family lived. Later, Mrs Franco would refuse to receive guests, no matter how important they were. Evita's stay had been enough.

Eva was presented with sumptuous gifts: an antique shawl, a gold and ivory fan, perfume, a leather valise decorated with the two countries' seals, and, most important, a beautiful rug with the reproduction of an El Greco painting. Later, they bid her good-night and retired to their rooms. Everyone, that is, except Eva. She called Lilian and bade her to stay next to her. It did not matter how many valets and police officers were guarding the place. She was scared that 'someone' was going to break into her room. But who? No one knows. But from now on, Evita would share her room with Lilian. That night, the two women pushed the dresser against the door, as if they were spending the night in dubious lodgings. And every night, during the three months that the trip lasted, Lilian would have access to her worries, dreams and plans, for Evita slept badly and scarcely. Later, Lilian talked about these conversations, which lasted until dawn and were dominated by two topics.

The first was Perón. Eva filled her mouth with his formidable and virile name. But she was unable to sleep for the thought that his enemies would take advantage of her absence to fool him. If she was deprived of sleep, it was because she felt responsible for Perón. She became obsessed by this thought toward the end of her life, during the illness that would kill her. And time would prove her right: the neurosis that consists of thinking oneself essential does not exclude the gift of clairvoyance.

The second topic of nocturnal conversation was history. From the first evening, Evita asked Lilian a very grave question that she would ask her again, during the following nights, and to which, half-asleep, her companion would answer in an increasingly failing voice. Eva would say, 'Lilian, tell me what you would like to do with your life?' 'I would be content to be a good mother to my children,' Lilian would respond again and again. And Evita would ardently sigh, 'Not me. I want to have a place in history.'

Evita at age fifteen, before her departure to the big city.

In one of her first dramatic roles as an ingenue, 1937.

Evita's movie debut in *La Cabalgata*

Colonel Perón's girlfriend in her living room
at the Posadas Street apartment.

In an evening gown designed by Paco
Jamandreu for her first gala at the
Colon Theater.

The starlet faces an uncertain future, 1945.

President Perón's wife becomes a newspaper editor, 1946.

The Spanish Ambassador and President Perón send off Evita on her trip to Europe, 1947.

At Barajas airport, next to Franco.

With Franco and his wife, dona Carmen Polo de Franco.

Evita speaks to the Spanish crowds gathered on Plaza de Oriente in Madrid, June 1947.

At the Escorial.

At the Vatican.

In Italy, Evita smiles despite the Communists' frosty welcome.

During a reception in Italy.

Evita in Paris.

At the Ritz Hotel with Edouard Herriot.

A Parisian evening.

Evita at Notre Dame, between Mrs. Suzanne Bidault and the Count of Paris.

At the Colon Theater, around 1949.

Perón and Evita, 1950.

Evita and her beloved poor.

A weekend in the country.

Dressed in Dior for the national holiday.

At the Colon Theater, May 25, 1951, surrounded by her ministers.

Powerful speech.

Already ill, but always working.

The official portrait.

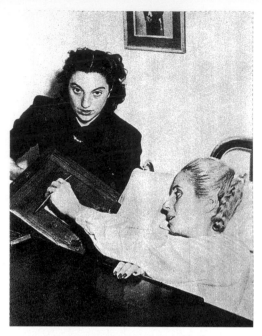

Evita votes from her hospital bed.

The "Day of Renunciation."

June 4, 1952. As Perón begins his second term as
President, a very ill Evita attends the ceremony.

Evita not long before her death.

Pedro Ara, the embalmer, watches over the corpse.

A shrine to Evita on every street corner.

When the subject of the invitation to Spain had been brought up back in Buenos Aires, Evita had told Ambassador Areilza that she wanted to receive the cross of Isabel the Catholic 'on this Occident Plaza that you have in Madrid.' 'Orient Plaza,' the count had corrected her, raising an eyebrow. Eva noted his objection and said, 'Same thing!' And now the moment had come. The day after her arrival, at the stroke of noon, she emerged from the Pardo with Franco to report to the Palacio Real, which in fact was located in the Orient Plaza.

It was very hot. Doña Carmen Polo de Franco was again wearing a black dress and a musketeer's capeline. Only the details were different. The neckline had changed from tri-angular to square, and her hat displayed a cascade of soft feathers instead of one straight one. Around her neck, she wore pearls.

Evita, however, had changed dramatically since the day before. Pedro Alcaraz had limited himself simply to retouching the French twist that surrounded the nape of her neck. But now, this quiff could be seen only if one was to her left. From the right, she disappeared under an enormous arrangement of feathers, which were as soft as Doña Carmen's, but without a hat, the solitary feathers softly caressed Evita's cheek and seemed to be the reason for her dreamy smile. She was wearing a flowing and shimmering printed dress, but we can barely see the dress's cut, since, despite the heat, Evita wore her sable cape throughout the ceremony. In the absence of the pyjama fetish, it seemed as if she still needed some kind of enveloping protection.

Still gripping her cape, she received the cross of Isabel the Catholic, as had been given to Perón on the day Evita showed up in her noodle necklace. The only difference was that the cross given to Evita was gold encrusted with precious gems. Clutching her cape, she listened to Franco's speech, which held nothing back in its praise of Perón. Then, still under her cape, she took the podium.

Her speech, written by Muñoz Azpiri, was a summary of all the familiar places in her motherland as well as a tribute to Isabel the Catholic, 'she who was the closest to God, during Spain's sacred times, when being close to God meant: to fight and to pray.' (She did not add, 'and to kill the Jews and the Indians.') In brief, the scriptwriter used every element of the rhetoric celebrated each October 12 on Ethnic Race Day. Next to Francoist rhetoric, Muñoz Azpiri's prose seemed dismayingly sober. In announcing Evita's arrival, for example, the famous Spanish writer Eugenio d'Ors had written: 'When delving into oneself to find the essence of Argentina, what one finds is none other than an ancient Spain, Rossinante's trot, the ardent desire for chivalry. Is anyone more like Don Quixote than a gaucho?' Only Sancho Panza and Old Vizcacha were missing from this stream of grandiloquent words. Whether it is Marrano or mulatto, the picaresque vein did not belong to such a solemn occasion.

After the speeches they went out on the balcony. The plaza was filled with crowds screaming, 'Franco and Perón!' Evita took the microphone. 'General Franco,' she said, 'is now feeling the same emotions that Perón felt when he was cheered by the *descamisados*.' We do not know if Franco appreciated this comment or if Evita was alluding to Perón's feelings only to utter once more this booming name she found so beautiful. When she finished improvising, as usual she waved to the crowd with her right arm barely moving, hardly bending it. This gesture was easily confused with the Fascist salute. The next day, the Spanish press was not shy about confirming this.

The newspapers reported that hundreds of thousands were in the crowd (there were forty thousand according to Marysa Navarro). In any case, the plaza was packed with people, a phenomenon that repeated itself throughout Spain wherever Evita set foot. A civil war had just ended, and the Spaniards were hungry. They also thirsted for a spectacle that television could not yet churn out. Evita fell into this scene perfectly with her bread and her circus. She was pretty and nice. And on top of this, Argentina was Spain's beloved daughter, and Evita proclaimed her Spanish origins (ignoring the fact that Duarte was a French Basque name). All the elements came together so that the visual joy was in line with the joy of the heart. It was theatre, emotional theatre.

Evita proved to be a strongly disconcerting actress in the show produced by Franco. That afternoon, she insisted on visiting the city's poor neighbourhoods. In this heat, Doña Carmen surely would have preferred to have a siesta, especially since a reception was scheduled at the Pardo that night. But her guest had enough energy for the two of them. Nor was Eva content to tour these slums by car; she walked into every dilapidated house, asked one hollow-cheeked man if he had work, another about his illness, and left behind a flood of pesetas insisting that it was not charity but social assistance. Justice. The poor had a right to ask. And once again she spoke of Perón, about his five-year plan, about the Perónist revolution. Doña Carmen wore her usual smile, as if it were were her mouth's destiny, but the corners fell just a bit when Evita asked Franco to pardon a Doña from the opposition: Juana Doña, the Communist sentenced to death. Unable to refuse a request from such a charming guest Franco spared Juana Doña's life.

At the party at the Pardo palace that night, Eva was not wearing the cross of Isabel. Franco welcomed her with an interrogating look. She understood immediately but did not lose her cool. She simpered, 'I should have worn it, shouldn't I? But it is not a big deal, I'll take care of it right away.' She snapped her fingers, and someone went to her room to get it for her.

She committed several blunders during her trip, and quite often she got out of it with a touching sincerity. Like the day she visited the cathedral in Madrid. The anecdote was recounted by Joaquín Romero Murube, who was the mayor of the city at the time. The bishop was waiting for her.

They had prepared a golden prie-dieu for her, and it went without saying that she would generously give alms. But she had just left a church where she donated a large sum. Inside the cathedral, she realised her mistake. So she banged her forehead and exclaimed, 'My God, I haven't got a penny left! I gave everything to the other church, the one we just visited. I thought that was the cathedral. Quickly, go to the Pardo and get my money!' Here or in another church she said to the Spanish worker who was escorting her, 'Please explain to me when I need to stand and sit, because, as you know, I am not very clever.' In all three cases she had taken the best possible route, humbly admitting, with all dignity, that she did not know how to behave. On other occasions, her haughty reactions revealed her inferiority complex. At the Prado, Ambassador Radío, the one who was late to the airport, again bore the brunt of the situation. The museum director had launched into an explanation of an El Greco painting when the ambassador, in the hope of entering in her graces, risked an opinion on the artist's work. 'Not a word!' Evita said. 'You know nothing about this. Shut your mouth and let the gentleman speak.'

At the Escorial, she was perfect, the spitting image of summer brightness in a print dress with a white background, white accessories, no necklace (just a brooch at the crux of the square neckline), and, what a surprise, a pretty capeline, white and supple, on her wide forehead. The poor women who had come to advise her to wear a chignon had been right! This was an exquisite Evita whose elegance was purified, who walked about Philip II's palace with a supreme indifference for this austere jewel. The Escorial inspired a unique commentary: 'So many rooms! We could make a great home for orphans here!'

She was treated to the complete folkloric programme, including, of course, the bullfight. For Evita, this was a new spectacle. The Argentinean Assembly of 1813 had forbidden bulls in an effort to eliminate all Spanish influence. However, the matador who was performing in her honour that day had been born in Argentina. His name was José Rovira, and this was not to be his day of glory. To start off, Evita was very late (later, she would exaggerate this odd behaviour). And when she appeared with her blonde scarf on her blonde head, the audience had eyes only for her. Rovira swung his hips to show off his wasp's waist and tight buttocks moulded by the shiny leggings, but no one noticed. 'They did not come to see me,' he said bitterly. 'They came to see her.' Nonetheless, the vain torero offered his 'president' his first victim. Most unfortunately, the performance lacked brilliance. The bull gave in from the start. It was the box of honour, inundated with carnations, that radiated and sparkled.

On June 15, Evita went to tour the regions with her entourage but without the Francos. On this occasion, she addressed a message to the Spanish women, where she defined the century as the 'century of victorious feminism.' These were daring words, quickly thwarted by others that were less so. In this speech, as in every one she spoke publicly in Spain, she pronounced *ll* the way a Spaniard would. This subtlety was intended to spare the Spanish from the strangeness of her Argentinean accent, but it also represented a certain obedience from a little girl who was reading her essay at school, enunciating all the words just as her teacher wanted her to. For now, she was pronouncing others' words with a strange accent.

And there she was in Andalucia. In Granada, in front of the recumbent figures of the Catholic kings, they asked her to pay close attention: 'See how Isabel's head is buried deeply into the pillow. The queen's brain, they say, was heavier than Ferdinand's.' Was this a malicious allusion to her own intelligence in comparison to her husband's? Whether or not it was, she did not hold back from 'betraying' him (she who was always so faithful), when she responded with the same malice, 'It's still like that.'

The farther south she went, the more she ignited popular idolatry. In Seville, she took a carriage from the airport to the Alfonso XIII hotel where a suite draped with red brocade and lined with museum furniture was waiting for her. People in flamenco costumes threw rose petals at her. One of them even wanted to offer the feather from Evita's hat to the Virgin of Macarena. We do not know if she was successful in dispossessing one to enrich the other, but one thing is clear: for her, one was just as sacred as the other. Another young woman, back in Argentina, had a similar wish, although a less fetishistic one: she wanted to see Evita. When she managed to stick her head inside her idol's car, she exclaimed, 'I *saw* her!' Then she fainted. It was the Virgin of Pilar that was honoured the most. In Zaragoza, Evita said a prayer in front of the altar. She had known a copy of the statue at the Los Toldos church. And there, perhaps in a studied outburst, but completely in the spirit of the other two women, she took off her gold and diamond earrings, and lifting her eyes towards the heavens, offered them to the Virgin of her childhood.

She visited Huelva, Toledo, Avila, Vigo, Santiago de Compostela. The moment to rejoin Doña Carmen had arrived. The two women met at the Barcelona airport. They entered the city in a convertible, followed by two hundred cars. The mayor welcomed them and the bishop offered them a Te Deum in the cathedral. The Argentine and the Spaniard stared grimly at each other. It was becoming more and more difficult to hide their antipathy. At this stage of the trip, Evita was about to have a nervous breakdown. She had done everything possible to behave properly, but anarchy was in her entrails, a malicious imp within her pushed her to boycott the Francoist machine.

After a moment of rest at the Pedralbes palace, the schedule called for a play, *A Midsummer Night's Dream*. This time Evita arrived at the amphitheatre of the national Palace of Montjuich two hours late. When Doña Carmen, who had waited for her, commented, Evita responded, 'Let them wait. We are not first ladies for nothing. No one sets my schedules, not even my husband.'

Luckily for Doña Carmen, Franco arrived the next day. He would not travel by plane since 1937 when an accident had cost his friend General Emilio Mola his life. At noon, the time of his arrival, Evita had not yet shown up. She was lunching on the *Hornero*, a ship that belonged to Dodero. And there, among family, her brother told of his adventures in the land of the *gallegos* – or rather, *gallegas* – and she laughed more than she had in a long time.

She was still not finished with the banquets, the Virgins, the reviews of the troops, and the speeches. On June 24, at the Pedralbes palace, saying confession to Father Benítez, she finally broke down. She could no longer stand the protocol. 'What have I done in my life, I who am an illegitimate child whom everyone has always called *Chinita*, what have I done to deserve all these tributes?'

Finally on June 26, she flew to Rome, exclaiming, her hand on her heart, '*Adiós, España mía!*'

Her bags were filled with regional costumes that the folkloric dancers from each region had placed at her feet during a party at Madrid's Plaza Mayor, the night when Evita showed up hidden under a floor-length mink coat. (These costumes were exhibited upon her return to Buenos Aires. The funds collected from the entrance fees were to fill the coffers of the Eva Perón Foundation, but they were insignificant. So Ambassador Areilza, who had not yet become the *gallego de mierda* that we know him to be, gave money from his own pocket, an act for which he was reprimanded by his compatriots.) Eva also brought home a pistol; a miniature reproduction of Don Juan Diaz de Solís's vessel (the explorer of the Río de La Plata who was eaten by the Charrúas Indians); several ounces of perfume; and most of all, an authentic Gobelin tapestry from the Prado depicting Darius's death.

The last gift came from winning a bet. Thinking that she was sentimental, the Galician dictator had said to her, 'If you are able to hold back your tears at the Escorial, I will give you this rug.' Obviously, he did not know her very well. Evita, crying crocodile tears? Perón could become emotional at the sight of the Argentinean flag. Had he been Spanish, the Escorial would have worked miracles. The two dictators may have shared the same abstract sentimentality, carried within symbols rather than within humans, the sentimentality evidenced by Dostoyevski when he described the old Karamazov, 'He was sentimental. Sentimental and bad.' As for Evita, she characterised her emotions well during this trip. When someone asked her, 'Don't these works of art move you?' she responded, 'No. I am filled with wonder, but I am not moved. I am only moved by the people.'

Later we would find out what could make her cry. According to her sister Erminda, Eva did not shed a tear when she found out she was going to die. But she cried when she returned to Argentina and announced that she was going to devote her life to the poor. She cried when she christened the homes for the elderly. She cried when faced with the destitution of the inhabitants of a destroyed village in the Andes, and she ordered a town to be built for them on that same spot, a small pretty town called Las Cuevas. When she left her bed to visit the children's homes for the last time, she cried at their neglect. She was moved only by her task and her mission and the realisation that her works wouldn't survive her. But the Escorial, she had no trouble winning that bet.

Eva was filled with new experiences. She had spoken to workers in Madrid at a technical school, in Granada in a factory, in Vigo at the House of Fishermen. And everywhere, she spoke of Perón and of her social works. From her husband's point of view, this leg of her trip was a success. When she was leaving, he sent a message to the Spaniards, welcoming them in Argentina: 'You have here a land that is an extension of the old Hispanic country that will welcome you with open arms if you so desire.' He needed arms, so he opened his widely.

As for Franco, he rubbed his hands in expectation of his wheat. But *Time* magazine published a story that must have dampened his glee. Before her departure, Evita had given him a ship full of wheat. Compared to the money the Spaniards spent flattering her, this was not a big deal. The dictator wanted a credit, the formal credit that Ambassador Areilza had finalised. And so he coldly responded, 'Thank you Madam, but we need nothing. Here in Spain, we have so much wheat we don't know what to do with it.' To which Evita is said to have responded, 'In this case, why not make bread with it?'

This joke actually was circulating in Madrilenian cafés long before Evita arrived. And besides, Evita was too shy at that time to dish out such repartee. But as often happens, jokes expose reality and even anticipate it. After her argument with Areilza, Evita ended up opposing the gift of wheat to the *gallegos*. And Franco complained, 'I do not understand why this woman has it in for us after all the attention we gave her.'

CHRIST'S VICAR

Count Carlo Sforza, Minister of Foreign Affairs of the Alcide De Gasperi cabinet, his wife, the Argentinean ambassador Rafael Ocampo Jiménez, and representatives from the Vatican were waiting for Eva at the Rome airport. The entourage travelled to the embassy at Piazza dell'Esquilino.

The embassy was decorated for the occasion and appeared worthy of receiving such an important guest. They had placed marble at the entrance and had removed one of the typical city public urinals from the sidewalk, the kind that hid the user's key parts and exposed only the focused face and the spread feet. Evita's visit was depriving Romans of their monuments. But that was not the reason for their reaction to her presence. Although she embellished the place, the embassy unfortunately was right across the street from a unit of the Communist party.

About five thousand people had gathered in the plaza to wait for Evita. They were not all chanting the same slogans. Maybe that's why Ambassador Ocampo erred at this point, his ear probably picking up only some of them. 'Go out on the balcony, Madam,' he said to the new arrival. 'The people are calling for you.' She would have gone out there had not a certain Mrs Alzaga, who either understood Italian better or who, not having a selective ear, heard the unpleasant chants too, interfered to prevent her from doing so. What were these people saying? Some were saying they were hungry, at least according to Román Lombille, one of those anti-Perónist authors whose hatred for Evita reveals a certain love. Others yelled 'Du-ce, Du-ce,' just as 'Pe-rón, Pe-rón' was said. Finally, others who were more in tune with the party line shouted, 'Fascist Perón!' or 'Neither Mussolini nor Perón!'

The next morning Evita had a meeting at the Vatican. Was it her unease caused by the Communists from across the street that prevented her from getting up on time or was it the bad news that Father Benítez had kept from her until now, that Dodero would not be received by the Pope as a reprimand for another time when he arrived for a visit with a young woman who was not his wife? In any case, when the Argentinean diplomat who was in charge of taking her to the Vatican came to pick her up at 9 A.M., she was still sleeping. No one had dared wake her.

She must have gotten dressed like lightning, while Pedro Alcaraz created a hair style with two uneven hairpieces (the one on the right was higher than the one on the left). Tied to her back was a black mantilla, a gift from Doña Carmen. On her chest, she wore the cross of Isabel the Catholic. And she wore a long black silk dress, almost like a nun's habit, just as her confessor had recommended. Everything about her majestic appearance seemed to be dictated by protocol.

Everything except her hair. When we look at a photo of Eva at the Vatican, a memory forcefully gallops toward us. The woman with the serious face, mourning from head to toe, and hair pulled up into two uneven shells – it was *La pródiga*.

Pope Pius XII was aware of her artistic past. Father Benítez had had a hard time counteracting the influence of a thick file filled with 'scandalous' photographs of Evita sent by Catholic anti-Perónists. Could the Argentinean oligarchy accept that the Pope, who was not happy to receive her, make her into a marquise? It was rumoured that Monsignor Coppello himself, who was always present at Perónist ceremonies, had asked ex-Monsignor Pacelli not to pay too much attention to the woman who had made him into a straw cardinal. Román Lombille goes as far as revealing the name of the priest in charge of placing the file in the hands of Monsignor Tardini, secretary of the pontifical state: a certain Cucetti. Introduced by Tardini, Cucetti is said to have been received by Pacelli. He would have showed him a memo signed by Monsignor X and Monsignor Y (that's what Lombille called them), with photos in which the actress – *Vade retro* – is wearing shorts. Christ's Vicar would have exclaimed, '*Ma questo non è possible!*' And then would have added these strange words, 'In this case, I am the only one who should sign this!' This said, he would have torn up the sheet with the signatures 'over Cucetti's humiliated and sad head.' That is why, still according to Lombille, Evita did not become a marquise. Things were awry in her past life. But Lombille's text leaves us with a question of why Pius XII, who was horrified by the sight of Evita's legs, would have destroyed the document from the mysterious prelates. And why would Cucetti, having successfully accomplished his mission, have sadly bowed his head?

Evita's oversleeping was not without its consequences. She arrived twenty minutes late. A tiny clergyman with a violet cape and small eyeglasses, Monsignor Bieniamino Nardoni, and a tall knight, all dressed in black, with a white gorget and a patch on his right eye, by the name of Prince Alessandro Ruspoli, were waiting for her in the San Damaso court, not revealing their impatience. Evita whispered, chuckling, to a member of her entourage, 'What's the patch for? Is it part of the uniform?' 'No,' he answered, not laughing. 'He's missing an eye.' 'Surely thanks to one of his spears,' she said pointing to the Swiss guard with her chin. 'No need to display them like that, if they don't even know how to use them.'

After a long walk through rooms and antechambers where other monsignors paid tribute to her, Evita found herself in the papal library, face to face with Pius XII.

That night, on the phone, she told Perón that Christ's Vicar's voice echoed 'as in a dream, faint and far away.' The Pope's portraits, which reveal an emaciated face, give no reason for anyone to believe that he had a warm voice. But how could one forget the balance he had to maintain between the Argentinean Catholics' indignant clamour and his own ties to the Nazi criminals who used the 'monastery route' to their Buenos Aires destination? Indeed this visit put him in a very compromising position. Christ's Vicar was stalling. Whether he was real or imaginary, the character of Cucetti humbly bowing his head when he achieved his goal gives us a faithful image.

What did Evita and the pope say to each other? Pius XII said a few words in Spanish to bless the visitor and her following. He murmured that he was closely following Perón's work, his 'favourite son' whom he considered a precious rampart against communism. He then offered a gold rosary to Evita, and the meeting was over. It had lasted twenty minutes, the same time devoted to queens. Benítez stressed this point to prove that the visit was neither a frustration nor a failure, as her critics claimed. But in *Historia del perónismo*, Hugo Gambini relates that Evita and Dodero had reached an agreement. If after the meeting Evita told him that everything had gone well, it meant that she would not be a marquise. If she said 'very well,' it meant that they had to donate

150,000 pesos. The answer was 'well,' and the donation was commensurate.

More troubling than the matter of her damaged ego is Jorge Camarasa's version, which is based on an article from *Izbor*, the magazine of Argentina's Croatian community. In this article, published in 1954, two years after Evita's death, the Croats wrote: 'We roamed all over Europe, visiting many countries, until the day our pain knocked on the door of the most noble heart that was beating in the whole world at that time, that of Eva Perón, when she was visiting Rome. . . . And it did not take long for the illustrious President of the Argentinean nation, Don Juan Domingo Perón, to open the doors of this blessed land to us.' In fact, Ante Pavelic, the Croatian Quisling, obtained a visa for Argentina on July 5, 1947, in Rome, ten days after Evita's meeting with the Pope. Armed with a passport from the International Red Cross, he arrived in Buenos Aires in September, in a priest's habit, using the name Aranjos Pal. Between 1941 and 1945, he had been responsible for the deaths of eight hundred thousand people in the concentration camps at Lobor, Jablanac, Mlaka, Brescica, Ustica, Stara Gradiska, Jastrebarsko, Gornja Rijeka, Koprivnica, Pag, and Senj.

To support this, Camarasa cites a dispatch from France-Presse, which was published in the newspaper *La Razón* in Buenos Aires on May 8, 1986. The American army's information service had not recommended arresting Pavelic, the ex-leader of the Croatian regime who was recognised by the Germans, due to his links to the Vatican (especially with Giovanni Battista Montini, the future Paul VI, and, as we have already seen, with Archbishop Draganovic, the heart of the Croatian network in Rome). It is thanks to these contacts that Pavelic was able to win over Argentina. However, Pavelic was at the top of the list of war criminals that the Allied forces had promised to extradite to Yugoslavia.

Why was the plural used in the *Izbor* article? Because Pavelic did not travel alone. The others who had knocked on Evita's heart's door were, among others, Vjekoslav Vrancic (decorated by Hitler for his participation in plans for a mass deportation), Petar Pejacevic, Ivan Herencic or Branko Benzón, all ex-dignitaries of the Reich. Benzón became Perón's doctor and the adviser for the Migrations Association, which was headed by Santiago Peralta, the anti-Semite who created obstacles for the Jews wishing to enter Argentina. These men, among others, collaborated with the *Alianza Libertadora Nacionalista* and the Perónist police, by advising them on methods of torture, in which they were very experienced and which the latter perfected.

Had Evita brought up the subject of the Croats during her meeting with the Pope as Camarasa suggests? It is hard to believe. She arrived in Rome at nightfall, and her meeting at the Vatican was early the next morning. But it is possible that she did meet with them at one point or another during her stay. The Croats' confirmations coincide with the date of the visas and of the trip. In Eva's defence, we can only cite her crass ignorance. In her role of kind fairy, she probably remembered only the gesture of her hand nonchalantly held out to some blue-eyed men who respectfully kissed it.

The day after her meeting with Pius XII, Evita received the great cross of Saint George the Great in Perón's name. Father Benítez assures us that she also received, in her own name, the habit of the tertiary Franciscan.

Later, during a press conference, she appealed to some, though not to others, when she announced she was against divorce. This was her warhorse (and Perón's before his tiff with the Church). But during a reception thrown by a feminist association, she reiterated her support of a woman's right to vote. 'My name,' she said, 'has become the rallying cry for women around the world. It is time for men and women to have equal rights.' The Argentinean press published daily dispatches about Eva's trip, including these words that, for Socialist women, caricatured a half century of political struggles.

If her hosts thought they were flattering her by offering her an *Aïda* under the stars in the Caracalla thermal baths, they were wrong. She arrived as late as she had to the Barcelona theatre. As her trip progressed, it became increasingly evident that she had no passion for artistic beauty. Besides fashion, there was no other show, exhibit, or diversion that moved her. She was travelling through an unknown world that did not evoke in her any literary memories, for she never turned away from her only obsession, social work. Her sole fascination was the orphanages. She closely examined these secular or religious institutions that were shown to her by request. When she returned, she said to Perón, 'Europe is old. The palaces are very beautiful . . . good places to build hospitals. And I saw what they do with the social aid . . . just enough so that I would not roll up my sleeves myself.'

It was hot in Rome, and she was already showing signs of fatigue. On June 28, after the visits to the orphanages and the screams at the *Aïda*, she became weak. Her doctor, Dr Alsina, advised her to end her tour, or at least to slow down its pace, but it was enough for her to hear these words, and Evita went against his orders. Accompanied by Count Sforza and, of course, by her entourage, she travelled to the North. She wanted to see the Argentinean booth at the Milan Fair. That evening, when she entered La Scala, the second act of *Orpheus* was ending. She was escorted to the royal box, where she enjoyed the show that much more since it was so short.

When she returned to Rome, she visited the Forum, the catacombs, and the museum of Villa Borghese. Once again she did not see the grace, the terror, or the nobility of the places she visited. It was as if she were blind. All she talked about was Perón. Eva could not spend her energy in amateurish raptures, as someone else with average ambition and culture would have. She needed to focus her energy. In an unexpected way, this trip was an initiation, as absurd as that might sound. Far from opening herself up to the world, she was enveloping herself tightly within her own ideas. Such an impoverishment was a sign of narrow-mindedness, but paradoxically also of greatness. To enrich oneself, from either a cultural or spiritual point of view, is not always desirable. Goethe understood this when he said, 'Genius resides in a conscious limitation.' The ignorant, haughty, resentful woman who ostentatiously exhibits jewels whose origins are suspect, rightly booed by anti-Facists, was trying to refine her talent, if not her genius: that of loving the poor, by putting herself in their shoes like no one else had ever done.

Her schedule included visits to Venice, Florence, and Naples. But on July 3, she met with De Gasperi. The Communist party was vehemently opposed to her presence in Italy. And the Democratic-Christian president admitted that he could not guarantee her safety.

The next day she received a telegram from her husband, asking her to pay a visit to James Dunn, the United States ambassador. Just like Christ's Vicar, Perón was stalling.

She agreed to one last day, July 5, to attend the canonisation of a Portuguese nun. The box of honour was to be occupied, rightfully so, by the princess of Braganza. But the Argentinean diplomat in charge said, with effectiveness rather than elegance, to his Italian counterparts, 'If you want wheat, make sure *la Signora* gets a seat in the box of honour.' Evita was seated in the top box, the princess in the bottom box, and Italy received its share of wheat.

Fatigue was the excuse used to cancel the rest of her Italian tour. On July 6, Evita went to Rapallo, where Alberto Dodero had a home, to rest. She visited Portofino, San Remo, and Genoa. The azure and green Riviera sparkled at her feet. She never sat in the sun, for her skin did not tolerate the sun's rays. But she went out and strolled, looking like a simple tourist who enjoyed shopping and passing the time.

SMOKE SCREEN

Perónism's adversaries have always said that Evita's trip was more of a smoke screen than a rainbow. Its true goal, they allege, was to deposit the fabulous fortune inherited from the Nazis in a Swiss bank. But it wasn't until July 14, 1972, that an Argentinean magazine, *Ultima Clave*, published a report regarding this charge. Its conclusions were never confirmed. We lay them out here only to open up an array of possibilities, and also because the article is based on a perplexing question that we readily share: why did Evita's itinerary become so frenzied after her stay at Rapallo?

On July 17, she returned to Rome in order to fly to Lisbon. Then it would be Paris, the French Riviera, Switzerland, and back to Lisbon to fly to Dakar where she would board a ship that would take her back to Argentina. It was an inexplicable zigzag. The explanation proposed by *Ultima Clave* is as follows. On June 10, in Rapallo, Evita was to have met Giovanni Maggio. A few days before, an Argentinean ship had anchored at Genoa. It was filled with ninety tons of wheat, a gift from Argentina to a famished Europe. The cargo was controlled by the members of the Argentinean Embassy. But, the article says, hidden within the blond grain was gold that was to be deposited in a Swiss bank account with Maggio's help. The objective of the Lisbon trip, as ill-timed as it was illogical, would have been to meet Italy's former King Umberto about the hidden treasure.

In fact, the meeting took place on July 20, at La Barraca, an inn located on the Portuguese beach of Guinco, about nine miles from Cascais. Besides the former monarch, his wife, Maria José, and two Italian generals, Graziani and Cassiani had lunch with her. The article does not say if a portion of the jewels were to have been deposited in Lisbon thanks to Umberto, or if the only objective of the luncheon was to effect, through her intermediary, the transfer to Switzerland. Finally, Evita would have reached an agreement with a few Swiss banks on August 7, 1947, in Bar-au-Lac. And, in fact, on that day she went to a reception thrown in her honour by two hundred bankers.

Umberto was not the only royal highness whom our disconcerting traveller met in Lisbon. Don Juan de Borbón also visited with her. An Argentinean diplomat had suggested that meeting with a pretender to the throne, who did not elicit Franco's empathy, could be misinterpreted, to which Eva allegedly responded with a shrug of the shoulders and the following, 'If the little fat guy is offended, tough luck.'

She stayed in the Portuguese capital for three days, arousing neither love nor hatred. The city was sleepy under the greyness imposed by António de Oliveira Salazar. She visited the 'Dining Rooms for the Joy of Working' (a Portuguese version of the Mussolinian 'after-work') in this gloomy atmosphere, then she flew off to Paris.

Previously, at Rapallo, a most confusing diplomatic game had developed in the shadows. The subject of the negotiations was Eva's trip to Great Britain, where the announcement of her visit had provoked a general outcry. The members of the Labour Party were against it; the right-wing moderates considered Argentina an important economic partner; and the uncompromising leftists considered the presence of a 'Fascist' in their country intolerable. Lord Strabolgi, a Socialist who had visited Argentina, had defended Evita, even calling her the 'South-American Eleanor Roosevelt.' This was an important parallel, for Mrs Roosevelt had been officially invited to England in 1942, and Evita wanted the same attention. As for the conservative bankers, they were more than happy to receive her.

The Foreign Office had finally announced that Evita was welcome. The London press published an entire programme of tributes, which was as long as it was contradictory. One day an official invitation by the queen was announced; the next day it was refuted. The Argentinean ambassador, Ricardo de

Labougle, went to Rapallo to convince Evita that she was not risking a snub. The queen would have tea with her. According to this version, Evita is to have said, 'If she is unable to officially invite me, I don't want to see her.' And when the ambassador insisted, she is said to have responded, 'If I said that I'm not going, then I am not going, and *basta!*' According to others, her prolonged stay at Rapallo would have pushed her date of arrival in London to August, at which time the queen would be on vacation.

Whatever the case, it was on July 17 that Evita decided on her departure for Lisbon. Why not see in this decision a simple noble, or even royal, whim? After all, a zigzag itinerary suited her. It is easy to imagine that Evita embarked on this insane expedition only to throw two kings into the queen's face. Although they were far from the throne, one Umberto of Italy and one Don Juan de Borbón were worth more than one Elizabeth of England.

But *Ultima Clave* offers yet another version. According to this article, Ricardo de Labougle would have been the diplomat in charge of glossing over the true meaning of the trip. These comings and goings, these explosions of a bruised ego had only one goal: to disorient the English bankers who were awaiting Evita's arrival, hopeful just like the Swiss, and for the same reasons.

Once again, *all* the explanations seem valid. The version of a plot to deposit the treasure in Switzerland does not exclude the psychological explanation. To reduce Evita's role to that of a simple instrument is one of the two typical attitudes that she aroused. Those who knew her and those who did not but spent much time studying her are divided into two groups. For the first group, she was used by Perón; for the second, she used him. It is probable that each used the other in his and her own way but that Evita surpassed the relationship of reciprocal utility by escaping the traps and the schemes through surprising detours. Indeed, if Perón's plan existed, she was the accomplice. Perón was even able to manipulate her from across the ocean, going as far as arousing some of her reactions. And yet, thanks to her insolent remarks and her bad moods, she had escaped from the heaviness of the Francoist machine. Likewise, she fled Perón's conspiracies by lending herself to them but also by evolving toward a mystical dimension of herself. Did she also escape him in the treasure affair? We'll come back to this.

PARIS'S NATIVES

Whatever the mystery of the trip, it certainly had an unexpected consequence: each European country reacted so differently that Eva's presence was a catalyst and a test. In France, the news of her arrival incited reactions that were halfway between gallantry and irony, with a pinch of indignation for good conscience.

France-Soir had published a photo of Eva seemingly naked under a fabric that she held close to her body. As we have already seen, the Bembergs had furnished the newspaper with this photo of Evita, for they considered the image damning. This was to ignore the fact that France rarely if ever scorns a half-naked woman. The Fascist's visit aroused protests from the French Communist Party, the CGT and other resistance associations. But, at the end of the day, everything transpired in a light mood. The people did not take the visit seriously.

As for the Bemberg family, their joke cost them dearly. These billionaires of German ancestry had built their fortune in Argentina in breweries. The father had died in Switzerland in the 1930s, and his descendants argued that they were exempt from paying taxes since this death took place out of the country. The trial lasted a long time, and in 1948, the Supreme Court ended up handing down a predictable verdict in favour of the state. That is when Congress, which was becoming increasingly obsequious with *la Señora*, decided that the ninety-seven million pesos paid by the Bembergs would be transferred to the Eva Perón Foundation. This was not surprising. In the photo in question, the woman draped with fabric that she holds with one hand on her breast and the other on her stomach does not look like an idiot. If the Bembergs had examined the photo more carefully, they would not have served it up to the press.

The chapter on Evita by Suzanne Bidault, wife of the Minister of Foreign Affairs, George Bidault, in her book *Je n'ai pas oublié* (I did not forget), wonderfully expresses the half-outraged, half-playful atmosphere with which the Parisians greeted her. Here is an example:

> In 1947, France needed Argentina or more precisely its wheat. That is why, despite the antipathy that the Perónist regime aroused, they had invited Evita. They had even decided to bestow upon her the Legion of Honour.
>
> A few days before her arrival, the Argentinean Ambassador came to see the Minister of Foreign Affairs to explain to him that he had better make the famous visitor an officer; and with his index finger, he traced a circle in the air, then rested it on the Minister's jacket: 'And pouf!' he said. 'You'll get more wheat!'
>
> The Minister courteously responded that Mrs Perón would have to settle for a ribbon of the Legion of Honour, which was a nice enough gesture in itself.

The beginning of Bidault's text seems even more delicious, for it expresses a feminine jealousy as well as a lack of information. 'Was Mrs Perón pretty? I would say yes. My husband does not agree but I think he's being difficult. It is true that there was something that spoiled her, something that the photos did not reveal: she had a completely wan face (was it leukaemia already?) under her dyed hair and she did nothing to change this because – she told me herself – her confessor allowed her to wear lipstick, but not blush!'

We can smile at these words, written many years later, since we know that on July 12, as Evita disembarked from the plane at Orly, George Bidault, who was waiting for her at the bottom of the steps, could not refrain from exclaiming, 'She's so young! So pretty!' As for the presumption of leukaemia, Bidault was only repeating the rumour that accompanied Evita's eventual illness and which her pallor seemed to justify.

Always worrying about the stage, she had waited a few minutes before making her entrance. She was dressed in white from head to toe. Only forty days had passed since she had come to Europe, and already an abyss separated this stylish woman from the tense one who arrived at Barajas Airport. It is also true that the same abyss separated the 'little fat' Spaniard from the worldly Frenchman with the twinkling eyes. But had she become as nonchalant as the photos in Paris suggest? Nothing is certain. She owed her new ease to a better tailor, and her stay in France would confine her to one of those nonspeaking roles that she was accustomed to from her theatre days. In Spain she was able to play the part of the spoiled child; in Italy, much less. Like every Argentine, she assumed she could speak Italian. Even though the effect was most often comical, conversations based on this confusion were possible. In France, she depended on either poor Lilian or the very anti-Perónist Argentinean ambassador's wife to communicate. She feared these interpreters with good reason.

The Argentinean ambassador, Julio Victorino Roca, was also waiting for her at the airport with other Latin American ambassadors. Forty cars escorted her to the Ritz hotel. A little girl gave her a bouquet of flowers. She stuck out her hand to Bidault for him to graze with his lips where, they say, Ante Pavelic had placed his. She thanked Vincent Auriol for his offer of De Gaulle's old car that Churchill used when he visited Paris. Then she went to her room to rest.

The next day, they threw a dinner for her at the Quai d'Orsay to celebrate the signing of a French-Argentinean commercial treaty. Argentina was extending a credit to France to buy wheat and beef, which was almost as important as the Franco-Perón protocol. The ceremony seemed to be traced on the currency of the lender, decorated with a sheaf of wheat on one side and a cow on the other. In fact, everything transpired within the limits of the most extreme hypocrisy, with a place for golden wheat and its reverse, spite. The European press had devoted much ink to Evita's lateness, both in Barcelona and in Rome. She had been warned that it was unacceptable to make the French wait. So she arrived 'amazingly on time,' according to Bidault. Seated next to Evita, the minister tried to sustain a conversation that the ambassador's wife 'did nothing to animate.' Quite the contrary. After a few efforts, Bidault heard the Argentinean woman wearily say to him, 'Don't tire yourself, that is enough!'

But Evita wanted to talk. If the conversation was flagging, it was not her fault, as Bidault suggests unfairly, 'Although she seemed eloquent with the *descamisados*, she had no gift for conversation. This can happen to famous orators.' Evita was simply not familiar with the Parisian tradition of 'flitting from one subject to another.' And since the ambassador's wife clearly abandoned her, Evita turned to Lilian to ask her to explain to the minister Mercante's achievements in the province of Buenos Aires. Lilian, who had enough flair to realise that it would not be appropriate to hurl propaganda on her hosts in the middle of dinner, took her time. Evita listened and insisted, turning red with anger and raising her voice, 'But Lilian, I am not hearing Mercante's name!'

After this uncomfortable dinner the guests were invited to the cabinet of ministers at the Luxembourg Palace. That is where the Legion of Honour was to be presented, under the eye of Rubens's *Marie de' Medici*, who seemed to be the only one looking upon the scene with goodwill. At this point,

Bidault's text abounds in acute visual observations describing the awkward moment that followed. 'Mrs Perón was wearing a mauve satin dress with no shoulder pads and, at the crucial moment, the assistants shot a maliciously curious look at the Minister: how was he going to get out of this? He would get out of it all right: the draped neckline had a few folds of fabric that he deftly pinched and thus pinned the cross in all decorum.'

On July 22, Evita was invited by President Vincent Auriol and his wife to a luncheon at the Rambouillet castle. It was a sweltering day, but she was nonetheless fresh in her pastel-coloured dress with a square neckline. Alas, besides her white capeline, she had placed a rose in her hair. In Barcelona, when speaking to the workers, and in Italy, during a stroll, she had already worn this useless rose, which neutralised the romantic effect of the wide-brimmed hat and gave her the look of a singer.

On her itinerary, Eva would not get out to stroll through the forest. Right after coffee, she was placed in a car with the two women who did not much care for her, Suzanne Bidault and Mrs Victorino Roca. A few minutes later, the three of them were wiping their wet faces. Dozens of cars were leaving the park at the same time, lifting a dull dust that entered the vehicles. The three sweaty Graces returned to the castle, their skin streaked reddish-brown.

The President and his wife were the only ones waiting for them. Mrs Auriol looked like Helena Rubinstein with her shiny and severe black chignon. She and her daughter-in-law forced themselves to find a topic of conversation, finally settling on fashion. Suzanne Bidault, the expert in jealousy, notes. 'The President, who spoke a little Spanish, bantered with the formidable Fascist, which did not seem to please his wife at all. When the guest left, she commented in an embittered tone on the bracelet Eva wore on her left wrist: I have obviously never seen anything like *that* before!'

The heat was an excellent pretext to skip a visit to the Louvre or any other museum. On the other hand, as usual she wanted to visit the poor neighbourhoods in order to hand out gifts. The next day Father Benítez had organised a visit to a school. Crates filled with sugar, lard, and ham had been prepared for her arrival. The children also waited for her, waving small Argentinean flags. But they waited in vain; there was no trace of Evita. The confessor telephoned her, but no one answered. He was desperate, so he took a taxi to the Ritz, and when he arrived, he grasped the extent of the disaster. That wretched Dodero had played another trick on him. Evita had wanted to see the designs of the famous designers, so the ambassador's wife had invited them to come to the Ritz. Dodero, who loved to satisfy Evita's slightest desire, had organized a fashion show. The most famous models from all the big fashion houses had already arrived and they were dressing in one of the ballrooms. Evita, who was thrilled, had forgotten about the school and the crates of ham. Benítez threw a fit, accusing Dodero of dragging Evita into his whims and Evita of letting herself fall prey to these whims. She sheepishly cancelled the fashion shows but she did not leave town without leaving her measurements at Christian Dior, who would become the creator of her most famous outfits.

With Suzanne Bidault, she visited another school in Sèvres, a Communist suburb at the time. Bidault remembers that Evita 'was clearly not very comfortable walking through the crowd, and probably due to her contradictory nature, she thought it appropriate to pronounce a sentence complimenting Hitler's regime. I understand Spanish, but I do not speak it, and I suffered cruelly by not being able to put her in her place as she deserved.'

To 'put her in her place,' they had her walk through the national Federation of Resistance Deportees, where, according to Fermín Chávez, she donated 100,000 francs. This organisation aided the victims of Auschwitz and Dachau. Thus, in one fell swoop, Eva found herself face to face with a reality about which she knew nothing. If she had heard about the Jews in her living room, it had no doubt been abstractly, most often from the point of view that the Nazis were the ones who were persecuted. In Argentina in 1947, only the victims knew. For all others, Europe was far away. And Perón was not concerned with the fate of the Jews. Thus it was here in Paris that Eva found out. They showed her the photos. She had never seen children like this, not even in the Flores shantytown. Did these images serve as a warning? Little did she know that five years after her visit, she would resemble the febrile skeletons that she was now seeing with her own eyes.

On July 24, the Argentinean Embassy threw a reception at the Ritz. As usual, Suzanne Bidault was there. 'Seated on a couch next to her, the chubby Edward Herriot was courting her: he spoke Italian, she Spanish, and they seemed to understand each other quite well.' In fact there is a photo of the couch and the friendly encounter. The writer and politician, rather overweight in fact, and no longer young, is looking at Evita with a sensuality that pervades his only eye we can see, his protruding lips, and his hairy hands. To his right, Evita looks as though she just stepped out of the Dior boutique. She is wearing white, no hat, her hair pulled back. She is perfect. She is animatedly speaking (about Mercante, perhaps?), playing with her ring, a usual gesture for her. Herriot was a heavy, dark mass, a bit animalistic with ignited instincts; she, a radiant beauty.

But her radiance did not come from her skin. Ambassador Areilza's description comes to mind: 'Eva was a disconcerting person, photogenic but not beautiful, with quite a spectacular, arrogant air, but sickly and with no sex appeal. I think,' he adds, 'that deadly sins exclude one another. An excess of avarice excludes an excess of gluttony, just as an excess of wrath excludes an excess of lust. She was devoured by the passion for power, and that left no room for anything else.'

The climax of the visit was the reception held in her honour at the Latin American House. Evita's dresses reveal everything about her, her fears as well as her audacity. That night, her gold lamé dress was staggering. Did she represent a Roman empress? The queen of Sheba? Salome? No, it is Cleopatra. Eva's Egyptian queen silhouette appeared sculpted by the diagonal folds of a form-fitting skirt, prolonged by a train that opened up like a fan. The dress was sleeveless and strapless, very tight around the waist and clearly held up by whalebone, and it was decorated by an embroidered bustier that pushed up her breasts – much more than her balled up socks had as a teenager. Her necklace, three heavy bracelets, long earrings, and gold sandals with heels encrusted with stones conjured up Rome or the Nile.

It was impossible to underestimate the effect this produced. If Evita, as happens with most baroque spirits, did not know when enough was enough, someone in her entourage should have persuaded her not to wear, on top of all this, a gold veil over her hair. Just like the rose to the right of the capeline, this veil was an old obsession. Paco Jamandreu had already succeeded in saving her from this odd ornament once, when she was getting ready to go to a gala at the Colón theatre. He was not afraid of her and had made a mean comment about the veil that she had then torn off her head, enraged, at the same time ruining the pile of hair her loyal hairdresser had styled. However, Eva would not have tolerated this honesty from the ambassador's wife or from Lilian. So she was rigged out in a ridiculous crown of stars or fairy wings. Only the gesture mattered, which meant: 'I am fashion.'

During this evening, Román Lombille observed her attitude closely. 'Eva, who was usually talkative, nervous, worried, always moving, remained hieratic throughout the full two hours of the reception.' Evita was frozen as if in a dream, because she was enjoying her own unique pleasure in dominating. To dress this absurdly was to exert power, a sensation that was intensified by a tradition of protocol requiring the wives of the

Latin American ambassadors who had just greeted her to bow, then back up three steps.

The journalists subjected her to their regular firing squad. Their questions woke her up, tearing her away from her dream. It was the first time that Evita answered irony with irony and that she admitted her lack of culture with perfect ease. Her favourite author? Plutarch. Had she read any of his works? Of course not, nor did she intend to. Her favourite music? The shortest.

After the reception, Dodero invited the group to the Pré Catelan, in the Bois de Boulogne. Eva's gold created a sensation. Customers went as far as to climb onto their tables so as not to miss the slightest detail. She smiled, still 'hieratic.'

Behind the scenes, there was someone whose influence on Eva was growing every day. He was the anticabaret, anti-fashion show, anti-Dodero Benítez. Throughout the trip, the passionate former Jesuit, converted to an ardent populist, was becoming Evita's conscience. His fanaticism joined that of the beautiful sinner, and no doubt also fuelled it. Perón appreciated Benítez, who gave him suggestions on wooing the Church. Yet, after Evita's death, the priest never saw him again. Why? Answering this question can help us better understand Evita's passion (in the religious sense of the word). Benítez never forgave Perón for the moral decadence he displayed in the fifties and the frigidity that he showed toward his dying wife.

The high point of Eva's stay in Paris was her visit to Notre-Dame, which was well planned by Father Benítez. It took place the evening after the luncheon at the Rambouillet castle.

Dressed in white, Evita arrived at Notre-Dame escorted by mounted soldiers with helmets and decked out in plumes. She arrived before her entourage and walked down the middle aisle. After having listened to the words of Monsignor Vaussart who welcomed her, she went, without hesitation, to kneel at the Virgin's altar. A few Argentines who witnessed this scene were dumbfounded and asked themselves how she could have found the altar in question without even having consulted the others, not even with a glance. An unexpected occurrence visibly moved her. Someone had dusted off the Notre-Dame organ, which had been abandoned long ago due to the war, and now the old cathedral resonated with the chords of the Argentinean national anthem. Evita bowed her head, dignified and gracious, as if to hide her tears. Among the assistants, a chubby prelate exclaimed in Italian: '*E tornata l'Imperatrice Eugenia di Montijo!*' (Empress Eugenie has returned). It was Monsignor Angelo Roncalli, papal nuncio and future Pope John XXIII.

Father Benítez was the only one to recall the meeting between Evita and Roncalli, which according to him was decisive. The meeting was long enough for these two people who were so different to come to understand each other. Like Evita, Roncalli came from humble origins, the son of peasants. At the Vatican, he did not overwhelm anyone with his brainpower. On the contrary, his roughness and his candour set tongues wagging.

Benítez said that this was the reason he was in Paris. Bidault had presented the Vatican with a long list of religious collaborators, asking that they be thrown out. The Pope, no doubt, did not appreciate this request. And his revenge had a name: Roncalli. When it came time to replace the nuncio in Paris, he picked this obscure archbishop who was finishing his duties in Alexandria and who was considered the last of the archbishops. At first, the rustic prelate was surprised by his selection, but he soon understood that it was a sign of the fiercest disdain to name a being as countrified as he to a post in a city as spirited as Paris. But as we know, history followed its own course. Without knowing it, a man with a beneficial intelligence was discovered, and the last of the archbishops would be the warmest of all popes.

Eva and Roncalli talked about charity projects, which Evita insisted on calling social aid, if not justice. She explained her ideas in detail. She thought constantly of the foundation that she would establish on her return. And Roncalli gave her two pieces of advice that she was to follow word for word. The first: do not burden yourself with official paperwork but preserve the flexibility of a nonbureaucratic organisation. The second, and more important: devote yourself without limits. He understood Eva's soul and advised her to go only as far as she could in herself, no matter what.

On the last day, Evita visited Versailles, which had been closed since the war started and was opened in her honour. She also wanted to see the grave of Napoleon, whom she admired very much, for Perón considered him one of his role models. Was not Perónism defined as a kind of Bonapartism? (She also admired Marie Antoinette, and she said so to Bidault, but she was careful to support her statement with reasons and, most of all, to recall her childhood memories.)

Finally, her visit had the unexpected consequence of changing the name of a metro station from 'Obligado' to 'Argentina.' A good student, Evita had pointed out to Vincent Auriol that the battle of Obligado had not been a French victory, as the French believed it to be, but an Argentinean one. Pierre Miquel can explain this in his history of the Parisian metro. 'This station is the only one with the name of a friendly country. There is no Brazil, United States or Great Britain station. Why Argentina? Argentina Street, from which the station takes its name, was originally called *rue de la Pelouse de l'Etoile* to evoke the country motif of the field located west of the Arc de Triomphe. It was given another name in 1868, Obligado. It is at Obligado on November 20, 1845, that a French-British squadron had deployed the marines to ensure access to the Río de la Plata during the Rosas dictatorship whose columns bloodied the Pampas and which, as was said in London, recruited its partisans by thrashing them even in the streets of Buenos Aires. The tyrant was denounced for he tried to close the country off from European interests: the victory of Obligado fully satisfied the City's financiers. Argentinean commerce was henceforth fully open to English and French companies. Finally, they could export to Argentina the kilometres of new barbed wire that would allow breeders to obtain better yields, and protect the cereal producers. In 1945, France was hungry: cargoes of wheat and beef were immediately requested to meet the needs of the French government. Paris recognised this and decided to devote a street to Argentina, without looking too closely at the new dictator who had taken over the country: Juan Domingo Perón. Later, the Argentinean government would take care of the decoration of the Argentina station. A special privilege.'

This text omits the rest of the story. On June 16, 1848, France lifted the embargo on the port of Buenos Aires. The Second Republic did not wish to remain in conflict with Argentina. And on August 31, 1850, Rear Admiral Le Prédour signed a peace treaty similar to the one that England had just reached, in which it accepted Rosas's demands. The two European powers withdrew their troops from the Río de la Plata, recognised Argentina's sovereignty over the interior rivers, and returned the island of Martin García that they had occupied in the meantime.

Miquel's text also avoids any reference to Evita. Yet she is the one who assimilitated the nationalist indoctrination that was necessary to remind Auriol that in 1848, at Vuelta de Obligado, France had not won the war but only a battle. In fact, the nationalists were not wrong on this point. A war handed over by colonialist powers in order to install their barbed wire inspires little sympathy. But that did present the opposition from being right, since Rosas was a dictator. Maybe France's attitude – in 1947, torn between a very relative famine and the temptation to give in to the Argentinean dictator, one hundred years after having given in to another – perfectly reflects partial reasons that become the truth once they are joined together.

Evita was in Monte Carlo, where the frivolous Dodero had taken her, when a ship anchored in Brest exploded, destroying part of the city. She sent a telegram and a check for 500,000 francs to Bidault for the victims. And before she left France, she added 200,000 francs for Paris's 'poor.'

After receiving the gold medal from the Principality of Monaco, she took the train to Geneva. It was August 3. The Argentinean ambassador, Benito Llambí had obtained an official invitation from the Swiss government.

TOMATOES AND MYSTERY

She strolled around for five days, five days that were among the most mysterious of her existence. Besides Geneva, her tour included Neuchâtel, Bern, Zürich, and St Moritz. In Bern, a young Swiss who had lived in Argentina threw rocks at her car, breaking the windshield and injuring the driver. Eva remained impassive. Farther on, in the same town, a more burlesque attempt occurred. Tomatoes were thrown at her. She again escaped without injury. However, Max Petitpierre, the Minister of Foreign Affairs, was seated next to her. This solemn man was drenched in red juice. The appalled members of the entourage ran up to them, but Eva kept her *Imperatrice Eugenia* mask. 'When you represent a State,' she said, 'you cannot be scared.'

Every newspaper in the world spoke of the tomatoes, the rock, and Max Petitpierre. Was there anything else? Yes, pure conjecture.

The first set of rumours has its roots in the bank accounts Evita opened. But the stories that relate this seemed too structured. How can one erect such perfect constructions on a base of unconfirmed reports? Nevertheless, the facts reported are numerous and important.

Glenn I. Infield, an American historian and a specialist in the Nazi era, prefers the confirmation of doubt. His theory relies on documents that, until now have remained unpublished, found in the National Archives in Washington, D.C., the

CIA, the FBI, Berlin, the Defense Intelligence Agency, the U.S. State Department, the Bureau for Military Security, and the Information Centre of Berlin. In his book about Otto Skorzeny – the leader of Hitler's commandos who became famous after freeing Mussolini in 1943 and whom he met face to face – he says the following: 'It is Rudolf Ludwig Freude . . . who first spoke to Evita about the money transferred to Argentina by the Third Reich. Freude handled the funds once they arrived in Argentina and oversaw the deposit at the Banco Aleman, with Heinrich Dörge, to double-check his task. . . . With her husband's complicity, she was able to convince Freude and Dörge that it would be safer to put the treasure in her name while they waited for Bormann's arrival.'

Time passed, and Bormann presumably still had not arrived in Buenos Aires. 'So Perón named himself administrator-guardian of foreign goods, with the forethought of appropriating these funds through confiscation in time. As for Evita, she persuaded Dörge and Freude, who considered themselves the true trustees of Bormann's confidence, to forget the whole thing!'

That is when Skorzeny showed up. He arrived in Argentina in 1948, having escaped from prison with the Americans' blessing. But he knew about the treasure's existence and had worried about it from his jail cell: 'Her [Evita's] trip to Europe bothered me. Was there a link with the part of our money that she was handling?' he said to Infield, who detected in this worry a confirmation of the reality of Bornmann's gold mine.

Once in Buenos Aires, it did not take long for Skorzeny to win over Perón, who admired him as Mussolini's liberator. The rest of Skorzeny's story becomes fantastic. He insists that he was Evita's lover. Even discounting this as wishful thinking, the fact remains that he played an important part in the Perónist regime as an instructor of the Argentinean police, just like the Croatian Ante Pavelic. And in July 1949, he thwarted an assassination attempt against Evita.

'Be that as it may,' Infield continues, 'from early 1950 . . . Evita and Juan Perón had returned to Skorzeny approximately one quarter of the funds sent by Bormann.'

When Evita died in 1952, Juan Duarte would have become the only keeper of the secret of the Swiss bank accounts. The unfortunate Juancito who was weakened by the death of his protectress and was being tracked down by Perón (and, according to Infield, by Skorzeny), obediently went to Switzerland, where 'he signed documents that gave Perón access to Evita's money and jewels, which were being kept in a Zurich bank's safety deposit box, as well as all the other Swiss bank accounts that had been opened in her name. This was to sign his own death wish.' We'll come back to this death, which occurred on April 9, 1953. On that date, four other people who were linked to this circumstance were no longer in this world: Heinrich Dörge, whose body was found in a Buenos Aires street in 1949; Ricardo von Leute, killed in 1950; Ricardo Staudt, also killed in 1950; and Ludwig Freude, found in 1952 in his home in front of a poisoned cup of coffee.

But why presage these events if we are still in Switzerland in 1947? For a very simple reason. The five mysterious days that Evita spent in Switzerland can be illuminated in the glow of these facts. Even if we decided to ignore *Ultima Clave's* supposed revelations about the ship anchored in the port of Genoa, Commander Giovanni Maggio, and King Umberto of Italy, the fact remains that Juan Duarte's last trip to Switzerland and the suicide or murder that would follow sounded an alarm. This signal was clearly heard by the Argentinean people, who always linked the two events with an intuitive finesse that historians sometimes lack.

The second network of conjecture refers to Evita's health in 1947. The rumours were vague, a feeling or an impression. Some had already sensed her illness. Thus, Raúl Salinas maintains that she experienced the first symptoms during her trip. The diagnosis albeit imprecise, had already been given, and her personal doctor, Dr Alsina, 'did not let go of her for a minute due to the injections she needed.' 'Morphine,' Lombille confirms. It is true that at the time, morphine was generously prescribed. Ana Macri, one of the pillars of the future feminist Perónist party, also confirms this: 'Before she left on her trip, Evita wanted to work. When she returned, it was not a want, it was a fever. It is certain that, already, she knew her days were numbered.'

That is all we know. We will later examine the games of hide-and-seek that Evita and Perón would resort to in order to hide what they 'knew.' Therefore, we can only attribute an intuition to this trip. But this intuition should not be neglected, for it is useful in understanding the dizzying change that Evita experienced in Europe. Once again it is useful to listen to the vox populi. The Argentinean people always pondered the reason for such a transformation. To frequent the world's great people (who, by the way, except for Roncalli, had only bored her and whom she mocked) and to have Dior as your tailor – these things could change a woman. But not to such an extent. There was something more. A light, a different aura. Father Benítez was beginning to play a major role in Eva's life. Would the priest have had a similar hold on a healthy young woman who had nothing but time?

THE RED CARPET

On August 10, she put the finishing touches on her zigzag trip by flying to Lisbon and then to Dakar. There she boarded the *Buenos Aires*, a ship that belonged to Dodero's company, on which six hundred immigrants were headed to Argentina. However, she did not accompany them to the promised land; she disembarked at Recife to fly to Rio de Janeiro. The Inter-American Conference for peace and security of the continent was taking place in the Brazilian capital. The Argentinean delegation was presided by Atilio Bramuglia, whom Evita hated so much that she had forbidden his name to appear in her newspaper, *Democracia*. But as a woman of the world, she knew how to hide this, and the two were able harmoniously to share tributes and banquets and even sit together for the conference's plenary meeting. George Marshall made a speech, and the Brazilian chancellor Raul Fernandes made a toast to Evita, who smiled under her veil flecked with velvet. After all, she had been the alternative to the Marshall Plan in Europe, especially in Spain. In Brazil, they knew this. The walls in Rio were covered with giant photographs of Evita with captions that read: 'To the Brazilian woman who fights, just like the Argentine, next to her people for a future of justice, of work and of peace.' Soon enough, however, swastikas appeared on these posters with '*Nacista*' written over her smile.

These infamous symbols were not the only sour note in Rio. In the wings, Lilian struck another. Among the Argentinean authorities who came to greet Evita was Ricardo Guardo. Raúl Salinas, a close friend of the dentist, relates that when Lilian saw her husband, she finally exploded in tears. She accused Evita of having tormented her throughout the horrible trip. Once she started, she could not be stopped. She went as far as to accuse Evita of having flirted with her husband. The peace conference in Rio marked the beginning of the war between Evita and Guardo, who ardently defended his wife. Later, when she arrived in Buenos Aires, Evita noticed Raúl Salinas in the crowd and made him climb into the car and sit between her and Perón. During the trip, she had spoken to her husband on the phone every night, but she was now seeing him for the first time in three months. Still, this was not the time for love but for rage. 'You have a friend who is a traitor,' she said to Salinas. 'Guardo.'

It was still August 21, and the traveller was welcomed by the Uruguayan authorities in Montevideo, the city she had visited with her acting troupe. This time, the posters in the streets no longer read *The innocents*. Now they proclaimed, 'To the Uruguayan woman.' Following was a message similar to the one addressed to the Brazilian woman. Evita lunched with President Luis Batlle Berres (in Brazil, she had met with Enrico Gaspar Dutra, his Brazilian counterpart). Then she boarded the *Ciudad de Montevideo* to cross the Río de la Plata.

On Saturday, August 23, at 4 P.M., the ship dropped anchor in the port of Buenos Aires. A red carpet was stretched out from the dock all the way to Customs. Perón, Doña Juana, the three sisters, and all the members of the administration were waiting for her on an improvised stage. The crowd was tremendous. All these people had read about Evita's success day after day. They felt like the parents of a young girl who had brilliantly passed an exam. Joy and pride filled their chests. Eva waved from the ship's bridge. She hurried to disembark even before they finished installing the gangplank. She was so impatient that she went the wrong way and had to turn around and come back to hug Perón.

She then spoke. Everything about her had changed, except for her words. She shelled them as usual: 'love,' '*corazón*,' 'message of peace.' Always reiteration, her enchanting power, and they listened to her reverently. And she was so haloed by the religious prestige of having 'triumphed in Europe' – the Argentinean dream – that they probably barely paid attention to her essential words, which she spoke in a voice muffled by her tears: 'On Monday, I will be among you again, ready to work.' They did not yet understand that from now on only her mission mattered.

During her trip, she had become exquisite. None of the ladies could even pretend to equal her. Her perfect elegance was not limited by the glamour of her clothing; it pervaded her entire self. A woman from her entourage observed that Evita no longer twisted the heels of her shoes, as if by completing the oligarchy's ritual she had finally found her balance. Aside from a few tomatoes, Europe had welcomed her like no other, not even

Victoria Ocampo. She was certainly flattered, but the hypocrisy and the pomp had made her laugh. Her ego had been gratified. Her resentment no longer had a reason to exist. It was time for her to roll up her sleeves and move on to serious things.

Her true history started on Monday, August 25, 1947, when she went back to work at the *Secretaría*. Until now, she had only practised her role. Now the curtain was up.

Part Three

Chapter 7

❖

FOUNDER

At the end of 1947, Evita made her choice. The chignon on the nape, which was already familiar, became the only hairstyle for her. According to some, Evita was inspired by an Argentinean lady, Hortensia Ruiz González de Fernández Anchorena, whom she met in Paris. But Pedro Alcaraz swore that he was the sole inventor of the chignon. He claims to have created it so that Evita, who left for the office early in the morning, would have perfectly combed hair until the evening, 'thanks to a hairpiece and a few hairpins.' Whatever the case may be, the chignon, woven like two intertwined hands, would go beyond fashion or practicality and transform itself into a symbol of the new Eva – and of the new regime.

Starting now, the characteristics of one woman and those of the other would stand out very dramatically and would accentuate the parallels between woman and the political system. The first would so incarnate the second that in order to observe Perónism, it was enough to look at Eva. In the period starting in 1948 and ending shortly before her death in 1952, authoritarianism would go hand in hand with her severe hairstyle. For Eva, it would mean to grasp the country in her fist. That is why she would wear an imitation fist on the nape of her neck.

When Evita was motivated by will power, everything she did disappeared without a trace. When inspired by love, there were no visible imprints, but a liberated energy floated around her memory, an opposite image to the severe chignon. Was it dangerous if the leftist Perónist youth, who ran with the torch in the 1970s, loved the only photo that depicted their *Pasionaria* with hair flowing over her shoulders? Their romantic vision of Perónism prevented them from seeing the hard image of the captured hair, so youth chose the free and flamboyant image of Evita that suited its needs. Once again, Eva incarnated an ideal. We find Evita frozen in two unique roles: that which is represented by the chignon, and that which, lacking a better option, we will call 'loose hair' – or love.

This runs the risk of imitating Perón when he ignored entire stages of life, describing Evita as if he had always known her to be blonde. However, the choice to do this is justified by one obvious fact: after Eva returned from Europe, the way she dressed, her behaviour, even her work did not change. Her life was suddenly split in two: before Europe and after. It seems that, all of a sudden, she inaugurated the 1950s through fashion. There were no more shoulder pads or square necklines. Instead there were rounded shoulders, cinched waists with flounces around the hips, and 'mermaid' skirts. Suddenly, Evita was sure of herself. Although her voice was hoarse, and her illness was leaving its mark on her face, she repeated over and over again the words that her mother once did: 'I do not have the time to stop' and 'I've started a race against time.' Time was rushing her, and she in turn was compressing time. Yet – and this is the contradiction – it was a revolutionary time, a time when she would repeatedly say, 'Now. Right away. We are trying to live a revolution.'

One month after her return she gave a memorable speech from the balcony of the *Casa Rosada*. In a still shrill and nervous voice, the voice of a doe hunted by the crowd, she read the following words: 'The nation's government has just handed to me the bill that grants us our civil rights. I am receiving it before you, certain that I am accepting this on behalf of all Argentinean women, and I can feel my hands tremble with joy as they grasp the laurel proclaiming victory. My sisters, I hold in my hands a few paragraphs that outline a long history of struggles, setbacks, and hope.' It was September 23, 1947, and she was presenting law 13010, which granted women the right to vote, to an enthusiastic crowd called by the CGT.

The certainty of acting on behalf of all Argentinean women that she claimed she felt was not believable. Eva never spoke exclusively to women, and she could not have been unaware of the other outraged women's reactions, especially those of the Socialist women. Besides, it was not certain that she knew the details of the 'long history of struggles' she mentioned. This was a history that dated back to September 1900, when Cecilia Grierson, the first female doctor in Argentina, founded the Women's Council after having discovered that the law prevented her from practicing her profession.

That same year, the Feminist Center was founded and was presided over by Elvira Rawson de Dellepiane. Did the names of Julieta Lanteri, Carmela Horne de Burmeister, Alicia Moreau de Justo, Luisa Berrondo, the sisters Tcherkoff, women who had fought, during different stages, for a woman's right to vote, mean anything to Eva? Did she know that the last bill presented by this group had been approved by Susana Larguía and Victoria Ocampo in 1938? It is possible that she did not. Besides, Eva was not at the heart of this law; she was in the heart of Perónism. In fact, in 1945, Farrell's government had announced it when Perón was vice president. The journalist Eduardo Colom insists that he was the instigator of this bill. Perón would be the first beneficiary, for, thanks to the women, he would win 60 percent of the vote during the elections.

Aloé was an old friend of Perón's and would be appointed

governor of the Province of Buenos Aires in 1952. This rough and docile man (the ideal Perónist) would find himself at the head of a gigantic journalistic empire named Alea SA. The name was a Latinism dear to Perón, who imposed the teaching of this classic language in the schools. *Alea jacta est:* the cards are on the table. Besides the Haynes group, Evita had ended up buying *La Razón, Noticias Gráficas*, the legendary *Crítica* to which the best Argentinean writers contributed, and more. They built a modern and imposing tower to shelter the one hundred dailies, weeklies, magazines, propaganda brochures, etc., published by Alea. Finally, *La Vanguardia, Argentina libre*, and many others were shut down by the government, under pretexts that were as preposterous as they were efficient, such as the fact that the bathrooms were out of order. As for the magazine *Qué sucedió en siete días*, it was shut down for having published a photo of Libertad Lamarque on the cover. The journalist Ambrosio Vecino told us that Quijano had given permission to reestablish the publication but that Evita had given the death blow.

Perhaps this is another trap, a way of using women, his and others. Or maybe it was he who fell into his woman's trap, a formidable trap born of absolute sincerity. Evita's feminism, although it is contradicted by her words, was visceral. But the rest of the story will show that in the race for power, the cheating of one and the honesty of the other went hand in hand.

The CGT, which had organised the assembly, had changed dramatically since the glorious October 17. In February 1947, Luis Gay, its secretary – and the union leader for the telephone workers, was replaced by Aurelio Hernández. Gay had dared to invite to Argentina a group of American, Mexican, and Italian unionists with whom Hernández wanted nothing to do. (This man who was close to anarchism had met Tito at a time when the Yugoslav lived in a Buenos Aires boarding house, and, later, he visited him in Belgrade.) Directly defying Perón's ban, Gay had received the union leaders, not suspecting that the hotel ballroom where the meeting took place had been bugged with microphones on the President's orders. The next day, he was summoned by Perón who simply said to him, 'Resign or I will smash your face in.'

Hernández was on the job for only one year. In 1948, José Espejo became the secretary of the CGT and remained so until Evita's death in 1952. Espejo was successful because he didn't make waves. With unions and other organisations, Perón was looking for men who reflected him. The same goes for Evita. Until then, her relations with the CGT had been distant. But with Espejo, she finally had a flattering CGT at her disposal, a CGT that reassured her by telling her that she was the 'fairest one of all.' And Espejo would increasingly become her magic mirror as well as Perón's.

TORTURE

On September 20, 1948, the noose was tightening on Cipriano Reyes. The government denounced a plot to assassinate Perón and Evita. Reyes and John Griffiths, the former cultural attaché to the American Embassy who had been transferred to Montevideo for having declared that Martin Bormann lived in Buenos Aires with the President's blessing, were among the twenty-one accused. Except for the American, who was not in the area, everyone was incarcerated. There was no trial. Reyes remained in prison until the fall of Perónism in 1955.

This episode was told by Walter Beveraggi Allende, who was exiled to Montevideo and tortured like the others. On September 13, Reyes was visited by two men who claimed to be air force officers. The first, Walter Pereyra, was indeed an air force officer, although he introduced himself under a fake name. The second was none other than Commissioner Salomón Wasserman. This was doubly confusing because as a Jew, he had not only succeeded in joining the police but also was working as a torturer. During a second meeting at the home of García Velloso, a notary who was a member of the Labour party, Wasserman and Pereyra revealed a 'revolutionary plan' to overthrow Perón. Before giving their consent, the members of the Labour party requested a meeting with the leaders of the movement. And Brigadier Francisco J. Vélez set up a meeting at the Organisation of Civil Aeronautics.

It was a setup. Reyes's group was taken to the special section of the federal police, where the leader, another Cipriano – the famous executioner Cipriano Lombilla – submitted their sensitive body parts to electric torture. Fifteen days later, Reyes was still suffering from monstrous inflammation of the genitals. Since Reyes himself neither confirmed nor denied this, Perónists took advantage and denied the entire affair.

It is hard to know for sure whose account is accurate. Long before Reyes' imprisonment, he had complained of having been attacked and hit on the head by a gang of Perónists. He would show up for the congressional meetings with his head bandaged as if he were a mummy. 'Wrong,' says Congress's former barber, Tito Di Ciano. 'That's completely wrong, I had just shaved Cipriano Reyes. I took off his bandages and there was nothing: not even one scratch. After that, he put the bandages back on and continued to play the victim.'

Beveraggi's story is so clear that we must attribute Reyes's silence to an understandable masculine pride, the same macho pride that made his jailers take photographs of the inmate next to a toilet. What did these torturers want to find out during their interrogations punctuated by electric shocks? They constantly referred to John Griffiths, whom they wished to implicate in the same scenario even though the prisoners denied ever having met him. However, when Perón announced the 'conspiracy' on the radio, neither the torturers nor Perón bothered with specifics. They accused the supposed conspirators as much of wanting to prevent the constitutional reform as of the opposite. Coherence was not important, but castigating was. There was no doubt that getting rid of Reyes while taking revenge on the most irritating American diplomat was a masterstroke.

During the colonial period, Argentina had known the Inquisition and its tortures only from afar. Lima was the capital of the important butchers. Buenos Aires, an uninteresting city due to its lack of gold and silver mines, had the right only to the torture rack. After its independence, the Assembly of 1813, which had banned bullfights, also abolished torture. The method was once again used in 1930 under Uriburu's regime and then in 1945 by Perón's police. Other torturers, such as Cardoso, Amoresano, Solveyra Casares, Simón Etchart, and Nievas Malaver (assisted by his dog, Tom), certainly deserved their fame under Perónism.

Yet they were not craftsmen. They barely knew how to simulate an execution, to prick someone with a long needle, to surround a member with a wet towel in order to strangle it little by little, to stick a wedge under one's nail, and, of course, to apply the electric prods, an Argentinean invention according to an old police manual published in France. As compared to the methods used by the Triple A (*Alianza Argentina Anticomunista*), created by López Rega beginning in 1974, and by the military dictatorship that followed, these modest attempts inspired nothing but pity. In fact, certain people shrug their shoulders when they bring up the tortures used by early Perónism. It is true that in 1977 the torturers from the Navy Mechanics School were picking up their task right at the point where their predecessors had left off: using electric prods.

There is other shoulder shrugging that is perplexing. When policemen's zeal exceeds their orders, some say simply, 'There are slipups in every regime.' Then why is it that there are no accusations of police going beyond their orders under the radical governments of Illía in the 1960s or Alfonsín in the 1980s? Besides, would it have been possible to exceed orders in a system of power such as Perónism, which monitored every individual under a magnifying glass? It was, in fact, one of Evita's roles to 'keep abreast of everything' in order to then tell Perón.

However, to control an entire country, with a husband who was a genius at deception, was not an easy task. The following anecdote, related by Raúl Salinas, clarifies this matter further. Perón had just 'discovered' Cipriano Reyes's conspiracy. He had called a meeting at the *Casa Rosada* to decide the next steps. But he seemed to hesitate. The 'herbivorous lion,' as he called himself, was not clearly displaying his intent to punish the 'plotters' as they deserved. Evita would not stand for this weakness. She ardently insisted that the 'assassins' receive an exemplary punishment, which, in her black and white point of view, was completely normal. But seeing that Perón was still hesitant, or pretending to be, she got carried away. She called him a coward, grabbed his general's cap off his head, and threw it out the window.

Impassive, the Argentinean President asked his aide to go downstairs and pick up his cap from the courtyard. We already know what punishment he inflicted on the Reyes group, but by acting this way, Evita was perhaps giving the impression that she honestly believed in the attempt against her life. It is possible that once again Perón created a scenario to excite Eva's indignation, to provoke her to the point at which she was white-hot mad and vociferously demanded what he was in fact willing to do but pretended not to be.

Once she reached this boiling point of anger she was capable of cruelty. The fanaticism, the sectarianism she admitted to and even claimed, allows us to suppose as much. And, in fact, an unsubstantiated but instant rumour accused Evita of having personally given the order to torture the employees of the Telephone Company. The sociologist Juan José Sebreli is certain of it. But, all the witnesses who were consulted, Perónists or not, unanimously admitted their ignorance on this subject, adding that most of the torture episodes occurred after Evita's death.

That is not the case for the aforementioned employees, who were imprisoned and tortured during her lifetime. Yet in *Los torturadores*, a very convincing summary of torture testimony, published in 1956, Raúl Lamas does not mention Evita. He does, however, refer to two of her cronies: Espejo and Nicolini.

The Telephone Company had been nationalised in 1949. Forty three employees refused to adhere to the Perónist party. Nicolini declared that they were breaking the law, and Cipriano Lombilla ordered a raid of their meeting place in order to plant incriminating documents. Irene Rodríguez, Nieves Boschi de Blanco, Dora Fernández, Paulina Manasaro, Segunda Gil, Luci Vial, and Raquel Soto, among others, were submitted to electric shocks in the vagina. One of them was pregnant and lost her child.

ASPHYXIA

The noose was tightening around the press at this time too. The day after the Revolution of 1943, the new military government had showed its colours by attacking the Socialist newspaper *La Vanguardia*, the Communist newspaper *La Hora*, various provincial newspapers, and *Crítica*, the Botana family's popular daily, whose director, Raúl Damonte Taborda, was forced to seek self-imposed exile in Montevideo. Still, the big newspapers remained independent. Some time later, the journalist Eduardo Colom presented to Perón a proposal to support his candidacy in the pages of his newspaper *La Epoca*. In order to do this, he requested a substantial subsidy. Perón did not need anyone to remind him of the press's role, so he accepted. In 1944, he had already appointed Muñoz Azpiri as Director of Propaganda under the administration's information subsecretary. Two other experts in this field, Oscar Lomuto and Roberto Pettinato, worked with him. Argentina had access only to the services of the United Press International and the Associated Press, but a project was born around the same time: the creation of an Argentinean information agency with the monopoly of radio information. This agency did not last, but during its existence it supported many nationalist newspapers (*Bandera argentina, El Pampero, Crisol*), Francoist (*Dario español*), and Nazi (*Deutsche La Plata Zeitung*), by providing them with free information.

According to the American historian Robert Potash, the Post Office, run by Nicolini, suspended the distribution of the anti-Perónist newspapers during the electoral campaign. Perón tried unsuccessfully to corrupt Yankelevich in order to transform Radio Belgrano into the official station of his movement. *La Prensa* and *La Vanguardia* rivalled each other in imagination during this campaign, by calling Perón 'the creator of the *candombe*' (the dance of Rosas Black partisans) or 'the auto-candidate apprentice statesman.' But after his electoral triumph, Perón pressured Farrell, who would be president for four more months, and made him sign a decree by which the surplus of paper used for newspapers became the property of the information subsecretary. The paper shortage was real, and Perón used it to strangle his adversaries' newspapers.

He did not stop at print media. In May 1946 he ordered various radio stations to program the state's radio news for the 8:35 P.M. bulletin. The radio broadcasts – it was written on the wall – had to 'abstain from all criticism.' The journalists who did not comply were subjected to trials and public contempt. Other intellectuals were chastised with humour. Borges, for example, employed by a municipal library, was named inspector of poultry in the Buenos Aires markets. He did not take this job and remained unemployed for Perónism's entire run. But in 1953, after an anti-Perónist demonstration, Victoria Ocampo was sent to prison with prostitutes.

In the meantime, *La Prensa* and the government continued to wrestle for power. Perón advised the workers not to buy the oligarch newspaper. But another unsuspected fight was taking place in the shadows, at the heart of Perónism, between Eduardo Colom and Evita. Here we follow Pablo Sirvén in *Perón y los medios de comunicación* (Perón and communication methods).

Colom wanted to expand his journalistic ventures by buying *La Razón*, an evening paper that was not for sale. He had contacted the director of the National Economic Council, Miguel Miranda, a Spanish industrial who had launched a sort of economic miracle before being disgraced. Evita liked to repeat that, when she needed money for her foundation, Miranda had only to tap a foot to get it. But Miranda was not interested in *La Razón*. He had just bought *Democracia* for Evita with Alberto Dodero and Orlando Maroglio. Eva was excited by the success of her newspaper, so she thought she would buy *La Epoca* from Colom, who refused such a transaction.

So she attended to another matter. Haynes Publishers was a very powerful group that published about ten newspapers and magazines, including *El Hogar*, the one in which Perón had published the first photo of Evita in an evening gown to shock the well-to-do ladies. In fact, the government bought 51 percent of the group's shares. Eva chose the editor, Major Carlos Vicente Aloé, nicknamed 'the Horse' by the opposition.

Simultaneously, a commission was created to investigate 'anti-Argentina activities.' It no longer had anything to do with investigating Argentinean Nazism, as the former commission headed by Raúl Damonte Taborda and Enrique Dickman had done, but rather imposed it. It was presided over by the former conservative José Emilio Visca and the attorney Rodolfo Decker, who was close to Mercante. The two men threw themselves into a campaign of intimidation. They disrupted and threatened editorial newsrooms. Visca went so far as to ban two books that he found in the Communist publishing house Lautaro. One must admit that the titles – *Existentialism*, by Henri Lefebvre, and most of all, *Treaty of Learned Ignorance*, by Nicolas de Cuse – certainly aroused his suspicion. Sixty provincial newspapers were made to disappear in 1950 for having inscribed under the title, *Year of the Liberator General San Martín*. The editor of *El Intransigente*, which was also shut down, was in prison, as were the socialist leaders Alfredo Palacios, Carlos Sánchez Viamonte, and Nicolás Repetto. The Socialist leader Américo Ghioldi had to leave the country. It is not surprising that in 1949, Eduardo Colom was also visited by Aloé and the very Evitist deputy Héctor Cámpora, who had come to buy *La Epoca*. This time, Colom understood the message and sold his newspaper for a mouthful of bread and left the scene.

History ends on an inevitable closure, that of *La Prensa*. Alberto Gainza Paz's newspaper, founded by his ancestors in 1869, had seen its pages reduced by half due to the 'paper shortage.' But the final excuse was neither his bold articles against the regime nor Visca's commission. It was Napoleon Sollazo, the leader of the newspaper vendors' union, who finished him off in 1951 by declaring that his union 'boys' could no longer distribute 'traitorous pages.' Gainza Paz was exiled and his newspaper expropriated. When they heard the news, many European and American journalists wore black arm bands as a sign of mourning.

The Perónist version of *La Prensa* came out on November 19, 1951. The editor was the gleaming secretary of the CGT, José Espejo. This issue of the converted newspaper was full of photos of Perón and Evita. The President's wife wrote, 'I hope the anti-nation party's infamy which for a long time preached injustice and the exploitation of the people will be replaced by the workers' preaching, inspired by Perónist doctrine.'

But that's not all. On the day Evita left for Europe, Radio Belgrano broadcast a speech by Perón, while the listeners heard a voice say, 'Don't listen to a word, these are all lies.' Somebody had intercepted the radiowaves, and the station was punished. It was closed, then bought out by Evita, who was nice enough to appoint Yankelevich as its director. He had just returned from the United States and was speaking about the wonders of television, when Evita, already very ill, cut him off and said, 'OK, I understand. Then televise the next demonstration on October 17.' And that is how Argentina became the second country on the American continent to have television.

A GOEBBELS FOLLOWER

In January 1947, the journalist Raúl Apold, an old acquaintance of Perón and Evita's, was named the information subsecretary's director of broadcasting. Muñoz Azpiri's star had stopped shining. 'I made a mistake,' he confessed, 'by rejecting an idea that someone had suggested. He wanted to create lapel pins bearing the effigy of the General. I refused in light of the psychological factors: I did not think they would be accepted because of Argentinean idiosyncrasies. The next day, Eva called me: "Are you crazy? What? You turned down a man who offered you such a great vehicle of propaganda? Perón is furious with you."'

Eleven hundred people worked with Apold. One of their fundamental tasks was to glorify Evita's activities at the Eva Perón Foundation. Besides, according to Raúl Salinas, the inventor of the name Eva Perón was none other than Apold. When Evita had left for Europe, her name was still Doña María Eva Duarte de Perón. But from the moment she came home, she agreed with Apold's idea and used only the shorter name. It was brief and pleasing to the ear, and it replaced the slowness of a traditional wife's name just as the chignon had replaced the curls. And yet, in Argentina, to abandon one's maiden name for the husband's name was not uncommon. Usually the 'de' was added. Thus the married woman became the husband's property, but a woman did not drop her father's name, and no one would refer to her using only her husband's name. We do not know Evita's reaction to losing the name Duarte, which had cost her so dearly to obtain, but we can suspect that she was not happy about it. In *My Mission in Life*, she establishes a very neat distinction between Eva Perón and Evita. Eva Perón was nothing but a social role of the President's wife, with which she did not identify. Then who was she? Evita, as the people called her, and which no other social class had the right to use. Evita, perhaps lessened by the diminutive, but exalted by the tenderness it implied. Evita, short and simple, without her father's, her mother's, or her husband's name.

Apold was always accused by the opposition of having mounted a propaganda machine akin to that of Goebbels. In fact, after the fall of Perónism, a study detailing the structure of the Ministry of Public Information and Propaganda of the Third Reich was found in his safe. He moulded Evita's image by presenting it with features of a good fairy in the films where the actor Pedro Maratea played the role of a poor worker suddenly overwhelmed by a revelation: Eva existed! Other times it was the actress Fanny Navarro, Juan Duarte's friend, who would go into ecstasies at the sight of the Lady of Hope shining with all her fires. Apold created thousands of ashtrays, handkerchiefs, brooches, matchboxes, and agendas imprinted with the 'royal' couple's profiles. The inventor of the slogan 'Perón accomplishes, Evita dignifies' inscribed in capital letters on giant posters was also Apold. Same with the children's game where the object is to crush the anti-Perónists.

Furthermore, the information subsecretary owned a division of Special Affairs that kept tabs on all the opposition's activity, as well as the Perónists'. Writers and teachers were among the files of this division. Apold centralised the allocation of tax-exempt cars to artists, journalists, judges, writers, and others who would show their appreciation to the regime. It was rumoured that the comedian Luis Sandrini owned five Mercedes Benzes and that General von der Becke received five per month. This was accomplished through the Ministry of Industry and Commerce. The businessman Jorge Antonio, who was very friendly with Juan Duarte and was involved with the Nazi treasure, was there for a reason. Evita, informed of the Mercedes Benz import business had called Antonio to get him involved in this type of activity.

Apold would play an even more important role after Eva's death. But for now it is enough to perfect the portrait of this man whom all the old Perónists describe as base. When Eva died, Apold phoned Anne-Marie Heinrich. She had known him as a teenager, when he was the commissioner of the Colón theatre, and she had no reason to be suspicious. 'We need all the photos of Evita that you have taken over the years, since the beginning of her career for we want to use them in a book about her,' he said. Anne-Marie Heinrich gave them all to him except one, which she never showed to anyone out of 'respect, and due to professional conscience': a photograph of sixteen-year-old Eva, pale and brunette, wearing a bathing suit. A few days later, the police arrived. They threatened to destroy Heinrich's files if she did not hand over the negatives for the photos. The photographer was left without a trace of her work on Eva that had chronicled all the years. The photos of Evita taken by Heinrich appeared in *Life* and *Paris-Match*, sold by Apold to add to his fortunes.

THE HUMILIATING MATÉ

The noose was also tightening around the radio, theatre, and film actors as well as around the singers, musicians, and dancers. They feared being blacklisted. Perónism had established the 'live number,' a sketch or musical interlude at the movie theatre right before the movie, to give the actors work. Perón had also decreed that in each concert or musical broadcast, 50 percent of the music had to be Argentinean. This was enough to make most of them toe the line. Eva hastened the unfortunate toward unemployment by the *no corre*, a veto that did not need an explanation.

One had to praise Perón on the radio for five minutes. The tango singer Tita Merello did not hesitate, but those who refused received telephone threats or lost their jobs. All the actors were obliged to wear a pin bearing Eva's image on their lapel, manufactured, it goes without saying, by Apold. Many, such as the singer Hugo del Carril and the tango lyricist Enrique Santos Discépolo, sincerely supported the regime. The majority, however, accepted it resignedly or openly took advantage of the situation. Perón himself had confided in Eduardo Colom, with a weariness coupled with victory (thus, his vision of humanity was confirmed): 'They only come to see me either to fink on someone or to pitch a proposition.'

In Junín, and to a lesser degree, Evita's mother played on the double-edged sword of fear and greed. A Junín resident relayed that in front of Doña Juana, the line of beggars prepared to do anything to please her got increasingly longer as the days went by. Forgetting that she had once scorned her, a doctor's wife had also come to ask for a favour. After listening to her, Doña Juana said, 'Pour a maté for me.' And so the doctor's wife immediately took a kettle and a gourd, poured the water over the herbs, and held out the maté to her hostess, once, twice, ten times until the satisfied matron stopped her with a wave of the hand. To understand the extent of this humiliation, bear in mind that to drink maté with two or more was convivial, but to serve it while standing and not sipping any – and Doña Juana knew this from experience – was the place of a chinita.

The women's vote had been approved by Congress. To celebrate, the new CGT had gathered its members in front of the Casa Rosada. There had to be a sign that everyone understood: the deliberations of the deputies and senators became a masquerade. Later, other dictatorships would dissolve Congress, but Perón did not deign to do so. He had defined his regime as a 'dictatorship of votes.' Having the majority in both houses, he could let the opposing legislators go hoarse with envy. And when they bothered him too much, as was the case in 1948 with the radical deputy Ernesto Sammartino, he simply rescinded their parliamentary immunity. Thrown out of Congress, Sammartino took revenge by making a famous speech in which he said, 'We are not here to reverently bow for the whip or to dance jigs to amuse Mrs Pompadour.'

Héctor J. Cámpora had succeeded Guardo as president of the House of Deputies. Like his predecessor, he was a dentist. He became the archetype of Perónist subservience and was especially Evitist. His peers said that when Evita asked him, 'What time is it?' Cámpora responded, 'Whatever time you want it to be.' In 1973, he would be Argentina's President for one month, before Perón came back to replace him. And he would surprise everyone with a geniality and a leftism that awarded him the nickname 'uncle,' the darling of the Perónist youth and Perón's warriors. But in 1948 and the years that followed, Cámpora was the most obsequious person in the regime, and that is saying a lot.

His wife, Georgina Acevedo de Cámpora, had replaced Lilian Lagomarsino symmetrically, just as her husband had replaced Guardo. From now on, Evita would show up at demonstrations with Georgina, nicknamed Néné. Isabel Ernst had also left the scene, and with the same symmetry her replacement was none other than Elena Caporeale de Mercante, wife of Domingo Mercante. Legitimate wife against mistress. According to Evita's new moral code, she was the winner with this change. But Elena did not limit herself to her role of wife. The wife of the governor of the province of Buenos Aires was ready to act in her province as Evita was in the entire country.

As for the courts, it is enough to relate this story told by Mike Gallaher, an air force officer who became a member of the Argentinean information services, to understand the degree of 'independence' with which the institution operated. The story goes back to 1948 or 1949. The High Court was presided over by Dr Casares. Eva came to the court to attend the inauguration of the judicial year. She took a seat with the ministers, when Casares softly intervened and sent her over to sit next to her spouse. Furious, Evita called Gache Pirán, the Minister of Justice, and said, 'Say, dear little Gache: that little President of the Court, over there, fire him right away! I don't ever want to see him here again!' The very embarrassed minister tried to smile and was able to stutter, 'Oh Madam! You're so funny!' A year later, Casares was out of a job.

In fact, Román Subiza, a great friend of Juancito Duarte, who had become Secretary of Political Affairs, had received a signed memo on which Perón had written the following by hand: 'For the enemy, not even justice.' According to Juan José Sebreli, a Perónist judge had declared during a trial what the *Revolución Libertadora* had done to him: 'I was not a judge, but a puppet who obeyed Subiza's orders.' And when in 1946, Perón had dusted off the old laws in order to dismiss four judges, among the four new members of the Supreme Court was Justo Alvarez Rodríguez, Evita's brother-in-law.

All justice seemed to have disappeared. Yet Perónism had erased the differences between legitimate and illegitimate children! Until now, the word 'illegitimate' showed up on the birth certificate. According to the journalist Enrique Oliva, when Evita found out that Cardinal Caggiano had mixed feelings on the subject, she blurted, 'One of two choices: we do as I say, or we write on the father's documents: "Illegitimate father."'

ENDLESS LOVE

The opposition maintained that Evita did the bad very well and the good very badly. It has already been shown that Evita did the bad very well. In fact, she also did the good well. Time was rushing Evita when she returned from Europe. Maybe that is why she understood others' urgency. The simple notion that the famished cannot wait tends to be ignored by those with full stomachs who cogitate economic plans in light of a radiant future. Evita remembered this haste and continued to live day by day just as she had in her bohemian days. She lived only in the present, as gypsies do. In fact, what Perón called the typically feminine 'small solution,' was also an immediate solution.

From the moment she arrived at the Unzué palace, Evita had begun to receive letters, from a child in the north who wanted a soccer ball or an old lady who wanted a mattress. For the most part, they wanted food or clothing. The surprising thing was the modesty of their desires and their concreteness. The dreams of the poor were not abstract. Eva could recognise this. As distraught as she felt in the midst of the hundreds of dresses, hats, and shoes, she knew what she wanted, just as in *La pródiga*. Now she wanted to provide the most generous abundance to the people who asked for so little.

To do this, she had accumulated a power that only Perón could contest. But for the time being, he was safe. By acting in his name, and by proclaiming increasingly louder that Perón was everything and that she was nothing, Evita was doing him a favour.

She began to amass a multitude of things in an unused garage of the presidential residence: shoes, sugar, pots, pants, flour . . . one runs the risk of what Borges called 'committing an enumeration.' Yet from here on, Evita's biography becomes enumerative. Evita's foundation provokes not only admiration but also a certain anguish, which surely reflects its founder.

When night fell and her husband went to bed, she would go down to the garage to classify and pack the objects that she would later distribute herself (10,000 boxes here, 9,000 there, 5,000,000 presents for Christmas 1947) during her trips to the provinces or the capital's suburbs. Atilio Renzi, the administrator of the residence, along with other employees would help her. Every night, Evita would summon them to this secret place that she had jokingly called 'store of delights,' which evokes *A Thousand and One Nights*. In fact, she lived her nocturnal adventures with such wonder and such passion that her hands trembled while packing the boxes with sugar just as the hands of the forty thieves handled the gold in the caverns.

This had its inception before the trip, when the lost souls came to knock on the door of the residence. It was *Democracia* that spread this news, and soon the union workers began giving Evita gifts, objects they made themselves, and these quickly filled up the 'store.' These activities were called social aid Crusades (or Works) of 'María Eva Duarte de Perón.' In September 1946, a decree proposed by Ramón Cereijo, the Minister of Economics, opened a special account at the Central Bank to which all the ministers had to contribute 'with a goal to obtain clothing, shoes, food, medicine' for the underprivileged.

The Eva Perón Foundation as it existed and functioned until the fall of Perónism in 1955 was officially established only on July 8, 1949. Before this, and simultaneous with Evita's activity in her post at the *Secretaría* and her Ali Baba cavern, Méndez San Martín, the man who had put an end to the Charitable Society, had reorganised the orphanages and the hospitals that depended on this association. And Teresa Adelina Fiora, a nurse, had in June 1948 founded the School of Nursing, baptised as usual, 'María Eva Duarte de Perón.' This school comprised a team of 858 nurses capable of replacing the doctors, of driving a jeep alone in the most rugged conditions, but also of parading, each October 17, behind the army's soldiers: the blue uniform, embroidered with the profile and the name of someone we know, the jodhpurs, the cinched jacket, and the proud and radiant expression that corresponded to that type of parade, whether they were Fascists or Soviets. The school changed names in 1950, when it was integrated into the foundation and was called '7 de Mayo,' Evita's birthday.

But the Eva Perón Foundation kept its fetishist name, as

well as its primary function – to accumulate things. And it became a 'store of delights' of enormous proportions, with fourteen thousand workers and assets reaching two hundred million dollars.

One thousand schools and eighteen school-homes were built in the provinces. The students, around three thousand, came from families who lived in adobe ranches and slept on the floor. Evita personally took care of each case and decided if the child had to spend the night at the school-home or go home. In Córdoba and Mendoza, she built student housing. But her two biggest passions were the student housing in Buenos Aires, which occupied five blocks, and the Amanda Allen Children's City, inaugurated on July 14, 1949. Allen was a nurse from the foundation who died in a plane accident as she was returning to Argentina after having brought her institution's aid to earthquake victims in Ecuador. When she learned this news, Evita, whom the grateful Ecuadorians had just named 'Citizen of the Americas,' had a fit of tears, the most violent of her life according to her sister Erminda.

A small city for the two-to seven-year-old children who lived there, the Children's City seemed to materialise from the memory of the huts built in a garden of Los Toldos. Eva was offering other poor children real houses. No one had done this before her, not for the poor, not for the rich. In this city, the little people could finally feel as if they lived in a world fit to size, with red tiles, white walls, and a few stones or bricks to accentuate the rustic aspects, a style halfway between Spanish and the ballet *Giselle* (green wood shutters with little hearts carved out). This was 'Evitist' architecture. If Perón had monoblocks built, Evita preferred the fashionable chalets. The city included a miniature bank, pharmacies, bakeries, a chapel, minipools, a school, a circus, and a large dining hall. Just as in every home inaugurated by Evita, the attention to detail implied a kind of perfectionism that bordered on obsession. (Mercante's son described her as red with anger, leaving the bathroom at the

CGT, screaming at the unionists, 'How is it possible that there are no small embroidered linen hand towels here? They must absolutely be here!') So in the Children's City, the windows had curtains with asymmetrical tiebacks; adorable little beds, little tables, little plates, little glasses; pretty frescoes depicting enchanted castles, elephants, clowns.

And the children! The little boys had slicked back hair with a perfectly straight part. The little girls wore white muslin dresses and short black hair parted in the middle with shiny and neat bangs. These little girls with their square haircuts and their immaculate dresses that seemed to have been washed by Doña Juana were multiplied images of those in Los Toldos.

'They're extras,' the regime's adversaries said. 'This Children's City is just decoration to impress visitors.' And it is true that in the propaganda photos, ordered by Apold, the children seemed 'symbolic,' as if they did not actually live there. This excess of cleanliness, of correction, expressed a popular taste. The more humble the origins, the more one aspires to the dark suit and tie and the white dress. In Latin American shantytowns, the mothers always dress their daughters in Sunday's best white muslin. The fairy tale requires a gathered skirt, a sash around the waist with a big bow in the back, a small round collar, and puffy sleeves.

The recollection of Lunazzi, a militant anarchist and pedagogic consultant at a toy factory, shows the extent to which Eva was interested in the details and the fierceness of her independence. Knowing that Evita would come to select a large quantity of toys, he created an educational game that focused on the *Libertador* San Martín (Perón had devoted this year to the national hero, to the point of disgusting those who had nothing against him in principle). Evita examined the toys one by one and picked out the most beautiful ones according to traditional criteria: dolls, balls, tricycles. As for the patriotic game, she did not even look at it.

These children, as many others, discovered the sea and the

mountains thanks to Evita. Besides the summer camps created in Ezeiza, near Buenos Aires, she had 'tourism units' built in Chapadmalal (not far from Mar del Plata), Uspallata (Mendoza), and Embalse Río Tercero (Córdoba). Each one of these units included a group of hotels that could lodge three to four thousand people – workers, retired folk, students, campers.

To wear real shoes was a dream as lofty as seeing the sea. And the 'Evita' soccer championships gave them the opportunity to exchange their espadrilles (or simply the crust of mud on the soles of their feet) for street shoes or white sneakers. One hundred thousand children signed up to participate in 1949, more than double in 1953. They came from every province. They were dressed for the trip to Buenos Aires and offered sports equipment, and the doctors and social workers took this opportunity to check their health and their living conditions. The games took place in the large soccer stadiums in Buenos Aires, accompanied by much publicity. And the little champions collected more than just scholarships, mopeds, or summers at the beach. They went home with the memory of Evita's smile as she signalled the kickoff for the finals and with a medal, gold of course, on which Evita's indelible smile was imprinted. Perónism was a profusion of medals, the sign of the alliance. All one needed to do was put one's hand around one's neck to find the proof that it had not been a dream. And if doubt still persisted, there were Evita's name and profile embroidered on the team's jersey.

Of course, it didn't take the championships for the foundation to look for health problems. Dr Ricardo Finochietto was Evita's medical assistant. In Buenos Aires alone, the foundation built four clinics. Similar hospital structures were opened in nine other provinces. In Catamarca and Termas de Reyes in the northwest and in Ramos Mejía (on the outskirts of Buenos Aires,) pediatric clinics were built. All twelve hospitals were very different from the old standard French hospital model. Eva got rid of the sinister barracklike rooms, and the brown or khaki walls. For Evita, to put more than three patients in one room was inconceivable. These hospitals were modern, luminous, had excellent equipment imported from the United States and wellpaid doctors, and were decorated with marble. Most important, care at these hospitals was free, including the medicine for the patients who came in to be examined.

In 1951, Mrs President Perón clinic chartered a sanitary train that travelled throughout Argentina offering its radiology and analysis services for free. In fact, the aid sent to Ecuador was not the exception. Evita sent clothing, medicine, and food to Peru, Colombia, Israel, Turkey, and any country on earth where other *descamisados* were in need due to a natural or provoked disaster.

The declaration of rights for seniors was solemnly proclaimed by the Minister of Labour in August 1948. And in July 1950, at the Colón theatre, Evita broke into tears when she handed out the first thousand pensions to senior citizens who were also crying. This was a typical Perónist ceremony where a wet eye was appropriate. Evita had just had an appendectomy, where her cancer was discovered. But if she was already thinking about the old age she would never see, her tears transcended her. Eva cried selflessly.

As much for the declaration of rights as for the granting of the pensions, Evita made speeches, invoking Perón using the vocative case, as one uses with God, and exalting Perón's immense love for grandfathers and grandmothers. This prompted the following words by American journalist Philip Hamburger: 'In Argentina everything is about love, love, love. (. . .) Constantly, crazily, passionately, nationally Perón and Evita are in love.' Certainly the regime's aim was to arouse emotion. The sentimental ritual crowned the pension for old age or the prize won by a little athletic champion with an even brighter halo. Still, the old gauchos who had come from the ends of the pampas where they had resigned themselves to die in oblivion, did not ask when receiving these unexpected pesos if it was really Perón who had a heavy heart when thinking about their suffering.

Whether Perón loved them or not, the seniors could spend the rest of their days in four shiny new homes. The one at Burzaco, near Buenos Aires, stretched over eighty acres and housed two hundred people. Its ambiance was so joyful and warm that Evita dreamed of a day when, maybe, she too could live there. Separately, she had issued a very painful blow to the oligarchy, the expropriation of the Pereyra Iraola's *estancia*. The landowners had held on to considerable land, as Perón had not kept his promise of agrarian reform. But this particular *estancia* was a symbol. Its hundred-year-old trees had been planted for happiness, and Evita transformed this paradise into a park for the seniors and opened it to all.

Other temporary homes were created to house unemployed and homeless women. According to Father Benítez, the luxurious atmosphere that reigned in these homes astonished Duchess Edmée de La Rochefoucauld, the latest in a long line of French philanthropists, who had come to visit the homes with Eva. She commented, 'When the rich think of the impoverished, they think of impoverished desires.' She added that she did not intend to act this way and, on the contrary, would give them all their own part of the dream.

One woman's stories especially moved her. This woman was a maid who had been kicked out of the home where she had worked all her life. The day she arrived at one of the foundation's homes, she had wanted to sleep on the floor and even roll up the carpet so as not to ruin it. How could she soil the satin (if not muslin) bedspread and the lace-embroidered sheets with her maid's body? In the end, she accepted the fundamental idea that Evita violently hammered into the heads of the humiliated and downtrodden: she *deserved* that bed. 'You have to understand,' the woman said to the duchess who was becoming more moved by the moment, 'this is my mistress' bed. This is the type of bed I always made for others. And all of a sudden I'm the one sleeping in it! Me! Do you understand what that means?' The duchess said, softly, 'I understand.'

Now, the maids had a union. The timid and silent provincial women with the slanted eyes had always hated their biased mistresses, but now they could look them straight in the eye, hands on their hips, and quote the new laws and request their Christmas bonuses and their paid vacations. The house mistresses preferred not to hire the vengeful 'shameless girls from the union.' This vengefulness was fuelled by Eva who, in a speech, had said more or less the following: 'Your duty is to come to the Plaza de Mayo on May 1. Ask your boss for permission. She will tell you that there is laundry to be washed. Wash it. Ask her permission again. She will remind you that a skirt must be ironed. Do it. Ask a third time. If she uses another excuse, open the refrigerator, take a can of beer, and hit her on the head with it.' Indeed, she had confessed to her collaborator Rosa Calviño de Gómez, 'There are some oligarchs who make me want to bite them just as one crunches into a carrot or a radish.'

However much she loved the home for women, Evita's darling was the Home for the Workers, on Avenida de Mayo. It accommodated five hundred young women who had come to work in the capital. Every floor had been decorated according to Evita's very precise directions: the first floor, in a provincial style, which was very fashionable at the time; the second floor, in an English style; the third, in a Louis XV style, and so on. 'The living room,' said a visitor quoted by Mary Main, 'could have passed for one of the rooms in the *Casa Rosada*. It was illuminated by many crystal chandeliers; on the Edwardian style piano there was an exquisitely embroidered mantilla, a museum piece which had been given to Evita during her trip to Spain; the Louis XV chairs were covered with a very pale brocade; there were figurines from Dresden on the shelves and tables, and in the corners, big vases from Sèvres. At each end, two oil paintings took up the entire wall: portraits of Eva and Perón.'

The former deputy, Angel Miel Asquía, said that Evita had come to inspect the barely finished work in the home when she noticed that the curtain in one of the rooms was slightly tilted. Before her assistants could stop her, she climbed up on a chair and fixed it herself. 'There,' she said triumphantly, 'the hem is not crooked anymore.' Intuition pushed Evita to respect the feelings of the humiliated in their most subtle forms. She was concerned about offending them with a mere awkward word or gesture. She was an expert in humiliations and knew the difference between a good or bad gift. If life had taught her something, it was to give well.

Father Benítez described Evita's unannounced inspections of the various homes. She would arrive in the middle of the night, to see if the children were peacefully sleeping; during meals, to inspect the menus and to seize the opportunity to count the supplies. Was there enough oil? Sugar? Dishwashing powder? And where was the chubby kid who usually sat right there? Does he have a cold? She went to his room to cuddle with him.

Her lists of supplies were endless. Her courtesan poets often called her the 'universal mother.' The foundation had opened a chain of discount stores in all the country's cities, but there were a few who remained isolated When one could not enjoy a vacation in Chapadmalal, or live in a temporary home, or get treatment in a marble clinic, or pay the cheap prices of the foundation's stores, simply because one had not reached the level of a worker or a peasant, then one wrote to Evita to request a meeting.

DEEP LOVE

On average, she received twelve thousand letters a day. Every single one was read and filed by a team of social assistants chosen by Evita because of their experience in suffering. To understand these letters and to not laugh at them one had to know pain. The assistants could have been in charge of responding to each letter and sending care packages or trucks with the requested items, but this was not the case, at least not exclusively. It was Eva's hand that had to give out the money, her ear that had to listen, her face that had to give faith in the existence of beauty. On the day one would start to despair for no letter had been received from the Lady of Hope, the letter would finally arrive, with the date and time of the meeting. If a little girl decided to add her own request for a doll to her mother's request for a sewing machine, then the request was almost always granted. The doorbell would ring, and there would be Evita, a dream doll with gold curly hair. Smiling, enjoying being there as an apparition.

Her days started around 7 A.M. Perón had already left (rain or shine, he rose at 5:30) when Evita received her first visitors. She would jump from her bed into a plain sky blue robe. Her pyjamas and her slippers were not luxurious either. Evita dressed only with a theatrical objective, and there was no need for any of that at home. At home, even when surrounded by people, she was uninterested in herself, as if her body did not belong to her, as if she were but an image of purity. The poet Héctor Villanueva recalled that one October 17, she was among ministers at the *Casa Rosada*, dressed and coiffed to appear on the balcony in front of one million people, but she wore plush slippers. The crowd could not see her bottom half, which represented the housewife with swollen feet. Her top half, the one the people saw, was Evita.

So her early morning visitors saw Evita, natural, just out of bed, before she put on her makeup. While she spoke with her exhausted group of important ministers, Pedro Alcaraz was undoing the small night braids before he styled Eva's chignon, a new one every day. Sara Gatti, the manicurist, would polish her nails and paint them fire-engine red. Irma Cabrera, the maid, would suggest the outfit for the day. Evita allowed herself to feel an instant of pleasure when she climbed into her bath. Her breakfast consisted of two gulps of *maté*. Once she was dressed, she took a tiny mirror from her purse, and, standing, in front of her guests, she applied a touch of red to her lips. No powder on her nose. Nothing on her eyes, which shone with candour, with malice, with anger, or with joy. A drop of perfume behind her ear, and she was ready to go or to have her interviews at the residence where a delegation of workers, whom she had woken up after the ministers, took turns bringing in a dress just arrived from Paris. This caused extraordinary scenes where workers who were supposed to demand a raise ended up guffawing, giving their fashion advice with a popular common sense close to Perón's, who, one day, when she was trying on a feathered Dior cape, said, 'But you look like an ostrich!'

In any case, these workers had confidence in Evita, for they always received more than they asked for. Under this regime, one had to ask for what one wanted. It was a duty as well as a right. But it was a right that, according to the opposition, excluded others. During one debate at the Senate, about a bill to levy taxes due to the foundation, the radical deputy Dávila had complained that the people shouldn't be dependent on the whim of someone who could change her mind or die. Their well-being should be required by law. He also voiced concern that any taxes be levied fairly, not only on the opposition.

Now there is a rosary of pious wishes targeting an Argentina better than the real one, an Argentina of rights, not of favours. An Argentina of truth, not of myth. Lilia Reta, a Socialist, clearly expressed her love for the ideal, that is rational, 'condition': 'Argentina's popular myths disgust me. The one about the legendary mother who dies in a faraway and dry land, under a lead sun, but whose body shades her child, while her milk continues to flow from her breasts to nourish him.'

Eva the perishable, the passenger, was, however, alive and well on that morning in 1948, 49, or 50 as she went to the *Secretaría*, where the crowd of a real Argentina awaited her. The old ladies who had come from the countryside, and who had waited for her since dawn had eyes to see. The ideal Argentina, blinded by hatred, still had not seen anything. They saw her get thinner and paler, and they asked themselves why every once in a while she would get up from her chair, put one knee on the chair, and double over. 'It looks like she's in pain,' they would say. 'It looks like she is killing herself over her work.' And then they would whisper, falling into a dream, a wish of a nature altogether different from the deputy's: 'Let's hope she can nourish us for a long time, and even after that.'

The *Secretaría* already carried the smell of the people who had come from afar when Evita arrived. It was an odour of poverty, which is not always a dirty odour, and one that Evita knew only too well: the smell of faded fabric that has been washed too many times, soaked with sweat, and practically burnt from exposure to the sun. Add to this the different odour according to the province of origin: cow or sheep smell, goat or horse smell, *maté* smell, coca leaf smell, rough red wine smell, *chicha* (a drink made of fermented corn) smell, the whole mixed with the smell of yellow soap. Some children had wet their pants, and there was also the aroma of milk, for in a side room, Evita had had stoves installed to heat up the baby bottles that lined the shelves up to the ceiling.

Thin and squeezed in by her severe suits, she crossed the heavy atmosphere as if she could smell only her own perfume. Her step was lively and quick. Illuminated by the camera's flashes or by the 'newsreel' cinematic cameras, Eva radiated light from her hair, her skin, her jewels, and her own self-assurance. She did not feel herself anywhere else. There was no doubt or error about where she was now; each gesture flowed from her spring.

She spoke to the union workers as if she were speaking to old friends: 'Hi, guys.' Once settled in behind her desk, she consulted her notes written in green ink. Behind her a thick cloud of secretaries and social assistants mulled about. The parade started.

Ambassador Areilza described the scene: 'There were groups of workers, union leaders, peasants and their children, foreign journalists; a family of gauchos in their ponchos, the father with the huge black and silky moustache; there were refugees who had climbed over the iron curtain, people from post-war Europe, intellectuals and graduate students from the Baltic countries, priests and nuns, exuberant and sweaty overweight middle-aged women, young factory workers and football players, actors and circus performers. . . . In the middle of the apparent chaos of this loud and confusing party, Evita paid attention to all that was asked of her, from a raise to the setting up of an industry, then a request for family housing, furniture, a position in a school, food. When it was not about authorisation for shooting a film, financial aid, complaints about abusive power, it was interviews, tributes, meetings, inaugurations, feminist political rendezvous, gifts and donations.'

Faced with this tide of problems, Evita's attitude varied. She quickly hunted down the 'suits' and made them wait. As for the 'humble,' she immediately put them at ease with a natural courtesy, acting as a woman of the people who just happened to get lucky and wanted to share her luck with others, to restore, repair, forgive. Milton Bracker of *The New York Times*, reported one of Evita's sentences, which expresses this real feeling: '*Those people*,' she said responding to a question, 'are my work. I am nothing, my work is everything.'

She had said 'I am nothing' to Perón that night at Luna Park. But now it was no longer a negative 'nothing' nor an aspiration to be 'filled' by the masculine 'whole.' It was a creative 'nothing.' She had established a method that appeared disorganised but in fact allowed her to become a corridor where one's riches would come back to others. These riches were not hers; she did not distribute her own money. Nonetheless, she conveyed them for eighteen hours a day until the day she died.

The poor always asked her for less than they needed, so she gave them more. To have them love her? No doubt. But also to heal her soul. She caught human situations and stories in midair and tried to resolve them in their entirety. A woman wanted a mattress. She was alone, no husband. 'Do you have a bed?' 'No.' 'One bed for the lady. Do you have children?' 'Five.' 'Do they have beds?' 'No.' 'Write down five beds. But wait! Is there enough room for all these beds in your home?' 'No, Evita, we live in one room.' Then there was a brief conversation with her assistants. 'You will be allocated to the new neighbourhood in Saavedra.' The woman would leave with visions of the 'Evitist' chalets, placed around a football field, and a church with a choice priest, Father Benítez, dancing in her head. That is when Evita would call out to her, 'Do you have money for the bus fare?'

Upon uttering these words, Evita revealed her 'poor girl' memory, for only someone who had gotten stuck without enough money to get back home could think of this. At that instant, her dress or her hat seemed to have been borrowed. From one moment to another she risked losing what she had by having to ask for the coins for her ticket. The woman who received a house to shelter her new mattress felt safe. She almost felt she could wink at her when leaving and say, 'Today for you, tomorrow for me.'

Evita's gaze evaluated a situation in its entirety, yet it also focused on details. A family asks for furniture, pots, roof tiles. The little girl was cross-eyed. Evita grants them their wish, then adds, 'And an oculist to cure little Miss.' A young girl asks for money to go see her fiancé who lives far away. 'Do you want to get married?' 'Yes, but his work is over there.' 'Find a job for the fiancé in Buenos Aires. And lodging. And furniture.' A toothless woman wants clothing for her children. 'Clothing, and a sewing machine so she can learn to make them herself.

And a dentist to make dentures for her. One must also look nice to please one's husband,' she added as she spoke to the poor woman, who obviously had not thought about that for a long time and who, upon hearing these words, pushed a strand of hair away from her eyes.

Evita seemed obsessed by sewing machines and dentures. She distributed the former as if it were a panacea. After all, Doña Juana had survived thanks to her Singer. There are thousands of anecdotes of her distributing dentures or responding joyously when a woman reluctantly asked for them herself, fearing that she was abusing her kindness. 'Of course, that's fine! No one asks me for teeth! On the contrary, we need people to request these things, so that doctors can study, do research.' She thanked the woman by joking that she asked for dentures for both herself and her old husband.

Inevitably, the wisdom that is attributed to her turned her into a psychologist of sorts. Among the poor, a few seemed more hesitant, less sure of what they wanted. Not mattresses, sewing machines, or dentures? Then what? Advice. These were 'secret audiences' who told her awful stories of injustice that made her redden with indignation. Evita listened, understood immediately, and respected the secret by shooing away the indiscreet with a single gesture, or isolating herself in an adjoining room with the distraught person in tears. And she would invent a solution on the spot, exactly as one would resolve a corporate problem, a solution that was both practical and psychological, as if she had absolute power even to cure the wounds of the heart.

Many times she would intervene personally in order to correct the outline of an existence. She would bring to her own home children found in the street or at the *Secretaría* and who desperately scratched themselves. 'Is it scabies?' she would ask Dr Lobo, who was always present for these meetings. When the doctor confirmed, she would say to the mother, 'Madam, won't you lend me your little ones for a few days?' At the Unzué palace, she could wash them, cure them, and spoil them. What were the fifty bathrooms for, anyway? Besides, she had already used these splendid bathtubs, to soak the poor in rags who, since 1946, had come to knock on her door. The scabby children or the smelly old women would leave cured and perfumed. However, this physical alteration was not the most important thing. Most of all, they left changed in their hearts. For just one bath or even a few days, they had lived at the President's house, in a palace that dreams are made of. It seems that Evita was re-creating with these people the magic space of the tribe nestled around Doña Juana. She purified, through baths and clean and neat objects, fighting every inch of the way against overflowing shapeless clothes and unkempt hair that represent poverty so close to sin. The bath was a symbol; the objects, as useful or 'rich' as they were, were also symbols. These scenes took place under the cameras' eyes, and yet they took place elsewhere, in a joyous, warm Eden, as if they were bathing in amniotic fluids. Evita and the poor were in osmosis, isolated from the world that did not and never could understand this mystery.

For Evita, this intervention was fully conscious, and she showed them princely delicacies to make them react. Rebellion is born out of comparison and knowledge. She had escaped Junín thanks to the white telephones she'd seen in Hollywood movies. Her poor also needed to be shaken by the vision of an abundance, which far from appeasing their rage would increase it. In this way Evita herself was revolutionary. Like happiness, luxury seems logical. Penury is an 'absurd wound,' just as the tango says and Evita's children went home with the feeling of having discovered something more than their poverty, which was suddenly unbearable.

Unfortunately, the photos of Evita stretching out her arm to give show only her profile. They do not reveal her eyes, which were increasingly sunken into their sockets. At the *Secretaría*, she worked hard, never lifting her head for the photographer, but the half-attentive, wonder-filled expression of the little girls who looked at her served as a mirror. Their mothers had thankful smiles plastered on their faces, but the little girls had time to study Evita, and they stared at her gravely to better record her image.

What did they see? A woman who was not scared of contagion. Did she notice a woman whose lip was split by syphilis? She kissed her on the mouth. The poet José María Castiñeira de Dios relates that he had tried to stop her, but Evita said to him, 'Do you know what it means to her when I kiss her?'

'I saw her kiss lepers,' says Father Benítez, 'people with tuberculosis, cancer. . . . I saw her take people in rags in her arms and catch their lice.' In the morning, Pedro Alcaraz combed her hair with a fine comb and vinegar, to kill the invaders. Once, Irma Cabrera wanted to clean Evita's face with alcohol, after she had kissed a man covered with pustules, but the one who was more and more frequently referred to as the 'saint,' grabbed the bottle out of her hand and threw it against the wall.

What else did the young inquisitive minds see? Often they felt scrutinised by the Virgin with the piercing eyes. For Evita would let moments go by in order to take time to figure out with whom she was dealing. 'She knew that people show you a different face if they are talking to you or if they forget that you are looking at them,' Angel Miel Asquía, the former deputy said. 'At the *Secretaría*, she had all the time in the world to study them when they did not know she was observing them. That is how she picked out the liars, the thieves, the honest or even the eventual collaborator.' For let's not forget that she was lying in wait for fervent supporters, especially women. When she helped the little old lady, she looked at her daughter, to track down the fervour underneath the gratitude. Her Women's Perónist party was born of this eye contact, and the only virtue Evita searched for was fanaticism.

Yet the dishonest folk inspired only pity in her, not disdain. She was becoming tolerant with those who attempted to abuse her generosity. They came back again and again to ask her for the same thing, thinking that she would not remember. Eva's memory surprised them. 'I already saw you,' she would say. 'No matter, I will give you one more thing, but you have to promise not to start this again.' This was the case for the woman to whom she gave money for the dentist. She came back, more toothless than ever. 'I already gave you money for your teeth. What did you do with it?' 'My husband took it.' 'Oh! And so he's sending you to get more! No money for you. An appointment at the dentist for this woman, we'll pay the bill ourselves.'

Renzi controlled the money (if there was any control), though Evita would take off a pair of diamond earrings and give them to a woman who had come back many times and who Renzi, stricter than Evita, would not appease. She took money from an overflowing envelope; she had no idea of the amount it held, and she didn't care. She gave each person whatever she wanted, in denominations of fifty pesos. When the gold mine was exhausted, she would dramatically tell the poor, 'Listen to me, I'm broke, but I'm going to get more from those people over there. See them? The suits?' And stimulated by the laughs of her brothers and sisters, who were squeezing in tighter so as not to miss this scene, she called a minister over, an important man, and said to him, 'Open your wallet.'

The men in suits had been warned, so they came over with two wallets, one of them empty. That is the one they would open when the time came, saying, 'Sorry, I'm broke too.' But you couldn't fool Evita. 'Give me your other wallet,' she would say with her palm out. Was she noticing resentment on the man's face? 'Come on, you earn enough as it is. Besides, what was your salary before you worked for us?'

THE CANDY WAR

Where did the money in the envelope come from, and who filled the depot on Uriburu Street? The novelist María Granata gives a Dantesque vision of these immense hangars that were divided into perfectly organised sections. In 1953, Apold had hired her to write a story about the foundation. She had walked around with her nose up in the air looking at all the shelves filled with pots, children's clothes, caps, cheese, or aspirin from the floor to the ceiling. From time to time, a voice would resonate over the microphone: 'Eighty-year-old black shoes, one pair. Soccer ball, child's, one. Set of six plates and six cups. A pair of sheets for a full bed.' By that time, Evita was dead, but her Foundation was still running. The assistants who worked at the *Secretaría* telephoned the depot to place an order, and the sky blue trucks would deliver the goods to the requesters. A very Catholic lady, Adela Caprile, a member of the liquidating commission of the Foundation that was established after the fall of Perónism, had a similar impression: 'I could never have believed that they could collect such a tremendous quantity of tennis rackets. It was a waste, craziness, but not a fraud. Evita cannot be accused of having kept one *peso* in her pocket. I would like to be able to say as much of all those who collaborated with me in the dissolution of the organisation.'

Who, then, contributed all these things in this living mess pure of all fraud? First of all, the workers themselves. From 1948, their contributions were no longer spontaneous. They were required to give the Foundation a calculated percentage on the raises Evita granted them. It was a demand for a favour, but the workers complained only much later, when their quality of life began to decline. In 1950, the CGT decided to give the Foundation the sum of each worker's salary corresponding to the bonuses of May 1 and October 17. Protests were raised, which were numerous and intense enough for Evita to make a show of climbing down and announcing that she would return the deductions that had been made. This was a strategic retreat. Espejo launched a series of declarations focused on embarrassing the workers, who ended up begging Evita to take their money. She responded in a speech on December 27, 'I will honestly admit that I did not expect anything less from you.'

She knew how to treat her workers. In January 1951, she left a banquet at the residence to meet with the striking railroad workers, in the middle of the night, on a disused track. She climbed into the service car they themselves used and reprimanded them by nodding her head, more disappointed than angry, as one does with naughty children. Seeing her so fragile, but so determined, they felt the same shame they felt over the matter of their contributions. The opposition complained about this 'maternalism,' but this was Argentina, in 1951, where the mother is the tango's heroine.

Of course, the leftist well-wishers thought that Perón and Evita bought the workers' movement to stop it. Perónism was a revolution of evil minds. Let's add a few details to this image of the strike. It had been organised by the *Fraternidad*, an association of railroad conductors who resisted Perónism, during a period of economic recession. The regime was experiencing increasing difficulties, and Evita insisted on working despite the shooting pain in her stomach. It was because she was afraid that this might mean the end that she reprimanded the workers by saying, 'Stop making silly mistakes that play to the adversary.'

But how far could Evita's will to take destiny in her hands go? According to the sociologist and historian Juan José Sebreli, the Foundation's shock forces, which had already suppressed other strikes, attacked the *Fraternidad*. After a very violent speech against the strikers, Perón laid off two thousand people and incarcerated three hundred of those who were Communist and Socialist and who were not asking for their mothers or fathers but simply for their rights. As for the others, like Evita they had known only authority or favours.

Besides the workers' 'voluntary' donations, the Foundation 'solicited' industrialists, who on request yielded much better dividends. In reality, what was shocking about these 'solicitations' was that, except for the cynical and authoritarian manner in which the requests were made, nothing distinguished this procedure from what other countries called 'a tax on large fortunes.' Beside the contribution that was demanded from the Bemberg family, the two most notorious cases were Arnaldo Massone's pharmaceutical laboratory and Mu-Mu candy. The former had the misfortune to preside over the very anti-Perónist Argentinean Chamber of Commerce. Around 1950, the Foundation asked Massone to provide vaccinations, for free of course. He refused. The next day, his laboratory was dark; there was no electricity. That is when an investigative commission showed up to examine his medicines, which were in bad condition since the refrigerators were not working. Don Arnaldo had just enough time to jump on a ship headed toward his Uruguayan exile, while his laboratory remained closed until the fall of the regime.

As for Mu-Mu candy, the same scenario occurred. The owners of the factory, the Grossman brothers, had expected to get paid by the Foundation for the candy they supplied. Suddenly, they were being accused of working in unhygienic conditions. An entire generation was traumatised. These delicious caramel candies that stayed stuck to one's molars for a long time were loved by Argentinean children. And now they were being accused of concealing rat hair! Three years later, the factory was able to open its doors again thanks to the Grossmans' generous offer to give the Foundation a percentage of their future earnings. But the deed was done, and the excuse given for the closing of the factory was such a stroke of inspiration that no one was ever able to dissociate the image of the caramels from that of rats. Even today, the story of Mu-Mu candy, like so many jokes about Evita, remains a symbol of solidarity for an entire generation of Argentines.

EVITA AT DAWN

Finally, around 3 P.M., Evita was persuaded to eat a bite at the Home for the Workers. In the early days it had been easy to have lunch with Perón every day, but now it was impossible. At that time, he was waking from his sacrosanct nap and going back to his office. Evita saw him less and less each day, sometimes during an official demonstration, or on Wednesdays, when the entire *Secretaría* would pay him a visit. Those days had a specific goal: to show the real boss, Perón, the accomplishments of his delegate, Evita. And as she related herself in *My Mission in Life*, this was Perón's opportunity to be in direct contact with the workers, to seduce them once more, explaining his ideas as a leader but also as a friend thinking out loud who specifically needed them to better form his thought. But since nothing was simple (as simplifying as Perón's speech was), these Wednesdays also had a hidden agenda, to show the former boss that his substitute was taking power. Since Evita never missed an opportunity to say that she was nothing, Perón never missed an opportunity to be satisfied with his wife's success.

Evita's lunch table was loud and animated. She barely crumbled a piece of fish with her fork, the same one she used to stir the bubbly mineral water in her glass. And when she left, the crumbs of a cookie that her fingers had broken remained on the tablecloth. Her gestures were nervous, and they tended to destroy the food and the drink placed in front of her.

On the days when she had neither an inauguration to attend nor a medal to hang on a young man, an old man, or a worker's chest, she received people in her den until two or three in the morning. A famous cliché depicts her in a car, waving to the photographer. She is going home after a long day of work. She is fresh and smiling under her small Maurice Chevalier-style hat. The clock on the English tower, behind Plaza San Martín, shows that the time is twenty to five.

In the afternoons at the *Secretaría*, the human scenery was always the same. A few solicitors had been waiting for her for hours, persuaded that she would eventually call out their names. Impatience was not the name of the game. Quite the contrary, for in Evita's eyes, those who persisted scored a point. They were tenacious, and knew what they wanted. In fact, it was Evita's race against time that made the wait longer. They were waiting now so as not to have to wait a lifetime for an economic solution that would be late in coming. This was the meaning of her 'direct aid.' While Perón put in place five-year plans that were going to take care of everything, Evita took care of those who were in a hurry. Her Foundation handled urgencies. Those for whom it was always too late got something out of it.

Waiting was nothing new in Argentina. The country had always known the *amansadora* tradition of taming or breaking cattle and horses, which was dear to government, especially President Yrigoyen's administration. He, too, would make everyone wait for hours, then grant their requests. It was a paternalistic tradition, and one of favours, arising from the tradition of conservative *caudillos* who, like Evita's father, Don Juan Duarte, handed out empanadas in order to get elected. The only difference was that Evita introduced herself as being Doña Juana's daughter as often as she said she was the daughter of a landowner. She remained loyal to her humble origins, a loyalty that was evident during her speeches and in most of her everyday attitudes, and which the people knew to be sincere.

The *Secretaría* was also the privileged place for her rendez-vous. Evita met with people who had nothing to request and who had no relation to the popular strata. By doing this, she admitted an educational objective, to place the Perónists who were remote from the common people face to face not only with poverty but also with the people's warmth. She would repeat another of Perón's phrases, one that did not lack truth: 'The best thing we have in Argentina is the people.' What truth did this phrase reveal? It was through Perónism that the Argentinean people revealed their virtues (and, it goes without saying, their faults). Since he felt he could confide in them, he could express himself with more ease than is possible for politicians today faced with a more sophisticated electorate. In Argentina, the colonial morals had been very simple. The massive arrival of immigrants had added a fraternal, democratic element to human relations. For all these reasons, the social codes had never been rigorous. And the authoritarian but popular Perónist regime did not have any problems establishing very open norms of behaviour that would have been inconceivable under the rule of a cultured elite whose democracy, more formal than real, banished the illiterate. The people in the street greeted Perón as his car drove by without any complexes: 'Ciao, Juancito.' 'Peróncito, please don't ever die!' 'We love you!'

Evita felt confused, she wanted to show this to warm men as one shows things to one's children. She was so proud of the sympathy, humour, humanity of her 'humble folk.' It is true that Perónist intellectuals (although for the opposition, these two terms were mutually exclusive) emerged amazed. That is how the Eva Perón Circle was born.

In 1950, José María Castiñeira de Dios was appointed as the cultural subsecretary. He was a young nationalist and Catholic poet who had supported the Perónist revolution since 1945 and had then distanced himself from it. It was Eva who appointed him to the position. As usual, she set up a meeting with him at the *Secretaría* and asked him to stay to help in the show of her *grasitas* ('little greasies'), as the poor liked to call themselves. It was a decisive day for the 'oligarch' poet (this was, of course, Eva's definition). He witnessed the promised scenes. A woman asked for three beds. 'Why only three if you have six children!'

From time to time, Evita asked Castiñeira, 'Now can you see these people's pain?'

But previously she had not treated him too kindly. First, she had asked him to have his wife come work for her. And Castiñeira, a self-proclaimed '*gallego* caveman,' responded that he did not want his wife to leave the hearth. So Evita answered, 'Why do you like Franco? I hate him, him and everyone around him.' He was simultaneously humiliated and fascinated, and that same night he wrote a poem in which he played with the names María and Eva and in which he compared this prodigious woman to a pelican who feeds its young from her entrails.

Evita had always loved 'poetries.' She was enchanted and ordered Apold to publish one hundred copies of the poem. Then she asked him to gather poets every Wednesday night at the Home for the Workers, on one condition: At these poetry readings, the topic had to be Perón. Not a word on another topic could be uttered.

Braving the discredit incurred when displaying Perónism in intellectual circles, many poets answered the call. As a result, seventeen volumes of laudatory poetry were published by Apold. On these nights, Evita sometimes departed from her self-imposed obligation to praise Perón and displayed a different personality. She joked, laughed loudly, had lively retorts. She enjoyed reliving her bohemian nights and her carefree life of days gone by. If she had once spent relaxing moments, she was now remembering them. Or maybe she was only now discovering them.

Fermín Chávez described a burst of laughter that had overcome her during one of these meetings, when she was listening to the speech of Dr Salomón Chichilnisky, a member of the Argentinean Israeli Organisation, which was formed by the few Jews who were Perónists. Evita was not an anti-Semite. Dora Dana, the widow of Moisés Lebensohn, the journalist from Junín, wholeheartedly confirmed this. The Jewish doctor, who had been born in Russia, transformed each *ué* diphthong into *oï*. *Abuela*, grandmother, became *aboïla*. At the end, Evita could not hold it any longer and burst out laughing. Chichilnisky looked up at her over his notes. So Evita turned toward Chocha Nicolini, who was sitting next to her. The daughter of her mother's old friend was like her own daughter. She scolded her: 'You little snot-nose! Will you never learn to respect adults? Go to the bathroom and stay there until the doctor finishes speaking!'

The famous poet and writer Leopoldo Marechal was not among the hero-worshippers. But he adhered to Perónism, and Evita was not about to forget it. His play *Antígona Vélez* was supposed to inaugurate the Cervantes National Theatre's season in 1951. The script had been given to Fanny Navarro, Juancito Duarte's friend, to play the lead, and Fanny had lost it. Since he did not keep a copy, Marechal had abandoned the project. One day, Eva called him. 'You are a great poet and a great Perónist,' she said. 'The show must begin on May 25. You must have the play in your head. Make an effort, and reconstruct it.' Marechal was won over by her energy and got right to work with the help of his wife, Elbia Rosbaco (the 'Elbiamor' from his poems). Two days later, the play existed once again.

According to the poet Héctor Villanueva, at the end of each meeting Eva selected her 'inner circle.' She pointed to each 'chosen one' with her finger, thus requesting that he or she accompany her back to the residence. Why did she choose some over others? Even they didn't know. So many years later, we can detect a common denominator among Villanueva, Castiñeira, and Rodolfo Decker (who did not participate in the circle but attended other meetings) in their physical appearance. At the time, they were all between twenty and thirty years of age and had smooth faces with turned-up noses. This type of young man did not attract her and instead inspired a feeling of fraternal camaraderie, thus posing no danger. Although the sessions often lasted until dawn, nothing indecent ever occurred. Evita's loyalty was such that the desperate non-Catholic opposition accused her of lacking femininity.

Thus, she chose her companions who kept her company until the small hours of the morning without risk (mature sportsmen like Péron or Kartulowicz were not among them). To remain alone in the light of dawn seemed like death. When she left the Home for the Workers, around 4 A.M., they would finally end the evening in a room at the Unzué palace. 'Shush!' she would say as she opened the door. 'The old man is sleeping.'

She idealised Perón enough, praised him to the skies for hours, and could finally give herself a few minutes rest by calling him 'old man.' In a speech given before 1949, she had called him 'the old General Perón.' She must have been punished, for from then on she always spoke reverently about him. Whatever the hour, she'd pick up her dog Tinolita to prevent her from barking and tell her gang of pug-nosed young brothers, 'Tiptoe. We'll cook up some French fries, some eggs, and drink some beer.'

The brothers would leave shortly before six, as soon as they heard the 'old man' moving about his room. They often ran into Juan Duarte just coming in, holding a finger up to his lips. Every morning, at six, Perón knocked on the door of Juancito's room, *maté* in hand. So Juancito would pretend to wake up and would have the barber come over so that he could sleep a little, at least while Perón was being shaved.

At seven Evita would call Castiñeira, Villanueva, or Decker and say in a singsongy voice, 'I'm not waking you, I hope. OK, then come over right away.'

In 1950, her illness had already been diagnosed. She no longer called her companions so early in the morning for a simple educational objective. She called them in emergency situations – when she was lonely.

Chapter 8

❖

RENOUNCER

On July 26, 1949, Eva's relationship with women took on a political aspect. The thousand Perónist women who had come to the party meeting at Luna Park went to the Cervantes National Theatre, where Evita was waiting for them as the founder of the Women's Perónist Party. What need was there to create a separate party from the men's? Rosa Calviño de Gómez responded with no hesitation, 'Because Evita said that men used women.' But this belief was not reflected in her words at the Cervantes theatre. The old *porteño* stage of noble Spanish decor was no doubt not the appropriate place for it. The women workers' problems, she told her supporters, were twice as painful as the workers'. They sacrificed themselves in the home, put up with their bosses' brutality, and earned a lower salary than the men. For all these reasons, women had to organise themselves in a completely different way. This, however, did not mean that Evita's role was independent of Perón's. 'For women, to be Perónist is, above all, to be faithful to Perón and to have a blind confidence in him.' Then came a eulogy for the leader in the style that was familiar, but exaggerated. In the preceding years, Evita had lauded Perón without moderation, but without deifying him either.

The year 1948 was the year of acquired power for her. The following year she created her party; this was a time of internal struggles and power games. Then in 1950 and 1951 came the pinnacle and the decline. It was in 1949 that Perón became, in Evita's words, nothing less than 'the sun.' The hyperbole of the eulogy awoke suspicion. Did she really adore him more and more each day? Was her love growing infinitely? Or was she also 'buying' her freedom, as she had during the Eva Perón Circle evenings, prolonged until dawn on the condition that they speak only of him? All this seems pretty clear when Rosa Calviño reports that Evita would tell her intimate friends, 'Perón is like the sun, it is true. It's better not to get too close so as not to get burnt.'

Thus, she had moments of candour when she admitted an image of Perón that was more burning than brilliant. Privately, she had used even harsher words when speaking to Guardo: 'Perón is a chicken.'

And yet, as strange as it may seem, her declarations of idolatry were sincere. She considered Perón to be the most brilliant statesman she knew. By exalting him, she exalted herself. It was her nature to exaggerate. Additionally, how else could she simultaneously hide her disenchantment and her feeling of being criticised by him? For the more ambitious she became, the guiltier she felt vis-à-vis this odd sun who worked in the shade. Besides, when she launched into her panegyrics, as delirious as they were, Perón neither frowned nor interrupted her, not even with a discreet gesture. Who better than his wife could speak on his behalf? So she did it because she needed to believe in it, because she knew that Perón's weakness was his vanity, and finally to play down his jealousy. During their trips or the ceremonies in the Plaza de Mayo, when the people ardently cheered Evita, Perón looked happy, too happy. It is impossible not to compare the ovations for his wife with the ovations for Perón himself. Evita was cheered more loudly than Perón. As the leader's smile widened, jealousy shone like a lightning bolt in his Indian eyes. Perón, envious? This is what made her tremble. She had confided to Raúl Salinas since 1946 that she feared her husband.

Once it was established that her personal ambition, a dangerous sin, was to be banished, she had all the right in the world to shape her party as she saw fit. To begin with, she proceeded to dissolve all the women's Perónist associations that had been formed up until that day, her sister Elisa's most of all. When she arrived at the Cervantes theatre, she had heard a group of women chant her sister's name with the same rhythm they chanted hers. Her blood had boiled, and the political career of the Junín *caudilla* ended on that day.

The ceremony on July 26 marked the beginning of a series of interviews where Evita tested women with one very specific goal, to find delegates who had the necessary moral fibre to carry out a countrywide census of all the potential women Perónists and to recruit them for the Perónist cause. The result was a team of twenty-three women (one for each province), chosen according to two specific criteria: fanaticism and aptitude for work. These delegates had to abandon their families, homes, and careers in order to devote their life to the cause. The way Rosa Calviño was selected clearly illustrates the methods used by Evita, the shepherd of souls.

Rosa and her husband owned a bakery in the Caballito neighbourhood, on the city's west side. She hung Perón and Evita's portraits on her walls. Atilio Renzi, the residence's administrator and Evita's essential collaborator to the foundation, was her client. One day he told her that he was moving into the Unzué palace with his wife. Time passed, and when he came back to see her she asked him for a job. She had a teaching certificate, but she had never used it. So she was appointed by Evita to work in a school. One day in 1949, Evita was waiting for her at the residence. Two other women were also waiting to meet her. Evita explained to them that they would have to work day and night at the Basic Units of the Women's Perónist Party. The two women refused. 'What about the schoolteacher?' Evita asked. 'I'd like to, but I have a three-year-old.' 'You'll have a house in the Saavedra region. That will be the unit's seat. You can work and take care of your child simultaneously.' So on January 27, 1950, the baker-teacher found herself at the head of the first Basic Unit of the Women's Perónist Party. She had penetrated Evita's inner circle, and, one year later, became the nation's senator.

Ana Macri's road to fame is also revealing. She had been employed by the Charitable Society and now worked at one of the hospitals that had been integrated into the Health Ministry by Dr Méndez San Martín. Evita asked the doctor for a list of 'honest women' to work with her. So Ana was nominated to the Transitional Home #2 on Calle Lafinur in Buenos Aires. After the assembly at the Cervantes theatre, she was one of the twenty-three delegates sent to Argentina's four corners by Eva. 'She gave us all a piece of paper,' she recalls. 'Each one was addressed to the governor of each province. We had to handle the rest on our own. If the governor was nice, he would help us get a car. But often, the Perónist men did not look upon us kindly, and they boycotted our work. When Evita put me in charge of the Santa Fe province, she said: "I've already sent a nice girl there, but she lacks charisma. She lets the governor of the Province, engineer Caenza, eat her alive. He is a cold Perónist who wants to appropriate our Party and use our women's efforts. Go and make them respect you."'

Ana Macri, a tiny blonde not even five feet tall, walked for miles, crossed rivers on a canoe, founded six hundred and fifty-eight Basic Units, and recruited five thousand women. Luckily, a fervent Evitist had preceded her in order to prepare for her arrival. She had rented a base for the party and had bought furniture, so that Ana could devote herself to her duty without wasting time. Driving her jeep, she made the rounds of all the villages in the province and went to the square and called the women over a loudspeaker. She repeated Evita's phrases to the newly arrived: 'In politics, a woman must be beside her man, but she should never accept that he meddle in her business. There are no men in the Basic Units: in politics, a woman's worst enemy is man.' Sometimes, the unit worked out of a home's dining room. But the husband was forbidden to enter during working hours.

The woman's party's base in the federal capital was inaugurated on October 29, 1949, by Teresa Adelina Fiora, the delegate for Buenos Aires, who also ran the Eva Perón Foundation's nursing school. Not long after this, Elena Caporeale de Mercante inaugurated the first provincial unit. These twenty-three delegates, helped by dozens of subdelegates, had two missions: to recruit members and to unearth feminine personalities capable of becoming deputies. How to choose them? 'I couldn't care less about diplomas,' Evita would say. 'Pick the hardest workers and the most fervent Perónists.' The procedure seemed like an initiation ceremony, like taking the mystical veil. The candidates had to know that they took the risk of reaching Congress. Evita required silence from her girls on this topic. She even kicked one of them out, a certain Señora de Coronel, for speaking about it too much. She wanted to eliminate ambition as the incentive for the eventual legislators. They were to be motivated by faith alone.

Among the nurses, the teachers, and the housewives who formed the heart of the group, there was also an attorney, Elsa Chamorro Alamán. And there was also a tango singer, Juana Larrauri, one of the rare people from Evita's artistic past who remained. But according to Ana Macri, the 'doctors' showed up only when 'the men' divulged the secret on purpose and spread the news of the eventual nominations as deputies and senators. As for Evita, intellect was the least of her worries, she asked only for ardour in one's task and obedience, and she knew how to get it.

In 1955, Delia Degliuomini de Parodi, a delegate in the San Luis province and Eva's most fervent collaborator, admitted the following to the *Revolucion Libertadora's* inquiry commission: 'Right after the elections in 1951, when the women senators and deputies of the Perónist party were elected, each and every woman legislator of the women's branch had to write and sign a letter to her parents or friends, making a treacherous statement about the Party. It was Mrs Perón's strict requirement which she communicated directly or through my intermediary: at the time, she was already ill. These documents were drafted at the Residence and given to Mr Renzi.' Renzi confirmed these astonishing declarations: 'The letters were a weapon for Mrs Perón so that, in case of disobedience, she could dismiss any one of the legislators.'

This was not an original procedure. Throughout most of the country, the people's representatives were chosen according to their mastery of the language. Evita even taught diction to her women. But she chose the ignorant ones, women who would never overshadow her. If a hint of this superiority began to show its ugly head, the woman was fired. Nonetheless, there was a margin of freshness, of genuine impertinence, that can be considered revolutionary. The world had never before been full of women bakers-cum-senators.

An Evitist innovation was that in the Basic Units, the neighbourhood women could learn to sew, cook, style hair, and any other skill that at least one of them knew well enough to teach. According to journalist Enrique Oliva, worker professors came to teach in espadrilles at the Cuyo University in Mendoza. They would start from the principle – an excellent principle, without prejudices – that each person knew how to do something and was capable of teaching it to others.

The women's party extended the Foundation's arm, for the census allowed them to control the country home by home. This was a useful tool for the police who watched each street and each group of houses. The Perónist regime had lists of the names, habits, and ideas of every individual. But this enumeration was good for something. Indeed, no one was invisible or anonymous, and indifference did not exist. An Indian woman from the northwest, living in a lost village on the Bolivian border, was going to get married soon. The delegate from the Salta or Jujuy province learned of this news. She communicated it to Evita, who called her women late every night. Soon before the wedding, the mailman knocked on the woman's door. He had a big box containing a wedding dress, a veil, a bouquet, and shoes. There was even some fabric to make the matron of honour's dress and a matching hat.

Evita was obsessed by seriousness and decorum as much as by dentures and sewing machines. Blamed and hated for reasons of 'morality,' she wanted her women to respect the norms. Ana Serrano, who was a very young girl at the time, related Eva's advice: 'Be careful! Be irreproachable in your behaviour and your manners. Dress elegantly. I made mistakes, but I was saved because I am Perón's wife. But for you, any false step, and they'll be all over you.' 'They' were an obscure force composed of disparate enemies: oligarchs, priests, soldiers, men. In 1951, during a meeting of the Superior Council of the Perónist party, the number of legislators – and women legislators – proposed by the movement was debated. Evita wanted to include eight women senators on the list but had to concede to six. 'Who did she have to accept this from?' 'The men,' Rosa Calviño responded. 'And Perón supported them by saying: "I will ask the president of the Women's Party to give up on these two senators. She will surely say yes: women are so generous!" Of course, Evita said yes. But, when she left the room, she started to vomit.'

A CENSURED REASON

The story of her book, *My Mission in Life*, is closely tied to the story of her Women's Party. In '*Historia del perónismo*,' Hugo Gambini describes a strange character, Manuel Penella de Silva. This Spanish journalist had led a very active life. He was the son of a famous musician whom he had never met and had been raised by his mother and four sisters. He later married in Germany and had five daughters, so he knew and understood women. After having written a book on Hitler (he was anti-Nazi and was thrown out of Germany for having predicted the fall of the regime), he had a sudden revelation: The Nazi empire did not have any women. 'Neither Agrippina, nor Lucretia. Hitler hid Eva Braun and all those who preceded her. The Führer, a symbol and example for the German man, had to be a male without a female.'

This revelation prompted him to study women's participation in all political regimes. One thing led to another, and he began to imagine a chamber devoted exclusively to women, since parliaments had two. He even thought about going to the United States to talk about his idea with Eleanor Roosevelt. He was in Zürich with his family, all seven of them rather famished, when he met the Argentinean ambassador, Benito Llambí, who said to him, 'I know the right person for you, Eva Perón.'

He gathered his last few pennies and went to Buenos Aires, where he wanted to present his project to Evita and write the biography of the 'Lady of Hope.' His first encounter with Perón, based, in fact, on a misunderstanding, outlined the future relationship. Perón always seduced his foreign visitors by expressing the greatest sympathy for their homeland – sometimes he even pretended that his grandfather was born there. Thinking that the name Silva was Brazilian, he launched into an elegy of Brazil. When he realised his error, he was so frustrated that from then on he always was unpleasant to the journalist. Penella de Silva was able to meet Evita only after a difficult struggle. She found out about his idea during her trip to Switzerland when Ambassador Llambí brought it to her attention. As soon as she returned, she courted Penella so zealously that Aloé suggested they no longer meet face to face in order to prevent gossip. She hastened to take this advice, for she was always careful about her reputation.

Evita was very impressed by the journalist's words. It was decided that he would write Evita's story, in the first person, placing his ideas, which she found fascinating, in her mouth. 'When he began to write, and to read the manuscript to her,' Gambini wrote, 'Evita would cry as if she were reading a saga:

"Yes! That's exactly how things happened! Exactly like this!"'
Nonetheless, she did not share Penella's writing criteria. He
was writing the book in a simple, slightly clumsy, and very
sentimental style that reflected Evita's candour and raw intelligence. She, on the other hand, wanted a neat, embellished,
bourgeois style, a style of writing that was identical to her way
of dressing and her moralising taste.

Perón opposed the book, as he did the idea of the Woman's
Chamber, which he considered ridiculous. Evita launched it
anyway, during the Hispanic-American Women's Congress
in Buenos Aires. The idea was that only women should be
admitted to the Senate, which would become a consulting
corps and an instrument for worldwide peace.

'Nonsense,' said Perón, and the idea and the manuscript
ended up at the bottom of a drawer.

According to Penella, Evita consoled herself by wangling
Perón's agreement for the creation of the Women's Party. It
was better than nothing, and Perón, who saw in this idea
an opportunity to obtain women's votes, was not about to
oppose it. The President was also endorsing a reality that was
impossible to hide: Eva had power.

But Penella was not satisfied by this arrangement, and he told
this to Evita one day when he was in a car with her, Raúl
Mendé, Minister of Technical Affairs, and Armando Méndez
San Martín, Minister of Education, who were going for lunch
to the Olivos residence, another presidential dwelling in a chic
suburb of Buenos Aires. On the way, Evita tirelessly repeated
the familiar phrases about obedience to Perón (which were no
doubt exaggerated due to the presence of the two witnesses):
'We have to work for Perón, we have to consecrate our will
to him. He leads, he knows where he is going. He is the
most extraordinary man in the world.' Tired of listening to
her, the journalist retorted, 'You never stop yelling this from
the rooftops. He, on the other hand, never compliments you
either in public or in private.' Evita was quiet for the rest of

the ride. When they arrived at Olivos, she did not invite the Spaniard in. Later he learned that during lunch she said to Perón, 'Penella thinks that you never compliment me.' And when the Spaniard scolded her for having said too much, she answered, as if it went without saying, 'What did you want me to do? It was better that Perón hear it from me than from Mendé.'

And in fact, Perón put Mendé (one of Perón's most obsequious servants) in charge of editing her autobiography in 1951. Evita was very sick, and she had told her husband that she wanted the book published before her death.

Father Benítez would have liked to be in charge of the 'corrections,' to reassure Perón, who detested the book's feminism and also to maintain the essence of a work he considered important. Raúl Mendé rendered it unrecognisable. He was not content to remove the fundamental concepts; he embellished it with delirious elegies to Perón. For example: 'In the same way that a woman reaches eternity and glory and saves herself from solitude and death by giving herself to a man for love, I believe no feminist movement in the world will reach glory and eternity, if it does not devote itself to a man's cause. . . . I believe that Perón and his cause are sufficiently great and worthy so that my Nation's feminist movement can wholly devote itself to him. Moreover, all women of the world should devote themselves to his Justicialism. By giving themselves up for love of a cause that belongs to all of humanity, they will grow as women.'

To Hector Gambini, these paragraphs come from a 'heated mind which defines a woman's adherence to Perón in terms of an exalted eroticism.' And he concludes, 'This coincides completely with certain subsequent manoeuvres of Perón's entourage, whose aim was to awaken in him a true sexual delirium. They hadn't yet started injecting him with hormones. The treatment was only verbal.' (We'll come back to Perón's 'sexual delirium' upon Evita's death and to the role that Mendé and Méndez San Martín played in this delirium.)

In October 1951, a month after her autobiography was published, Penella visited Eva one last time to say good-bye before he returned to Europe. He found her pale and sad. It was the illness, but it was also the feeling of not having had enough courage and letting herself be turned down by Perón. She said only this to him: 'Thank you for the book. It is the child I never had.' At the exact time she said this, she was incubating the fruit of her rebellion: uterine cancer.

What was left of Evita in this book that was mandatory reading in schools? Sometimes, a simple and direct word, lost within the pages, hits us through its freshness. It is as if we are listening to her free from all rhetoric, candid and passionate. Even so, her reactionary declarations on the devoted maternal woman who lives for her children in the heart of the hearth are not revealing. First of all, because their origin is easy to imagine. Second, because even if Evita did genuinely write them, they are uninteresting. The biographer of an intuitive but uncultured being is obliged to capture him or her beyond words. As Father Benítez said, do not look for Evita in phrases; she is whole in her actions. One would also add, in her subconscious gestures and in her death. It was not abnegation or 'feminine generosity' or her 'taste for sacrifice' that made her vomit in the middle of the street when she lost the battle for the two positions in Parliament.

In her biography of Evita, Marysa Navarro correctly notes the similarities between the language in Eva's autobiography and in her speeches, especially the written speeches she read. Her articles in *Democracia* and the Perónist history 'lessons' she taught, starting in 1951 at the Higher School of Perónism are also related. The whole of this 'work' was, in fact, drafted in a uniformly basic language. So Navarro concludes that the pen is the same, it is Evita's. There is another explanation: if this writing demonstrates such uniformity, it is simply because the prose of the hacks who produced it was cut with the same scissors. Had it been less flat, it would have been suspicious. And yet, certain words reappear, signalling an attempt to express a self that could only have been Eva's. It is not a sentimental expression, but a physical expression that is all about sensations, especially painful ones. We recognise in them a corporeal element that only she could express. She must have transmitted it to her writers, who, finding no danger, transcribed it. A hint of this was evident in Muñoz Azpiri's texts destined to spread propaganda 'for a better world.' 'Something anguishing and hard,' she would say, 'that germinated in the viscera.'

Similarly, Eva's autobiography speaks of viscera and bruised bodies: 'The thought of injustice has always induced a strange sensation of asphyxia in me, as if, not being able to find a cure for the pain that I saw, I could no longer breathe.' 'As far as I can remember, every act of injustice hurt my soul as if I was being pierced with something. I have a memory of an injustice that revolted me and tore me apart from each period of my life.' 'That is why I scream until my voice goes hoarse, and until I lose my voice, when the indignation I carry within me bleeds into my speeches, each time stronger, almost like a wound of the heart.' 'There is only one worthy thing in me: that is my love for the people and for Perón which burns my soul, my skin and inflames my nerves.' 'I have spent my physical energy to re-animate my defeated brother's. My soul knows this, my body felt it. I offer to you all my energy so that my body may be a bridge stretching towards a common happiness. Cross it.'

BEHIND THE CURTAIN

Perón and Evita seemed always to address each other through little secrets or coded messages where it was unclear whether something was being revealed or being faked, all to disguise the essence. Jorge Luis Borges said, 'Perón was not Perón and Eva was not Eva. They were mysterious, anonymous individuals, whose faces and secret names we do not know.' It does seem, however, that it was easier to discern Eva than Perón. They performed in the same shadowy theatre, but behind the sham of the fairy, there was still always a woman.

And yet, although she was frank and he a cheater, they became similar within the third personality that was their relationship. This should make sense to most couples, always composed of two, to which a third is added stemming from the two. Thus, in the struggle for power that had united them, Evita chased the guanaco in her own way.

Angel Miel Asquía described the little dramas she would perform in order to convince Perón that a certain minister or a certain worker was not working out. But Perón, believing himself infallible, was extremely opinionated (according to Sergia Machinandearena, his stubbornness sometimes rendered him inflexible, while Evita, less vain, listened to advice). So, Evita often searched for other routes, such as telling Cámpora that someone or other was betraying Perón. The loyal servant would go immediately to tell Perón, and Perón, caught off guard, would say, surprised, 'That's funny! Evita thinks the same thing.' Encouraged by the success, Evita used this procedure again and again to denigrate or exalt one or another Perónist. Perón quickly became suspicious, and after several of these encounters, he finally walked Cámpora to the door, bowing reverently as usual, and whispered, 'That's good, Cámpora, mission accomplished. Give my respects to Evita.'

The image of a stubborn Perón seems to contradict that of the 'amorphous and cosmic' man, described by José Pablo Feinman, who the world thought was on its side, since he seemed to agree with whatever was said to him. In reality, Perón remained inaccessible. The film director Mario Sabato defines Perón well. Having just criticised X in front of Y, Perón would receive X and embrace him. But over X's shoulder, he would wink at Y, who believed he was the holder of Perón's true thoughts. The enigma remained within the solution: Which of the two was he betraying? Or was he betraying both?

Lost in this apathy, Evita fought with all her strength to 'save' Perón from his foggy side, a nonexistent zone in which he would lock himself. After all, she was 'responsible' for her husband. By increasing her intervention, she was only loving him and trying to annihilate his adversaries. He needed to be 'covered' so that no one could see the real him: 'Don't get too close, he is the sun!' But it also was for fear of being ousted that she exaggerated her surveillance. She lived, according to Penella, 'in a state of permanent anger,' furious with the true or imaginary enemies and often confusing herself as an antagonist. Finally, she was the one who had chosen Raúl Mendé as a successor to José Figuerola, the Francoist Spaniard who had worked with Perón at the *Secretaría* and whom Evita had decided to fire by arguing that he was not an Argentine. And hadn't Méndez San Martín himself been part of Evita's team, before becoming the organiser of Perón's 'sexual delirium'?

If the apathetic Perón threw her off balance and frustrated her, the hard and disdainful Perón hurt her just as much. 'Perón's only fault,' she confided to Rosa Calviño, 'is that he was a military man.' This is a strange way to address a long list of faults, pretending not to get into the specifics. The Perón of strict habits, neurotic about order and cleanliness, who showered and changed his clothes six times a day, was in fact a military man. He had a hurtfulness that Evita worked hard to conceal. One day, a poor man kissed his cheek, and Perón began to yell, 'That's disgusting! I can't stand being kissed by a man!' And so, she explained to the man that the leader had not meant to mortify him. At the time, the custom of kissing among friends, among men, did not exist. Men, military or not, kept their distance, even avoiding physical closeness with their children.

A close friend of Erminda Duarte related an anecdote about

the couple riding in a car to San Vicente. They got caught in traffic, and Perón ordered the driver to take a forbidden road. A young police officer pulled the car over to issue a ticket. 'Can't you see who I am?' Perón said furiously. 'Yes,' the officer said, 'but nonetheless, you broke the law.' Perón asked for his name and, despite Evita's pleading, drove to the precinct to have him fired. For the rest of the trip he kept muttering, 'Dirty black!' When they got to San Vicente, Evita surreptitiously phoned the precinct 'on Perón's behalf,' to rehire the police officer and apologise.

In fact, at San Vicente, she used the phone endlessly to the point that Perón disconnected it. She noticed this, fixed it herself, and covered it with a cushion to muffle the ringer. The telephone was an old obsession. On her trip to Europe, she had called Perón and Congress every day. The Evitist deputies interrupted their hearings to run to the phone, and Evita gave them instructions that she always checked up on the following day.

Not so Perón, who did not consider himself irreplaceable. In San Vicente, he rode Manchita, his blond horse with one brown spot, which he had ridden in August 1950 during a tribute to San Martín. Perón on horseback was quite an intoxicating sight for a woman! Standing, his thick size and his short arms, which he crossed over his stomach (his hands joined together at his belly), were obvious. In ordinary street clothes, he lacked elegance. But on horseback, in jodhpurs and accordion boots, he became himself, and that was irresistible. Evita, thinking of the poor, who could not wait until Monday, looked at him without seeing him.

Sailing with Perón, or accompanying him to a car race or to a boxing fight bored her just as much. Every Saturday afternoon, she left the Foundation to see a film with Perón. She could tolerate love stories, but he liked adventure films. She was nervous and passionate, he was relaxed and phlegmatic; they were as different as night and day. But the two were stuck in a repetitive game where each tries to manipulate the other – and each ends up frustrated.

Around 1949, the Evitist court was formed by Cereijo, Finance Minister and the foundation's administrator, Cámpora, Miel Asquía, Espejo, and Nicolini. Miranda, the one who found money for the Foundation just by tapping his foot, was not, however, an 'Evita man.' He worked only for himself and paid for it (accused of embezzling funds, he had to seek exile in Montevideo). To be a part of Evita's circle did not necessarily mean to have all of her confidence. Sometimes she told a secret to one of her followers to see how long it would take to come back to her in the form of gossip. She treated them with a mixture of happy camaraderie, maternal indulgence, childish seduction, and a slightly sadistic severity. She shook her finger and said, 'I've been told that you have been misbehaving lately. Be careful, OK? I am very good, but . . .' Or she would purse her lips and say, 'Come on, please, be nice, do this work for me for tomorrow.' Or she'd be blunt: 'Tell me, what is in your head? Shit?'

She also amused herself by submitting them to rough tests. Eva offered a delicacy that had been given to her by the Japanese ambassador to Juan Oscar Ponferrada, one of the poets in her circle. The poet tasted it, practically spat it out, and said, 'That is the foulest thing I've ever tasted.' Evita burst out laughing. 'I think it's gross too. But I told Cámpora I thought it was delicious, and he ate seven of them.'

This was mischief from an all-powerful woman expressing her disgust for servility. Meanwhile, elsewhere, she encouraged adulation. Was she capable of friendship? She thought she was. In reality, she was capable of giving, which is not the same thing. To give is also to exert power. She did not appreciate being asked favours unless the requests came from the needy who flocked to her Foundation. But with some, she established humble relationships full of freshness. Then she revealed herself to be simple and cordial, joking like any other young woman.

Fermín Chávez wrote that, 'The Evita that I knew had nothing to do with the "woman with the whip," nor the "black myth" woman, nor the dominatrix that some described her as, nor the psychotic personality which appears in a few bookish, pedantic, and pretentious rantings and ravings.'

On the other hand, when she told Salinas, 'The General does not have friends. He neither loves nor hates anyone,' she was attempting to express a recurring side of Perón's personality. As complicated as he was, in human relationships he revealed two primary aspects: seduction and coldness. The latter characteristic was the source of his supposed cowardliness. Courage requires ardour. An icy man has no reason to risk his life, and Evita feared his lack of spark, his refusal of all affection. It was to cure this that she frequented Doña Juana Sosa. After she became a widow, Perón's mother had married an agricultural worker twenty years her junior. Perón never saw his mother; perhaps he was ashamed to show his overweight mulatto woman to the Argentinean people. His brother was not as unpresentable, but Perón did not introduce him either. Ironically, he gave him a job at the zoo and ordered his aides not to let him come into the Red House.

Let's not forget the literary and 'Latin' aspect of this relationship. With Perón the master, Evita, the admiring student, would listen to him open-mouthed while he explained the sacrosanct books inherited from his father, most of all Plutarch's *Parallel Lives*. That is why, in her speeches, Evita reverently referred to Alexander the Great. Maybe Perón's reserve and capacity for self-control were Hellenistic virtues. She vehemently believed in her husband's intelligence. Early in his life, Perón had conceived a high idea of himself, probably because he spent time only with military men. In the army, he was passed off as an intellectual, but actually he was more cunning than anything else. He had an average, pragmatic intelligence that was only out of the ordinary to the extent that he believed so himself. As with beauty, so with intelligence:

what is important is to be convinced of it oneself. Evita knew something about this, for she had had the will to become beautiful.

Strengthened by this image of himself, Perón understood that the country dreamed of a debonair father, whose physique and language were typically *criollo*, a charming father of fun who was authoritarian when need be. He was in no doubt about all this. If he had failed to shy away from 'destiny' in 1945, it was because he experienced a moment of weariness and had not yet understood the enormity of the role that was waiting for him. So he took on the role of the actor who lets sympathy flow like a tidal wave. Perón sincerely enjoyed playing Perón, mirroring emotions capable of convincing millions of Argentines. Eva invented her elegance and her beauty but not her love for the people, which was real. The truly brilliant actor was Perón.

At the Teodoro García Street apartment, he played with electric trains with Raúl Salinas. To celebrate the nationalisation of the rail-roads, a badge was made with Perón's portrait on one side and a train on the other. This made Perón laugh like a child. The English laughed too, under their breath, for they had sold Argentina the dilapidated trains instead of repaying a debt to Argentina of many millions of pounds sterling (a debt that still remains unpaid). Did Perón realise the enormous swindle that, according to the conclusions reached at a recent summit of Brazilian economists, ruined other developing countries in addition to Argentina? Did he celebrate the nationalisation for purely electoral ends? Or, blinded by his arrogance and an odd candour that contrasted with his wiliness, did he let himself be deceived by people who were more cunning than he, as was the case with Ronald Richter?

This German 'scientist' had succeeded in convincing Perón that he was capable of producing atomic energy. Perón had an atomic plant built for him on the island of Huemul, in the south. The country lacked cement to build homes, yet tons of mortar were shuttled to Huemul. With his raincoat and his tousled hair, Richter looked like a mad scientist, and he made everyone laugh – except Perón, who for once was very serious. Evita would say, 'The General is very naïve.' Needless to say, nothing came of this endeavour.

Finally, this protean man could also be paternal. Perón scolded Evita for working all night, and he even wrote about it in his memoirs: 'My wife, I almost lost her. . . . One day I said to her: "Eva, rest and dream that you are my wife." Her face became serious. "It's exactly like that," she answered. "That is exactly how I feel I am your wife."' Perón also resorted to pleading with Mrs Mercante: 'Tell Evita not to stay up so late.' Evita just pouted, 'He's so annoying!'

This man, in love and worried about his wife's health, scolded her in public for not taking care of herself. An essential part of the story is Evita's illness. Illness and power became the two themes of the rest of their life together.

CROSSED WIRES: THE ILLNESS

It is hard to specify when the first signs of illness appeared, since Evita's health had always been delicate. The generally accepted date is January 9, 1950. On that day Evita was inaugurating the new seat of the taxi drivers' union when she fainted in front of Dr Oscar Ivanissevich, Minister of Education. Three days later, Ivanissevich removed Eva's appendix and also diagnosed cancer of the uterus.

Ivanissevich is said to have told Evita that she had a cancer that would require an operation, adding that Doña Juana had undergone a similar procedure and was now well. Evita is said to have responded, 'You will not touch me. I am fine.' A few months later, the doctor was back to insist on the operation, and Eva is alleged to have hit him with her purse. Ivanissevich, irritated, dropped the subject.

Eva continued her gruelling schedule. She believed herself

to be omnipotent, a woman who could control everything, including her illness. To stop, even for an instant, would have been the end. Could she give in to her enemies by leaving them some room? Never! She would do anything, including cheat to throw off her doctors. In the morning, she hurried to eat before the nurse arrived to draw her blood. And during her long days at the *Secretaría*, she took her temperature by putting the thermometer in backward. Denial killed her body, but anything else would have killed her heart and soul. She told the poet Héctor Villanueva, early one morning, when they were walking through semideserted Buenos Aires, unrecognised by the passersby, 'I do not want to stay in bed drinking hot toddies. I want to help people today, not tomorrow. And that is how I want to die.'

It is even easier to understand Perón's denial, why he never forced her to have an operation or even slow down. His first wife, Aurelia, had died of uterine cancer. A repetition of this was beyond imagining. Since he could recognise every symptom, he much preferred Eva to be at her Foundation all day and most of the night. He was not a man who accepted powerlessness, or fate, or God's will. Or maybe it was simpler than that. Perhaps he just couldn't watch the woman he loved die.

CROSSED WIRES: POWER

The second chapter of crossed wires begins with the constitutional reform of 1949. Perón wanted to enact social laws that he had been advocating since 1943, as well as the rights for seniors that Eva had proclaimed. The preamble of the new Constitution also had to include the definition of a Perónist Argentina: 'Socially just, politically sovereign, and economically powerful.' Finally, Perón wanted to abolish the article that, in the old Constitution of 1853, prohibited a president from running for reelection.

Perón being Perón could not simply admit that he wanted to be reelected. No one would have blamed him for this natural ambition. But since it was impossible for him to act with such clarity, the whole situation became convoluted.

According to Rodolfo Decker, who was close to Mercante, Perón was not interested in a second presidential term. He wanted to roam the planet, spreading his doctrine and studying new world realities, especially in developed countries. Mercante, who was president of the assembly in charge of modifying the old Constitution, appeared to be his successor. Evita had always said that Mercante was 'Perón's heart' and his heir apparent. Who else could have replaced Perón as president? Later, Perón thought he would return. But not for now. He had planned it all.

It turned out not to be that simple. Juancito Duarte and his three musketeers – Ramón Subiza, Héctor Cámpora, and Raúl Apold – feared a Mercante presidency more than they feared Evita's death, for their careers would be over. Thus, they tried to disparage Mercante in front of Evita, suggesting that he wanted to overthrow Perón.

Influenced by her brother and his three friends, Eva gave in to the fear that if Mercante became President, he would taint her husband's prestige. So she influenced Perón in this direction. Perón had always been secure in Mercante's loyalty, but soon he began to doubt him. Meanwhile, Evita met with a few members of the constitutional assembly and persuaded them of the necessity to abolish the famous article so that Perón could be reelected. When these members presented the abolishment article in question, Mercante was surprised, but seeing that Evita supported it, he did too.

He still believed that Perón and Evita wanted him to be the next Argentinean President. But if this were not the case, then he would obey without complaint.

This version contradicts the generally accepted one in which Evita struck Mercante off the register for the vice presidential candidacy to make room for her own candidacy. But the story adds an element that can explain the reasons behind the imprisonment of the radical leader Ricardo Balbín.

In 1949 and 1950, Balbín made three incendiary speeches against Perón. He was the radical candidate for the job of governor of the province of Buenos Aires, which was then held by Mercante. The latter had led the province remarkably well and wanted to be reelected for another two years. So Perón had Balbín put in jail. Carmen Llorca wrote that 'this incarceration was an example of presidential shrewdness for he had noted that Balbín's prestige had declined. . . . In order to balance the powers, and in order that Balbín reclaim his lost prestige, he offered him the role of a martyr, which always moves the masses.' Why would Perón want to restore the power of a dangerous opponent?

Juan Duarte and his friends were not satisfied with having pushed Mercante out of contention for the presidency. They were also plotting to oust him from the province's government. And Balbín's speeches gave them their ideal excuse. The federal judge of San Nicolas, where Subiza was influential, considered these speeches injurious to the President and ordered the radical leader's incarceration. Mercante begged Perón not to sign the order for incarceration, so that no one could ever say that Mercante was elected governor only because Balbín was put in prison. This affair hurt his prestige more than Balbín's! So Perón promised him. However, on the eve of the elections, Balbín was imprisoned. The order came from the judge in San Nicolas – who would not have done it without Perón's order.

Despite Balbín's 'moving martyrdom,' Mercante was reelected governor of the province of Buenos Aires. He held this office until 1952, when he was replaced by Aloé. But he never became 'Perón's heart' again. As for Evita, she now considered Mercante a 'traitor.'

Raúl Salinas's version adds a new element. According to him, although Perón often said he didn't want to be reelected, the opposite was true. However, Evita and Mercante believed him and considered a Mercante-Eva Perón ticket. This resulted in consternation, intrigue, rumours, and backstabbing through the entire government.

THE GLORY OF FAILURE

Whatever story is true, and each probably includes some kernels of truth, one thing is certain – Mercante was out. This left 'a hole that only Evita could fill,' according to Marysa Navarro. In 1950, Héctor Cámpora, Angel Miel Asquía, and other loyal followers organised tributes to Evita that pointedly suggested her candidacy for the vice presidency.

This was her moment of glory. Almost all the ministers were on her side. She had replaced those who were suspect with loyal Evitists. Only Borlenghi (a former Socialist who would spend his last days in Cuba, in poverty) was untouchable. He maintained a relationship with Eva that was fraught with both fascination and antagonism, and was able to keep his job for a long time. With him, of course, were the military ministers that only the army could dismiss. As for the rest she had been successful, and Perón did not oppose her.

The official campaign for the Perón-Eva Perón ticket kicked off on August 2, 1951, when two hundred unionists from the CGT came to see Perón. They asked him to accept reelection and expressed 'the vehement desire' that Evita be part of the ticket. Perón said neither yes nor no. Even in the intimacy of his own home, he said nothing to Evita. If 'no' was not spoken, then she thought she had a free hand.

They set a date of August 22 for Perón and Evita to declare their respective candidacies. For once, the direct drama would not take place on the balcony of the Red House, for they feared that the traditional square would not be big enough to hold the crowds. Instead they chose Avenida 9 de Julio, that piece of the pampas that is as wide as a block of houses and crosses the city from north to south. Room was needed to stage Evita's passion.

Although Buenos Aires is usually a sunny city, the sky is often hazy in August, the heart of winter. However, as expected, it was beautiful that day. The people had found a name for these radiant days, 'a Perónist day.' The Perónist ceremonies always benefited from this golden caress. And neither Perón's or Evita's smiles nor her blonde chignon could have shined so brightly without this loyal sun. These were overwhelming images of Perónism, so different from those of German Nazism. Italian fascism took advantage of good weather; but Mussolini, who feared the jubilation that seemed to render him effeminate, never unlocked his jaws. Perónism was a smiling fascism, one all the more palpable due to the fact that a woman was involved.

It was a Fascism during which the masses lived happily with their apartment houses and their stylish chalets, their clinics, their Christmas bonuses, their paid vacations, their easy retirements, their holidays spent at the beach, their championships, their children's games, and their feeling of helping to put together a stage where fascism played the leading role.

Close to one million people gathered facing the enormous stage that was built on the corner of the immense avenue and Moreno Street. The entire scene took on gigantic proportions. The undulation of the flags, the raised arms of the human throng, the plane that wrote 'CGT, Perón and Evita' in the sky, the voices of the button, poster, and souvenir salesmen were all part of the ritual. It was the perfect Perónist day, a day to celebrate the new faith. 'For a Perónist,' Perón had said, 'there is nothing better than another Perónist.' Perónism was inexplicable and defined in terms of 'feelings.' It was all about a mystical communion.

At five o'clock, Perón walked onto the stage, followed by various ministers and workers. But without Evita. José Espejo took the microphone to point out her absence, due to Evita's 'modesty.' He announced that they would go look for her. A few minutes later, she appeared and was applauded. She was dressed in black, with a bare head, and was very pale.

Espejo, her mirror, opened fire by declaring that the people had united in an open session, just as they had on May 25, 1810, when Argentina began its revolutionary war. Eva responded with a long speech. She alluded to that May 25, when the people had asked the first patriots, the founding fathers who were among them, what it was all about. Now, she said, the people knew exactly what it was about. It was simply about the management of 'the destinies of the Nation,' now and forever, by General Perón. Her words of incendiary love for Perón and the people and of her furious hatred for the oligarchy came as no surprise. But the crowd liked it that way. Since 1948, when Evita's power began to grow, she had acquired the right to speak during the big assemblies of October 17 and May 1. The people wanted to relive this nostalgic scene each time, to see themselves once again in the role of a tribe who idolised their priestess. In fact, the nostalgia was accompanied by a revolutionary music that went beyond words: the accent and the rhythm expressed revolt. A stranger who did not understand Spanish would have thought this woman was speaking of an insurrection. Evita spoke extending her hands, palms facing up. But the nervous tension, the trembling of her hands, demonstrated that there was nothing soothing about it. Was it an imploring or a menacing gesture? Screams of rage and pain burned her throat. Following her rasping voice, her skin turned red.

Perón's veiled voice calmed the crowd. Nothing was trembling or bleeding in him. He spoke of the 'strong and virtuous' people. The 'herbivorous lion' could be carnivorous in his calls to violence, which would become stronger and more frequent after Evita's death. But on August 22, 1951, his role was limited to accepting his candidacy and to observing, stunned, the sequence of events. A voice interrupted him: 'Speak, Evita!'

When the President had finished his speech, Espejo took the microphone to signal that Evita still had not said anything about her candidacy. He added that the CGT wanted an answer by the next day.

But they had not counted on the crowd, which responded in one breath: 'No! Not tomorrow! Now!'

No one could describe the wrench of her voice when she said, 'Do not make me do what I never wanted to do.' And she asked for four days to think.

'No! Now!'

She had to repeat *'compañeros'* four times before they would listen to her. *'Compañeros*, I am not renouncing my job to fight, I am renouncing the honour.'

'NO, no! Today! Now! Or we will strike!' the human sea cried.

She wanted to explain her reasons. 'In the world, they said I was a selfish and ambitious woman. You know it is not true. But you also know that I never did what I did in order to hold a political position in my country. Tomorrow, I do not want a worker from my nation to be defenceless when faced with envious and mediocre people who never understood me and will never understand me, who see greedy intentions in everything that I have done—' She was interrupted by protests of love, and her request was once again denied.

So she took the bull by the horns. 'This is all a surprise for me. For a long time I knew that my name was insistently mentioned and I did not deny the rumours. I did it . . . because there is no man who could even come close to Perón.' (What she meant to say was, because all men were mere planets orbiting around Perón the sun.) 'But never in my humble Argentinean woman's heart, did I consider accepting the position.' Then she handed the microphone back to Espejo.

'We will not budge until Evita replies favourably to the working people's wishes,' he said, very worried.

All Argentina witnessed the nervousness that reigned on that stage, thanks to the movie cameras, and heard the battle of voices, and Perón's dominating voice, thanks to the microphones: 'Stop! Let's wrap this up!' Someone who was close to Cámpora confirmed that Perón told Evita in a low voice, 'Basta.'

The essence of the scene was perceived by every Argentine, and the evidence was clear. Evita prolonged her dialogue with the people with the ultimate hope of convincing Perón. She did not succeed, and her personal October 17 turned into a failure. When she left the stage, she fainted. According to Father Benítez, this was due to the pain. 'She had not stopped feeling as if something was piercing her stomach, needles.' And also due to her lost hope.

Well before her speech, she had heard echoes of the army's rage at the announcement of such a scandalous candidacy. She referred to it in her own way, by speaking of 'insults and slander' and by textually adding, 'When the unrestrained tongues became unrestrained . . .' The uniforms' anger had a rational basis. If Evita were elected vice president, and if Perón died before her, she would take over the Argentinean presidency – just as Isabelita would twenty years later. And she would review the troops – just as Isabelita would. The idea alone of this affront made the servicemen pale.

However, Perón had never worried about the army's reactions. On the contrary, he had played with fire. Not only had he married Evita, ignoring his colleagues' horror, but he also enjoyed provoking them every chance that he got. Raúl Lagomarsino recalled Perón's laughter when he gave away coupons for luxurious cars to simple sergeants purely to mock their superiors. Of course, a military plot was brewing and would soon become a reality. Yet the servicemen were the first to be surprised when Perón paid so much attention to their outraged clamour.

Why suddenly listen to them, even when he knew who would die first? And knowing it so clearly, why not give Evita this last gift? And why did he let things get as far as the stage where the star herself did not seem to know the outcome?

Perón had not foreseen the intensity of the dialogue of love between Evita and the people. To find himself obscured by the radiance of this passion was not part of his plan. And nothing disconcerts a calculating man like the sudden appearance of the unexpected. Jealousy was the basis of his obstinacy.

However, he did not tell Evita to give up her candidacy. That would have been too simple. The day after the most important triumph of her life, which was also her greatest defeat, Evita confided in Ana Macri, 'I haven't slept in three nights. Perón has abandoned me. I've asked him what to do one thousand times, and one thousand times, he answered, "Your conscience will tell you what to do."' After Ana Macri related this, she was silent for a long time. She finally said by way of a conclusion, '*Pobrecita. Pobrecita.*' Poor thing.

Nine days later, Evita addressed a radio message to the Argentinean people, announcing her decision to renounce the candidacy. 'I have only one personal ambition,' she said, holding back a deluge of tears. 'On the day when they write a marvellous chapter of Perón life, they will say the following about me: next to Perón, there was a woman who was devoted to communicate the hopes of the people to him. Of this woman, we only know that the people lovingly called her Evita.'

And one month after this affirmation of the unique name that belonged only to her, she took to her bed to begin to die.

PERÓN'S SHIRT

The country crumbled away with her. The joyful extravagance of which she had been the protagonist was becoming
impossible for Argentina. Purchasing power had been growing
smaller and smaller since 1946, and inflation was galloping
out of control. That is why the government had launched a
campaign against 'speculation,' and that is the reason Evita had
organised a chain of stores in the neighbourhoods. Perón had
banked on an economic 'solution' that was revealing itself to
be illusory, that is, a third world war. But Argentina, enriched
by World War II (despite the English debt), was becoming
increasingly impoverished and had no remedy. They said that
Evita embodied Perónist Argentina: on September 28, when
they were administering a blood transfusion due to her extreme
weakness, General Benjamín Menéndez was at the head of a
military uprising to overthrow an anaemic regime.

According to Decker, Perón knew about this even before the
rebel troops emerged from their quarters, but loyal to himself,
he let them come. His only disdainful comment on this attempt
was: '*Chirinada*' (from the name of a certain Sergeant Chirino
who fifty years earlier had attempted a coup that was just as
unfortunate). When everything was again in order, General
Berdaguer, in charge of military justice, came to ask him to
sign Menéndez's death sentence. At the end of the meeting, as
Berdaguer was leaving, Perón yelled out, 'Oh! I forgot to tell
you, these hands will never be tainted with a man's blood. I
will not sign the sentence.'

The CGT had summoned the assembly at the Plaza de Mayo
to denounce the traitors. Perón spoke to a crowd that was
surprised by Evita's absence. Everything had been hidden from
her. She did not learn of this until the end of the day, and then
she spoke on the radio to thank the people. In a hoarse voice,
she asked her listeners, 'Pray to God to give me back my health.'

But she quickly added, as if her desire to get better seemed a reprehensible ambition, 'Not for me, but for Perón, and for you my *descamisados*.'

On September 10, Perón awarded her the Great Extraordinary Medal for her Renunciation with a capital *R*. From now on, everything that she would say or do would be written in capital letters. But the bitter satisfaction she got from having been transformed into the image of Sacrifice would not prevent her from secretly calling the unionists Isaías Santín, José Espejo, and Florencio Soto, as well as a loyal serviceman, General Humberto Sosa Molina. What did she want from them, in the prostrate state she was in? She ordered the purchase of five thousand automatic weapons and fifteen hundred submachine guns to distribute to the people in case of a military coup.

When Evita died, Perón seized these arms and bequeathed them to the police force. This was poor strategy, for in 1955 this institution turned against him. Why would he refuse to arm the people, as Eva wanted, in order to defend the revolution with his own hands? To avoid the social explosion that, as a good reformist, he had never wanted. Evita confided in Rosa Calviño, 'I am the oligarchy's enemy, not the General.'

The assembly of October 17 was dedicated to honour Evita's Renunciation. For the first time in his life, Perón covered her with elegies in his speech. He who never complimented her, gave thanks to 'this incomparable woman for every instant.' Dressed in a dark grey suit, as if in mourning herself, she listened to him in ecstasy. When she wanted to speak, not a word came from her mouth. And finally, she spoke the words that would remain in Argentina's memory and that the opposition contributed to its perpetuation through mockery: 'I have left the shreds of my life on the road.' 'We must attain victory, whatever it costs, whoever may fall.'

When her speech was over, she fell into Perón's arms.

✥

Once again, the vice presidential candidate chosen was Hortensio Quijano. This candidacy seemed doomed. Quijano still hung on to a few characteristics of a *caudillo correntino*, his moustache, sideburns, and bushy eyebrows. Quijano had cancer, too. Father Benítez recalls that he would sigh, 'Poor Evita! To have a race to death with a poor old man like me!' Perón knew perfectly well the state of Quijano's health. To choose him meant that he was appointing no one to the post. Or more precisely, not Evita, not Mercante, not any rival.

THE ARM IN A CAST

On November 3, Evita was admitted to the Presidente Perón clinic, which had been built by her Foundation.

A medical report, signed by Abel Canonico and Jorge Albertelli, two of the doctors who assisted at the operation, was published in the newspapers, *La Nacion* and *La Prensa*.

At the end of August – that is, immediately after her political hopes had been dashed – Evita had had vaginal discharges. According to Dr Canónico, the gynaecologist Humberto Dionisi had examined her. Dionisi noticed an ulceration on the cervix and requested a biopsy. Dr Julio Lascano González, in charge of the analysis, had given his diagnosis: endophytic carcinoma. In other words, a malignant tumor. They had decided to destroy the affected area with radiation treatments.

Albertelli gave her the first treatment on September 28. Later, he was asked to move in to the residence, where he would live for the rest of her illness.

For the time being, the analyses did not reveal that the cancer had spread. However, surgery was necessary. Canónico suggested they call George Pack, an eminent surgeon at the Memorial Cancer Center in New York. Pack and Canónico settled in at the Olivos residence and examined Evita under general anaesthesia, at the request of the patient, according to

Albertelli. In fact, her friends tried to hide the name of the illness from Evita. She knew nothing about Pack's presence or even Abel Canónico's. Why such secrecy? Canónico explains: 'First of all, at that time, the mention of an oncological procedure was inexorably associated with suffering and fatality. Second, given the patient's vigorous and hyper-active temperament, the suggestion of a cancerous procedure would have strongly affected her highly sensitive spirit.'

The results of the examination were clear. She needed a hysterectomy. Pack returned to the United States to take care of his patients, then returned for the operation a month and a half later, in early November. Wasn't this a long time to wait?

'Although we told Mrs Perón that she had a fibroid,' Albertelli writes, 'she sensed that we were going to perform major gynaecological surgery. At her request, we called in Dr Finochietto, a prominent general surgery specialist, to eliminate the gynaecological aspect of the surgery.' In other words, in case anyone was watching, her illness had to appear to be less serious. Father Benítez confirms that she was not fooled.

'I know the enemy with whom I must fight,' she said. 'The doctors are lying and I am lying back. We are all lying. But we all know the truth.'

Canónico continues the story. 'They removed the uterus and some nearby lymph nodes. A biopsy, performed by Dr Grato Bur, confirmed that the carcinoma had spread.'

Pack returned to the United States having accepted no fee. The postoperation scenario looked promising, and, as Father Benítez said, 'the surgeon had cut more rather than less to be certain.' Although the root had been excised, the cancer could of course return, though not immediately. When he left, the surgeon said only, 'Tell her to eat. If she is not afraid of gaining weight, she will live one hundred years.' Evita remained unaware of the presence of the optimistic American who had removed her female organs. She assumed Finochietto had been the one who removed a part of her that no one, in her presence, would refer to by name.

On November 11, they brought the electoral ballot box to the foot of her bed. The night before, just thinking about the elections had caused such a severe attack of nerves that she thought she was dying. But the next day, she celebrated the first time in the country's history that women were participating in an election. 'That's it, I voted,' she murmured, then she burst into tears. A photo shows her profile, a pointy nose, sunken eyes, two little braids crossed at the nape of her neck and crushed by her pillow. The worker who had come to take her vote was the young writer David Viñas. 'I was sickened by the adulation that surrounded her,' he said. 'But one image did move me: that of the women who, kneeling on the sidewalk, touched and kissed the ballot box that held her ballot.'

Perón had a landslide victory, due in large part to the women. Although exalted by the triumph, Evita immediately understood the meaning of the ten thousand blank ballots. 'Those are the people who have been disappointed by Perónism,' she said. 'We lost the best ones.' And Father Benítez adds that this silent refusal denounced 'Perón's self-worship, the moral cancer which was more severe than Evita's physical cancer, and also ate away at him.'

By Christmas, she was able to speak on the radio and go out into the residence's garden to give gifts to the children: toys, cider, and panettone that she distributed every year by the millions. In the eyes of the opposition, this was to 'train the people to beg.' In reality, to eat Evita's panettone had more to do with communion than it did with begging.

In mid-January, she took a trip aboard the *Tequara*, On the banks of the delta, the people welcomed her with a shower of flower petals.

Reclining or settled into the cushions at the Unzué palace, she still received about a hundred workers or ministers every day.

But by mid-February, the pain returned. Then, the terrible nightmares, the lack of appetite, the weight loss that Renzi hid by distorting the scale. The new biopsy revealed the recurrence of a neoplasm that risked spreading. The doctors said, 'She has one month left.'

She held on for many months, for dying a petty death was as impossible for her as living a petty life. She loved extremes, and her efforts to extend her days were as violent as her struggle to end them.

On April 3, she went to the funeral of Hortensio Jazmín Quijano, who had won the 'race to death.' The next day, still very elegant, she read the manuscript of her autobiography in a room on the first floor of the residence in front of a chosen audience. At the end of the day, she considered this book, which was reworked by Mendé, as another wish come true. To her left, Prince Bernard of the Netherlands courteously listened to her. 'He adored Evita,' confirmed Irma Cabrera, the maid. He had just awarded her the Great Cross of the Orange-Nassau Order, but he had come specifically to sell her the five thousand handguns and the fifteen hundred submachine guns that she had ordered.

On April 25, for the first time in Argentina, thirty-one women received their parliamentary mandates.

On May 1, she dragged herself to the balcony of the Red House to make her last speech. Her menacing air contrasted with her skeletal thinness hidden under a shapeless robe that covered the burns from radiation treatment. Her sister Blanca kept a shred of her blackened skin for a long time. The metaphor the opposition so ridiculed, 'the shreds of my life,' proved to be a literal reality.

Subconsciously, people closed their eyes when they listened to her. 'If we need to,' she yelled, 'we will make justice with our own hands. God, don't let those incensed people raise their hands against Perón. Watch out for that day! On that day, my General, dead or alive, I will go with the working people, I will go with the women of my people, I will go with the *descamisados* of the Nation and we will not leave a brick standing that is not Perónist.'

Perón was holding Eva up by the waist. They left the balcony together. 'In the room, the windows closed,' he writes in his memoirs, 'one could still hear the voice of the people calling for her. One could also hear my breath. Evita's was imperceptible. In my arms, there was nothing left but a corpse.'

On May 7, she celebrated her thirty-third birthday.

She weighed eighty-two pounds on June 4, when Perón began his second presidential term. On that same day, Raúl Apold had brought Evita a book about Perónism's accomplishments. When she saw a photo of herself, she said, 'Look at what I was then, and what I am now.' To distract her, Apold told her it was cold outside. 'The General told you to tell me that,' she said angrily. 'But I will not stay in this bed, unless I am dead.' And she got up to get dressed.

Perón commuted between the residence and Congress in a convertible. Eva could hardly stand up straight. But for this last role, she did not want to be sitting next to a standing Perón. So they gave her more morphine. They also created a plaster support in which they had her stand. Her large fur coat hid the belt that held her to the window placed behind the driver. Some said that they had plastered her right arm, too, for despite her weakness, she constantly waved to the crowds, never resting her arm.

Chapter 9

❖

THE MARTYR, THE MUMMY, THE SAINT, AND THE GRANDMOTHER

June 4 had passed and Eva could give in to her agony. That night, Father Benítez says, she did not sleep. Happiness kept her up. 'She had just given this triumph to her husband and her people.' She could breathe. She had been blocked from becoming vice president, from holding a position in her own name, but no woman, in Argentina or elsewhere, had ever attained such power. To feel satisfied also meant to be at the limit. She could go no farther.

When she returned from the clinic, she moved to a princely room with gilded furniture and silky red curtains. 'I had to get sick,' she said, 'to get an acceptable room.' This is where she would receive her visitors during the period when her condition seemed to be improving. Later, she moved to a room far enough away that she would not disturb Perón. He could not tolerate her screams, her smell. Uterine cancer, in its terminal phase, emits a terrible odour, and a doctor can detect the illness from the moment he or she enters the patient's room. Pavón Pereyra described a young woman visiting Evita, who lay in her bed as if crucified, unable to move, all her wounds open. When she leaned down to kiss her, the visitor could not hold back a grimace. 'Oh!' Evita said. 'She was nauseated when she hugged me.'

'Of course not,' answered another woman present, 'she has a tick.'

'Maybe, but she got it right when she got close to me.'

So in the other wing of the palace, a little room was made up for the nurse and Evita. 'Everything was very simple,' said one visitor. 'Very unattractive and shabby,' specified another. 'Perón was so tight-fisted that he ordered them not to make her bed with good sheets. "What good does it do?" he would say, "Her wounds ooze, and she would soil them."'

Was Perón afraid to get near her? Most people agree that he was. Always impeccably groomed, he controlled his nerves by keeping a distance. According to Father Benítez, late one night Evita managed to drag herself to Perón's room. Terrified, he began to yell, 'Get *this* out of here!'

So *this* Evita drafted a long text entitled 'My message,' which Perón had not wanted to publish for he considered it too incendiary. Perón published only a 'will,' whose first few words announced the tone: 'I want to live eternally with Perón and with my people.' To both, she bequeathed her jewels, which would form a permanent fund for the construction of popular housing. The rest of Evita's message was lost for many years but was finally recovered.

Having only Muñoz Azpiri or Raúl Mendé as models, Eva borrows their 'style' by setting it on fire. Hers were not words but cries – against the Church and against the army. She spoke without beating around the bush, but not without rhetoric. In their veracity and sincerity, her words could have been those of a prophet. But a scream is not language. Her cancer spoke for her.

They say that the dying recollect their lives in a succession of rapid images. Thus, we can imagine Evita trying to recall her moments of splendour, the times she graciously held out her chest so that a man wearing a tie could put a cross, a medal, or even a scarf with the country's colours around her neck. There were not many awards left for her to receive. Prince Bernard had decorated her in the name of Her Majesty Queen Julienne. When she was already very ill, she had left her bed to put on a beautiful low-cut, garnet-coloured velvet dress to receive the Order of Omeyyades from the Syrian ambassador. The Aztec Eagle of Mexico, the Great Cross of the Order of the Peruvian Sun, the Great Cross of the Order of Malta, as well as the Colombian, Haitian, Brazilian, Dominican, Ecuadorian, and Lebanese distinctions . . . How many times had she heard people describe her as 'honourable,' 'virtuous,' 'most illustrious'? Her own country, only eight days before her death, honoured her with the necklace of the Order of the Libertador General San Martín. It was made of emeralds, rubies, diamonds, and enamel, with the crests of the provinces, the Argentinean crest, a condor, laurels, a sabre, and on the very bottom, a sun with sixteen platinum and diamond rays and sixteen gold rays encircling the golden effigy of the Liberator.

Meanwhile, everyone kept lying to her. The entire country held masses for her health, broadcast over the radio. But the people at the palace unplugged Eva's radio so that she would not know about it. And each day, they brought her a special edition of the newspaper purged of all the bulletins reporting on her condition. Perón had asked Paco Jamandreu to bring her the most beautiful fabrics and the most original designs so that she could pick out a new wardrobe. They also showed her travel brochures. 'Look at India! Egypt! That's where we'll go.' She would acquiesce and play the game, believing without believing, defying the pious liars with allusions to her death, and scrutinising their reactions. Once she said to Apold, 'Last night I dreamt that I was dying and that you published the news.' Apold started to babble an answer when Juancito whispered in his ear, 'Watch out. She's

testing you.' Another time she gathered her family to announce
that she was dying. Doña Juana screamed so loudly that Eva
laughed out loud, 'But no! It's a joke.' She called her friends to
give them souvenirs and medals engraved with her signature. In
early July she called Father Benítez to take confession. 'You know,'
she murmured, 'that I am at the bottom of a well. Neither doctors,
nor anyone but God can take me out of it.'

She often spoke of religion. She discussed it with Juan Duarte,
who himself had been struck by syphilis and was aghast at divine
injustice. 'On the contrary, He is just,' she would argue. 'He is
even a stickler for justice! If not, He would have saved me: I am
the wife of the President! But I accept suffering, if it is for the love
of my people.' A taste for soap opera characterised her until the
end. But when the claws pierced her stomach and the nape of her
neck more and more deeply, her language changed. 'However, I
will ask Him for a truce. Let Him give me a vacation. I am too
little for so much pain.'

She would also say, 'If God gives me my health back, I will
never wear jewels or beautiful dresses again. Nothing but a skirt
and a blouse.'

Eva, who had always had fairly thick ankles, sighed when
contemplating the bones in her legs now visible underneath
her skin. 'With all I did to refine them, and look at them
now.' Alluding to 'Captain Evita,' a famous march that had
been dedicated to her, she joked, 'Presently, I am not even a
sergeant.'

One of the last photographs of her shows her sitting on a couch.
It is no longer Evita, but a skeleton trying to smile. Her chignon is
gone, and in its place, a badly tressed, too-thin braid has appeared.
Her kneecaps are visible under her slacks. She is wearing a wool
sweater and sport shoes with white socks. Her back, curved by the
pain, gives her an air of humility. Her pointed nose and protruding
upper lip, as if someone had pulled them forward, do not belong
to the woman who once was so elegant.

She organised eight-hour shifts so that her sisters and her

friends could stay close to her. Meanwhile, against her husband's advice, Lina Machinandearena had gone to see Evita. The two women had not seen each other for quite some time. To think that Evita had once worn Lina's jewels to play *La pródiga*! Lina returned home screaming, 'That woman is all alone! I found her abandoned, in a miserable bed! She was so happy to see me, as if no one ever visits her.' It was practically true. Besides her intimate group, the doctors tried to avoid letting people see her, so as not to excite her too much or divulge her illness. She languished not in her solitude but in the nostalgia of all those she would never see again. She had known so many people. Where were they now?

On June 18 she fell into what appeared to be a coma. The doctors thought that she was dying, and they tried to revive her. She woke up surrounded by strange machines, conscious of an unusual movement and anxiety. 'What's happening to me?' she asked. 'I have to get up. If I stay in this bed, I am dead.' And she got up.

The doctors no longer hid the truth from her. They were stunned by all that she knew about uterine cancer. It seemed she had taught herself about it all along. In fact, in 1945, she assailed Anne-Marie Heinrich with very precise questions. They had been lying to a courageous and well-informed woman.

On the eve of her death, she called Perón in alone, hoping to have a final heart-to-heart conversation with him. According to Carmen Llorca, he had not come to see for two days. She told Perón, 'I wanted to see you for a little while.' Then, 'Do not forget the *humble*,' as if worrying about the forgetfulness that her absence could easily cause.

Was there reproach in her voice? Castiñeira de Dios, the former Minister of Culture, acknowledged that, 'Perón loved Evita, but less than she loved him. He was more distant. While she was in agony, he smoked and talked in the hallway, aloof.' An intimate friend of Erminda and Blanca went farther: 'At that time, he already had his young coeds, and he did not think twice about talking about them to Pedro Ara, in front of her.' Ara was the Spanish doctor who mummified Evita's cadaver.

Saturday, July 26, around eleven A.M., Elisa came to replace Blanca. Doña Juana left the room for a moment.

'Poor old lady!' the dying woman sighed.

'Why poor?' said her sister, who knew what Evita meant. 'Mom looks good!'

'I know. *Lo digo porque Eva se va.*'

Those were her last words, and her most beautiful. *Eva se va*, Eva is leaving. Perfectly musical, an ultimate understanding of her name, a syllable that comes back like an echo.

✣

There is deception regarding the time of her death. It was officially announced at 8:25 P.M., but some people believe that she died in the late morning, others in the afternoon, and still others at 7:40 P.M., the time when Pedro Ara had telephoned Aznar, the Spanish ambassador, to tell him, 'She just died. I am taking her to the bathroom for her first autopsy.' Whatever the actual time, it was not yet 8:25. But that was the time of her marriage to Perón, and it was the time she chose for her death.

BEAUTIFUL FOREVER

Beginning on July 26, 1952, until the fall of Perón's regime, the evening news was interrupted so that the anchor could remind the audience 'It is 8:25 P.M., the time when Eva Perón entered immortality.' A national mourning was decreed for one month. The CGT ordered all its Perónists to wear a black tie or another sign of mourning for three days. 'All the Perónists' meant everybody. The poet María Elena Walsh was fired from the school where she taught for not wearing an armband. She was one of many.

In the meantime, Dr Ara went on with his task.

According to Perón, Evita would have refused to 'waste away underground.' In any case, she knew she would be exhibited. That is why she had asked Sara Gatti, her manicurist, to give her nails a new coat of nail polish.

The manicurist arrived at the residence at dawn on July 27. (By then Pedro Ara had made Evita's body 'definitively incorruptible.') She wanted to file Evita's nails, but her long, thin fingers were rigid, and Ara had to separate them. Then it was Pedro Alcaraz's turn. He dyed her hair to make it radiant and styled her chignon from the happy days gone by. The two of them, Pedro and Sara, worked as if 'in a dream,' like Sleeping Beauty's manicurist and hairdresser, giving her a beauty that would last a hundred years.

Dressed in a white shroud and Argentina's blue and white flag, she was laid to rest in a clear glass casket. Between her fingers, they placed the rosary beads given to her by the pope. She was exhibited in the hallway of the *Secretaría*.

(Even this was not without controversy. According to Sebastian Borro, the Perónist right did not want to hold a wake within the walls of the Ministry of Labour. It was too symbolic. And the political future started to take shape on that same day. When Espejo and Santín came to say good-bye to Evita, they were almost not let in.)

The hallway was flanked by stairways. In the middle was the transparent casket. People walked up one side, looked in the casket, and walked down the other side, taking with them an indelible memory, an image that held within it every fairy tale, Cinderella, Sleeping Beauty, Snow White, all of them. It was a parade of images that Apold could not miss. The Argentinean Goebbels hired Edward Cronjagar, the cameraman from 20th Century-Fox who had filmed Marshal Foch's funeral, to capture the event. The result was a film entitled *And Argentina's heart stopped*.

For thirteen days, Argentina's heart stopped beating. These

were also 'Perónist days,' but of an opposite sign. The rain did not stop falling, as if the weather blended in with the sorrow. The line of visitors stretched in a zigzag under a roof of umbrellas and newspapers for almost two miles. The people waited for ten long hours, frozen, starved, sick. The foundation and the Red Cross took care of the old people and distributed coffee and sandwiches. By the time they reached the casket, they were chilled to the bone, exhausted from fatigue and from having cried so much. She was so beautiful, so young, so small. The mourners would kiss the glass cover, then faint. When they finally left, it was nighttime, and it was as if they were orphans. Blinded by tears, they saw thousands of torches burning, which would be turned off in unison, at exactly 8:25, as well as flowers, thousands of flowers. The smell of rotting flowers permeated the streets. And her portrait, with her smile was displayed on the Plaza de Mayo. From the moment the sky cleared, the neighbours from Maciel Island – those who had crossed the Riachuelo in 1945 – said that they saw Evita's face in the full moon.

On August 9, the casket was placed on a gun carriage. With all her honours, surrounded by a sea of flowers and two million spectators, she was taken to Congress, then to the CGT where she was to rest waiting while the monument was constructed. It was a brand-new building that she had given to the workers. The unionsts had a hard time obtaining the right to shelter Evita, but they ended up winning, for her last wish was to be laid to rest among the workers. Someone commented that her remains were more political than human. Dr Pedro Ara was waiting for her in a laboratory that he designed. He had been waiting for her a long time.

This anatomy professor, who was now working as an embalmer, was renowned around the world and was even said to have been in charge of Lenin's mummification. Ara would neither confirm nor deny this flattering rumour. On the other hand, it was indeed he who, having settled in Argentina with

a vague honourific position of cultural attaché, had embalmed
the body of the composer Manuel de Falla. It was also said that
he had mummified the body of a young teenager from Córdoba
whose father, crazy with grief, dressed her every night and sat
her at the dinner table. One thing was certain, he kept a 'beggar's
head' at his home that he would place neatly on the bar next to
the bottles of sherry. It must have been the contemplation of
this marvel that persuaded Perón to hire him.

In his book, *El caso Eva Perón*, Pedro Ara tells about the time
he was able to observe Evita (in fact, watch her like a spider).
One October 17, the serendipity of diplomacy allowed him
to find himself next to her on stage at the Red House. The
moment Evita began to speak, he said to himself that now her
resistance would be put to the test. If she really did suffer from
serious anaemia, as it was said, she wouldn't be able to speak
for long without resting. He expected her to take advantage of
the countless ovations that always interrupted her speeches.
Ara was there to see her fatigue, her shortness of breath, her
panting pulse under her neck's thin skin.' To his great surprise,
if not his disappointment, Evita did not flinch.

Evita did not die on that October 17, far from it. But time
passed, and finally the day came when no one could ignore
that the end was near, and that is the time when, according to
Ara, the idea to mummify Evita began floating around in the
air. Various official emissaries had suggested it to her. Finally,
Ara was contacted by Raúl Mendé, but didn't actually see Evita
until the day of her death. Gabriel García Márquez wrote in
Clarín, a Buenos Aires newspaper, 'The man who embalmed her
stood guard in her antechamber during the long weeks that her
illness lasted, for he had to proceed with the mummification the
instant she died, to render the conservation more convincing
and more durable.'

During the thirteen days that the corpse was exposed at
the *Secretaría*, zealous workers had taken the glass cover off
to clean the inside. Anticipating the emission of gases, they

had had air circulating through the coffin to prevent the glass from fogging. Ara was not pleased when he heard about this. He had given strict orders not to expose the body to air. The damage, especially aesthetic damage, could be irreparable.

This was not to be tolerated. That is why Pedro Ara had a perfect technical laboratory built in the CGT, to which only he and Perón had keys. The most profound secrecy would surround the long hours during which Evita would remain submerged in boiling pools of God knows what mysterious liquids.

Pedro Ara did not furnish any details about the contents of the pools. It is Dr Domingo Tellechea, who was in charge of restoring the mummy many years later, who divulged the information. The corpse had been dissected by the ancient method of 'Spanish mummification,' in which preserving solutions are sent through the entire circulatory system, all the way to the capillaries. Some areas of the body were filled with wax. Then the entire body was covered with a layer of hard wax. This procedure took an entire year, during which time Doña Juana, Elisa, Blanca, and Erminda came to pray and cry regularly behind the closed door.

Finally, in July 1953, Evita was ready. The monument was not; post-Evita Perónism had lost its verve. So she was kept at the CGT, where they built a kind of chapel. On the wall was the Virgin of Luján with the rigid triangular coat to whom she had been devoted. Evita lay under a glass bell, on a tiny bed of silk. She wore an ivory tunic with wide sleeves, designed and sewn by Thana Palud, a Spanish 'lady' who was friends with the embalmer. 'She seemed to sleep,' according to the expression inevitably used by Perón when he saw her.

Only a selected audience was allowed to see her. They contemplated her with a religious respect, as if she were a wax Madonna. They still cried. During this time, the CGT's facade remained covered with flowers from top to bottom. Meanwhile, the visitors could not help but look suspiciously at Ara, who always seemed to be hovering nearby. Eva's body remained in that chapel, under Ara's watchful eye.

On September 16, 1955, when Perón was overthrown, Juana Larrauri had the integrity in the midst of indescribable confusion, to settle the debt of fifty thousand dollars due to the embalmer. Ara hurried toward the Unzué palace, where he came across army trucks and excited crowds of people. It was a chaotic atmosphere, as if it were the end of the world. It was raining, of course. The sky, always a Perónist, changed with the events. Gone were the sunny days; it seemed that it had not stopped raining since Eva's death.

The residence was surrounded by soldiers, but due to the disorder, Ara slipped by them. Thinking that Perón was no longer there (it was believed that he had already escaped abroad), he asked to see Major Renner to ask him the burning question: what to do with Eva now? Where should she be taken to protect her from the perverse and morbid enemies? But much to Ara's surprise, Renner responded that Perón was in fact there.

Perón neither met with him nor gave him the slightest indication about the destiny of Eva's body. He had someone tell Ara that he would call him, but the circumstances dictated otherwise. He was forced to seek exile without seeing his wife's embalmer. He never got in touch with Ara, not from Paraguay or Panama, his first places of exile, or from Madrid, where he lived for almost twenty years. Pedro Ara stayed alone, the only person responsible for Evita, and this was seemingly far from unpleasant for him.

'THIS WOMAN IS MINE'

For some time, nothing disturbed the doctor's tranquillity. Every day he climbed to the second floor of the CGT building, waved to the guards whom no one had thought of replacing, and settled into his office not far from Evita to read or meditate on life. No one ever came to interrupt his reflections. Ara had tried to approach the new president, Eduardo Lonardi, to tell him that Evita was in his hands, but the relative secret with which the embalmer had surrounded the operation had been fruitful. Perónism's opponents did not know that she was there, or they were sceptical, thinking that they were looking at a statue when actually seeing this perfect body. The government finally ordered a medical examination. Doctors Nerio Rojas, Julio César, Lascano González, and Osvaldo Fustinoni arrived at a pitiful conclusion. Yes, it was her all right. This woman continued to annoy. She had been a living scandal and now she was a dead scandal. What to do? In doubt, they refrained from action.

Lonardi had assumed his role as President on September 23, 1955. On November 13, he was replaced by General Pedro Eugenio Aramburu, a representative of a political line that unabashedly favoured the rights of the winners. Admiral Isaac Rojas, vice president under Lonardi, remained in his position, and he represented the hard line better than anybody else. (Castiñeira de Dios said this about the ferocious anti-Perónist: 'I saw him with my own two eyes when he was decorated by Evita. He said: "*Señora*, this is the biggest honour of my life!"')

Three days after Aramburu came to power, the CGT was besieged by the army. Espejo was no longer its secretary after Evita's death. He had fallen with the other survivors of the team, for Perón (the Perónists modestly say 'his collaborators') had purged their conscience of any sign of Evitism.

A wide variety of uniforms currently came to contemplate the mummy. Horror, amusement, and incredulousness alternated with a religious respect. As ardent as their hatred of Evita was, the sleeping woman gave an illusion of sanctity by which few of them were unaffected. One of these visitors was Captain Francisco Manrique, the leader of the military. He described her as follows: 'She was the size of a twelve year old girl. Her skin looked like wax, artificial. Her lips were painted red. If you tapped her finger, it sounded hollow. Ara, the embalmer, did not part from it as if he loved it.'

The conflict created by the existence of it was the fear of deification. The *Revolución Libertadora's* military feared that every place would be designated a shelter for these remains and would be transformed into a shrine. Isaac Rojas expressed this fear in one oddly just sentence: 'the cadaver had to be excluded from the political scene.' And to think that Evita had fought her damnedest not to be excluded and even believed for a time that this was the goal of Dr Ivanissevich's diagnosis in the first place!

Lieutenant Colonel Carlos Eugenio Moori Koening was the son of a German soldier who had been killed during World War I. He was massive, red skinned, and had become the chief of the army's Information Service. He had already seen Evita in her diminished state when Pedro Ara showed up at the *Casa Rosada* to inform Lonardi that Perón had left Eva's body to him. Moori Koening had silently observed it all, not commenting. But throughout these months of hesitation, an idea sprouted in his mind that he ended up proposing to Aramburu. Its name was 'Operation Evasion.' The idea was to take the emotionally explosive remains and make them disappear for good. Not to profane them or burn them, after all they were Christians! But to eliminate them from the scene forever. Aramburu agreed.

On November 24, at midnight, Moori Koening climbed to the second floor of the CGT, followed by a group of soldiers. Pedro Ara had been informed of Aramburu's decision and was there. He wanted to make sure that the rules were followed. The body would be placed in the same casket that had held it during the exhibition at the *Secretaría*. Moori Koening had hired a welder to solder the cover.

This last night with the dead woman held two surprises for the embalmer. Perón was the only one, or so he thought, to have a key that gave private access to the garage of the offices of the union leaders. This door had to be opened in order to allow the army truck that transported the casket to pass. The casket had been recovered that same afternoon from the funeral parlour that had stored it. But the door was closed, and no member of the guard had a key. Desperately, Ara tried his. 'My astonishment was endless,' he writes. 'This door opened with the same key that opened the door to the laboratory and the chapel on the second floor.' In other words, Perón had not insisted on a special key. He had not worried about the security of the 'operation.' This negligence underscored the indifference which he evidenced for the mummy's destiny.

The second surprise for Ara was that the welder did not show up. They would not be able to transport Evita in the sealed casket. Her body would be touched, by hands and eyes.

There were about twenty men witnessing the scene: the soldiers who had come with the general, the policemen, the guards, and the workers of the CGT who had come to help lift the casket. Moori Koening spoke to the workers, 'We wanted you to be here tonight so that you could witness the Christian respect with which we do things.' With that, he removed the Perónist flag that covered her (the Argentinean flag had been removed during a previous soldier's visit).

Ara's recollections are as follows: 'Eva's body appeared, dressed in her new tunic which covered her bare feet. I signalled to two workers who came over to help me.

'Without touching her as such, one of them took her by the ankles over the tunic. The other worker and myself took her by the shoulders. And this is how we carried her thin body, slowly, very carefully, from the platform to the bottom of the casket, without disturbing her hair or her dress. My assistants were pale and covered with perspiration due to the respectful emotion and the fear they felt. More than one tear fell, and not only from the eyes of fanatic Perónists.'

The truck driven by Captain Frascoli left the CGT garage

with the open casket. It remained parked until dawn in the courtyard of the navy's First Infantry Regiment. Moori Koening admitted much later, when the full extent of his nervous ailment was already known, that when morning came, they found a candle and a bouquet of flowers next to the truck.

The wandering cadaver made the rounds of various military buildings. She was hidden in an office of the army's information service on Sucre Street for twenty days. They had to change the location often to shake off the Perónists in search of their Señora, but Moori Koening confirmed that at each place, the flowers and the candles would appear as if by magic. 'I kept her at Viamonte Street, 25 de Mayo Street, always watching her, protecting her, hiding her,' he said. 'They wanted to take her away from me. I don't know what they wanted to do with her.'

All this persuaded Moori Koening to cease moving Evita around. He took her to his office on the fourth floor, at the headquarters of the information service on the corner of Callao and Viamonte streets. She was placed in a wooden case that had contained audio equipment and on which was inscribed: 'The Voice of Córdoba.' She stayed there until 1957.

In February 1956, Moori Koening went to Chile under Aramburu's orders to meet Doña Juana who had been exiled to Santiago with her three daughters. The general had received her authorisation to secretly bury Evita in a dignified manner. In decree number 37, Aramburu ordered Moori Koening to place the remains in plot #275, section B, of the Chacarita cemetery. But Moori Koening did not follow these orders. He kept Evita. He contemplated her. He may even have previously buried her in a random field near General Paz Avenue. He would say only this: 'I buried her standing up, because she was a man!'

Did he later have the woman, whom he thought he was hon-ouring as a soldier by not laying her in the tomb, disinterred? Did he keep her in his office for a longer period of time in order to have her near his thoughts, as Ara did? To meditate on a woman's courage that made his soldier's imagination even more masculine? The second man to fall in love with the corpse would end up saying in a faraway murmur, 'She is mine. That woman is mine.'

Meanwhile, Francisco Manrique thought Evita was indeed in plot #275, until he went to see Moori Koening, who revealed his treasure. Informed of this by Manrique, General Aramburu dismissed Moori Koening, whom he now considered to be mentally ill, and replaced him with Colonel Cabanillas. Major Arandia and Captain Frascoli, too, were kicked out of the army.

Manrique then called Major Hamilton Díaz and Colonel Gustavo Adolfo Ortiz. These two soldiers would be in charge of accompanying the mummy to Europe in collaboration with an Italian priest introduced to the *Casa Rosada* by Father Rotger, an Argentinean priest. Besides these people, no one would know where Evita was.

A few weeks later, the Italian priest returned to Buenos Aires carrying an envelope containing all the details of the final destination of the remains. However, President Aramburu refused to open it. He gave it to a notary and asked him to give it to the next Argentinean president four weeks after his death.

'THE PATRIARCH'S AUTUMN'

In the meantime, where was Perón? Economic hardships had increased since 1951. As wages rose, prices climbed even higher. At that time, Evita had been there to take on her role as an intermediary, if necessary scolding the strikers. When she died, everything seemed to deflate. The workers no longer had a spokesperson, an intermediary. Perón tried to meet with them more often, but more importantly he wanted to dismiss the CGT's leadership, which was used to getting along with Evita who always took the side of the workers.

October 17, 1952, was devoted to honour the memory of the absent heroine. Perón read the will and announced the creation of the Evita Foundation, independent from the Eva Perón Foundation. The jewels she had bequeathed to the people would be kept at the Perónist museum that they planned to inaugurate at the future monument. They would represent collateral for housing loans granted to the 'humble.' But behind the curtain of honours and good intentions, a true drama was taking place. On the plaza, groups of determined men booed Espejo, who was soon replaced by Vuletich. The new CGT had to take note of the change, for the politics of the redistribution of riches, nationalisation, and the state's control over the economy, carried out by Perón and supported by Evita, were no longer possible. From now on, the CGT was to stimulate foreign investments, especially American. Perón had once said that he would rather cut off his hands than let things come to this.

Evita sensed all this from her deathbed, and her rage intensified her physical suffering. That is why she had called Castiñeira de Dios, whom she had not seen in a long time. 'They distanced us,' Evita told him sadly. 'But I want to see you head the Foundation. I will do anything so that evil Méndez San Martín doesn't get his hands on it.'

In the end, it would in fact be Méndez San Martín who would take hold, if not of the Foundation, then of Perón. Méndez San Martín who, with Raúl Mendé or Teisseire, represented the right wing of Perónism, López Rega's precursors.

For when Evita died, Perón seemed to personify the country. But strangely, without Evita, Perónist Argentina seemed to be deflating. Suddenly Perón's stoutness lacked muscle, he was nothing but an empty goatskin. He was pathetic with his glasses at the end of his Indian nose, sitting at Evita's desk at the *Secretaría*, trying to do what she did (Evita's project with Castiñeira never succeeded). There was a day, long ago, when she had tried to be like him. Now he was incapable of imitating his imitator. She had accurately predicted the future when she screamed and sobbed in agony, 'Who, who is going to take care of my poor?'

Nonetheless, the Foundation continued without her – and without Perón – until the demise of the regime. It was often accused of possessing the trappings of a personality cult; nevertheless after Evita's death, it continued its activity. It was accused of waste and disorder, yet almost a half century later, it would be acknowledged that Argentina never had a more organised institution. The Foundation functioned as it pleased, unaffected by bureaucracy – but it worked. But after Eva's death, it had to live up to a dream of reallocation of wealth that became increasingly impossible. A frenzied energy was always required to take care of it efficiently. Since that energy was missing, Perón created another trick to hide the death behind a curtain. He asked the people to continue sending letters to Evita as if she were still alive. The envelope should be addressed to 'Señora Eva Perón, Presidential Residence, Agüero 2502, Capital.'

In the photos taken on the few days when Perón actually received Evita's poor, it is evident that his back no longer held him up. His mouth is constantly open, not because of a protruding jaw but due to stupor. Had he loved her after all, and was the emptiness detected on his face and body the proof? Did the manipulations, the traps, the jealousies create a kind of love that only Eva and Perón could understand? And now that he found himself without support, without bones, without air, did he wish to disappear?

Méndez San Martín quickly understood what the widower needed. Perón, who was almost sixty, still wanted to taste the green fruit. He was returning to his first passion, child loves, with a voracity that age and the terror of corrupted skin only intensified. His desire was for freshness, puerility, silliness. Dolls that seemed never to wilt and that liberated him from the other doll that was too heavy a burden to carry. Thus the Union of High School Students (UES) was born.

As the Minister of Education, Méndez San Martín worked hard to transform the UES into a political tool (Perónise the students) and an effective relaxation for Perón. Membership was not obligatory, but in the schools, the student delegates would tell the hesitant few in a barely veiled menacing voice, 'You better sign up.' There were very few students who did not have a UES card. It was a magic card that opened the doors of the presidential residence in Olivos.

In the photos from this period, Perón can be seen in his visored cap. His waist was thicker, and his arms seem to have shrunk like a pair of fins. He had people call him *Pochito*. His half-childish, half-cynical sense of humour ended up turning against him and making him appear grotesque. The autumnal patriarch was surrounded by a crowd of teenagers dressed in white T-shirts and black shorts, gym clothes. Everyone seemed happy. Perón was happy because he was breathing the smell of youth, and the students were happy because they sensed that they were about to receive gifts. In addition to the 'Pochito cap,' the mopeds he gave to the girls by the hundreds were part of the legend. How could the truth not be seen? Father Benítez himself even writes that Perón's thirteen-year-old mistress lived in the Unzué palace. She was a brunette with big black eyes and pronounced eyebrows. She would amuse herself by trying on Evita's clothes while the 'old General' tenderly watched. Atilio Renzi, Evita's loyal collaborator who still ran the household, resented this as if it were a stab to the heart. He cried before Benítez.

In the eyes of the Church, these young students in their sporty uniforms whose hedonism was actively stimulated were lost souls. And on his side, Perón had grievances against the Vatican. Already in October 1950 he had frowned on the idea of inaugurating the eucharistic congress that was supposed to take place in Rosario. Catholics had felt outraged by the welcoming speech the President had addressed to the Basilio Scientific School during their conference at Luna Park. They had concluded that Perón belonged to that esoteric movement and had taken advantage of the opportunity to cry scandal.

Perón, frustrated by Catholic propaganda, did not want to go to Rosario. Only Evita's insistence, encouraged by Father Benítez, had prevented him from hitting a sour note. The presidential couple inaugurated the eucharistic congress beside Monsignor Ernesto Ruffini, and the young Catholic schoolgirls gave delirious ovations to Evita, which horrified the nuns. After all, Evita had experienced an anticlerical crisis around 1951. Raúl Mendé, a former seminary man, had persuaded her that Perónism was the new religion to the point that she would remove the crucifixes from the hospital walls. She who had led, at the same time as her campaign for women's right to vote, a plan to institute religious teachings! It was not until she was faced with death that she liberated herself from Mendé and got closer to Benítez and to God.

Before going to Rosario, Perón had written a letter to Father Benítez. This is what he wrote: 'I noticed very indiscreet behaviour on the Vatican's behalf. You know that my government is "in quarantine" there. But that is not all: according to a report from our Ambassador Arpezani, the Pope personally declared that our government was totalitarian. Minister Paz also heard this and was as surprised as I was, *not by the affirmation but by its indiscretion*'. Why wasn't Perón surprised by this affirmation? Because as a convinced totalitarian, he had no problem admitting it. On the other hand, 'the indiscretion' shocked him. But what indiscretion? Did he believe the Vatican had no right to denounce a President as a totalitarian since they had sent him thousands of Nazis?

Let's come back to Evita's death, to the UES, and to the moment when Perón gave in to his long-simmering irritation against the Church. Attempts to explain the reasons for this confusion were many. The letter implies that, for the ecclesiastical hierarchy, Perón was no longer the sort of person with whom they wanted to associate, but that the Church was not in a position to find fault in him. And according to Benítez, it was Méndez San Martín again, the black beast, who worked hard to persuade him to dismiss the Church.

A word about Father Benítez. The priest's absolute allegiance to Perónism and his relentless work at the Foundation as its spiritual leader were detrimental to his relationship with the ecclesiastical authorities. They were unhappy about the closing of the Charitable Society, for they had had close ties to it. Despite his cordial relations with Cardinals Coppello and Caggiano, Benítez had never been promoted up the hierarchical ladder. He believed the Church was distancing itself from Christ. He wanted a popular church. There was no doubt that his feelings influenced Evita far beyond Raúl Mendé's actions, actions whose aim was to intoxicate her with Perónist fanaticism and then to manipulate her.

On June 11, 1955, the Catholics organised the traditional procession of Corpus Christi. But the procession turned into a violent anti-Perónist demonstration, so much so that Perón, who was at the end of his tether, accused them of having burned an Argentinean flag. According to Father Benítez, 'On June 16, 1955, at 4 A.M., someone knocked on my door. It was Trenti Rocamora, who had replaced Martínez Zuviría at the National Library. He was very close to Méndez San Martín with whom he shared infamy. I let him in and he asked me if the Church owned a title to the Buenos Aires Cathedral property. I answered: "No, but the place that was designated for the cathedral is mapped on Juan de Garay's map of the founding of Buenos Aires. Why do you ask?"

'"Because the State is going to expropriate it."

'I told him that was crazy, that it would create an international scandal. And I stayed at home to pray. At noon, I heard the news about the bombing of the Plaza de Mayo. The cathedral's secularisation had been decided, at that precise moment and on that same day.'

Did the air force know what Perón was proposing when

it took advantage of an assembly on the plaza, an expiatory ceremony after the flag burning episode, to attack the regime, massacring men, women, and children along the way?

The day after the massacre, the fires started again, and the old colonial churches of San Ignacio, Santo Domingo, and San Francisco were burned down by enraged Perónists, no doubt the same ones who had set fire to the Jockey Club on April 15, 1953, during a demonstration to show support for Perón and whose goal was to neutralise the rumours started by Juancito Duarte's death.

A BULLET IN THE HEAD

On April 9, 1953, Juan Duarte was found dead in his apartment on Callao Street. He was kneeling next to his bed in his underclothes. There was a .38-caliber Smith and Wesson revolver on the floor to his left. A white shirt and a suit were strewn over a chair behind him. On a little table there was a letter addressed to Perón in which he explained the reasons for his act. He was disgusted with life. He had been honest and had never stopped loving and respecting Perón. He had come with his sister, and now he was leaving with her. Judge Pizarro Miguens concluded that it had been a suicide. Juancito was stricken with syphilis, which allowed Perón to feel sorry for him. 'Poor boy! He was a provincial guy. In Buenos Aires he lost his head.'

But the poor boy had just been accused by the government of participating in shady deals involving beef exports. Perón, who was posing more and more, had screamed during a speech that he would go as far as to bring down a member of his own family if he engaged in speculation.

'Juancito was never involved in beef exports,' says Raúl Salinas. 'Bertolini, Erminda's husband, yes, but not him. The police planted compromising documents which belonged to

Bertolini on Juancito's desk. And on the eve of his death, Juancito confided in a friend: "Tell Raúl that the General abandoned me." Even if they didn't actually kill him they pushed him into killing himself.'

However, an analysis of the circumstances surrounding his death rules out suicide. To begin with, the bullet that killed him was from a .45-caliber gun. Additionally, it is impossible that a man who, according to the judge, was sitting on the edge of the bed, shot a bullet into his right temple and ended up on his knees, his forehead resting on the bed and the revolver to his left. When he was questioned, Pizarro Miguens gave the following extraordinary explanation: 'In movies it is easy to see how a man who gets a bullet to the head turns over under the effects of shock.' Since the judge's cinematic knowledge was so vast, he did not request an autopsy. Never mind that Juancito's valet confirmed that on the night of his death, his boss was wearing a striped shirt, not a white shirt. No matter that other witnesses said that they did not see the body kneeling, but in another position. Never mind that, late that night, many neighbours in the building heard a noise in the stairway and saw something heavy being dragged, or that they saw Ambassador Margueirat, Apold, Cámpora, and a stranger whom they called 'Gallego' in the hallway, carefully examining papers with a flashlight.

Judge Miguens did not request a handwriting expert to review Juancito's letter. It was so obvious, however, that it had been revised, that the government ended up 'admitting' to it; they thought they should correct the spelling errors. Did Juancito write it under duress? Had they imitated his handwriting? Had he been killed elsewhere and then taken to his apartment? Whatever the case may be, the judge called the undertakers before the family was able to see the body. Doña Juana screamed in the middle of the street, 'They killed my two children!' María Rosa Daly Nelson, a friend of the Duartes who lived on the sixth floor and had recognised three of the men in the hallway, testified to the investigative commission in October 1955, 'The day after his death, I saw Juana Ibarguren de Duarte and Elisa Duarte de Arrieta. They were desperate. They told me word for word, "Apold killed him."' Perón had dismissed Apold after the attempted coup in June 1955.

And what about the treasure and Juancito's trip to Switzerland right before his death? Did he have the bank account there? To whom on the 'right' had he confided his secrets? And did they want to get rid of him, since they expected nothing else from him, just like Glenn I. Infield before him, or were they getting rid of him to get hold of the bank account numbers in the first place? Were they eliminating him to serve as an example? Juancito was trying to leave the country with his friend Elina Colomer when the police arrested him, accusing him of beef trafficking. A newspaper suggested that he was killed by a shot to the back, then finished off by another to the head, when he was trying to board a plane to escape.

In fact, Juancito had always trafficked in less perishable goods, with his friend Jorge Antonio. Also Evita had appointed him inspector of the Mar del Plata casino (where Doña Juana, a big gambler, spent many happy moments). It was a custom-made position for a charming, unbiased fellow like him. These things had never been a mystery to anyone. To accuse him of trafficking the year after Evita's death, and precisely upon his return from Switzerland, was extremely significant.

Upon Juancito's death, Jorge Antonio's star began to shine very brightly. In the October 7, 1955 issue of the tabloid magazine *Ahora*, the following appeared: 'Jorge Antonio emerged at the beginning of 1948. A job at the Industrial Credit Bank allowed him to be tied to the Presidency's Technical Secretariat, where he worked under José Figuerola. Through his stay at the *Casa Rosada*, he and Juan Duarte soon became very close. When he was found after Juan Duarte's "suicide," Jorge Antonio is said to have gone to see General Perón to tell him that he had a number of property titles that belonged to the dead person.

He then proved himself to be a very adept administrator which had not been suspected, and he revealed an authentic financial genius.'

The magazine *Hechos en el mundo* reported on October 24: 'Soon after Juan Duarte's death, Doña Juana Ibarguren de Duarte had her son's estate opened. We understand the surprise occasioned by civil suit #16 presided over by Dr Ots Ortiz, when the extent of his property became clear. Juan Duarte, the man who had had millions in his hands, and who the American press called "the richest bachelor in Latin America," had a credit of 850,000 pesos from the Bank of the Province of Buenos Aires. As a mortgage for this loan, he had had 80,000 at the First National Bank, two cars, and a plane valued at 620,000 pesos. But the whole world knew, or at least sensed, that he had money in local banks. Why had he opened them if he had nothing to put in them? . . . It is known that all the men in the former dictator's entourage, whether it was Aloé or Nicolini, disposed of considerable capital. The only one in the open was Juan Duarte. Where had his fortune gone? Who had taken a hold of it?'

Doña Juana had given up her portion of the inheritance of Evita's jewels. Perón had requested this, though he had not signed a waiver for his own share. Later, Doña Juana engaged in an endless trial against Perón for Evita's estate. The relations between the son-in-law and the mother-in-law left much to be desired. In 1959, in a letter addressed to Pope John XXIII begging him to help find Evita's remains, she wrote: '*Before* Perón's fall, and for reasons that are not appropriate to bring up here, my situation, and my daughters' situation, were already being threatened.' Doña Juana died without knowing what had become of her daughter's remains and before the outcome of her trial against Perón. Erminda and Blanca (in the meantime, Elisa had also died) ended up winning the case.

But what kind of inheritance was this? Unlike Juancito, Evita herself had drafted a declaration of goods, in which she claimed a house on Teodoro García Street and 1.3 million pesos in jewels and cash. However, at the fall of the regime, the *Revolución Libertadora* exhibited and auctioned her possessions, including dresses, furs, shoes, hats, and jewels. Between December 9 and 19, 1957, the liquidating commission sold, or tried to sell, 65 kilograms of gold and as much of silver, a 48-carat emerald, 3 platinum ingots, 1,650 diamonds, 120 gold bracelets, and 100 gold watches. Before the auction, the commission's special account opened for this auction had 11,155,608 pesos; afterward it had 100 million. A report states that this sale could not even be compared to the sale of King Farouk's possessions. In her biography of Evita, Libertad Demitrópulo confirms that these funds disappeared without a trace.

In a study published by the magazine *Todo es historia*, Adolfo Rocha Campos maintains that in 1949, Perón released a statement of his possessions to the public. This statement was spoken like a sermon, at the time when he was ascending to the presidency. He declared the house in San Vicente and a few insignificant possessions. Evita also signed a declaration of goods, but hers remained in a sealed envelope.

Rocha Campos estimates Evita and Perón's fortune in 1952 at $12,271,280 and $11,265,438 respectively, plus the house in San Vicente and a piece of land in the province of Córdoba. The *Revolución Libertadora* froze all these possessions by decree in 1955, a time when anti-Perónists were seeing red. On the other hand, in 1973, when Perón returned to Argentina, the climate was one of pacification, and his adversaries, who were worried about falling back into the excesses of the past, vied for spiritual elevation. Law 20503, which rescinded the freeze on the assets, was the product of an opinion and a state of mind equal to the previous law but on the opposite side of the spectrum. Perón's widow, Isabel, was to inherit half of these assets, the other half was to go to Evita's sisters.

However these numbers do not reveal the origin of the possessions. 'During his eighteen years of exile,' writes Rocha

Campos, 'Perón had time to acquire assets, personally or through his friends, such as Jorge Antonio, among others. Separately, certain funds deposited abroad were put in Perón's name.' In 1974, when he became President for the third time, it seems that Perón did not provide full disclosure of his assets. No one criticised him for it. To differentiate oneself from the old anti-Perónists whose fervour became ridiculous with the passage of time, it became trendy to simply shrug one's shoulders at the mention of these riches.

In her letter to Pope John XXIII, Doña Juana also alluded to a subject that was as painful for her as the disappearance of Evita's body, the blasphemy of her son's mortal remains. After Perón's demise, a certain 'Captain Gandi' had obtained Juancito's skull under the pretext of proving that his death had been a crime and not a suicide. But people saw the skull sitting casually on the captain's desk. The same insanity that had taken hold of certain Perónists was now affecting anti-Perónists. The same, but opposite. Since they had overthrown the 'corrupted' regime, people were now 'virtuously' insane. One begins to resemble one's enemy the moment one tries to differentiate oneself from him too drastically.

EXILE NOW AND FOREVER

Juancito's 'suicide' caused an emotional uproar in the country. Félix Luna describes it: 'A heavy atmosphere of deception and clandestine get-rich schemes reigned in the official spheres. The names of the highest placed bigwigs, the presumed front men, were supposed to be secret, but everyone knew.

'And in the House of Deputies, a Perónist legislator had the inopportune idea to quote one of the most used Perónist slogans during his speech ("In the new Argentina only the children are privileged"), at which point, feigning innocence, a deputy from the opposition asked the age of one of the people suspected of having gotten rich by a most unspeakable association.'

The atmosphere was such that on April 15, the CGT organised a demonstration in support of the president. The opposition set off a few bombs, and that is when Perónist groups burned down the Jockey Club, a symbol of the oligarchy, of 'elite' culture, with its high-priced art gallery left in the ashes. This was the beginning of the end.

On September 16, the day when the *Revolución Libertadora* led by General Lombardi broke out, Perón refused to arm the people. When his supporters asked for weapons, he responded that he did not want a bloodbath. Perhaps he was afraid that the people would not defend him as ardently as they had in 1945. Probably he feared for his life. So he gave up. All the Perónists and a good number of anti-Perónists were unanimous on one point: if Evita had won the vice presidency, the *Revolución Libertadora* would not have happened.

Ambition was considered 'masculine.' However, Argentina cherishes San Martín's surrender and exile and Rosas's exile in its memory. Now it was Perón's turn.

When they heard about his flight, an enthusiastic crowd gathered in the streets. This was a different crowd, made up of people who had not tasted Evita's panettone or lived in her stylish chalets. They cried, 'Freedom! Freedom!' For ten years they had felt asphyxiated. Now they could finally breathe.

Perón hid out at the Paraguayan Embassy and boarded a gunboat headed for Asunción. Later he went to Venezuela, the Dominican Republic, and finally Panama, where he met a dancer. Her name was Estela, but she was called Isabel. He must have liked her fragile body and her birdlike face, with eyes that a sly expression rendered even smaller. He lived with her but refused to marry her so as not to offend the Evitists. He finally married her only when he was granted political asylum in Spain, a Catholic country, and had to be reconciled with the Vatican. In fact, Pope John XXIII ended up revoking the excommunication that the Argentinean Church had imposed on Perón in 1955.

Once he was out of the country, he began to organise the Perónist resistance. But today, Guillermo Patricio Kelly, former resistance fighter and nationalist turned defender of Israel, questions his methods. 'Perón left because he did not want to see the blood of the Argentinean people flow. But the minute he arrived in Paraguay, he began to ask for the anti-Perónists' head. So the blood could flow, as long as he was far away, safe and sound.'

In Madrid, Perón did not often visit his friend Franco. He lived in a villa in Puerta de Hierro and grew roses. That is where a better Perón surfaced, a Perón who calmly explained how to prune plants, a neat, steady, calm man, enjoying his daily life and using funny rustic sayings to express himself. Alas, a better Perón, the one who knew how to make mayonnaise, was not the Perón loved by Evita. She had loved the imaginary man. She called him only Perón, almost never Juan – and even less Juancito. Oddly, Aurelia Tizón, his first wife, had done the same. In the end, he was the outcast.

López Rega, who was obsequious and devoted, wove his fabric around him as Méndez San Martín once had. According to Rosa Calviño, López Rega had started as a simple police officer, smiling at the entrance of the residence, offering *maté* to the visitors. He went a long way, and he would go farther, always lurking.

But despite the saccharine sorcerer, Perón had shaken off his torpor and woken up. He managed Argentina from afar. There was not a strike in the country about which the Argentinean government did not feel obliged to confer with Perón. This is another subject that did not induce tenderness in Patricio Kelly: 'He caused a strike, let's say in the beef sector. The government would send him a delegate to rectify things. And Perón would say: "Always send the union leader, and I will see what I can do." In exchange, he would ask them to lift part of the freeze on his and Jorge Antonio's assets. During this time, the people waited for him. They risked prison and their lives for him. And Perón called them the *gilada*, the clowns.'

The clowns dreamt of seeing Perón return to Argentina on a black plane. At the Chacarita cemetery, the Perónist regime had erected a bust of Evita that the clowns regularly covered with flowers. The *Revolución Libertadora* had replaced the bust with a trash can, so the flowers were simply placed on the can. By savagely burning every bedspread, every athletic jersey with the 'Eva Perón Foundation' inscription on it, the *Revolución Libertadora* actually assured the survival of Perónism, because the fury engendered resistance. The anti-Perónists demolished the Unzué palace and the house on Teodoro García Street. They destroyed iron lungs in hospitals afflicted with the damned inscription (shortly thereafter, a polio epidemic broke out and many children died for lack of respiratory assistance). They repainted the foundation's sky blue trucks another colour. They forbade the press to mention Perón and Evita's names, so Perón was referred to as 'the ex-dictator' or 'the beaten tyrant.' Each word, each name, each absent building became a fearful presence – the same way God's presence can be fearful.

The poorest rancho, no matter how isolated, had a photo of Evita illuminated by candles. In the daytime as in the nighttime, millions of altars were lit for the mythical mother who nourished her children even after her death.

WHITE, BLACK, RED

Two myths opposed each other: white and black. The first depicted Eva as a virgin in the flesh, as maternal tenderness, the very meaning of sacrifice. The second reflected a prostitute, a social climber thirsting for power.

Both the white myth and the black myth were born of the same principle. The first loved Eva for her purity, and the second hated her because she was impure. For both, sex was reprehensible. The virgin and the whore were but opposite images of one ideal. Borges saw Evita as a prostitute. But to exalt her or to denigrate her seemed aimed at something beyond humanity. She was religiously loved; she was religiously hated. In *Los mitos de una mujer* (Mother myths), Julie Taylor concluded that women and the dead create unease and disorder. As a 'feminine cadaver,' Evita's symbolic power remained intact.

How to exorcise it? In *Fantasías eternas a la luz del psicoanálisis* (Eternal fantasies in the light of psychoanalysis), Marie Langer wrote, 'Everyone had two contradictory images [of Evita] deep down inside, some of them projected the good and repressed the bad, and others did the opposite.' Maybe the moment has come to not repress anything, not even a smile. The dead cease to haunt us, as feminine as they may be, the day we surprise ourselves by laughing at them, tenderly.

The *Cordobazo* of 1969, a revolutionary movement that threw the entire population of Córdoba into the streets against the army, marked the birth of a new race of Perónists who would create Evita's third myth, the 'red myth.' These new Perónists (called Montoneros after the nineteenth-century freedom fighters) were leftists. They all had their youth in common, and those who chose the guerrilla path felt pure, committed to a mission. Dostoyevski described them in *The Demons*. In general, they were middle class or bourgeois. Their parents had been anti-Perónists. All the more reason to try to seize what had escaped the previous generation, to know that Perónism was a movement of national liberation. Didn't Perón's welcoming the Nazis worry them? No, they saw in it only an old man's drivel.

They succeeded in creating an army of forty thousand men, an army against the army. This was post-Cuban Revolution, post-May 1968. Perón, whom they went to see in Madrid, told them that he agreed with them completely. They loved his ironic wisdom and thought they could infiltrate his movement to radicalise it.

But Perón did not have the moral fibre of a romantic hero, and although they claimed to be Perónists, they used Evita as their flag. The same taste for self-sacrifice and death, the same ardour, the same Robin Hood spirit. They thought they were imitating her when they stormed the supermarkets, kidnapped billionaires, and distributed their booty in the shanty towns.

Evita liked to construct. She was a builder. This new group wanted to destroy to erect a new society. If she had lived, she certainly would have stayed to the left, but not to this extent. However, this part of her legacy was not of her choosing. By using her image, the Montoneros discovered a revolutionary energy that Perón did not possess. Of the three myths, probably the least absurd is the red one. Despite her insolent outfits, which Perón considered 'cabaret' costumes, or maybe because of them, everything about Evita said *Pasionaria*.

Besides dreaming about Evita, the Montoneros dreamt about themselves. Dreaming became their life – and their death. This dream did not lack beauty, albeit sombre beauty, but it no longer exists. In today's Argentina, as in the rest of the world, a bloodless left is questioning itself. Eva deserves to be respected by the actual Socialist left or the left composed of Perónist dissidents who, faced with a 'heartless' liberalism, as she herself would have said, are beginning to react. She should not be mythologised, for myths, whether they exalt or denigrate, are disrespectful, nor analysed objectively either, for to respect a human does not mean gravely to rub one's chin.

THE WOUNDED BODY

For the young Perónists, there was an enormous injustice to repair. They had to find Evita's body. Perón's indifference vis-à-vis Pedro Ara had been confirmed. He had never used his power over the Argentinean authorities (through his power over the people) to demand that she be returned. The Montoneros were going to remedy this situation. And the only one who knew where she was hidden was Pedro Aramburu.

On May 29, 1970, two men in uniform showed up at the former president's home and forced Aramburu to follow them in a truck with covered windows. Eight hours later, they arrived at a rancho lost in the Pampas. They told their prisoner that he would be judged by a revolutionary trial. Mario Firmenich, their leader, began the interrogation the very next day. Aramburu answered every question. He spoke of Juan José Valle's execution and the execution of twenty-one other Perónists in 1956, and he admitted to the role he played in the operation. But when they asked him where Evita's body was, he remained 'paralysed,' according to Firmenich. He made a sign for them to stop the recording and whispered, 'For reasons of honour, I cannot say.' Since they insisted, he promised to think about it. In the early morning, he revealed that the Vatican had been in charge and that Eva was buried in a cemetery in Rome, under an alias. They later discovered she was in Milan. But what he did not reveal was the name of the notary to whom he gave the envelope containing the information about the location of Eva's resting place. Aramburu did not know where she was. He had not wanted to know. Since he insisted on keeping quiet, he was condemned and executed. The Montoneros broadcast a communiqué announcing that his remains would be returned to his family 'on the day when the remains of our dear *compañera* Evita are returned to the people.'

Meanwhile, the police found Aramburu's remains, and the notary kept his promise to hand over the envelope four weeks after the death of the former president, to General Alexandro Augustin Lanusse, who was then in power.

Lanusse had wanted to strike a deal with Perón for a long time, for Perón did not allow anyone to govern Argentina. He was still giving orders from Madrid. Lanusse opened the envelope, summoned Colonel Cabanillas, gave him the name of a priest and a cemetery, and Cabanillas went to Milan with Father Rotger, the same man who had intervened during the cadaver's first trip.

In the meantime, the Italian priest had died. There was only one solution, to look through the cemetery's registry for the names of all the women who had been buried in 1956. They came upon a certain Maria Maggi de Magistris, Italian, widow, emigrated to Argentina, dead for five years before finding a tomb in Milan.

Colonel Cabanillas, who had let his moustache grow, introduced himself to the cemetery authorities as Carlos Maggi, Maria's brother. He requested authorisation to transfer his sister's remains to Spain. On September 2, 1971, a group of men found themselves before the neglected plot #86, section 41. Eva was there.

The funeral parlour's truck transporting Evita crossed the Italian-French border. From the moment she arrived in Spain, she was escorted by many cars. Perón was not informed until the last minute.

This body, which he had so desired to escape, had caught up with him. During his wanderings through Latin America, he had never let go of a photo of Evita, a tiny driver's license photo. 'He kept this over his bed, hung on the wall,' Roberto Galán said. In Madrid, this small photo was always on his desk. Diminutive love. Superstitious love, too, just in case. But the body, no. To think that the Montoneros killed for that. Now they were sending it to him as if they were requesting a favour. No one had asked his advice, which he would not have given anyway.

Perón, Isabel, López Rega, Jorge Paladino, the Argentinean ambassador Rojas Silveyra, Colonel Cabanillas, and two priests from the Merced were at Puerta de Hierro to greet the body. This time, Evita arrived not in a hearse but in a bakery truck. Perón tried to open the casket and hurt himself on the zinc cover. López Rega drew appalled glances when he proposed using a blow torch. Finally, they went to look for a crowbar that could open the rusty cover. Eva's body reappeared.

When he saw her, Perón exclaimed. 'Those bastards!' Then, he began to cry. While he signed the form for the body's identification, Isabel undid Eva's chignon, which had become wet. She refused to sign the document. 'If I did not know her when she was living,' she argued, 'how could I recognise her now?'

✛

Why had Perón exclaimed, 'Those bastards!'? Even this issue causes controversy. Pedro Ara, who had moved to Madrid, was summoned to assess the damage. According to him, the neck had not been slashed, the breasts showed no signs of violence. Everything was reparable.

Yet, Blanca and Erminda, who had come to Madrid to see their sister, released a statement in 1985: 'Our intention is not to reopen the old wounds that never stop causing us pain. But we cannot allow history to be distorted. That is why we are testifying to the gross mistreatment inflicted on our dear sister Evita's remains:

- blows of a hammer to the temple, and four on the forehead
- a large gash on her cheek and another on her arm, at the height of the humerus
- her nose almost completely sunken in, the nasal septum fractured
- her neck practically severed
- a finger on her hand, cut off
- her kneecaps, fractured
- her chest slashed in four places
- the soles of her feet covered with a layer of tar

- the casket's zinc cover traces of three perforations, obviously intentional. In fact, the inside of the casket was completely wet, the pillow had been ripped apart and wood chips from the padding were stuck to her hair
- the body had been covered with quicklime and occasionally showed burns
- her hair was like wet wool
- the shroud was stained from rust and corrosion.'

In 1971, Dr Isidro Ventura Mayoral, Perón's lawyer, had denounced anti-Perónist insanity by describing the body's condition. In a speech spoken at a Basic Unit, he agreed with the sisters. And he considered his testimony so important that he ended his speech with these solemn words: 'We want this information to be transmitted from mouth to ear, just as it was during the wars of the gauchos.'

But nothing happened. Perón never brought up the sunken nose or the deep gashes that revealed the shreds of flesh. He kept the mummy in the attic of his villa at Puerta de Hierro where, according to Tomás Eloy Martínez, López Rega attempted to transfer Evita's soul into Isabel's body. But the task was overwhelming.

RETURN TO THE COUNTRY OF OBLIVION

In 1973, Héctor Cámpora was elected president of Argentina. His term of office lasted one month. This 'month of Cámpora' – a renewed Cámpora, having become leftist – would remain in Argentineans' memory like a sign, a field where one could see the virtues and the errors of a true revolution. One month later, Perón came to reclaim the place that was his. Cámpora had been a puppet, elected only to bring back Perón.

The day he returned to the country, after twenty years of

exile, both left-wing and right-wing Perónists found themselves face to face once again at Ezeiza airport. Perón had said that he agreed completely with both groups, but the right was better equipped: they had even hired the services of mercenaries and former members of the OAS. And they were counting on López Rega, who had become the creator of the Triple A, a well-organised parapolice force.

A million people lined the road that led to the airport, joyous people that only Perónism knew how to assemble. They came from every province: brown skinned, jubilant, warm, and raucous with emotion as they were in 1945. They had brought their *bombos* and were getting ready to enjoy a celebration that would give their lives meaning. They had been looking toward the sky, their hands held up to their foreheads, waiting for that black airplane for twenty years.

The massacre that ensued was horrible. Perched on the trees, the right-wing mercenaries shot at the clowns, young intellectuals, young workers, young peasants. Perón had not organised the slaughter; his entourage had. But he had freely chosen these right-wingers, today and yesterday. To throw all responsibility on them would reduce him to a puppet. True, he was old and senile, which had been evident since 1955. However, at the moment of truth, the doddering Perón and the pragmatic Perón, that is, the man who was open to anything, combined to form one perfectly coherent whole.

On the enormous posters, there were now three faces: Perón in the middle, Isabelita on the right, Evita on the left.

Perón had returned with Isabel – who would become vice president – leaving behind the problematic cadaver in Spain. He had promised to bring it back to Argentina, but he never alluded to it again. However, Isabelita proved more interested. She wanted to revive Evita's myth, which she attempted to emulate if only in her bulging, mouse-coloured chignon.

The Montoneros had longed to see their blonde and luminous love once more. And to perfect this macabre story, they desecrated Aramburu's tomb and removed his corpse, which they vowed to keep until the day Evita's was returned to Argentina.

Perón could not disguise his irritation with these 'fake' Perónists, who were eager to annoy him by reviving the old issue and who wanted to turn Perónism into the left-wing movement it was not. He chased them off the Plaza de Mayo by calling them 'beardless youth' during a speech (in fact they all had beards, Cuban-style).

The fake Perónists ended up winning, at least on the issue of Evita's body. After Perón's death, it was returned to Argentina. Isabel, or rather Doña María Estela Martínez de Perón, had become president, and the task of bringing Evita's dream to fruition was now her responsibility.

On November 17, 1974, a charter flight brought Evita from Madrid to Buenos Aires. They took her to the Olivos residence, where Dr Domingo Tellechea began the repairs that Perón had neglected in the three years that had passed since her body had been discovered.

Dr Tellechea's report corroborates Erminda and Blanca's statement about the body's condition. But he adds a detail that confirms Moori Koening's words, 'I buried her standing, because she was a male.' Here is the detail: 'Her feet were ruined by the vertical position that had to support the body and by the bad treatment.'

A brand-new Evita, her hair restyled, dressed in the same white tunic that Isabel had put on her, her nails freshly polished, was thrown out of the Olivos residence on March 26, 1976, when Isabel Perón was overthrown by General Videla, thus inaugurating the military dictatorship that would result in the disappearance of thirty thousand people.

❖

On October 22 of that same year, Erminda and Blanca received the casket and deposited it in the Arrieta vault (that of Elisa Duarte's husband's family) in the Recoleta cemetery. On the Recoleta vault, a very small plaque announces her presence. The crowds no longer rush to see her. Only a few nostalgic old folk, mostly women, come to burn a few candles from time to time. However, lively foreign journalists still come by, as do television and film people. The wish Evita confided to Lilian that night so many years ago was fulfilled. She belongs to History.

BIBLIOGRAPHY

GENERAL WORKS

Avni, Haim. *Argentina y la historia de la imigración judía.* Buenos Aires.

Belloni, Alberto. *Del anarquismo al peronismo.* Buenos Aires: Editorial A. Peña Lillo, 1960.

Bianchi, Susana, and Norma Sanchís. *El Partido Peronista Femenino.* Buenos Aires: Centro Editor de América Latina.

Bidault, Suzanne. *Je n'ai pas oublié.* Éditions La Table Ronde.

Boimvaser, Jorge. *Las manos de Perón. (¿y porqué Señor Alfonsín?).* Buenos Aires: BB Editores, 1991.

Boizard, Ricardo. *Esa noche de Perón.* Buenos Aires: H. del Valle, 1955.

Buchrucher, Cristián. 'Nacionalismo y peronismo,' in *La Argentina en la crisis ideológica mundial (1927–1955).* Buenos Aires: Editorial Sudamericana, 1987.

Cafiero, Antonio, and Hugo Gambini. *Desde que grité: ¡Viva Perón!* Buenos Aires: Pequén Ediciones, 1983.

Camarasa, Jorge. *Los nazis en la Argentina.* Buenos Aires: Editorial Legasa, 1992.

Carril, Bonifacio del. *Memorias dispersas. El colonel Perón*, Buenos Aires: Editorial Emecé, 1984.

Collection. *Historias del peronismo*. Buenos Aires: Editorial Corregidor, 1973.

Damonte Taborda, Raúl. *Ayer fue San Perón*. Buenos Aires: Ediciones Gure, 1954.

Dos Santos, Estela. *Las mujeres del tango*. Buenos Aires: Centro Editor de América Latina, 1972.

———. *Las mujeres peronistas*. Buenos Aires: Centro Editor de América Latina, 1983.

Flores, José. *Operación 'Rosa Negra.'* Buenos Aires, 1956.

Gambini, Hugo. *El 17 de Octubre de 1945*. Buenos Aires: Editorial Brújula, 1969.

Hollander, Nancy. *La mujer, ¿esclave de la historia o historia de la esclava?* Buenos Aires: Editorial La Pléyade, 1974.

Horowicz, Alejandro. *Los cuatro peronismos*. Buenos Aires: Editorial Legasa, 1985.

Infield, Glenn I. *Skorzeny, chief des commandos de Hitler*. Paris: Editions Pygmalio/Gérard Wattelet, 1984.

Jackisch, Carlota. *El nazismo y los refugiados alemanes en la Argentina, 1933–1945*. Buenos Aires: Editorial Belgrano.

Jamandreu, Paco. *La cabeza contra el suelo. Memorias*. Buenos Aires: Editociones de La Flor, 1975.

Lamarque, Libertad. *Autobiografía*.

Lamas, Raúl. *Los torturadores*. Buenos Aires: Lamas, 1956.

Langer, Marie. *Fantasías eternas a la luz del psicoanálisis*. Buenos Aires: Editorial Nova, 1957.

Luna Felix. *La Argentina de Perón a Lanusse*. Buenos Aires: Editorial Planeta, 1990.

———. *Crónica de un año decisivo*. Buenos Aires: Editorial Sudamericana, 1972.

———. *Perón y su tiempo. 2 vols*. Buenos Aires: Editorial Sudamericana, 1986, 1990.

Manning Paul. *My Search for Martin Bormann*. Photocopy of the original consulted by Jorge Camarasa (*Los nazis en Argentina*).

Martínez, Tomás Eloy. *La novela de Perón*. Madrid: Editorial Alianza Cuatro, 1989.

Medina, Enrique. *Gatica*. Buenos Aires: Editorial Galerna, 1991.

Mercier Vega, Louis. *Autopsia de Perón*. Barcelona: Editorial Tusquets, 1975.

Miquel, Pierre. *Histoire du métro de Paris*. Éditions de la RATP.

Molinari, Aldo Luis. *Caso Duarte*. Buenos Aires: 1958.

Peicovich, Esteban. *Hola, Perón*. Buenos Aires: Editorial Jorge Alvarez, 1965.

Pombo, Ana de. *Mi última condena*.

Potash, Robert A. *El Ejército y la política en la Argentina*, 1928–1945. Buenos Aires: Editorial Hyspamérica, 1971.

Quattrocchi-Woisson, Diana. *Un nationalisme de déracinés. L'Argentine, pays malade de sa mémoire*. Paris: Éditions du CNRS, 1992.

Reyes, Cipriano. *La farsa del peronismo*. Buenos Aires: Sudamerica-Planeta, 1987.

———. *Yo hice el 17 de Octubre*. Buenos Aires: Memorias, GS editorial, 1973.

Rozichner, León. *Perón entre y el tiempo*. Buenos Aires: Centro Editor de América Latina,

Sábato, Ernesto. *El otro rostro del peronismo. Carta abierta a Mario Amadeo*. Buenos Aires: Editorial Gure, 1957.

Santander, Silvano. *Técnica de una traición, Juan D. Perón y Eva Duarte agentes del nazismo en Argentina*. Buenos Aires: Editorial Legasa, 1985.

Sebreli, Juan José. *Los deseos imaginarios del peronismo*.

Sirvén, Pablo. *Perón y los medios de comunicación: 1943–1955*. Buenos Aires: Centro Editor de América Latina.

Sommi, Luis V. *Los capitales alemanes en la Argentina*. Buenos Aires: Editorial Claridad, 1943.

Walsh, Rodolfo. *Los oficios terrestres*. Buenos Aires: Editorial La Flor, 1986.

Wiesenthal, Simon. *Los asesinos entre nosotros*. Barcelona: Editorial Noguer, 1967.

WORKS ABOUT EVA PERÓN

Acossano, Benigno. *Eva Perón, su verdadera vida*. Buenos Aires: Editorial Lamas, 1955.

Ara, Pedro. *El caso Eva Perón. Apuntes para la historia*.

Barnes, John. *Eva Perón*. Buenos Aires: Editorial Ultramar, 1987.

Borroni, Otelo, and Roberto Vacca. *Eva Perón*. Buenos Aires: Centro Editor de América Latina, 1970.

Bruce, George. *Evita*. Ediciones Picazo.

Chávez, Fermín. *Eva Perón en la historia*. Buenos Aires: Editorial Oriente, 1986.

———. *Eva Perón sin mitos*. Buenos Aires: Editorial Fraterna, 1990.

COPI, *Eva Perón*. Paris: Christian Bourgois, 1969.

Demitrópulos, Libertad. *Eva Perón*. Buenos Aires: Centro Editor de América Latina, 1984.

Deutsch, Mario, Alejandro, Garbarino, Alejandro Raggio, and Hebert Tenembaum. *Eva Perón, una aproximación psicoanalítica*.

Doumerc, Beatriz. *Eva Perón*. Barcelona: Editorial Lumen, 1989.

Duarte, Erminda. *Mi hermana Evita*. Buenos Aires: Centro de Estudios Eva Perón, 1972.

Fraser, Nicholas, and Marysa Navarro. *Eva Perón*. Editorial Bruguera.

Ghioldi, Américo. *El mito de Eva Perón*. Buenos Aires: Ediciones Gure, 1956.

Jamandreu, Paco. *Evita fuera del balcón*. Buenos Aires: Ediciones del Libro Abierto, 1981.

Llorca, Carmen. *Llamadme Evita*. Barcelona: Editorial Planeta, 1980.

Lombille, Román. *Eva, la predestinada. Alucinante historia de éxitos y frustraciones.* Buenos Aires: Editorial Gure, 1955.

Main, Mary. *La mujer del látigo.* Buenos Aires: Ediciones La Reja, 1955.

Mignogna, Eduardo. *Evita, Quien quiere oir, que oiga.* Buenos Aires: Editorial Legasa, 1984. Screenplay of the film of the same title.

Naipaul, V. S. *The Return of Eva Perón.* New York: Knopf, 1980.

Navarro, Marysa. *Evita.* Buenos Aires: Editorial Corregidor, 1981.

Ottino, Mónica. *Evita y Victoria.* Buenos Aires: Grupo Editor Latinoamericano, 1990.

Pagano, Mabel. *Eterna.* Buenos Aires: Editorial Nueva Sol, 1982.

Pavón Pereyra, Enrique. *Evita la mujer del siglo.* Buenos Aires: Editorial Ruy Diaz.

Pichel, Vera. *Evita íntima.* Buenos Aires: Editorial Planeta, 1993.

———. *Mi país y sus mujeres.* Buenos Aires: Editorial Sudestada, 1968.

Saccomano, Guillermo. *Roberto y Eva.* Buenos Aires: Editoriales Legasa, 1989.

Sebreli, Juan José. *Eva Perón: ¿Aventurera o militante?* Buenos Aires: Editorial Siglo XX, 1966.

Taylor, Julie. *Los mitos de una mujer.*

Tettamanti, Rodolfo. *Eva Perón.* Buenos Aires: Centro Editor de América Latina, 1971.

WORKS BY JUAN PERÓN AND EVA PERÓN

Perón, Juan Domingo. *Del poder al exilio. Cómo y quiénes me derrocaron. La comunidad organizada.* Buenos Aires: Ediciones del Pueblo, 1970.

Perón, Eva. *La razón de mi vida*. Buenos Aires: Editorial Peuser, 1951.

———. *Discursos completos*. 1946–1948. Buenos Aires: Editorial Megafón, 1985.

———. *Clases y discursos completos*. Buenos Aires: Editorial Megafón, 1987.

———. *Historia del peronismo*. Buenos Aires: Editora Volver, 1987.

———. *Mi mensaje*. Buenos Aires: Ediciones del Mundo, 1987.

DIVERSE PUBLICATIONS

'Historia del peronismo,' edited by *Hugo Gambini*. In *Primera Plana*, 1967.

'Evita,' #7, Organo del Ateneo Eva Perón. No date.

'Eva Perón hoy,' *Vicente Zito Lema, Cuadernos de Fin de Siglo*, Buenos Aires, 1973.

'Etnicidad e inmigración durante el primer peronismo,' by *Leonardo Senkman*, in *Estudios Interdisciplinarios de América Latina*, Hebrew University of Jerusalem.

'Las relaciones Estados Unidos-Argentina y la cuestión de los refugiados de la post-guerra: 1945–1948,' by *Leonardo Senkman*, in *Judaica Latinoamericana*, Separatum, Hebrew University of Jerusalem.

'Perón y Evita en la historia bonaerense,' Homenaje del Gobierno del pueblo de la Provincia de Buenos Aires, October 1990.

'Mayoría,' Año de la Liberación. July 26, 1973.

'Eva Duarte, actriz,' by *Gerardo Bra*, in *Todo es Historia*, August 1986.

'Perón y los judios,' by *Emilio J. Capstiski*, in *Todo es Historia*, June 1988.

'Prehistoria de Eva Perón,' by *Jorge Capstiski*, in *Todo es Historia*, #14.

'Perón y su exilio español,' by *Marcela A. García* and *Aníbal Iturrieta*.

'La fortuna de Perón,' by *Adolfo Rocha Campos*, in *Todo es Historia, #313*, August 1993.

'Perón, Braden y el antisemitismo: opinión pública e imagen internacional,' by *Ignacio Klich*, in *Ciclos*, año II, vol. II, #2, 1st semester 1992.

'Perón y los nazis,' by *Tomás Eloy Martínez*, in *El Periodista*, Buenos Aires, August 1985, #49 and 50.

'*Marcha*. Catorce hipótesis de trabajo en torno a Eva Perón,' by *David Viñas*, Montevideo, 1965.

'La Fundación Eva Perón,' unpublished university thesis, *Mónica Campins, Horacio Gaggero, Alicia Yano*.

'Eva Perón: catholicisme traditionnel et mythologie christiano-justicialiste,' unpublished university thesis, *Lila Caimari*.

'Hernán Benítez: le peronisme comme meilleure façon de faire le christianisme,' unpublished university thesis, *Lila Caimari*.

'La infancia de Perón en la Patagonia,' by *Tomás Eloy Martínez*, in *2001*, año 6, #63, October 1973.

'Perón, el hombre del destino,' collection of 45 volumes edited by *Enrique Pavón Pereyra*, Editorial Abril, Buenos Aires, 1973.

'Ciuadad infantil Amanda Allen,' Presidencia de la Nación, Secretaría de Informaciones.

'Cuando Descartes firmaba Perón,' by *Fermín Chávez*, in *Clarín*, March 9, 1989.

Unpublished from Eva Perón's sisters to Dr Raúl Matera, July 29, 1985 (property of Fermín Chávez).

Unpublished letter from Juana Ibarguren to Pope John XXIII, March 22, 1959 (property of Fermín Chávez).

Unpublished letter from Raúl Matera to Monsignor Lino Zanini, 1971 (property of Fermín Chávez).

FILMS

Evita by Juan Schroeder
El misterio de Eva Perón by Tulio de Michelis
La Pródiga, La República perdida by Luis Gregorich and Maria
    Elena Walsh
Quien quiera oír que oiga by Eduardo Mignona

MAGAZINES AND NEWSPAPERS

Ahora   *Página 12*
Antena   *El País*
Buenos Aires Herald *Paris-Match*
Careo   *Paroles françaises*
Clarin   *La Prensa*
La Démocratie   *Primera Plana*
Gaceta ilustrada   *Radiolandia*
Gente   *La Repubblica*
Hechos en el mundo   *Río Negro*
El Hogar   *Siete Días*
Life   *Somos*
La Nación   *La Stampa*
Noticias   *Time*
                       Voìx Ouvrière

PEOPLE CONSULTED

José María Acosta, journalist; Luis Agostino, Eva Perón's tailor;
    Gloria Alcorta, writer; Julio Ardiles Gray, writer and jour-
    nalist; Angel Miel Asquía, former Perónist deputy; Osvaldo
    Bayer, historian and sociologist; Father Hernán Benítez,
    Eva Perón's confessor; Dr Benjamin, psychoanalyst; Isidro

Blaisten, writer; Marta Boto, artist; Héctor Cámpora, son of the former Argentinean president, Héctor Cámpora; Martin Caparrós, writer; Delfina Caprile, member of the former liquidating commission of the Eva Perón Foundation; Héctor Cartier, painter of Eva Perón's portrait; José María Castiñeira de Dios, poet and former Perónist secretary of culture; Ramón Cereijo, former Perónist minister; Fermín Chávez, historian; Tito di Ciano, Congress's former barber; Victor Claiman, journalist; Luis Clur, journalist; Rodolfo Decker, attorney and former Perónist deputy; Miguel Angel Estrella, pianist; Sara Facio, photographer; Juan Pablo Feinman, writer; Javier Fernández, diplomat; Gisèle Freund, photographer; Roberto Galán, television host; Mike Gallaher, former member of the Information Services; Hugo Gambini, journalist; María Granata, writer; Anne-Marie Heinrich, photographer; Eduardo Jonquières, painter; Dr Larrauri, doctor; Félix Luna, historian; Lunazzi, militant anarchist; Sergia Machinandearena, film producer; Ana Macri, Rosa Calviño de Gómez, Ana Serrano, and Sarita Romero, former members of the Women's Perónist party; Graciela Maglie, sociologist; Maguid Jacobo and Dora Barranco, militant anarchists; Dr Rodríguez Mancini, doctor; Pedro Maratea, actor; Mercante, son of Domingo Mercante, former governor of the province of Buenos Aires; José Enrique Miguens, sociologist; Angel Núñez, writer; Enrique Oliva, journalist; Pedro Orgambide, writer; Rodolfo Pandolfi, journalist; Enrique Pavón Pereyra, Juan Domingo Perón's biographer; Elena Piaggio de Hogan, friend of Eva Perón; Lilia Reta, militant socialist; Carlos Righi, former Perónist minister; Alberto Rocamora, former Perónist minister; Isaac Rojas, former Argentinean vice president; Elbia Rosbaco de Marechal, poet; Raúl Rossi, actor; Dr León Rozichner, psychoanalyst; Dr Gerardo Ruiz Moreno, psychoanalyst; Raúl Salinas, former Perónist secretary of culture; Ernesto Sábato, writer; Mario Sábato, filmmaker; Valentin Thiébault, journalist; Alejandro Valenti, filmmaker; Ambrosio Vecino, journalist; Héctor Villanueva, poet; María Elena Walsh, poet; Dr Ordiales, Dora Dana, Héctor Lebensohn, Rogelio Leguizamón Cabrera, Elsa Sabella, Roberto Carlos Dimarco, Müller, Amicucci, neighbours from Junín; Father Meinrado Hux, Pirula Villa, Rufino Herce, Tito de la Torre, Ema Vinuessa, neighbours from Los Toldos.

Father Hernán Benítez: unpublished interview with sociologist Lila Caimari. Chávez Fermín, Raúl Lagomarsino (former minister), Fernando Torres and Sebastián Borro (union leaders), José María Castiñeira de Dios, Guillermo Patricio Kelly (Perónist politician), Leonor Troxler (militant Perónist): unpublished interview with sociologist Marta Echeverría.